Best Practices in Change Management 2016 — 9th Edition

1120 participants share lessons and best practices in change management

ISBN: 978-1-930885-64-6

Editors – Tim Creasey, Robert Stise
Study design – Tim Creasey, Robert Stise
Data visualization – Tim Creasey, Robert Stise, Tyler Lehman
Regression analysis – Tyler Lehman
Contributors – Alex FitzSimons, Alyssa Thomas, Courtney Schultz, JD Jacob, Josh Garside, Matthew Flood, Mike Davis, Rachel Grossman, Rashelle Esparza, Robert Stise, Ty Lehman
With assistance from – Alana Birky, Ali Semonchick, Allison Seabeck, Dan Gamble, Greg Henning, Jeremy Carson, Jorge Garza, Jude Larrimore, Mark Dorsett, Mary Brittenham, Michelle Haggerty, Rob Green, Ron Boyle, Scott McAllister, Sierra Barrick, Susie Patterson, Tim Martin
Copy editor – John Garger
Reviewed by – D. Scott Ross, Jude Larrimore, Merril Alligood
Photography by – Shelby Perez
Cover and introduction pages designed by – Ruth Waddingham

This edition of Best Practices in Change Management aggregates findings from the 2015 study and previous studies (1998, 2000, 2003, 2005, 2007, 2009, 2011 and 2013) to create a compendium of benchmarking findings, and one of the most comprehensive bodies of knowledge on change management. Findings brought forward from the 2007, 2009, 2011 and 2013 editions of the report are noted with the following text: "Source date: 20XX."

Table of contents

Tables and figures

Letter from Prosci

The imperative for organizations to realize results from change and engage a workforce in the process reverberates loudly across industry, organization size and geography. As a change leader, you play a pivotal role in ensuring your organization realizes its unique vision of a different and brighter future. Prosci's mission, and the purpose of this study, is to enable organizations and individuals to build their own change management capabilities. We endeavor to uncover best practices that help you become better at leading change.

Best practices provide a starting point for understanding the fundamental concepts of leading people through change. The collective successes of other change efforts provide checkpoints to guide your planning. Lessons others have learned give you insights into tackling delicate change scenarios and help you avoid common pitfalls. Data from nine studies across 17 years encompassing over 4500 change agents who have undertaken significant organizational changes demonstrate authoritatively the value of investing in the people side of change.

The 2016 edition of Best Practices in Change Management study represents the largest body of knowledge about managing the people side of change. Thank you to the 1120 contributors who devoted time and energy providing valuable insights and data. New to the report this year, we explore the influence of culture on change management, complementary business roles that support change and more while continuing to redefine and add to the largest body of knowledge on core change management practices.

Whether you study specific topics as a learning exercise, use the book as a reference or rely on the tools and processes derived from the results, I trust that you will find insights that make your change management more effective, your projects more successful through better adoption and usage, and your organizations more adept at managing its portfolios of change.

Thank you,

Allison Seabeck
President

Study overview

Participant profile

One thousand one hundred twenty (1120) participants from 56 countries took part in Prosci's 2015 Best Practices in Change Management benchmarking study. This report combines findings and data from the 2015 study with Prosci's previous eight studies to form the largest body of knowledge related to managing the people side of change based on insights and experiences from more than 4500 participants.

2015 study – 1120 participants
2013 study – 822 participants
2011 study – 650 participants
2009 study – 575 participants
2007 study – 426 participants
2005 study – 411 participants
2003 study – 288 participants
2000 study – 152 participants
1998 study – 102 participants

Figure i.1 shows the geographic distribution of participants in the 2015 study. Proportionately, participation dropped from Australia and New Zealand, Asia and Pacific Islands and the Middle East. Participation increased from the United States, Europe and Africa. Participation from Canada and Latin America did not change.

Figure i.1 – Geographic representation of participants

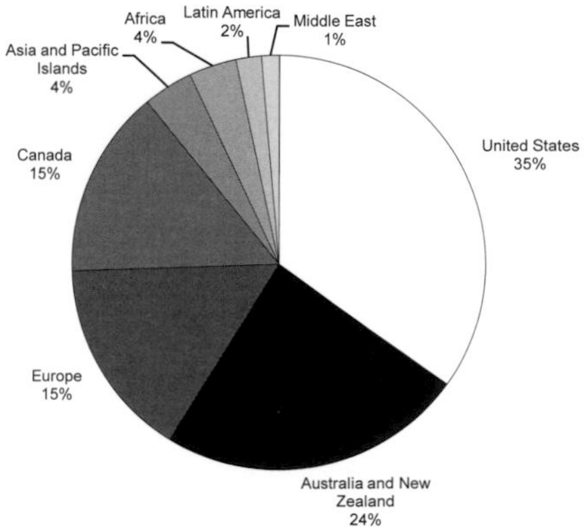

Participants represented a variety of roles in relation to the change on which they reported. Figure i.2 shows the role of participants throughout the last five benchmarking studies. The top four job roles of participants were:

- Change management team leader
- External consultant
- Project team leader
- Change management team member

Figure i.2 – Role of participants

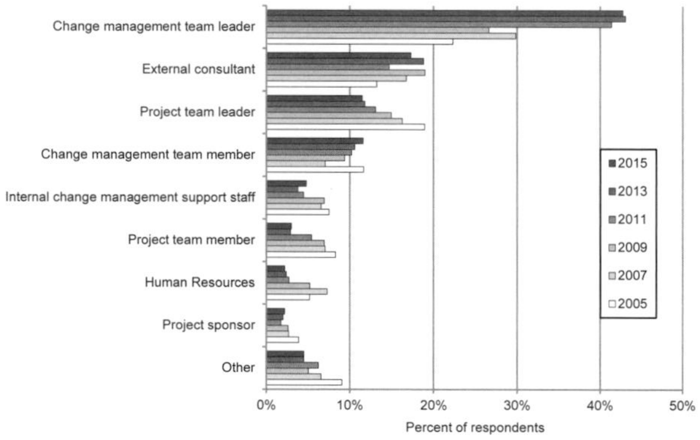

Study objective

The objective of this study is to uncover lessons learned from practitioners and consultants so current change management teams can benefit from these experiences. Emphasis is placed on what is working and what is not in all areas of change management. The 2015 report also presents emerging trends in change management, identifies changes that occurred and describes the future direction of the discipline.

Since change management is a holistic system that requires involvement by change management practitioners, project teams, executives, managers, supervisors and frontline employees, this report details the engagement and role of each of these groups in change management.

New sections in the report

As with previous studies, the 2015 research effort expanded the scope, depth and body of knowledge for change management with new research areas. New research focuses of note in the 2015 study include:

1. Impact of **culture** on change management
2. Importance of **cultural awareness and global literacy** in change
3. Development and leveraging of **change agent networks**
4. Engagement of **complementary roles** in change management work
5. Customization of change management for **vertical industry** segments
6. **Certification** in change management

1. Culture
- Perception of change management in regional cultures
- Aspects of change management that did not fit with various cultures and unique reasons for resisting change management
- Factors that aided in adoption
- Impact of six specific cultural dimensions on change management, including the unique challenges and adaptations for change management based on:
    - Individualism/Collectivism
    - Power Distance
    - Uncertainty Avoidance
    - Assertiveness
    - Performance Orientation
    - Emotional Expressiveness

2. Cultural awareness and global literacy
- Impact of cultural awareness on change management and how cultural awareness influenced change management
- Definition of global literacy

3. Change Agent Networks
- Reasons to use a change agent network
- Definition of the change agent network
- Roles of the change agent network
- Expectations of the change agent network
- Building a change agent network and criteria used to select members of the change agent network

4. Complementary roles
- Examination of how five complementary roles impact change management and the change management process:
    - Internal consultants
    - Human Resources Business Partners
    - Internal communications
    - Business Analyst
    - Organization Development

5. Vertical industry customization
- Industry-specific challenges when employing change management
- Top changes on the horizon segmented by vertical industry

6. Certification in change management
- Prevalence of certification including which certifications were attained
- Recommendation of certification
- Value of change management certification

Additional new findings of interest:
Trends in the discipline, deployment approaches, functional group locations and rationale, job roles, drivers of change management, effectiveness factor regression analysis, measurement of Return on Investment (ROI) factors, budget sources and influence, contributors to starting early, impact of social media, attributes of top tier training, engaging project teams.

Report structure and highlights

PART ONE: Current State of Change Management		
Chapter 1	Insights	*Foundational findings in change management benchmarking research*
Chapter 2	Trends	*What is happening at the forefront of a maturing discipline and how it is evolving*
Chapter 3	Organizational Change Capability	*Move past a project-by-project approach to build change capability into your organization DNA*
PART TWO: Change Management Application		
Chapter 4	Motivation and Justification	*Build buy-in for the results you deliver with project teams and senior leaders*
Chapter 5	Effectiveness and Measurement	*Projects with excellent change management are six times more likely to meet objectives*
Chapter 6	Methodology	*Increase change management effectiveness with a standard methodology*
Chapter 7	Budget, Resources and Team Structure	*Size and secure the right resources for optimizing your change management efforts*
Chapter 8	Change Management Activities	*The specific steps effective change managers take to influence project success*
Chapter 9	PM and CM Integration	*The power of complementary disciplines working in partnership toward a common objective*
PART THREE: Roles in Change Management		
Chapter 10	Sponsorship	*Active and visible sponsorship is the single greatest contributor to success*
Chapter 11	Managers and Supervisors	*Managers and supervisors legitimize the changes impacting the teams they lead*
Chapter 12	Change Agent Network	*Extend project support and credibility through an engaged group of advocates*
Chapter 13	Consultants	*Strategically leverage experienced change professionals to drive change performance*
Chapter 14	Complementary Roles	*Collaborate with internal support functions to enhance change management outcomes*
PART FOUR: Adapting and Aligning Change Management		
Chapter 15	Culture and Change Management	*Navigate the complexity of managing change within the context of culture*
Chapter 16	Customizing CM by Industry	*Adapt change activities to the unique challenges of your industry*
Chapter 17	Aligning CM with Specific Approaches	*Change management intersects with Program Management, Lean, Agile and CPI*
Chapter 18	Managing Complex Changes	*How to adapt when the project presents difficult change management scenarios*
Chapter 19	Saturation and Portfolio Management	*Mitigate the cumulative and collective impact of an ever-increasing volume of change*

PART 1

CURRENT STATE OF CHANGE MANAGEMENT

INSIGHTS

FOUNDATIONAL FINDINGS FROM CHANGE MANAGEMENT RESEARCH ON THE MOST CRITICAL STEPS TO DRIVE SUCCESS

SUMMARY

Greatest contributors to success and greatest change management obstacles provide a research foundation for your change management work. These core best practices continue to shape the practice and growth of the change management industry. Longitudinal data reveals how key findings have changed over time. Start here for advice and lessons learned from seasoned change leaders.

HIGHLIGHT

For the ninth consecutive study, active and visible executive sponsorship was identified as the greatest overall contributor to change success.

Greatest contributors to success

Greatest contributors to success

As in previous studies, participants in the 2015 study identified the greatest contributors to a successful change management initiative. Participants identified seven top contributors and one secondary contributor. All contributors were consistent with previous studies with a slight change in ranking.

1. **Active and visible executive sponsorship**
   As in previous studies, participants identified active and visible sponsorship as the most important contributor to change management success more than three times as often as other contributors. Participants reported that a dedicated and supportive sponsor was critical to a successful change initiative. Participants reported that a sponsor should come from the correct level within the organization and have sufficient influence to affect the budget and other members of executive leadership.

2. **Structured change management approach**
   Participants stressed the importance of applying and sticking with a structured change management approach. Employing a structured methodology creates a formal process and provides a shared language that supports application of change management on a project and throughout the organization. Participants noted that the ideal structured approach is customizable, scalable and proactive in its deployment.

3. **Dedicated change management resources**
   Participants reported that having and maintaining the appropriate level of funding were crucial to the success of their change management initiatives. Participants highlighted the importance of having an experienced and dedicated change management resource who was involved in the initiative from the beginning. Participants identified that having influential resources who could act as part of a team and speak for and represent diverse business areas and impact groups, was also important to the success of change initiatives.

4. **Integration and engagement with project management**
   Participants reported that integrating and engaging with the project team and leaders were important contributors to the success of a change management initiative. Participants also stressed the importance of engaging with the project team at the beginning because it allowed for the merging of work streams.

5. **Employee engagement and participation**
   Participants cited employee engagement and participation in the change as key contributors to a successful change initiative. This focused on working to engage employees in the change by highlighting "what's in it for me?" (WIIFM), identifying and building relationships with impacted groups, and ensuring those groups received the appropriate level of training.

6. **Frequent and open communication**
   Frequent communication was cited as a top contributor to a successful change initiative. Beyond frequency, participants cited consistency, openness and transparency, and the regularity of communication as important to success. Additionally, participants identified important topics for communication to address including expectations, plans and how the change will affect employees.

7. **Engagement with middle managers**
   Participants identified a need to engage middle managers, ensuring that there was an appropriate level of buy-in, commitment and involvement from middle managers. Participants also identified the importance of turning managers into change champions who act as early adopters and vocal advocates of the change to their direct reports and other impacted groups.

Additional contributors to success reported

When listing other contributors to success, participants in the 2015 study also reported a secondary contributor: awareness of the need for change management. An understanding and appreciation of the need for change management drove many of the other top contributors. Participants identified the need to demonstrate the Return on Investment (ROI) of change management, the business case for employing and using change management and the potential of improved project success as key factors in building change management awareness.

Contributors to success over time

The table below shows the ranking of contributors to success throughout the last nine benchmarking studies. Active and visible executive sponsorship ranked number one in each of the nine studies. The ranking of the top three factors in the 2015 study mirrored the 2013 findings, with slight movements in the remaining factors.

Table 1.1 – Contributors to success over time

Contributors to success	2015 rank	2013 rank	2011 rank	2009 rank	2007 rank	2005 rank	2003 rank	2000 rank	1998 rank
Sponsorship	1	1	1	1	1	1	1	1	1
Structured approach	2	2	3	3	2	2	5	-	-
Dedicated funding and resources	3	3	4	4	4	-	-	-	-
Project management integration	4	6	-	-	-	-	-	-	-
Employee engagement	5	5	5	5	5	4	-	2*	2
Communication	6	4	2	2	3	3	4	2	-
Middle management	7	7	6	-	-	-	-	-	-

* This item was combined with "Frequent and open communications around the need for change" in the 2000 study.

Greatest change management obstacles

Greatest obstacles to success

Participants identified the most challenging obstacles they faced when applying change management.

1. **Lack of active and visible sponsorship**
   More than twice as often as any other obstacle, participants reported lack of effective executive sponsorship as the number-one obstacle to successful change management. This included sponsors delegating duties, being present at kickoff then stepping away from the project and not helping to get other employees and sponsors on board. Many participants reported that these mistakes came from executives lacking an understanding of the role of an effective sponsor.
2. **Lack of change management resourcing**
   Lack of investment and resourcing for change management was cited as an obstacle to success, including both financial and human resources. Change management resources were often insufficient to apply change management. Allocated resources were often the first to be cut when budget concerns and competing projects arose.
3. **Manager and supervisor resistance**
   Resistance at the mid-level and frontline manager positions was the third most common obstacle participants identified. A manager's focus on daily operations and lack of inclusion during decision-making resulted in managers being predisposed to resistance. Managers also lacked awareness of the important role they played in the change process. Consequently, managers often took sides, speaking out against the change and failing to participate in cascading communications that the change initiative required.
4. **Employee resistance**
   Resistance from frontline employees was also cited as an obstacle. Participants reported this was largely due to a lack of employee awareness of the need for change. Participants also reported that the majority of frontline employees were already experiencing large amounts of change, which increased their resistance to any new change.
5. **Lack of buy-in from project teams**
   Lack of the project team understanding the important role change management plays in the success of a project was another obstacle for change managers. Project teams often involved change managers very late in the process, or even worse, after a previous rollout had already failed. Change management was viewed as a soft science and did not have credibility with people who were project minded.

Other obstacles

A number of obstacles did not make the top five, but were frequently identified:

- A large amount of change happening in an organization, frequently referred to as change fatigue or saturation
- Change resistant culture
- Organization complexity including globally dispersed authority structures and multi-lingual work forces
- Unclear or changing future state
- Lack of change management competency or understanding in the organization

What to do differently on the next project

What change practitioners would do differently

Participants reflected on their experiences in managing a change and detailed what they would have done differently.

1. **Planning/strategizing**
   Participants reported that the greatest activity they would have done differently would be to have spent more time planning and strategizing their approach to the change. Participants identified the need to create a comprehensive strategy for managing the change by identifying resources necessary for the change, by aligning with key project deliverables and results of the change, and by properly identifying and preparing leaders responsible for the change.

2. **Leader involvement**
   Participants indicated that all leaders, including managers, sponsors and stakeholders, needed to be engaged throughout the change process. Participants highlighted the need for early leader involvement to provide clear objectives of the change and ensure that all groups involved were aligned with how to reach those objectives. To have such leader involvement, participants stressed the need to educate leaders on their proper role in the change process and the responsibilities of that role. One participant stated, "*Spend more time educating the sponsors on their role and activities (and less time on CM theory and tools).*"

3. **Early change management involvement**
   Participants reported that it was important to involve change management early in the change process. Participants emphasized the need to begin change management efforts earlier in the change process. They would have planned on using change management at an earlier stage in the process and having the change manager engaged in the process at an earlier time in the change lifecycle.

4. **Education**
   Participants would have provided education on what change management is, why it is important and the benefits of change management. Participants also indicated that they would have provided education on how change management supports the specific change occurring, including education on why the change was necessary, what the scope of the change would be and how change management supports the specific change.

Advice for practitioners

Most important activities at the beginning of engagement

Source date: 2011

Experienced practitioners in the 2011 study identified the three most important activities they would recommend that a new practitioner complete at the start of engagement to improve the success of change management. The most common start-up activities were:

1. **Communication**
   Strategize for effective and efficient early communication. Avoid saturating the audience. Use language that is understood at all levels. Be sure to discuss and agree on roles and expectations. Be explicit about deliverables. Define what involvement looks like. Listen to all levels. Develop a means for accepting input from stakeholders. Develop easy-to-understand plans and be visible and vocal about those plans. Establish a communications plan quickly to develop common language.
2. **Analysis and assessment including stakeholder analysis**
   Identify critical success factors of the project, and then assess for alignment with these factors. Complete impact and readiness assessments. Gauge and understand the scope of the project. Determine what might interfere with or impact employees' capacities to adopt change. Spend more time in the analysis phase, and convince others to do the same.
3. **Relationship development and coalition building**
   Identify and get commitment from the right sponsor. Establish a relationship with key team members including business leaders and middle managers. Customize a strategy to address leadership resistance. Develop a team of change champions, agents and leaders. Develop team principles and rules. Present benefits and change management methodology to key players. Meet with stakeholders often.

Biggest challenges or hurdles

Source date: 2011

In the 2011 study, experienced practitioners commented on the biggest challenges or hurdles they would recommend that a practitioner be aware of and watch for at the start of a new engagement. The most common challenges or hurdles included:

1. **Poorly selected, waning or disengaged sponsorship**
   Watch for sponsors who lack authority, have insufficient change management knowledge or do not believe in the change. Many participants offered comments similar to "*make sure the sponsor is at the correct level in the organization,*" and "*beware of sponsors with no interest, authority or impact on individuals.*"
2. **Lack of understanding, buy-in or recognition of the value of change management**
   Challenges include organizations with low change maturity, change saturation and lack of strategic prioritization. One participant stated, "*It is too easy for anyone to think they can 'do' change management. However, it is a specialized skill that requires experts and deserves to be treated properly.*"
3. **Lack of resources for the change management team including budget, time allotment and dedicated personnel**
   One participant's comment summarized the theme: "*The challenge is change management resourcing not getting the needed attention, it is too often underestimated and understaffed.*"
4. **Lack of project and change management team integration**
   The biggest integration challenge was lack of collaboration, including the change management team not being asked to participate in key decisions. Hurdles also included: "*being ignored by project managers,*" "*project managers who don't know what change management is and is not, and who don't understand the change*

management role" and "*[being] sidelined by project teams who speed through to meet deadlines rather than purposefully plan for change.*"

5. **Resistance to change at all levels, including passive resistance**
   Participants noted resistance to the specific change in addition to resistance to change management efforts and activities. Challenges also included verbal support of the change but unwillingness to participate in change activities.

Advice for new practitioners

Source date: 2011

Experienced practitioners participating in the 2011 benchmarking study provided the two most valuable pieces of advice that they would give to new practitioners. Top responses were:

1. **Communicate early and often**
   Agree on who communicates what and when. Engage face-to-face at all levels in the organization. Try to answer the question "what's in it for me?" (WIIFM) at all levels. Identify who can credibly communicate messages about the change. Listen to both formal and informal communication about and within the project.
2. **Get involved early**
   Get involved early to participate in or drive vision, outcomes, planning and stakeholder analysis; involvement midway through the project is too late to do this effectively. The change management team needs to be involved at the onset of an initiative. Establish change management as an integral part of the project from day one. Engage stakeholders, sponsors and employees up front. Involve impacted employees in the change process as early as possible. Engage middle management immediately.
3. **Integrate change management with project management and strategy**
   "*Don't underestimate the power of project management to override the people side of projects.*" Align with the project manager and closely integrate with the project activities. Meet with the project manager frequently (at least twice a week was recommended most commonly). Participants advised that new practitioners should view project and change management as parallel processes. Be clear on the scope of the project and any changes to the scope.
4. **Establish buy-in**
   Ensure that the "why" for the change is clear. Educate others on the change management process and the value and rationale for applying change management to the project. Use a recognized methodology and justify the need for a formal change management program early. Create understanding of the Return on Investment (ROI) of change management, and establish what change management will deliver.
5. **Work with sponsors**
   Participants advised new practitioners to be clear about sponsor activities, and consider the level of sponsorship. Ensure sponsors understand their role and what is expected of them. Work closely with the sponsors and be confident in the direction given to them. Secure sponsorship early and document expectations and specific activities. Ensure the sponsorship is meaningful to all levels of the organization.

Biggest gap new practitioners would like to fill

Source date: 2011

New change management practitioners in the 2011 study identified the biggest gaps they would like to fill. The top gaps were:

1. **Change management knowledge, tools and skills**
   Participants identified a lack of knowledge and training in key change management skills, tools and methodologies as a gap for new practitioners. They reported needing more expertise in the field of change management.

2. **Selling change management to the organization**
   Participants sought approaches to engage with project teams, stakeholders and sponsors and build buy-in for change management with these groups. Participants expressed a desire for "*more experience influencing sponsors and leaders,*" and sought the ability to position change management as a permanent function by "*clearly articulating benefits of a structured change management approach.*"

3. **Sponsorship and leadership engagement**
   Participants identified the ability to engage and coach sponsors as a key gap for new practitioners. Lacking understanding of how to influence decision-makers and build a coalition of support from leadership, participants expressed a desire to learn approaches for creating sustained engagement from sponsors.

4. **Creating effective communications**
   New change management practitioners identified a gap in creating of honest and effective communication. They desired improved skills in selecting and implementing appropriate communication tools and correct alignment of timing and messages for specific audiences.

5. **Project management integration**
   The ability to integrate change management with project management effectively and efficiently was identified as a gap for new practitioners. Participants described this gap as including competencies both in bridging the differences between the methodologies used in each area and in managing the overlap of the two disciplines.

TRENDS

WHAT IS HAPPENING AT THE FOREFRONT OF AN EMERGING AND MATURING DISCIPLINE?

SUMMARY

Explore benchmarking data about where the change management industry is advancing today and how it will grow over the next five years. Trends toward greater use of formal methodologies, greater integration into project management and more resources dedicated to the people side of change point to the next frontiers of development for change professionals. These trends present ways change leaders must continue to evolve in order to stay relevant. Use research-backed data to develop your change management practice and deliver added value to your organization.

HIGHLIGHT

Greater awareness of the need for change management was again the top two-year trend projected; increased integration with project management was the top five-year trend.

Internal two-year trends in change management

In each study beginning in 2007, participants identified change management trends that they witnessed in their organizations. Since 2007, the top change management trend has been greater awareness or recognition of the need for change management. Participants in the 2015 study identified eight trends in change management.

1. **Greater awareness of the need for change management**
   Participants noted an increase in the awareness of change management as a core competency. This increase derives from greater understanding of the value and benefits of change management and greater acceptance of change management practices occurring at all levels. Along with greater acceptance, participants reported broader awareness and credibility of the discipline.
2. **More resources and positions dedicated to change management**
   Participants reported that more resources and positions are being dedicated to change management. Greater investment is being made in acquiring formal change management staff members. Executives are committing more funds to change management. Participants note more resources allocated to support more changes, creation of more positions, formal change roles attached to departments and increased levels of change management capability.
3. **Enhanced integration with project management**
   Change management worked more in tandem with project management, including more recognition of the criticality of change management as a partner, integration of tools and practices between the two disciplines and initiation of change management earlier in project plans. Participants also observed the establishment of a Project Management Office (PMO) with a dedicated change team and integration of a Change Management Office (CMO) with Project Management Offices (PMOs).
4. **Greater importance or effort to establish a CMO or dedicated functional group**
   Participants noted efforts to establish a Change Management Office (CMO), citing several reasons including building capability and credibility and creating an enterprise-wide view.
5. **Broader application of change management**
   Participants observed broader applications of change management across the organization. Broader thinking about the application of change management to other areas included involvement of a larger number of employees, broadened definitions of stakeholders, a change in thinking regarding performance appraisals, use of change management for changes that are not formal projects, gamification and use of change management to facilitate business engagement in new ways. In some cases, change management was required for complex projects.
6. **Use of formal methodology or structure to manage change**
   Participants reported an increase in the use of structure and adoption of established methodologies to manage change, driven by a need for common language and tools. A structured approach, in conjunction with project management, resulted in increased capability. Participants identified both external methodologies and internally created methods and tools.
7. **Increased leadership support for change management**
   Participants noted an increase in senior leadership support for change management including greater understanding of sponsorship and the impact of strong leadership. Participants identified change management as a focus at the executive level, with more desire for and emphasis placed on sponsor involvement.

8. **Greater demand for change management training or education**
   Participants reported an increase in the training and education of change management practitioners, including training sessions designated for change leaders, more formal change management training events, increased interest in training broader audiences and integration of change management training into existing learning and development programs. Participants also cited increased solicitation of change management training and services and, in some cases, mandatory change management training for employees. Increased change management education was reported at all levels of the organization, driven by greater understanding of the value and impact of change management.

Challenges facing the discipline

Participants also mentioned some challenges they faced associated with these trends:

- Change management is not valued leading to senior leaders and impacted groups giving lip service to change management, lack of resources, lack of adequate time, lack of information, being the first group to have resources cut, decentralized resources and minimal investment in change management
- Unqualified change managers
- Confusion around change management activities, communication, training and methodologies
- Resistance to the change and change management
- Tensions between change management and project management
- Limited internal capability
- Leadership turnover
- Departments being overly protective of change management practices

Trends from previous studies

The top trends identified in the 2013 study were:

1. Greater awareness of the need for change management
2. Broader application of change management
3. Increased leadership support for change management
4. Greater effort to establish a Change Management Office (CMO) or dedicated functional group
5. Increased use of methodologies and tools to manage the people side of change
6. Greater emphasis on training, communications and reinforcement plans
7. Increased focus on impacted individuals
8. Recognition of the need for change portfolio management

The top trends identified by participants in the 2011 study included:

1. Greater awareness of the need for and value of change management
2. Increased use of methodologies, tools and language
3. More engagement and earlier integration with project management
4. More resources and positions devoted to change management
5. Greater demand for change management training and certification
6. Increased leadership support for change management
7. Underestimation and allocation of change management resources

The top trends identified in the 2009 study were:

1. Growing recognition of the need for change management
2. Greater demand for change management competency building (training)
3. More dedicated resources for change management
4. Increased use of change management tools
5. Greater application of change management on projects
6. More integration between project management and change management
7. Growing change saturation
8. Increased use of a standard change management approach
9. More frequent establishment of a change management group
10. Increased focus on management of the portfolio of change

The top trends identified in the 2007 study were:

1. Growing recognition of the need for change management
2. Increased use of more structured and formal processes
3. Better understanding of what change management really is
4. Enhanced integration with project management
5. Greater recognition of change management as a new competency
6. More frequent creation of formal change management job roles and titles
7. Earlier application on projects

Projected discipline trends over the next five years

Participants in the 2015 study identified the top trends they expect in the discipline of change management over the next five years. Although a large number of trends were identified, six were mentioned more often than the others.

1. **Integration with project management**
   The top trend expected in the next five years is integration of change and project management. Participants anticipate a continuation of an increase in the integration between the two disciplines. Participants identified an increase in the number of project managers developing skill sets for managing change and recognition by project managers of change management's role in project success as reasons for further discipline integration.
2. **Continued maturation of the discipline of change management**
   Participants expect that over the next five years, the discipline will continue to mature. Three factors related to maturation were cited more often than others:
   - **Increased use of a structured methodology**
     Participants stated that over the next five years, organizations will demonstrate and commit to the use of a particular methodology to provide structure for their change management efforts.
   - **Increased use of tools**
     Similar to the use of a structured methodology, participants expect that the availability and use of tools to assist with change will increase. Participants highlighted the development of common tools to measure change impact, change readiness, benefit tracking and communication. The tools will become easier to use and interactive. Participants expect the quality of tools to increase.
   - **Increase in the general use of change management**
     Participants expect that the overall use of change management within organizations will continue to increase, which will contribute to maturation of the discipline.
3. **Focus on building internal capabilities and core competency**
   Over the next five years, participants anticipate an internal focus on building capabilities and competencies for change. Participants expect greater emphasis on change agility and capacity within organizations, including development of internal change teams and creation and refinement of change management roles that will be integrated throughout the functional areas of the organization. It is expected that a skill set for change management will be developed at all levels and the majority of projects will incorporate change management efforts. There will be heightened focus on executive and manager roles within change. Participants believed there will be continued focus on development of internal Change Management Offices (CMOs).
4. **Recognition and acceptance of change management as a discipline**
   Participants expect that over the next five years, change management will be viewed with greater acceptance including recognition on an international scale and career path. There will be an increase in the availability of change management jobs and an overall increase in the number of change management networks.
5. **Increased executive awareness, development and engagement**
   Participants expected an overall increase in awareness at the executive level over the next five years. The engagement level of executives will increase, and participants believed there will be a requirement for executives to be able to lead change efforts within organizations. There will be focused efforts to enhance and support development of sponsors to be effective leaders of change.

6. **General awareness of the need for and value of change management**
   Participants expect that over the next five years, awareness of change management will continue to increase. Change management's value will be recognized, and understanding of the need for change management within organizations will develop.

Additional five-year trends identified by participants included:

- Creation of a guiding professional standard for change management
- Increased focus on and emphasis of change management Return on Investment (ROI)
- Continued focus on and development of change management metrics
- Focus on enterprise change management including change portfolio management
- Growth in the number of change management practitioners and certifications in change management

5-year trends from previous studies

The top 5-year discipline-related trends identified in the 2013 study were:

1. Continued maturation of the practice of change management
2. Focus on building internal capabilities and core competency
3. Expansion of change management as a profession
4. Continued elevation of acceptance
5. Further integration with project management
6. Greater application of change management

ORGANIZATIONAL CAPABILITY

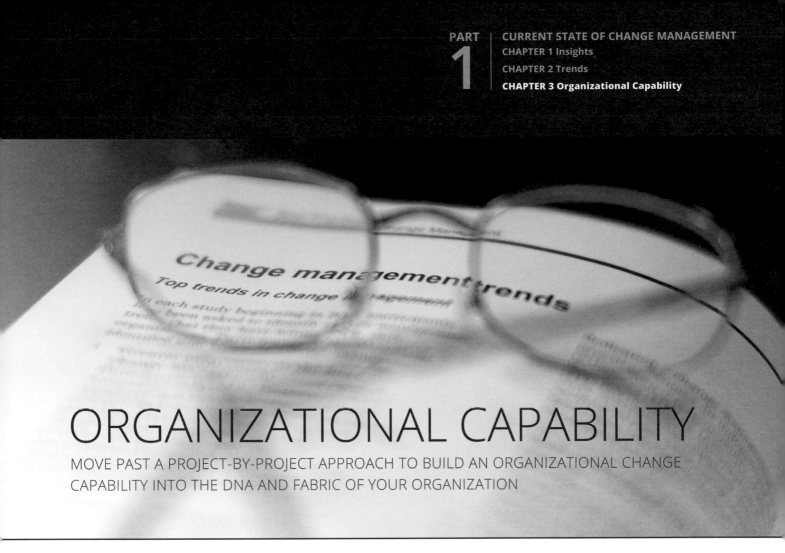

MOVE PAST A PROJECT-BY-PROJECT APPROACH TO BUILD AN ORGANIZATIONAL CHANGE CAPABILITY INTO THE DNA AND FABRIC OF YOUR ORGANIZATION

SUMMARY

Leaders recognize that consistently delivering change results is a valuable competitive differentiator and a key to strategic success. Uncover best practices in approach, structure and function for deploying an organization-wide change management capability. The latest data on change management maturity provides benchmarks by organization size and geographical region. Enable your organization to increase its change management maturity by approaching the deployment of change capability with structure and intent.

HIGHLIGHT

Training, education and standardization of a methodology were the top three steps for building an organizational capability in change management.

Organizational maturity

Change management maturity

Figure 3.1 shows how 2015 participants rated their organizations (or for consultants, their client organizations) on the Prosci® Change Management Maturity Model™ (see Appendix E for a full description). Levels of the Prosci Change Management Maturity Model describe overall deployment and maturity of change management within an organization:

Level 5: Organizational competency

Level 4: Organizational standards

Level 3: Multiple projects

Level 2: Isolated projects

Level 1: Absent or ad hoc

Participants' Change Management Maturity Model levels in 2015 were similar to levels in 2013. Those reporting Level 2 increased by 3%, which was offset by a reduction of Level 5 by 2% and Level 4 by 1%, as shown in Figure 3.1.

Figure 3.1 – Prosci Change Management Maturity Model

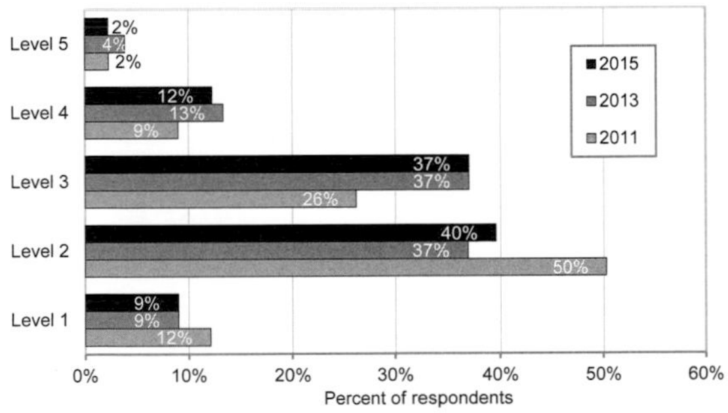

Factors that influenced movement in organizational maturity

Participants in the 2015 study identified key factors that caused the organization's maturity level to move up, move down or stay the same.

1. **Change management benefit awareness**
   Realization and awareness of the value added by using change management methodologies was a primary driver behind an organization's maturity. An increase in awareness of the benefits from change management practices led to an increase in organizational maturity. Lack of awareness of the benefits of change management caused maturity to stagnate or even decrease. Benefit awareness often arose after organizations experienced multiple projects or initiatives that failed, for example, exceeded time frames, budgets and resources.
2. **Leadership and dedicated teams**
   Changes in leadership and leadership engagement, creation of a dedicated change position and the use of outside contributors were factors that led to increases in maturity. Organizations' maturity levels moved down or stayed the same when change management teams were disbanded or key change champions left.
3. **Methodology use**
   Using a more standardized approach, training additional stakeholders, integrating change management on the project team and aligning the direction of the organization contributed to increases in organizations' maturity. Maturity levels decreased or stayed the same when companies took an isolated approach or used an inconsistent methodology across the organization.
4. **Business growth and structural change**
   Mergers and acquisitions, growth in the size of the organization and an increase in the number and scope of projects applying change management were associated with maturity levels increasing.

5. **Resource allocation**
Additions of change management resources, such as budgets, time and the number of resources, were cited as contributors to increases in an organization's maturity. Cutting budgets, resources and time allocation to change management caused maturity to decrease.

Maturity level two years ago

Greater detail is provided in Figure 3.2, which shows changes in Change Management Maturity Model levels during the last two years. Thirty-two percent of participants reported that their organization remained at the same level. More than half (57%) reported an increase of one level, and 10% increased two levels. One percent reported an increase of three or four levels. Participant responses in 2015 were similar to those in 2013 as shown in Figure 3.2.

Figure 3.2 – Prosci Change Management Maturity Model progression

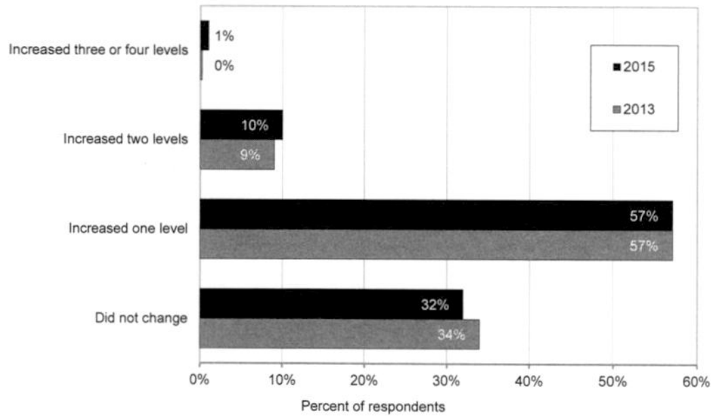

Maturity Model data by region

Prosci Change Management Maturity Model data provided by participants in the 2013 and 2015 studies were segmented by region. Table 3.3 shows the averages and standard deviations for each level in the model along with the percentage of participants represented by that region.

Table 3.3 – Maturity Model averages by region

Region (percent of study participants from that region in 2015 study)	**Average Maturity Model level** 2015 *(2013)*	**Standard deviation** 2015 *(2013)*
All regions (100%)	2.59 *(2.66)*	0.89 *(0.95)*
United States (35%)	2.70 *(2.69)*	0.86 *(0.93)*
Australia and New Zealand (24%)	2.56 *(2.68)*	0.93 *(0.95)*
Canada (15%)	2.57 *(2.62)*	0.82 *(0.93)*
Europe (15%)	2.37 *(2.66)*	0.92 *(0.94)*
Africa (4%)	2.89 *(2.59)*	.88 *(1.21)*
Asia and Pacific Islands (4%)	2.65 *(2.88)*	.94 *(1.03)*
Latin America (2%)	2.67 *(2.67)*	.96 *(0.78)*
Middle East (1%)	2.64 *(2.31)*	.91 *(0.63)*

Editor's note: The distributions should not be interpreted as fully representative of change management maturity in each region, given that in regions with fewer participants, data would more likely be provided by organizations with higher interest and maturity in change management than by other organizations in that region that did not participate in the benchmarking studies.

Table 3.4 shows a more granular view of Prosci Change Management Maturity Model data by region with a breakout of the percent of each region that classified themselves as a Level 1, Level 2, Level 3, Level 4 or Level 5 maturity.

Table 3.4 – Maturity Model data segmented by region

	Level 1	Level 2	Level 3	Level 4	Level 5
Africa	8%	26%	43%	23%	0%
Asia and Pacific Islands	10%	32%	45%	8%	5%
Australia and New Zealand	11%	38%	37%	11%	3%
Canada	7%	41%	41%	10%	1%
Europe	14%	48%	25%	11%	2%
Latin America (Mexico, Central, South America)	24%	28%	38%	10%	0%
Middle East	13%	40%	34%	13%	0%
United States	5%	39%	39%	15%	2%

Maturity Model data by industry

Table 3.5 shows Prosci Change Management Maturity Model data for those industries representing 1.5% or more of participants. Percent of study participants from that industry is shown in parenthesis.

Table 3.5 – Maturity Model data segmented by industry

	Level 1	Level 2	Level 3	Level 4	Level 5
Aerospace (2%)	5%	47%	37%	11%	0%
Banking (6%)	6%	25%	37%	26%	6%
Consulting (6%)	12%	45%	31%	7%	5%
Consumer Goods Manufacturing (2%)	0%	32%	45%	23%	0%
Education Services (5%)	10%	50%	34%	6%	0%
Finance (6%)	6%	33%	40%	18%	3%
Government - Federal (5%)	9%	42%	31%	18%	0%
Government - Local & Municipal (4%)	21%	45%	29%	5%	0%
Government - Military (2%)	11%	50%	28%	11%	0%
Government - Other (2%)	12%	41%	41%	6%	0%
Government - State (6%)	10%	53%	27%	10%	0%
Health Care (7%)	5%	41%	47%	6%	1%
Information Services (3%)	17%	42%	30%	3%	8%
Insurance (5%)	6%	40%	42%	10%	2%
Manufacturing (4%)	15%	26%	40%	15%	4%
Non-profit (2%)	19%	52%	29%	0%	0%
Oil and Gas (6%)	5%	38%	41%	11%	5%
Pharmaceutical (2%)	0%	37%	21%	31%	11%
Professional, Scientific & Technical Services (2%)	12%	56%	12%	16%	4%
Retail Trade (3%)	3%	35%	47%	15%	0%
Telecommunications (3%)	7%	29%	57%	7%	0%
Transportation & Warehousing (2%)	0%	58%	21%	21%	0%
Utilities (4%)	13%	34%	42%	11%	0%

Table 3.6 includes the average Prosci Change Management Maturity Model level and the standard deviation for each industry.

Table 3.6 – Maturity Model averages by industry

Industry (percent of study participants from that industry)	Average Maturity Model level	Standard deviation
All Industries (100%)	2.5	.89
Aerospace (2%)	2.52	.77
Banking (6%)	3.01	.99
Consulting (6%)	2.48	.96
Consumer Goods Manufacturing (2%)	2.9	.75
Education Services (5%)	2.36	.75
Finance (6%)	2.77	.92
Government – Federal (5%)	2.58	.89
Government - Local & Municipal (4%)	2.18	.83
Government – Military (2%)	2.38	.84.
Government – Other (2%)	2.41	.79
Government – State (6%)	2.37	.80
Health Care (7%)	2.57	.74
Information Services (3%)	2.44	1.08
Insurance (5%)	2.61	.82
Manufacturing (4%)	2.68	1.04
Non-profit (2%)	2.09	.70
Oil and Gas (6%)	2.73	.91
Pharmaceutical (2%)	3.17	1.06
Professional, Scientific & Technical Services (2%)	2.44	1.04
Retail Trade (3%)	2.73	.75
Telecommunications (3%)	2.64	.73
Transportation & Warehousing (2%)	2.63	.83
Utilities (4%)	2.51	.87

Maturity Model data by revenue

Table 3.7 presents the distribution of change management maturity by size of the organization as determined by annual revenue.

Table 3.7 – Maturity Model data segmented by revenue

	Level 1	Level 2	Level 3	Level 4	Level 5
Less than $10 million	18%	41%	23%	14%	4%
$10 million - $25 million	19%	40%	30%	8%	3%
$25 million - $50 million	19%	47%	23%	9%	2%
$50 million - $100 million	12%	50%	31%	6%	1%
$100 million - $250 million	16%	47%	36%	1%	0%
$250 million - $500 million	7%	54%	30%	9%	0%
$500 million - $1 billion	8%	39%	44%	8%	1%
$1 billion - $2.5 billion	9%	45%	35%	8%	3%
$2.5 billion - $5 billion	5%	38%	43%	13%	1%
More than $5 billion	4%	29%	41%	22%	4%

Maturity Model data by number of employees

Table 3.8 presents the distribution of change management maturity by size of the organization based on number of employees.

Table 3.8 – Maturity Model data segmented by number of employees

	Level 1	Level 2	Level 3	Level 4	Level 5
1 - 99	13%	41%	35%	10%	1%
100 - 499	21%	41%	30%	8%	0%
500 - 999	14%	49%	30%	5%	2%
1,000 - 2,499	12%	50%	33%	4%	1%
2,500 - 4,999	7%	45%	38%	9%	1%
5,000 - 9,999	5%	44%	35%	15%	1%
10,000 - 19,999	7%	36%	43%	11%	3%
20,000 - 34,999	2%	33%	44%	18%	3%
More than 35,000	5%	24%	42%	23%	6%

Editor's note: The distributions are insightful and the most robust data available, but they should not be interpreted as representative of a random sample of change management maturity for each region, industry or organization size. Summation data is impacted by the amount of representation from each group and may not be a random sample specifically for groups where representation is low.

Deployment approach

Working to deploy change management

Just less than half of participants (47%) were actively working to deploy change management throughout their organization (Figure 3.9).

Figure 3.9 – Actively working to deploy change management

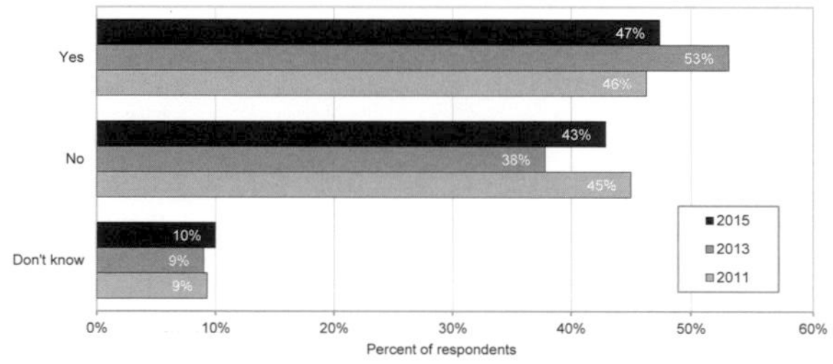

Those organizations that were working to deploy change management scored higher in the Prosci Change Management Maturity Model (Table 3.10). Sixty-five percent of those actively working to deploy change management rated their organization as Level 5, 4 or 3 in the model, in comparison to 41% of those not deploying change management. Only 3% of those working to deploy change management rated their organizations as Level 1, in comparison to 14% not deploying change management.

Table 3.10 – Organizations actively working to deploy change management by maturity level

Prosci Change Management Maturity Model Level	Actively working to deploy	Not actively working to deploy
Level 5	4%	0%
Level 4	19%	5%
Level 3	43%	29%
Level 2	31%	52%
Level 1	3%	14%

Steps to deploy change management within a capability development effort

Participants in the 2015 study identified the steps they took to deploy change management capability.

1. **Training and education**
   Respondents recommended instituting training in a cascading fashion beginning with senior leaders in the organization, frequently conducting change management workshops and using education tools such as eLearning modules and social media.
2. **Use of a specific methodology**
   The most frequently identified characteristics of an effective methodology were its consistency and intentional design. Certification programs were identified as supporting a common and consistent methodology.
3. **Use of a structured change plan**
   Participants used a structured change plan to deploy change management which included conducting readiness assessments, clearly defining success and standards, and leveraging an integrated plan that addressed both project management and change management.
4. **Active and supported leadership**
   Participants noted the importance of having the active and engaged support of leadership throughout deployment of change management, including obtaining buy-in from senior or executive leadership. Participants frequently noted the importance of providing support for leadership, generally in the form of training sessions or seminars specifically developed for leadership.

5. **Communication**
Examples of effective communication regarding deployment included face-to-face meetings, showcasing the change management framework internally, clearly defining roles within the change project and highlighting the benefits of change management through success stories.

6. **Having appropriate resources**
Participants noted the importance of obtaining appropriate resources for deploying change management capability. Examples of resource activities included determining the change management budget, training practitioners and external consultants and procuring licenses for tools and content.

Length of effort

Of those actively working to deploy change management, 14% were just starting the effort, in comparison to 15% in 2013 and 23% in 2011. Thirty-two percent were within the first year of deployment, compared to 36% in the 2013 and 32% in the 2011 studies. More than 16% were over than three years into deployment, compared to 16% in 2013 and 14% in 2011 (Figure 3.11).

Figure 3.11 – Length of deployment effort

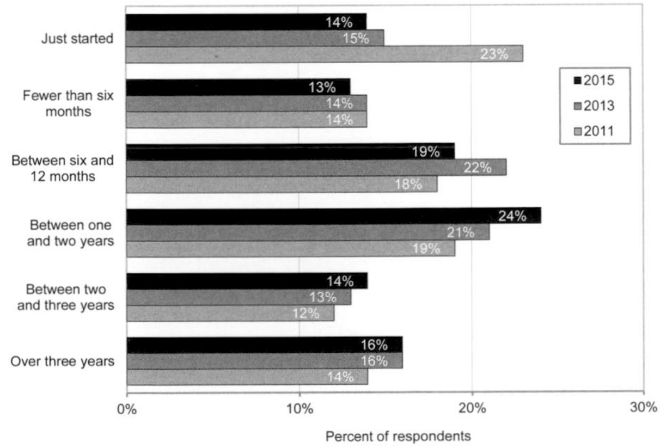

Originator of the effort

Human Resources (HR), Project Management Office (PMO) or Organization Development (OD) were cited by just over half of participants as the originators of the effort to build organizational change management capability and competency, as in the 2013 study. The other top originators were executive leadership and Information Technology (IT), shown in Figure 3.12.

Figure 3.12 – Originator of the effort

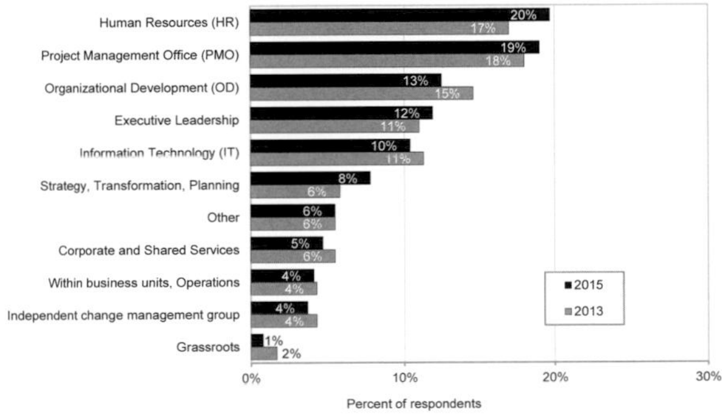

Activities with the largest impact

When participants were asked what activities had the greatest impact on change management deployment, five primary activities were identified.

1. **Visible leadership support**
Senior leader commitment to change management was identified as the activity with the largest impact when deploying change management across an organization. These leaders set an example for others to follow by being involved during deployment, understanding the importance of change management and addressing issues early during deployment.

2. **Training**
Participants indicated that training had a large impact on deployment. Training was provided to key resources within the change scope and was often tailored to individuals. Early and frequent training decreased the amount of potential resistance to change management.

3. **Engagement on projects**
   Engaging and applying change management on initiatives aided deployment. Clear and open communication channels, both formal and informal, ensured that employees aligned with the organization's direction. Engagement on projects also provided change experience to key stakeholders.

4. **Implementation of tools and methodology**
   Participants used structured change management tools and methods for change deployment. Activities included assessing awareness of employees, preparing surveys, implementing strategies specific to a particular method and aligning the entire organization with a consistent methodology.

5. **Demonstration of successes**
   Proof of success played a role in change management deployment. This entailed applying change management on a project and rigorously documenting results. Evidence of success improved the reputation, credibility and visibility of change management.

Important activities at the launch of change management

Participants identified the most important activities during launch of change management.

1. **Executive buy-in**
   Participants reported that it was important to gain executive buy-in and advocacy when broadly deploying change management. Executives needed to communicate the benefits of fully funding change management. Doing so before deployment ensured it was viewed in a positive light by the business.

2. **Creating one coherent message**
   Participants reported the need to solidly advocate for a single message about the need for change management. Multiple messages often confused or diluted change management. This made it harder for change practitioners to motivate impacted groups to participate in change because desire stemmed from different or conflicting awareness messages.

3. **Proof of success**
   Participants provided data on the clear benefits and Return on Investment (ROI) of change management. They shared examples of past successes when change management was applied on projects to build both awareness and trust of the change management methodology and what it could accomplish.

Use of a pilot group and proofs of success in deployment

Participants in the 2015 study reported on whether or not they used a pilot group when deploying their organizational change capability. Figure 3.13 shows that one third of participants did use a pilot group.

Figure 3.13 - Use of a pilot group

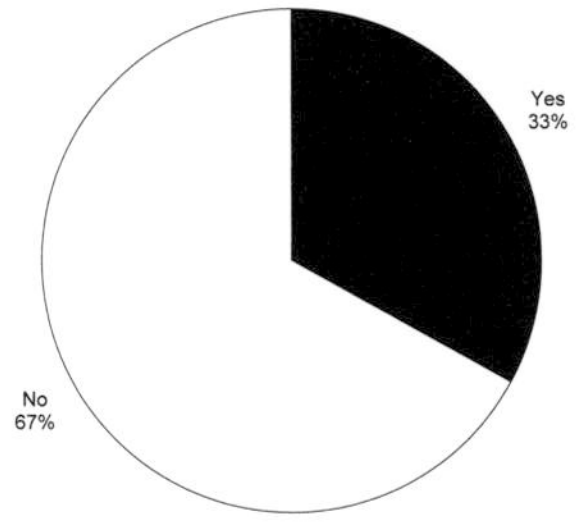

Participants stated how they would classify proofs of success when deploying change management broadly across the enterprise.

1. **Qualitative feedback**
   Participants considered positive qualitative feedback as proof of success. Feedback included post-implementation interviews, word of mouth and surveys designed to elicit descriptive feedback for impacted groups and primary stakeholders. Participants also used

quantitative, data-driven feedback but found qualitative feedback more valuable in demonstrating proof of success.

2. **Project success**
   Participants reported that project success was deemed adequate proof of success. Participants who implemented a methodology for the first time identified the importance of a first-success project to demonstrate the value of change management. Participants who worked to implement an organizational change management capability reported that multiple and consistent project successes were more important than one successful project.
3. **Cross-project implementation**
   Participants reported that cross-project use of the methodology acted as additional proof of success. Although many participants hoped to see organization-wide adoption of the methodology, they also gauged success by several projects adopting select change management practices.

Consistent change management methodology or approach

Participants in the past two studies were asked whether all projects in the organization that apply change management followed a consistent change management methodology or approach. Nearly two thirds reported that they did not follow a consistent methodology on projects throughout the organization (Figure 3.14).

Figure 3.14 – Consistent methodology across organization

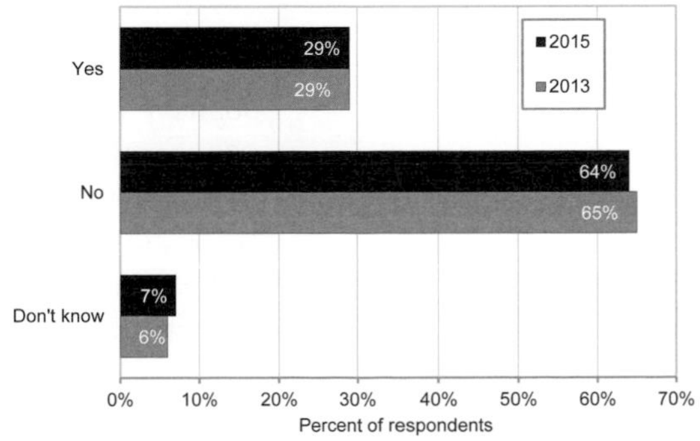

Success of deployment efforts

Source date: 2011

Participants working to deploy change management evaluated their overall level of success (Figure 3.15).

Figure 3.15 – Success of deployment

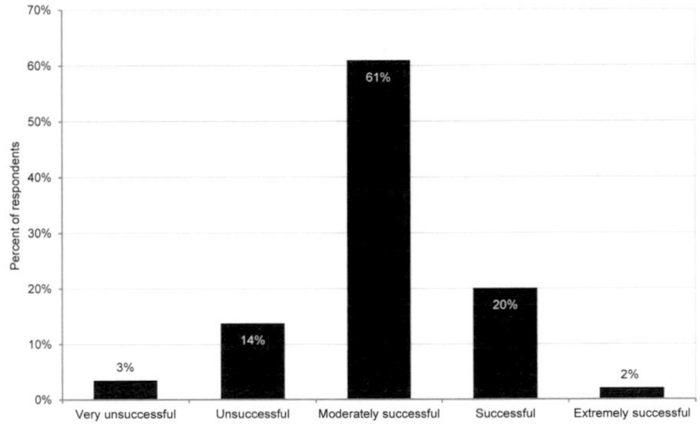

Contributors to successful deployments

Source date: 2011

The greatest contributors to deployment success identified by participants who classified their deployment as successful or extremely successful were:

1. **Sponsorship and leadership commitment**
   Participants noted a strong sponsor presence, executive support and senior leadership support of change management. A clear vision created by senior leaders contributed to success.
2. **Proof of success**
   Many participants highlighted the impact of showing the value of change management on deployment success, documenting and sharing proven successes on key projects, measuring the impact on project results and clearly calling out the impacts.
3. **Implementation approach that included collaboration**
   A number of participants identified having a clear implementation plan which included coordinating and collaborating on the design approach with various parts of the

organization. A passionate and effective deployment leader and team contributed to implementation success.

4. **Clear and open communication**
Communications included information on change management and how it was being deployed in the organization.

5. **Engagement of project teams**
Integrating or embedding change management with the work of project teams contributed to success and gave project leaders and team members the ability to learn though application.

Obstacles to deployment

Source date: 2011

Participants who considered their deployment moderately successful, unsuccessful or very unsuccessful shared the greatest obstacles they faced, the top three of which were:

- **Lack of understanding of and buy-in for change management**
Change management was not understood or valued in the organization. Change management was perceived as simply good management, nice to have but unnecessary, irrelevant or extraneous work. Employees throughout the organization, particularly project managers, did not see the value of change management and were not committed to applying it.
- **Poorly resourced and executed deployment effort**
Deployment either had no dedicated resources or had too few resources, and insufficient time was committed. A failure to treat deployment as a project also reduced the impact. Deployment failed to arrive at an organizational standard or consistent approach.
- **No leadership commitment or consistent sponsorship**
Leadership was not committed to deployment, and sponsorship was inconsistent or absent.

Additional obstacles to deployment identified by participants were:

- **Lack of application of change management** – including inconsistent application, lack of resources for application, insufficient time for change management and lack of integration with project management.
- **Lack of expertise** – including not having sufficient change management competencies and turnover of change management resources.
- **Conflicting priorities** – the organization was too busy with other change projects, and those other efforts took priority.
- **Lack of focus or prioritization** –change management deployment was not made a priority or given adequate attention.
- **No participation by managers and supervisors** – managers and supervisors did not have the capacity to take on change management responsibilities and were not engaged effectively.

Mistakes to avoid when deploying change management

Source date: 2011

Participants commented on mistakes they suggest others avoid when building change management capabilities and competencies. The top six were:

1. **Failing to treat the effort as a project**
Participants suggested that it was important to treat the effort to deploy change management like a project and a change to be managed, which included creating a plan and approach and assigning time and resources. Do not attempt the effort without clearly defining the vision, outcomes, objectives and milestones. Avoid underestimating the necessary work, effort and resources required. Use change management to support change management deployment.

2. **Moving forward without sponsorship**
   Participants warned against change management deployment without appropriate sponsorship. Sponsors need to be at the right level and active and visible in their support. An attempt without adequate sponsorship results in numerous challenges.

3. **Failing to build the case for change management**
   Build an understanding of what change management is and why it is important. Secure buy-in for change management and create a business case. Participants emphasized the importance of building on successes and demonstrating the impact of change management.

4. **Approaching the effort with only one aspect of the solution**
   Change management deployment cannot be limited to training that lacks real-life application. Training must be applicable and meaningful. Provision of tools without appropriate training and coaching was also identified as ineffective. Change management should not be viewed as solely a Human Resources (HR) competency.

5. **Failing to provide an effective methodology**
   Deployment must provide repeatable processes and tools that can be used by employees throughout the organization; deployment requires a solid methodology as its foundation. Ensure consistency of application of the methodology. Avoid forcing a methodology that does not fit the organization and is not adaptable.

6. **Making change management a separate activity**
   Change management should not be viewed as a separate activity. It should be positioned as "everyone's job" and embedded as a competency necessary to be successful in the organization, regardless of a person's role in the organization. Competency models that clarify responsibilities and roles during change management for each audience in the organization enable this embedding of change management as part of everyone's job.

Additional considerations included:

- **Engage the right people** – deployment should include representation throughout the organization and should have the support of key influencers. A skilled lead team should champion the effort. The effort should not take place too low in the organization.
- **Take small steps** – avoid "biting off more than you can chew." Participants cautioned against being overly ambitious at the beginning of the effort, instead preferring small steps to move the effort forward.
- **Understand the current climate, culture and competency** – be sure to assess, understand and tailor the approach based on the current competency and culture of the organization

Percent of projects applying change management

Participants in the 2015 benchmarking study shared the percentage of projects in their organization that were applying change management (Figure 3.16). Participants reported on average that just over one in three (35%) of the projects in their organization were applying change management.

Figure 3.16 – Percent of projects applying change management

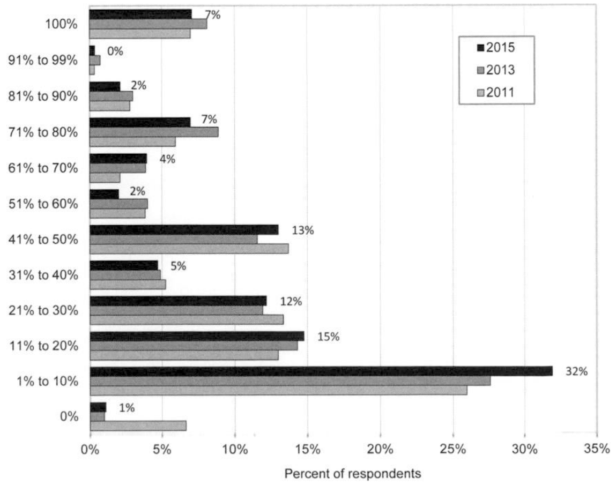

Table 3.17 shows a segmented view of the percent of participants reporting that 10% or fewer, 25% or fewer or 50% or fewer projects in the organization were applying change management. The data shows a slight decrease in change management application between the 2013 and 2015 benchmarking studies.

Table 3.17 – Percent of projects applying change management

Percent of projects applying change management	Percent of participants in 2013 study	Percent of participants in 2015 study
10% or fewer	29%	33%
25% or fewer	49%	55%
50% or fewer	71%	78%

Recognition of the value and need for change management

Participants rated the level of recognition of the value and need for change management in their organizations. Participants reported on five groups: project leaders and managers, executives and senior leaders, middle managers, frontline managers and supervisors, and solution developers and designers. Figures 3.18 through 3.22 show participants' views of the level of recognition for these groups from the 2015, 2013 and 2011 studies.

Figure 3.18 – Project leader and project manager recognition

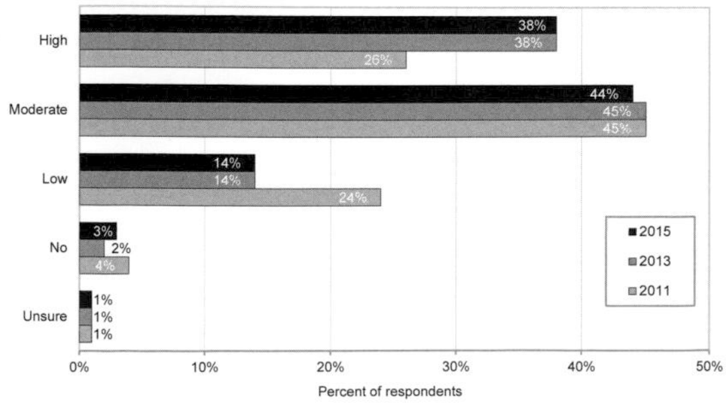

Figure 3.19 – Executive and senior leader recognition

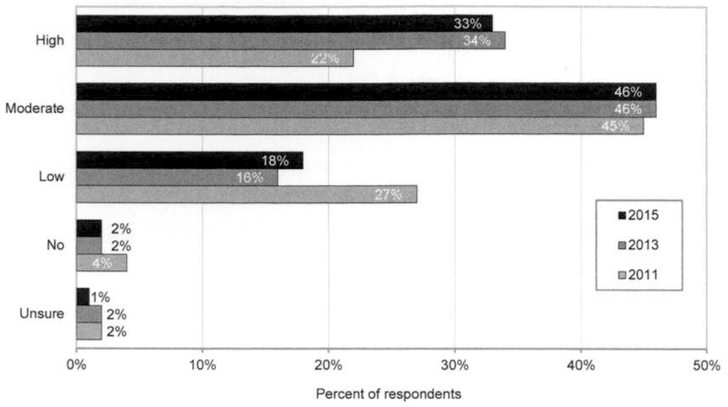

Figure 3.20 – Middle manager recognition

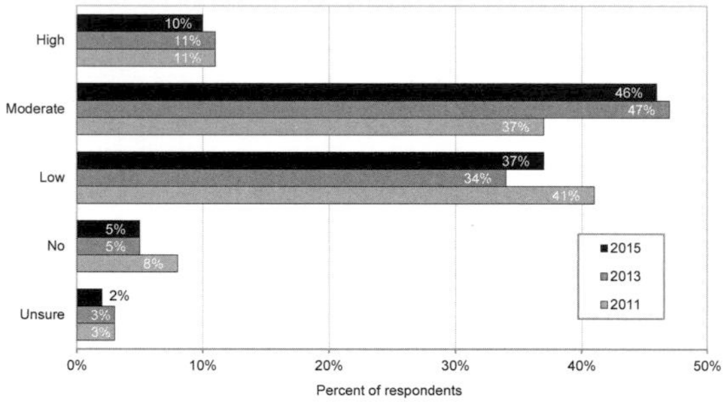

Figure 3.21 – Frontline manager and supervisor recognition

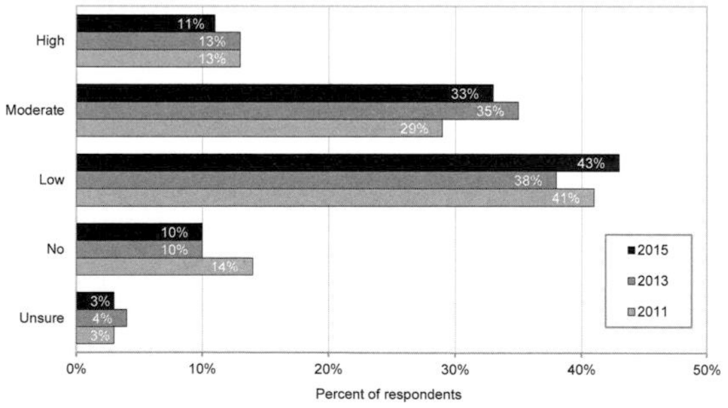

Figure 3.22 – Solution developer and designer recognition

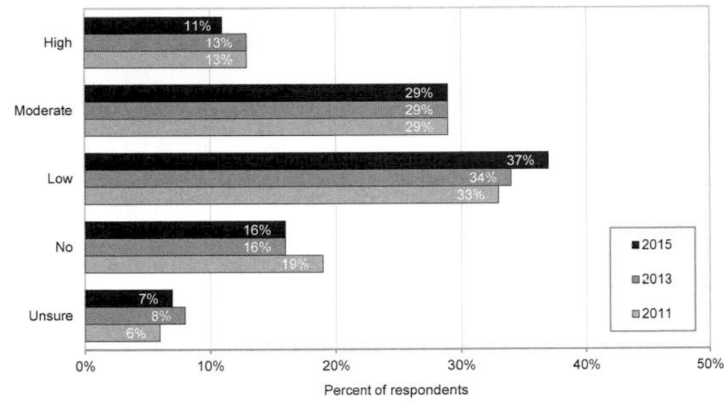

Overall findings for 2015, 2013 and 2011 are shown in Figure 3.23. Participants who ranked project leaders and project managers as having moderate or high recognition grew from 71% in 2011 to 82% in both 2013 and 2015. Seventy-nine percent ranked executives and senior leaders as having either moderate or high recognition of the value and need for change management, a slight decrease from 80% in 2013. Fifty-six percent of participants ranked middle managers as having either moderate or high recognition, a slight decrease from 58% in 2013.

Only 44% of participants ranked frontline managers and supervisors as having moderate to high recognition. Even fewer, 40% of participants, considered that solution designers and developers recognized the value of change management.

Figure 3.23 – Moderate to high recognition of the value and need for change management

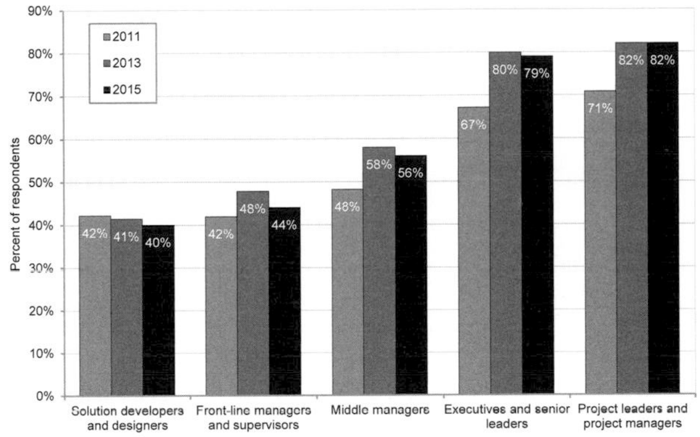

Trends in the recognition of the value and need for change management

Table 3.24 shows 2015 participants' views of the level of recognition of the value and need for change management in comparison to two years prior for key groups within the organization. Participants indicated an increase in recognition of the value and need for change management by the groups: project leaders and project managers, and executives and senior leaders.

Table 3.24 – Development of the recognition of the value and need for change management

	Less	No change	Slightly more	Significantly more
Project leader and project manager	5%	18%	55%	22%
Executive and senior leader	5%	18%	52%	25%
Middle manager	6%	38%	48%	8%
Frontline manager and supervisor	6%	47%	39%	8%
Solution developer and designer	6%	49%	36%	9%

Change management functional group

Change Management Office or functional group

Thirty-eight percent of participants in the 2013 study reported having a Change Management Office (CMO) or functional group (Figure 3.25), an increase from 36% in the 2013 study.

Figure 3.25 – Prevalence of Change Management Office or functional group

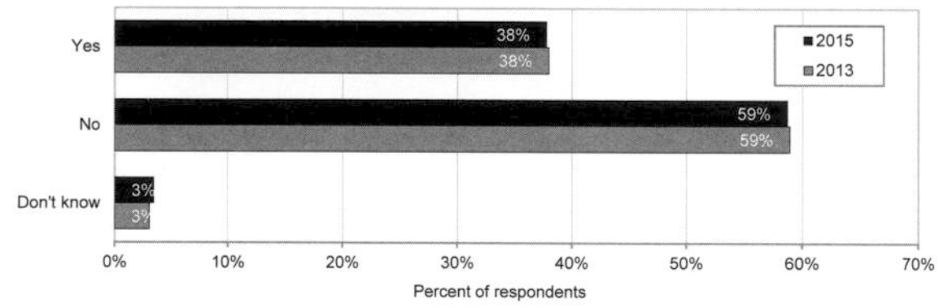

Change Management Office or functional group by region

Figure 3.26 shows the percentage of participants from each region that reported having a CMO or functional group. Participants from Africa and Latin America reported the highest rates.

Figure 3.26 – Change Management Office or functional group by region

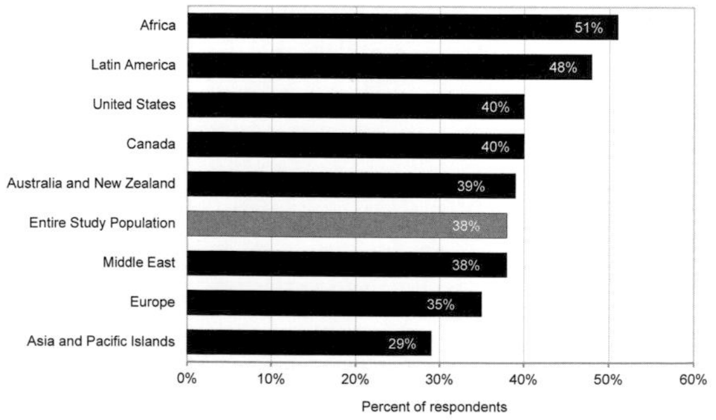

Change Management Office or functional group by industry

Figure 3.27 shows the percentage of participants from each industry who reported having a CMO or functional group. Banking, utilities, retail trade and government - federal reported the highest rates.

Figure 3.27 – Change Management Office or functional group by industry

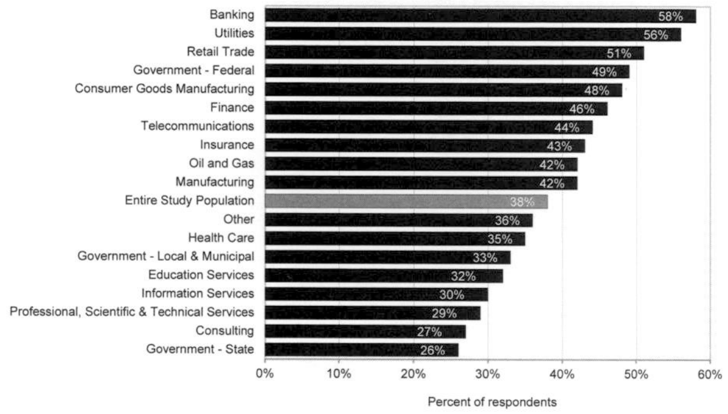

Change Management Office or functional group by organization size

CMO or functional group data were segmented by organization size (both annual revenue and number of employees). Figures 3.28 and 3.29 show the percentage of participants who reported having a CMO or functional group based on size.

Figure 3.28 – Change Management Office or functional group by annual revenue

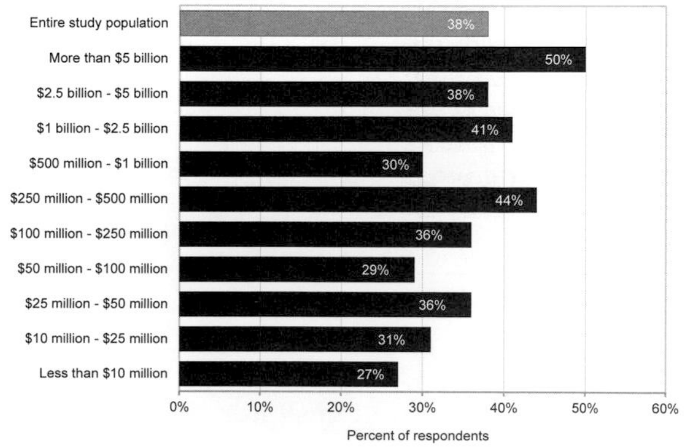

Figure 3.29 – Change Management Office or functional group by number of employees

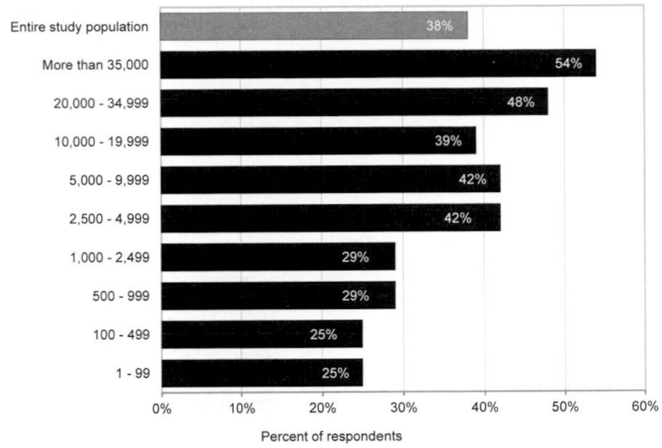

Change Management Office or functional group by Change Management Maturity Model level

Figure 3.30 shows the percentage of participants who reported having a CMO by Change Management Maturity Model level. Organizations reporting higher levels of change management maturity also reported the highest rates of having a CMO or functional group.

Figure 3.30 –Change Management Office or functional group by maturity level

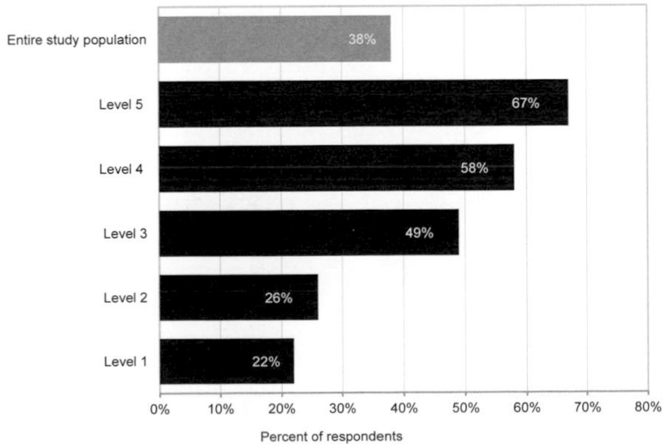

Primary responsibilities of functional group

Participants in the 2015 study reported on the responsibilities of the CMO or functional group. Table 3.31 shows the most common responsibilities. The three most common responsibilities were: own and maintain the change management methodology, own and maintain the change management tools, and provide consultative support to resources on project teams. Participant responses in the 2015 study were similar to those in 2013. The categories that saw the largest increases were provide coaching to sponsors in fulfilling their role (9% increase), own and maintain the change management methodology (7% increase) and provide coaching to managers and supervisors in fulfilling their role (7% increase).

Table 3.31 – Responsibilities of the Change Management Office or functional group

Responsibility	2015 *(2013)*
Own and maintain the change management methodology	83% *(76%)*
Own and maintain the change management tools	77% *(74%)*
Provide consultative support to resources on project teams	74% *(74%)*
Provide change management resources (people) on specific projects	71% *(66%)*
Maintain a change management community	66% *(67%)*
Provide coaching to sponsors in fulfilling their role	63% *(54%)*
Provide coaching to managers and supervisors in fulfilling their role	59% *(52%)*
Track change management progress on projects	57% *(57%)*
Own the change management curriculum	49% *(49%)*
Track and manage the change portfolio	46% *(43%)*
Other	5% *(6%)*

Location of functional group

Participants with a functional group dedicated to change management provided data on where the group resided within the organization (Figure 3.32). The top four responses were:

- Project Management Office (PMO)
- Human Resources (HR)
- Strategy, transformation and planning
- Information Technology (IT)

Figure 3.32 – Location of Change Management Office or functional group

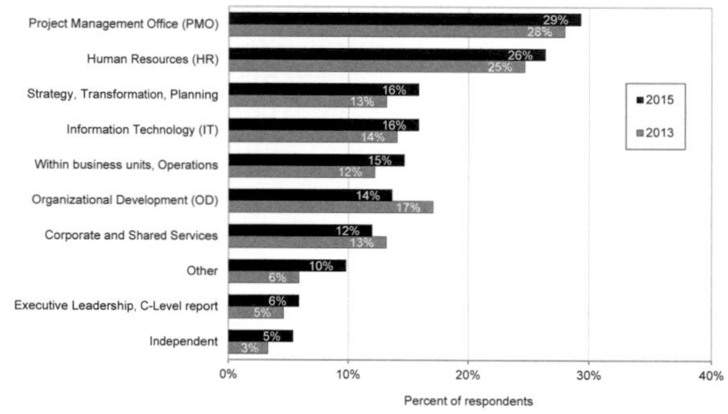

Editor's note: Participants were able to select multiple responses, resulting in a total of more than 100%.

In the 2015 study, the functional group was found most commonly in Project Management Office (PMO), Human Resources (HR) or the Strategy, Transformation, Planning department. Overall, responses in the 2015 study were similar to findings in the 2013 study.

Participants in 2015 reported that CMOs were more spread out in comparison to 2013; 10% fewer respondents indicated having a CMO in one location in 2015 in comparison to 2013, as seen in figure 3.33.

Figure 3.33 – Number of locations for Change Management Office or functional group

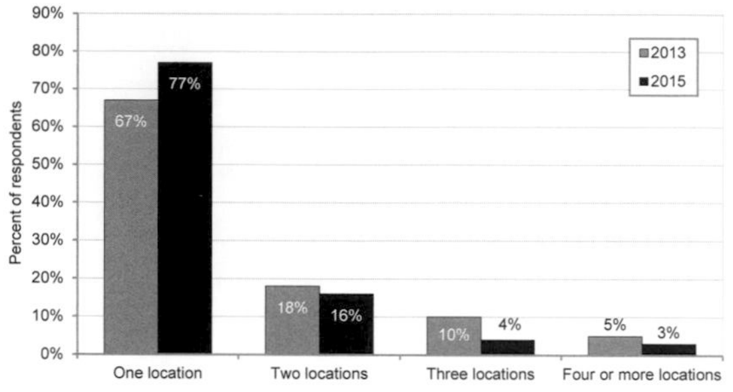

Reasons for group location

Participants in the 2015 study with CMOs or functional groups identified the following reasons for its location in the organization.

1. **Alignment with function or objectives**
   The location was selected because its existing function or objectives aligned or overlapped with those of change management. In some cases, the location was selected because it gave the project and the change management team a degree of independence, aligned with the future state or supported integration of change management with project management.

2. **Existing resources or position of influence**
   Participants selected the location based on the presence of existing resources or position of influence in the location. Participants identified employees with previous change management experience and financial resources as two of the most important influences on the choice of location for the group. A central location within the organization or a position with advisory roles was a consideration when determining a location that would lead to the greatest impact of change management.

3. **Initiation or leadership directive**
In many cases, location was chosen based on the department initiating the effort or the department managing and leading deployment. In other cases, location was chosen based on an executive decision.

4. **Politics and historical reasons**
In some cases, location was selected based on internal politics or historical reasons. Examples included power plays, long-standing policies within the organization and the location being selected at initiation of deployment.

5. **Perception of change management**
In some cases, participants noted that location was selected based on a common perception of change management, sometimes correct and sometimes incorrect. A commonly held misconception was change management's "*perceived affinity with HR*," and as a result, Human Resources (HR) was the default location for change management. Other respondents noted that location was chosen to give prominence and legitimacy to the change effort or to combat a negative perception of change management.

Location criteria

Source date: 2013

Participants who created a CMO or functional group listed the following reasons for selecting its location in the organization:

1. **Ability to support projects across the organization**
A central location with reach and access to projects across the organization was ideal. A location was often chosen because it was cross-functional and supported multiple business units. The location provided neutrality and independence.

2. **Alignment with function, objectives or job roles**
The location was selected because its existing function, objectives or job roles aligned or overlapped with those of change management. In some cases, the location was selected because employees had existing skills and responsibilities that overlapped with and could be applied to change management. Overall, participants chose a location based on its commonalities with the change management practice.

3. **Amount of change and associated risk**
Location was selected because it required the most change management. It was either launching the greatest number of projects or the projects being launched from the location were highly impactful. The nature and magnitude of the changes were considered. The risk exposure created from the amount or type of change resulted in the decision to place the change management functional group there.

4. **Originator of change management effort**
Participants selected the location based on who introduced change management to the organization. The location that developed an interest in change management, introduced it to the organization or invested resources to make it a formal practice was selected. Existing support, interest and understanding were viewed as advantageous.

5. **Directive from executive sponsors or senior leaders**
Executives or senior leaders who initiated and sponsored deployment also selected locations. Executives who understood change management and had capacity within their divisions led the organization's change management.

Advantages of locations

Participants in the 2015 study selected the location they felt would be most effective (Figure 3.34). Just under one-quarter of participants chose the Project Management Office (PMO), followed by the strategy, transformation and planning function at 21%. 2015 participant responses were similar to those in 2013. The rationale for each location follows Figure 3.34.

Figure 3.34 – Most effective location for the Change Management Office or functional group

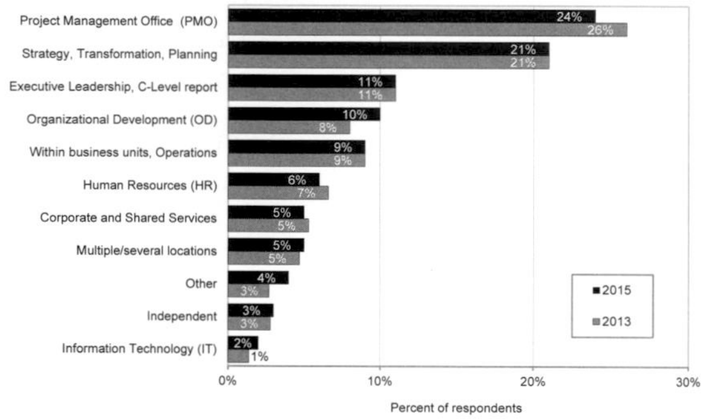

Project Management Office (PMO) or project delivery

"Projects are the means where organizations structurally manage change—the PMO can best guide the integration and delivery of change management as part of the project lifecycle."

- Location provides access to projects, and most changes originate in the PMO
- Change management aligns with the purpose of the PMO—supporting the implementation of change and aligning adoption of those changes with project success
- Location provides easier integration into project methodology
- Change management can be integrated more effectively into project plans
- PMO has wide cross-organizational reach and representative perspective
- Change management can be infused earlier in the project lifecycle
- PMO has an established reputation and credibility, and is respected

Strategy, transformation and planning

"This level is organizationally close to exec leadership team, has significant support, and reaches across all communities. This would ensure change management is engaged early in projects/changes."

- Change management can be aligned better with the strategy and direction of the organization
- Change management can be attached at the beginning of planning
- Location provides proximity to executives
- Location grants access to many projects, particularly highly visible and important ones
- Location supports an enterprise perspective on changes that occur across the organization
- Strategy, transformation and planning group has influence and credibility, and provides visibility
- Change management can become part of the culture and mindset of the organization

Executive leadership, c-level report

- Location ensures adequate sponsorship for enterprise impact
- Location allows access to the sponsors of change
- Executive leadership has clout, power and authority
- This group has influence and credibility and provides visibility
- Location provides a strategic view and gets readings on the pulse of the organization

- Location supports cultural and mindset changes
- Location provides proximity to budget control and resource decisions

Organization Development (OD)

- Location supports alignment, integration and collaboration with current OD functions
- OD is involved in numerous changes and strategic efforts
- Location supports an organization-wide reach and perspective

Within business units, operations

- Business units and operations have the most knowledge of affected areas and proximity to the user base
- Location supports building organization-wide change management capability
- Location allows for enhanced sustainment of change
- Location provides insights for understanding company culture

Human Resources (HR)

- Location synergizes with HR's purpose which relates to the people side of the organization and human capital, and focuses on employees
- HR has enterprise scope and reach
- Location supports alignment with skill development, training, roles and responsibilities

Corporate and shared services

- Corporate and shared services provides a common offering available to all projects
- Location has enterprise reach and scope
- Location supports the ability to share resources to manage the peaks and valleys of change management requirements during projects

Independent

- Location protected against being hindered by internal politics and agendas; it is objective and impartial
- Location allows change management to be applied on various changes across the organization or enterprise

Information Technology (IT)

- Location provides proximity to the largest projects

Size of functional group

Participants with a functional group dedicated to change management indicated the number of employees in the group (Figure 3.35). More than half (56%) indicated five or fewer employees. The most frequent response was two to five employees (48%). Overall, the proportion of the sizes of functional groups remained stable between the 2013 and 2015 studies.

Figure 3.35 – Number of employees in the functional group

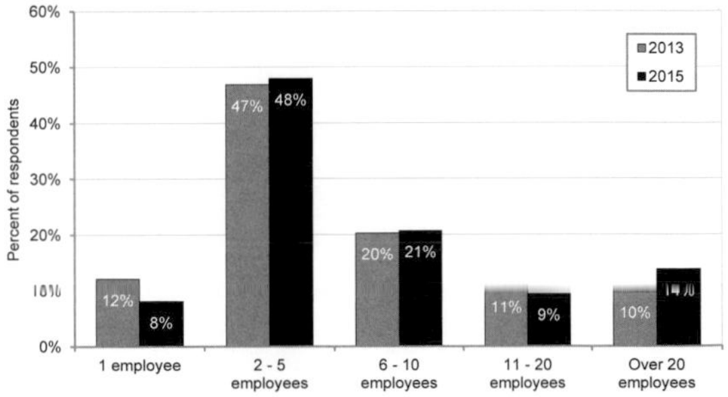

Name of functional group

Source date: 2011

Participants in the 2011 study shared names by which the office or functional group was called:

1. A title using the words *change management* including:
   - Change management
   - Change management office
   - Change management department
   - Change management team
   - Enterprise change management
   - Organizational change management
2. A title using the word "Change" including:
   - Business change
   - Change team
   - Change group
   - Change unit
   - Change leadership
3. A title using one of the following words related to change: transition, improvement, transformation, performance or strategy

Definition of change management throughout organization

Source date: 2013

Two thirds of participants indicated that they disagreed or strongly disagreed that the organization shared a common definition of change management, a decline from 73% in the 2011 (Figure 3.36). Although 2011 and 2013 data show an improvement in terms of having a shared definition, these data indicate that organizations still experience varied interpretations of change management.

Figure 3.36 – Common definition

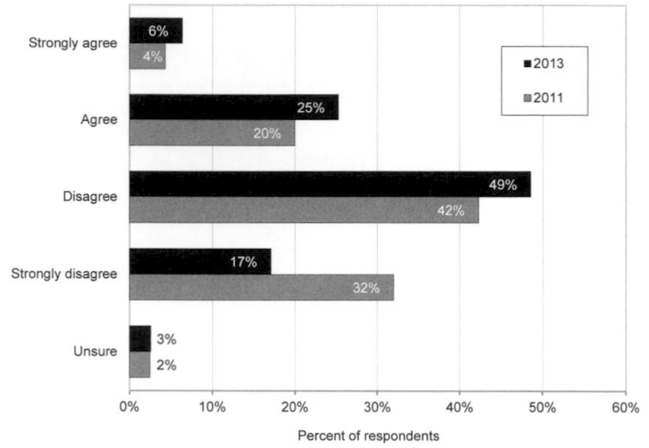

Figure 3.37 shows the percentage of participants who reported having a shared definition of change management throughout the organization segmented by organizational change management maturity. Participants in organizations with higher maturities tended to agree that their organization had a shared definition, more so than participants in organizations with lower maturities.

Figure 3.37 – Shared definition by maturity level

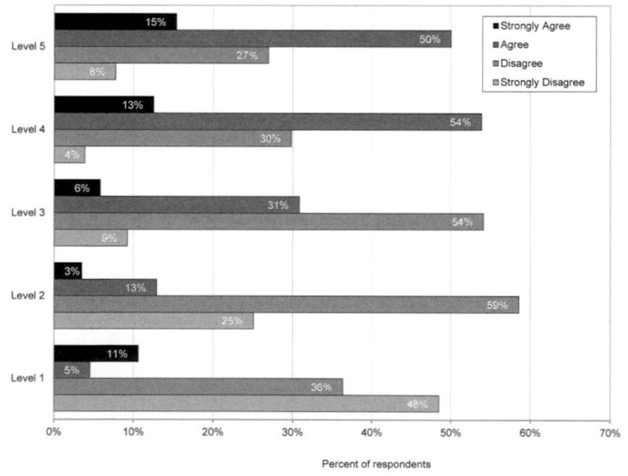

Participants in the 2013 study were asked if they noticed a change in the level of a commonly shared definition of change management in the past two years (Figure 3.38). Sixty-five percent indicated that the definition had become slightly or significantly more shared throughout the organization.

Figure 3.38 – Change in common definition

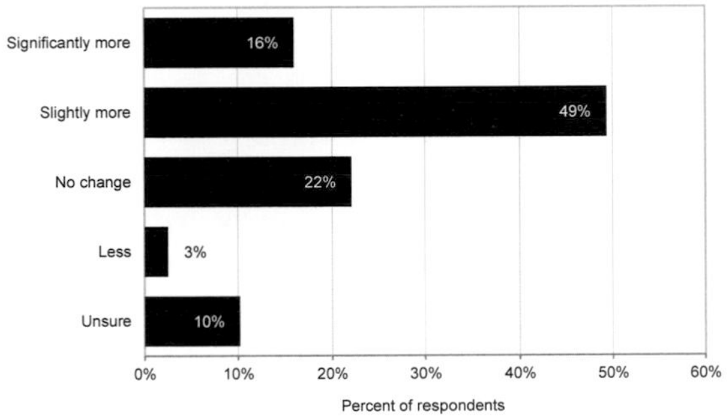

Training on change management

Attended change management certification

For the first time in 2015, participants indicated whether they had attended a change management certification program. Nearly three quarters of participants had attended a change management certification program (Figure 3.39).

Figure 3.39 – Certified in change management

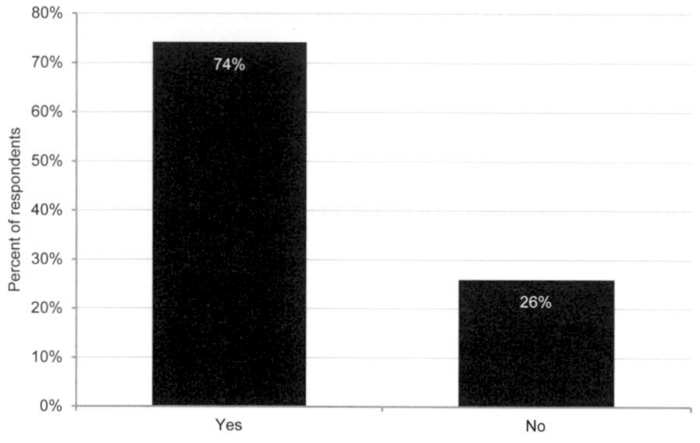

Participants also shared whether they would recommend that others become certified in change management. An overwhelming number of participants, 86%, said they would recommend change management certification to others (Figure 3.40).

Figure 3.40 – Recommend that others become certified in change management

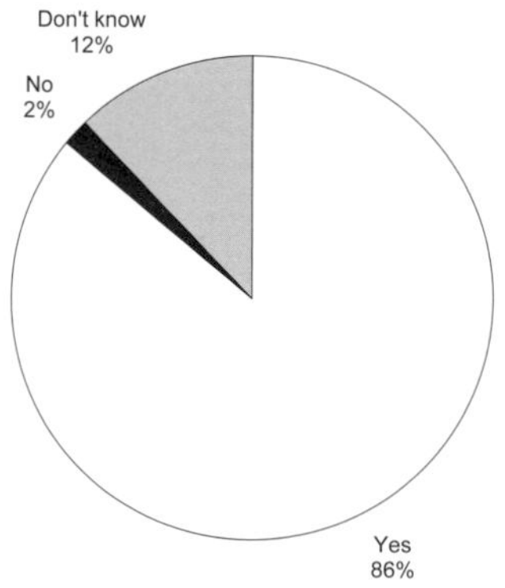

Value of certification

For the first time, participants who attended certification described why they would recommend that others attend certification.

1. **Structured approach gained**
   Participants felt that certification provided a clear, formalized methodology and process for doing change management. They also felt that others would gain the knowledge about change management's theory and framework necessary to do good change management. Attending certification also provided a structured way of thinking and deepened the understanding of the dynamics of change.
2. **Build skills and credentials**
   Participants felt that getting a certification in change management not only added to their professional credibility but also equipped them with a variety of important skills that were applicable within and outside of change management settings. Participants found that having a certification was an important step to advancing their careers and building confidence in their own ability to succeed at change management.
3. **Acquire common and universal tools**
   Participants felt that they gained tools, templates, techniques and ideas that apply immediately to change projects. Certification also provided exposure to methodologies, tools and techniques, while getting the opportunity to learn from other experts in the field. It also provided common practices and tools, and language and frameworks, for change management.
4. **More likely to achieve desired outcomes**
   Participants felt that by attending certification, they could help their organization recognize the value of change management. They could help their organizations become aware of how change management can make them more likely to achieve desired outcomes. Certification increased proficiency, raised the overall

standard of work and created better results. By attending certification, they were able to help their organizations not only create but see the value in creating a standardized approach to managing change.

Certification programs attended

Participants who had attended a certification program identified the program they attended. Although many individual providers were listed, eight were listed five times more often than others:

- Prosci
- AdPro
- AIM
- APMG
- Being Human
- Change Guides
- CMC
- LaMarsh

Several participants listed various university programs, workshops and degrees from which they obtained change management certification. For a full list of certification providers that participants attended, see Appendix C.

Groups trained in change management

2015 data show a significant increase in training provided to change management resources but decreased change management training for project teams, managers and supervisors, executives and senior leaders and impacted employees. Figure 3.41 shows the percentage of participants who reported that change management training was provided to each group, comparing 2015, 2013 and 2011 study results.

Figure 3.41 – Groups that received change management training

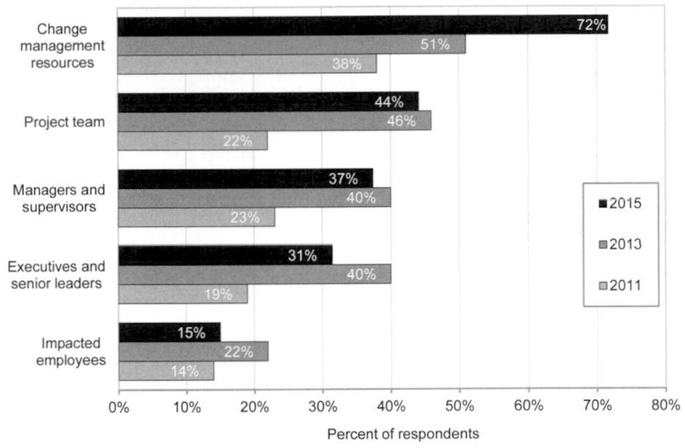

Other groups receiving change management training included change champions and members of the change network. These groups usually consisted of individuals who were not formally change management practitioners but who were involved in other areas of the organization, able to influence impacted groups and seen as role models and advocates for change. Individuals from the Human Resources (HR) department were also commonly trained.

Training vehicles used

Source date: 2013

Participants in the 2013 study identified what training vehicles were used for each group. Resoundingly, informal information sharing and coaching, and formal classroom training, were the most common approaches for delivering training across groups (Table 3.42). Informal information sharing and coaching were used by between 52% and 71% of participants, depending on the group. Between 46% and 69% used formal classroom training. Web-based training and self-paced training were used significantly less.

Table 3.42 – Training vehicles used

	Percentage that used informal information sharing	Percentage that used formal classroom training
Change management resources	60%	69%
Project team	71%	49%
Executives and senior leaders	66%	46%
Managers and supervisors	61%	61%
Impacted employees	52%	65%

Other types of training included workshops, webinars, briefings, meetings, forums, discussions, lunch and learns and awareness-building sessions

Change management training topics

Participants in the 2013 study identified the topics covered while training each of the five groups. The following top five topics were identified:

- **Change management plans**
  Most groups were educated on the change management plans that were being created or already in place. The plans most often presented were communications, training and resistance management.
- **ADKAR®**
  Each group was trained in the Prosci® ADKAR® Model to understand how each element of the model applied to their roles in change.
- **Methodology**
  The five groups were trained in the change management methodology that was being used. The Prosci 3-Phase Change Management Process was the most frequently cited methodology.
- **Tools**
  Most groups were trained to use tools for evaluating change prior to implementation. Training covered readiness assessments, impact assessments and other stakeholder analysis tools.
- **Change management principles**
  Each group was taught the foundation of change management: what it is, why it is applied, benefits of using a change management methodology and principles concerning the psychology of change.

Length of training

Source date: 2011

Participants shared the number of days of change management training provided for each of the five groups and the number of days they recommend for each group. Table 3.43 contains averages for the number of days of change management training provided and the recommended number of days of change management training for each group.

Table 3.43 – Average days of change management training

	Actual days	Recommended days
Change management resources	3.73	5.06
Project teams	2.41	3.44
Executives and senior leaders	1.22	2.13
Managers and supervisors	2.04	2.95
Impacted employees	1.70	2.52

The following sections provide more details regarding training vehicles, topics and duration of delivering training to change management resources, project teams, executives and senior leaders, managers and supervisors, and employees.

What participants would do differently next time regarding change management training

Participants indicated four major adjustments to how they would provide change management training for future initiatives.

1. **Increase training for additional groups**
   Provide more training to key stakeholders and include additional audiences, such as project sponsors, project managers, employee supervisors, mid-level managers, senior-level managers and relevant executives, in training efforts.
2. **Deliver training differently**
   Deliver training in more personable settings and continuously throughout the project, and use training specialists to implement plans. Participants would provide more interactive components and incorporate technology systems such as web-based and e-learning approaches.
3. **Tailor content to individual roles**
   By tailoring training more specifically to individuals, there would be greater awareness regarding how to address issues when they arise. Training recipients would feel more connected with the change were more aligned with the methodology used.
4. **Plan for training earlier**
   Plan training activities earlier in the project lifecycle to provide more time to assess current knowledge and training requirements. Although participants would plan earlier, they would also schedule the delivery of training at the appropriate time in the change lifecycle.

Change management resource training

Source date: 2013

Participants in the 2013 study identified vehicles used to deliver change management training to change management resources (Figure 3.44). Formal classroom training was used most often to train change management resources.

Figure 3.44 – Type of training for change management resources

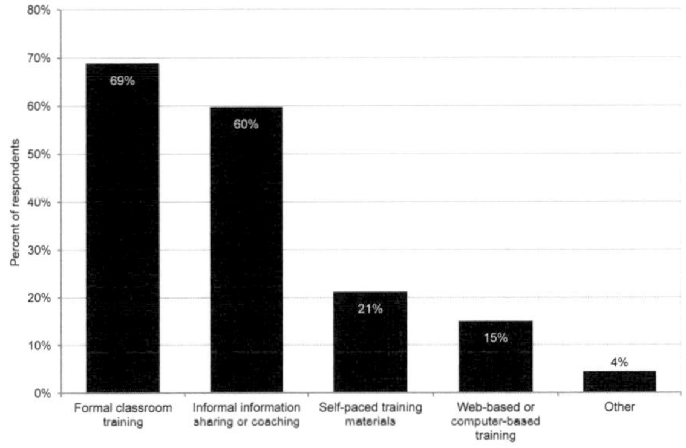

Participants in both the 2011 and 2013 studies identified key learning objectives or topics for change management training regarding change management resources. The top four responses were:

1. Change management methodologies and processes
2. An overview of the basics of change management
3. Change management tools
4. Communication plans and skills

Participants in the 2011 study shared the number of days of change management training provided for change management resources (Figure 3.45).

Figure 3.45 – Days of training for change management resources

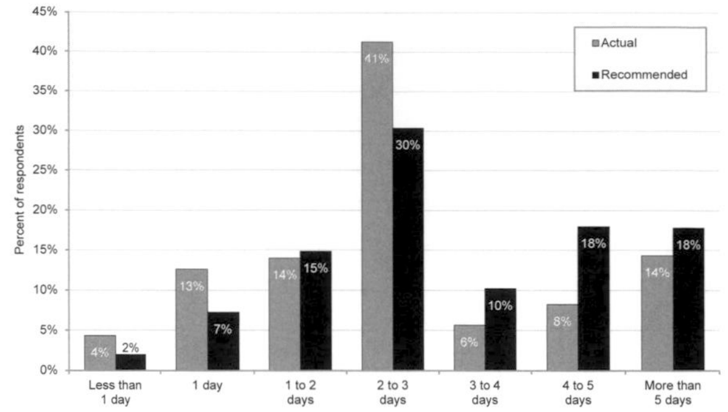

Project team training

Source date: 2013

Participants in the 2013 study identified vehicles used to deliver change management training to project teams (Figure 3.46).

Figure 3.46 – Type of training for project team members

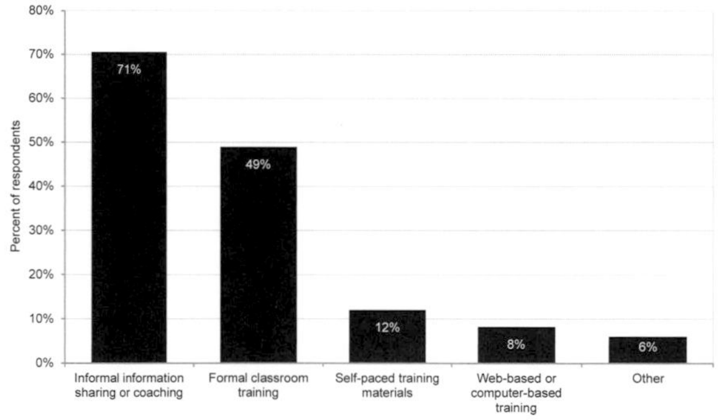

Participants in both the 2011 and 2013 studies identified key learning objectives or topics for change management training for project team members. The top six responses were:

1. Change management plans (communications, training and resistance management)
2. Awareness of the need for change management
3. Change management processes and methodologies
4. Roles in change management
5. The individual change experience
6. Support tools

Participants in the 2011 study shared the number of days of change management training provided for project teams (Figure 3.47).

Figure 3.47 – Days of training for project team members

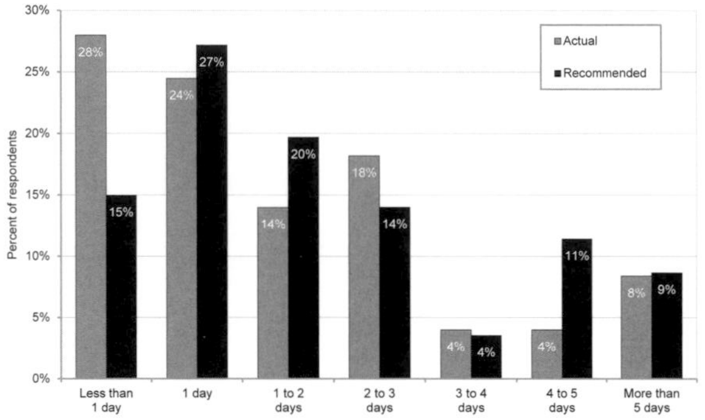

Executive and senior leader training

Source date: 2013

Participants in the 2013 study identified vehicles used to deliver change management training to executives and senior leaders (Figure 3.48).

Figure 3.48 – Type of training for executives and senior leaders

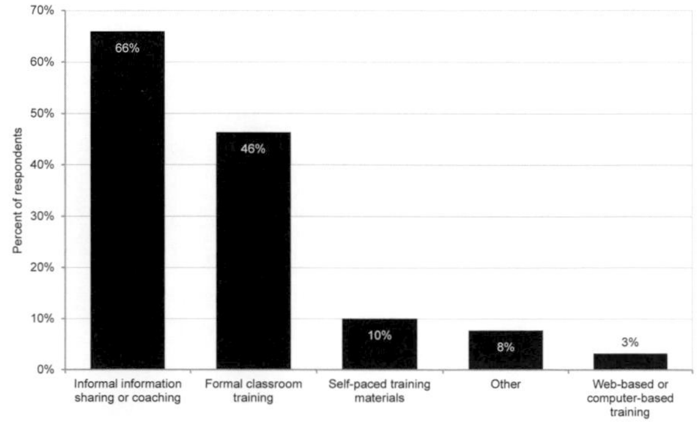

Participants in both the 2011 and 2013 studies identified key learning objectives or topics for change management training for executives and senior leaders. The top two responses were:

1. The roles and responsibilities of the sponsor during the project, with emphasis on the critical nature of the role, was cited more than twice as often as the next training topic
2. Greater understanding of the change management methodology selected

Participants in the 2011 study shared the number of days of change management training provided for executives and senior leaders (Figure 3.49).

Figure 3.49 – Days of training for executives and senior leaders

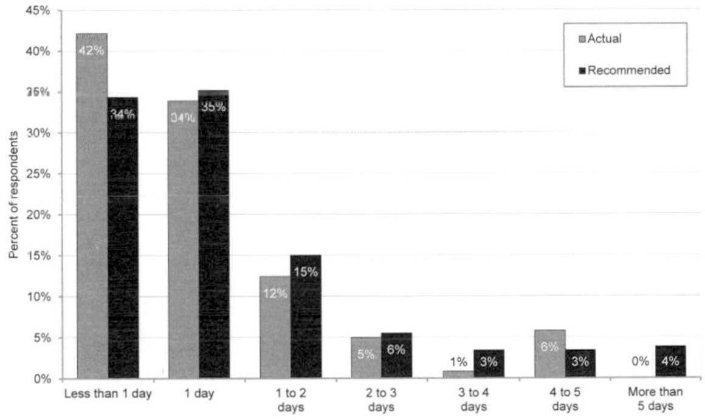

Manager and supervisor training

Source date: 2013

Participants in the 2013 study identified vehicles used to deliver change management training to managers and supervisors (Figure 3.50).

Figure 3.50 – Type of training for managers and supervisors

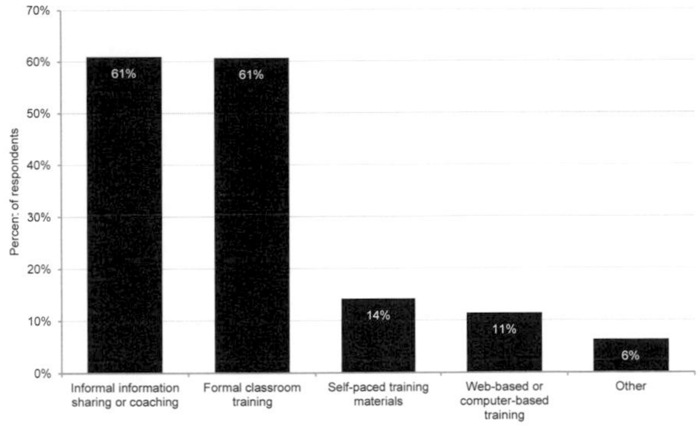

Participants in both the 2011 and 2013 studies identified key learning objectives or topics for change management training for managers and supervisors. The top five responses were:

1. Leading and managing change
2. Roles in change management
3. Awareness of the need for change management
4. The change experience for individuals
5. Methodology and process

Participants in the 2011 study shared the number of days of change management training provided for managers and supervisors (Figure 3.51).

Figure 3.51 – Days of training for managers and supervisors

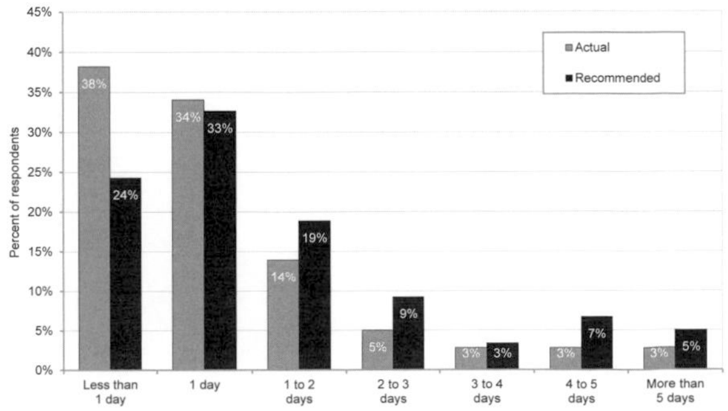

Employee training

Source date: 2013

Participants in the 2013 study identified vehicles used to deliver change management training to employees (Figure 3.52).

Figure 3.52 – Type of training for impacted employees

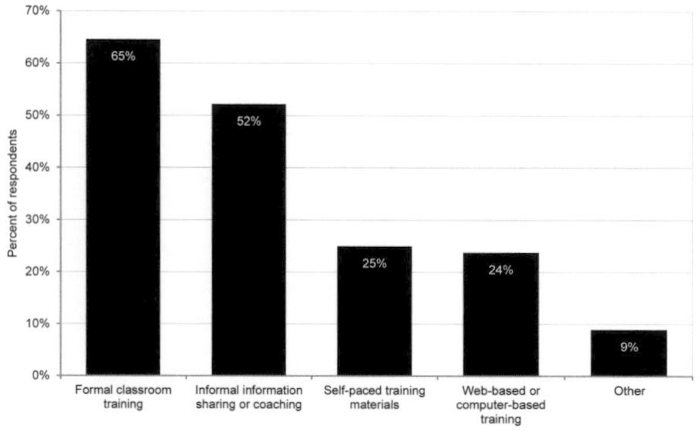

Participants in both the 2011 and 2013 studies identified key learning objectives or topics for change management training for impacted employees. The top five responses were:

1. How individuals move through change
2. What change management is
3. Specifics on how to operate in the new environment
4. Roles in change management
5. Why the change is happening

Participants in the 2011 study shared the number of days of change management training provided for employees (Figure 3.53).

Figure 3.53 – Days of training for impacted employees

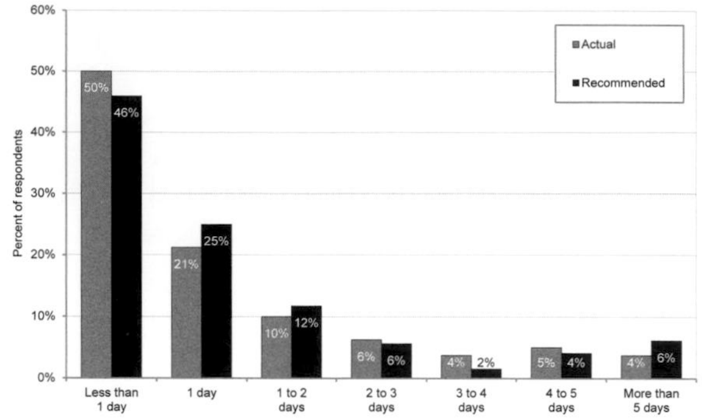

Change management job roles

Most important skills for a great change management practitioner

Participants identified attributes of a great change management practitioner. The top five were:

1. **Change management competency**
   Being knowledgeable or experienced in change management was the most desired attribute. Great practitioners have experience with coaching employees through the change. They also understand basic change theories, have experience applying tools and have knowledge of multiple methodologies. Holding an accredited certification in change management is valued.
2. **Interpersonal skills**
   Practitioners must be empathetic and approachable with an ability to read emotions and manage conflict. Practitioners need excellent relationship-building and collaboration skills. They should also be influential regardless of formal authority.
3. **Communication skills**
   Effective communication skills are required. A great practitioner is competent with both written and oral communication and able to listen to and elicit responses from employees. They articulate change messages clearly to a variety of groups. Practitioners should also be able to create and deliver an engaging presentation.
4. **Business acumen**
   Practitioners must have a developed sense of business. They should be comfortable working with frontline employees and c-level executives. A basic understanding of common business areas, such as project management, sales and marketing or information technology, is desired. They should also understand the organization's culture.
5. **Flexibility**
   Practitioners should be adaptive and flexible and demonstrate resilience and perseverance. They must be comfortable working with ambiguity and be pragmatic decision-makers.

Permanent position or job role

Participants in the 2015, 2013 and 2011 studies answered whether their organizations had a permanent position or job role specific to change management. In the 2011 study, 43% of participants reported having a permanent change management job role. In the 2013 study, that amount grew to 52%, and in the 2015 study 53% reported a permanent position or job role for change management (Figure 3.54).

Figure 3.54 – Organization has a permanent change management position or job role

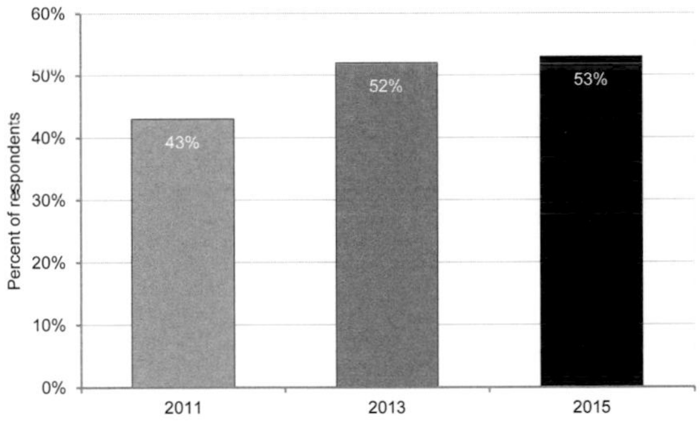

Figure 3.55 shows the percentage of participants with a permanent position by region. Participants in Africa (69%), Australia and New Zealand (67%), and the United States (54%) reported higher rates of permanent change management positions than the overall study population (53%).

Figure 3.55 – Permanent positions by region

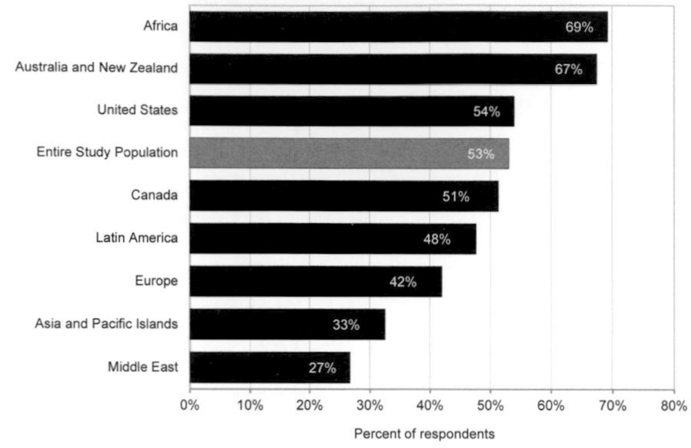

Figure 3.56 provides segmentation by industry relative to the overall study average.

Figure 3.56 – Permanent positions by industry

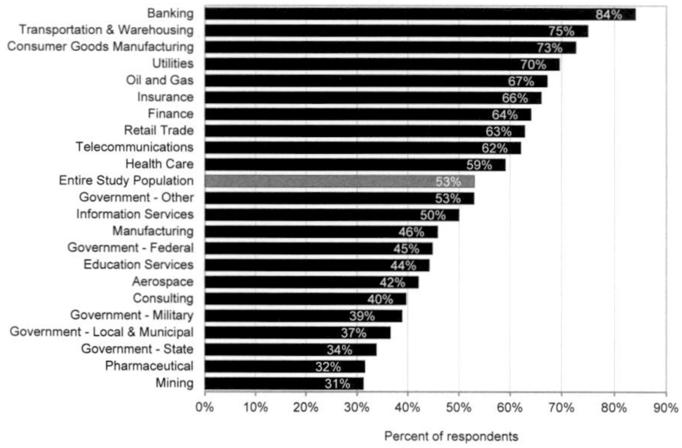

Figures 3.57 and Figure 3.58 provide segmentation according to organization size (annual revenue and number of employees). The data show a trend of organizations with higher revenue or more employees being more likely to have change management job roles.

Figure 3.57 – Permanent positions by annual revenue

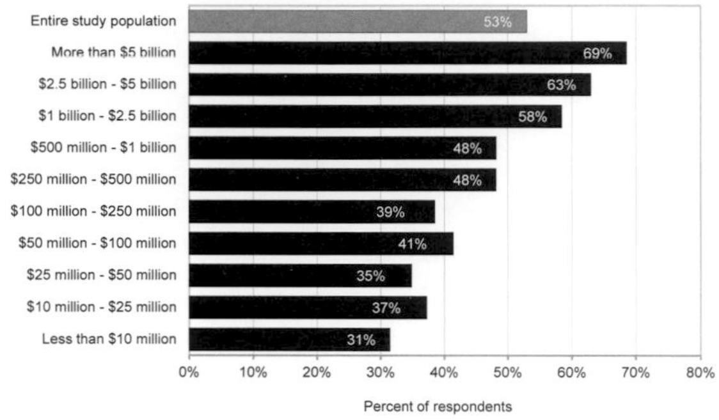

Figure 3.58 – Permanent positions by number of employees in organization

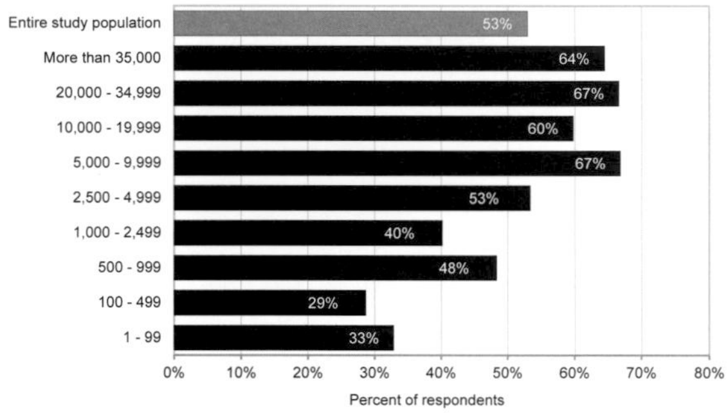

Finally, the data were segmented by organizational change management maturity level (Figure 3.59). More mature organizations were more likely to have change management job roles.

Figure 3.59 – Permanent positions by change management maturity level

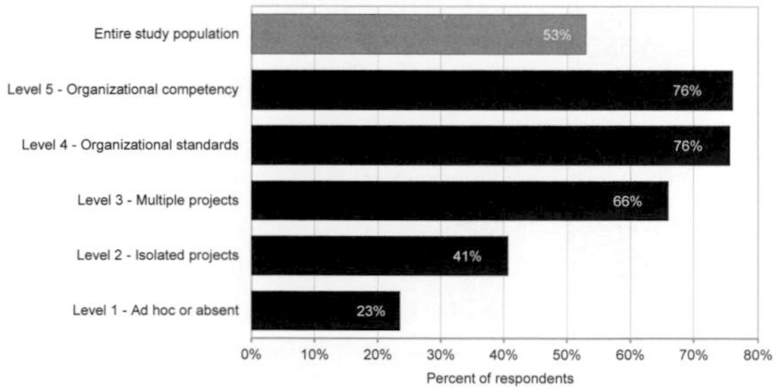

Duration of permanent position

Participants explained how long their organizations have had permanent change management positions or job roles (Figure 3.60). Most organizations have had permanent positions for fewer than three years (57%).

Figure 3.60 – Length of time permanent positions existed in the organization

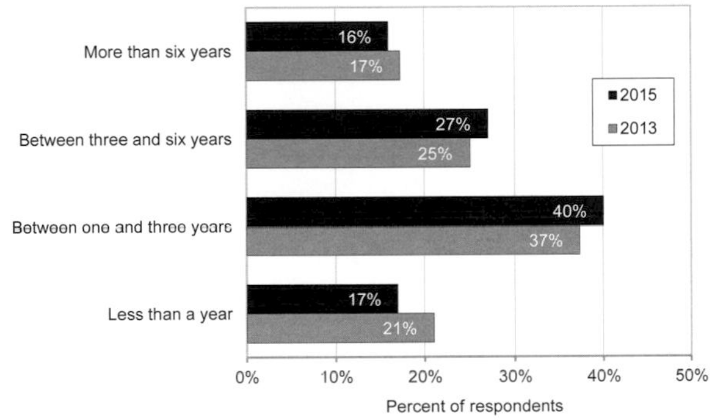

Organizational locations of permanent position or job role

Participants identified how many locations within their organizations had permanent change management positions (Figure 3.61). Sixty-six percent reported having change management job roles in only one location.

Figure 3.61 – Number of locations in the organization that have permanent job roles

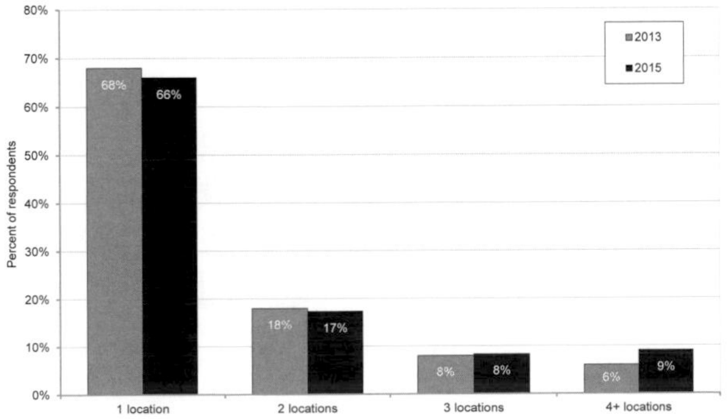

For those with job roles in one location (Figure 3.62), the most common location was the Project Management Office (PMO), followed by Human Resources (HR) and within business units, just ahead of Information Technology (IT).

Figure 3.62 – Location at which a change management job role resides

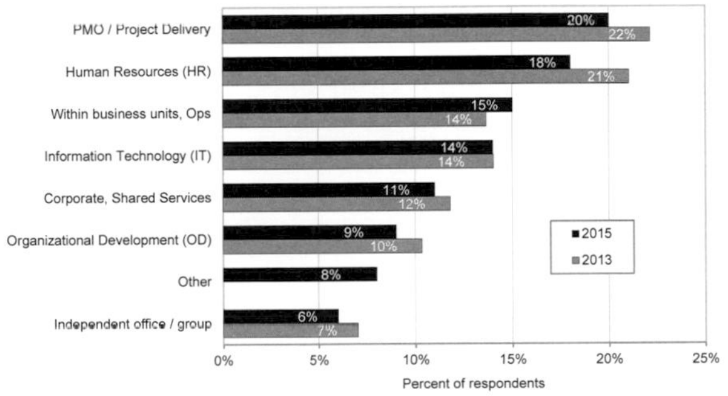

Editor's note: The category "other" was not offered to participants in the 2013 study.

Of the 17% of participants who reported having job roles in two locations, they were most commonly located in a Project Management Office (PMO) and business units (BUs). Other common combinations were business units (BUs) and corporate shared services, and Project Management Office (PMO) and Information Technology (IT). See Figure 3.63 for common combinations.

Figure 3.63 – Common location combinations

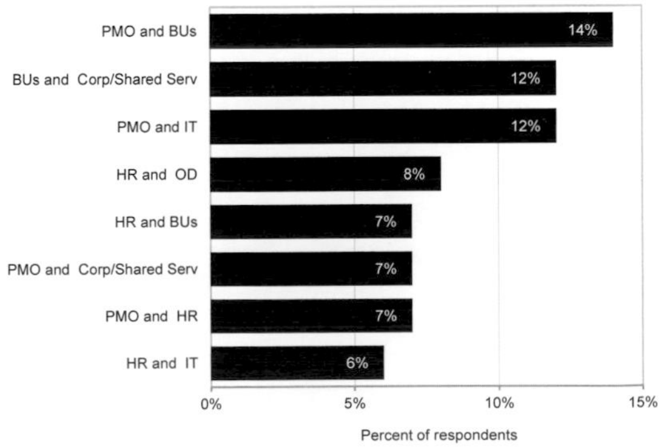

Editor's note: Figure 3.63 shows only the most common combinations which represented 73% of respondents.

Projects supported

Participants shared how many projects the change management resource typically supported at one time (Figure 3.64). A majority of participants (63%) reported that the resource supported two to four projects. It was less common for the resource to support only one project (17%) or more than five (20%).

Figure 3.64 – Number of projects supported by change management resource

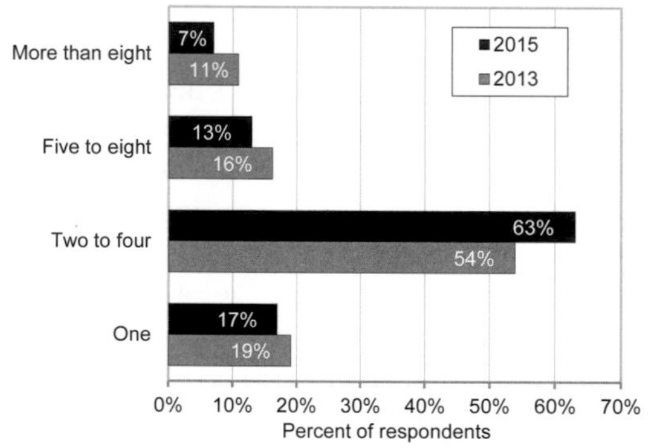

Annual salary

Participants reported on the annual salary for a change management position in their organizations (Figure 3.65). The average salary reported in 2015 was $106,997, a 1.2% increase from the 2013 average salary of $105,700. The most common salary range was between $100,000 and $149,999.

Figure 3.65 – Annual salary of permanent position or job role (in U.S. dollars)

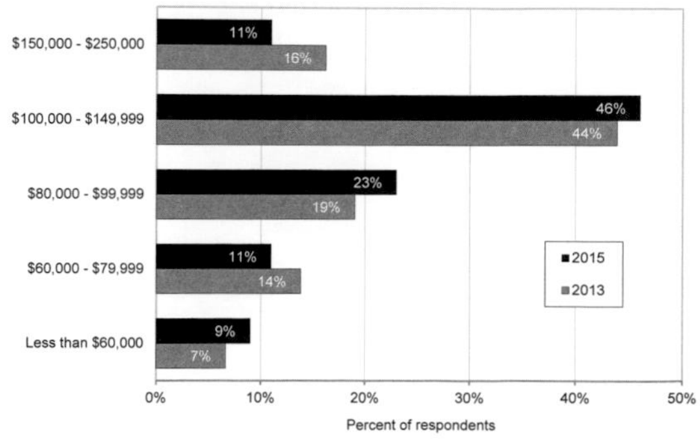

Job description

Participants in the 2015 study identified key elements of their job descriptions in change management roles. Six elements were identified most commonly.

1. **Support change management at the organizational level**
   The most common response was to support change management at the organizational level. This consisted of building change management skills, creating and/or implementing an enterprise framework, supporting other change management practitioners, maintaining a change management network, building change management capabilities, providing change management tools, building awareness of the need for change management and facilitating continuous improvement by capturing lessons learned.
2. **Apply a structured methodology and lead change management**
   The second most frequent response was to manage change management and apply change management tools in support of the project or initiative.
3. **Support communication efforts**
   Participants supported the design, development, delivery and management of communications to individuals at various levels of the organization.
4. **Support training efforts**
   Change management positions supported training by providing input, documenting requirements, managing training programs and supporting design and delivery.
5. **Interpersonal skills**
   Interpersonal skills were noted, which included possessing the ability to influence others, being a team player, having emotional intelligence and building relationships.
6. **Change experiences**
   The final element was change experience to understand the "ins and outs" of change methodologies and tools and to leverage and adapt processes to different situations.

Additional items included:

- Complete change management assessments by conducting change analyses and identifying key stakeholders
- Assess current awareness of the change and identify areas of resistance and readiness
- Create alignment of goals, objectives and strategic initiatives
- Identify and manage adoption, use and reinforcement of change
- Provide leadership and direction to enhance effectiveness of change
- Influence and engage stakeholders and leaders
- Perform autonomously, independently and flexibly in ambiguous dimensions
- Allocate budgets and resources efficiently
- Identify, analyze and prepare risk mitigation tactics

A number of participants indicated that the job description was different for every project, a work in progress or undefined.

Change management career paths

Participants indicated whether their organizations have career paths for change management job roles (Figure 3.66). Less than one in five participants reported that their organizations had a career path for change management professionals. Over one quarter of organizations did not have career paths but were developing them.

Figure 3.66 – Change management career paths

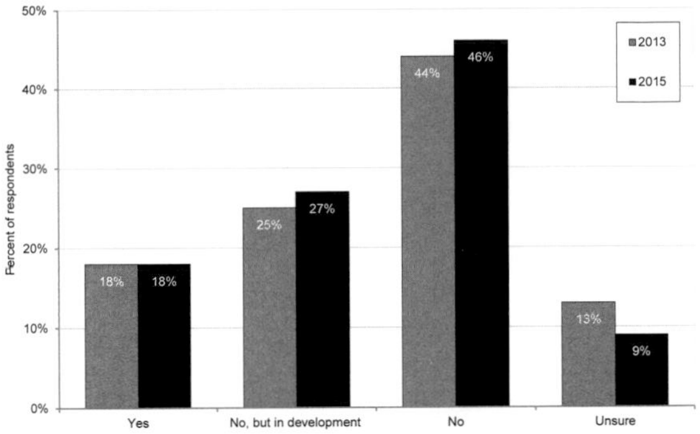

Figure 3.67 compares an organization's change management maturity in 2015 to whether it had career paths (findings exclude responses of *unsure*). The majority of organizations with high change management maturity levels had career paths. More than 40% of Level 4 organizations and more than 80% of Level 5 organizations reported having career paths. Only 17% of Level 3 organizations and 6% of Level 2 organizations had career paths.

Figure 3.67 – Career paths by change management maturity

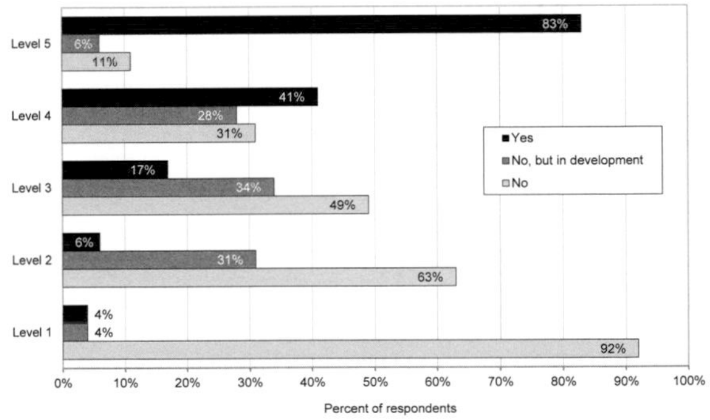

PART 2

CHANGE MANAGEMENT APPLICATION

MOTIVATION AND JUSTIFICATION

GAIN BUY-IN AND COMMITMENT FOR CHANGE MANAGEMENT BY FOCUSING ON THE RESULTS AND OUTCOMES YOU DELIVER

SUMMARY

How do you convince leaders to invest in the people side of change? Study respondents reveal the most influential motivating factors behind their organizations' use of change management. Uncover how to use risk mitigation and cost avoidance tactics for justifying investment in change management to project teams and senior leaders. Clarify what you deliver and present the case for change management in data-driven, results-oriented language that speaks directly to your leaders.

HIGHLIGHT

73% of participants had to justify change management to project teams while 67% had to justify change management to senior leaders.

Motivation

Drivers for applying change management

Participants in the 2015 study identified drivers that caused change management to be applied to their specific project. The top two drivers, complexity of change and awareness of change management as a discipline, were cited twice as often as other contributors. The top four drivers were:

1. **Changes facing the organization are complex and varied**
   Participants cited their need to change as the primary driver of change management. The size and scope of the change acted as key elements in recognizing their need for change management. Other responses included improving management, mitigating risks and complying with regulations.

2. **Awareness of change management as a discipline**
   Participants cited awareness of the discipline of change management as a significant driver for change management on projects. Participants cited failures of projects without use of change management as the primary driver. Previous success of change management efforts and recognition of the business case for change management were also cited.

3. **Recognition that change and people are connected**
   Participants cited a relationship between change and the people it affected. Examples included adoption, critical analysis of project successes and high anticipated resistance.

4. **As a mandate or directive**
   Participants felt that change management often came as a directive from upper leadership or executives. This push from leadership occasionally came as a direct response to practitioners lobbying for and explaining the benefits of change management.

Justifying change management

Justifying change management to project teams

Nearly 73% of participants in the 2015 study indicated that they had to justify change management to some degree when interacting with project teams, an increase from 2013 when participants had to justify change management 64% of the time, as shown in Figure 4.1.

Figure 4.1 – Degree of justification needed for project teams

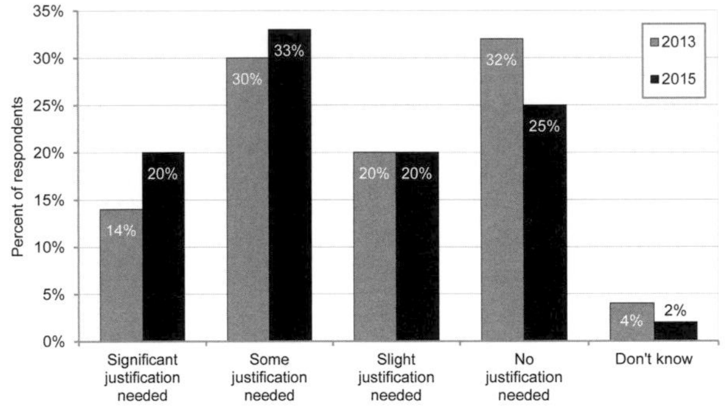

In cases where justification was needed

Source date: 2013

Participants justified change management to a project team in a number of ways. The most common justifications, in rank order, were:

1. **Change management improves the results and outcomes of a project**
   Overwhelmingly, the top method for justifying change management was to connect it to successful implementation of the change. Delivery on key performance indicators (KPIs) and project outcomes were the focus. Practitioners emphasized the contribution of change management to benefit realization, Return on Investment (ROI) and sustainment of results. Some extended justification to include the overall importance of the project including the bottom line impact and risks to the organization if the project failed. Effective change management was positioned as a way to reduce the project time frame, accelerate results and control the budget. Some participants used external data on the success rates of projects that applied change management to solidify their case.
2. **Change management increases the focus on the people side of change**
   Participants expressed to project teams that change management placed a necessary focus on people issues of a project. The necessity of employee preparation, buy-in, engagement, adoption and embracement of the solution was part of the justification. Change management was positioned as a way to increase the focus on stakeholders and on the impact to them.
3. **Change management minimizes risks associated with change**
   The risks of not managing the people side of change were used to justify application of change management. These risks included overall project failure, delays, avoidance and mitigation of intended improvement. Attrition and resistance by employees were also highlighted risks. Change management was positioned as a way to minimize the productivity dip associated with change implementations.
4. **Change management enhances the personal success of a project team**
   The final approach for justifying change management was focusing on the personal impact a project team would experience if it incorporated change management. Participants using this approach highlighted "what's in it for me?" (WIIFM) to project leaders, including helping them succeed and building their credibility in the organization. This approach also included reducing the workload and potential rework for the project manager through application of change management and use of change management resources.

Additional topics used to justify the need for change management included organizational history, culture, capacity and lessons learned from previous changes.

Participants also commented on their overall strategies for introducing change management to project teams. To justify change management, participants provided clarity around change management. Many had to provide a clear definition of change management, while others focused on clarifying the intent, focus, role and need for structure and resources. Providing clarity included explaining the specific activities of change management and the value they would bring.

In cases where no justification was needed

Source date: 2013

One third of participants reported that they did not need to justify change management to a project team. The top reasons were:

1. **Pre-existing awareness and experience**
The need for and value of change management were already acknowledged in the organization. Experiences with change management, including historical successes when applying change management and historical failures when not, created this awareness. This reason was cited three times more often than others.
2. **Requirement by sponsor or project leader**
Practitioners did not have to justify change management when its application was required or requested by senior leaders who recognized the need or influenced a project manager along those lines.
3. **Already embedded on project**
Change management did not have to be justified because it was already part of the project. In some cases, change management was a standard practice integrated into the project methodology and applied as part of all changes. In other cases, change management was attached to a project through project planning, most commonly as a requirement in the request for proposal (RFP).
4. **Necessity due to the nature of the change**
Change management did not have to be justified for projects with large impacts. In particular, participants identified the scope, degree of impact and number of employees impacted as factors that made the case for change management. For some projects in which adoption was viewed as key to success, change management was considered necessary and did not need to be justified.

Justifying change management to leadership teams

Seventy-six percent of participants indicated that they had to justify change management to their leadership team, in comparison to 61% in 2013 (Figure 4.2).

Figure 4.2 – Participants who had to justify change management to leadership teams

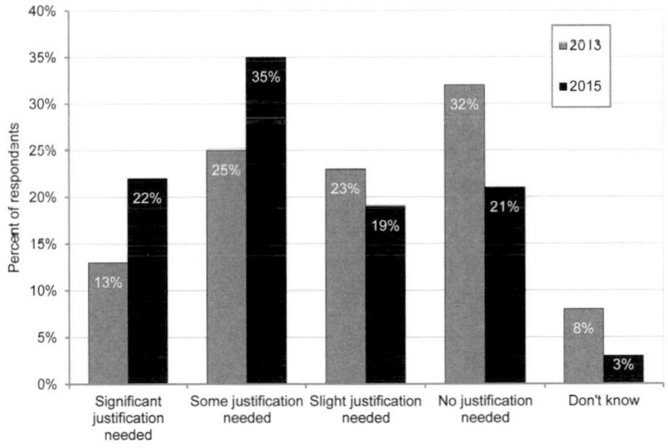

In cases where justification was needed

Source date: 2013

Participants who had to justify change management to senior leaders identified the following topics as the focus of their justification:

1. **Benefit realization and financial outcome**
The focus for justifying change management to senior leaders was the positive correlation between change management and benefit realization. Participants demonstrated how change management supports adoption and use, linking change management directly to achieving project outcomes, realizing project benefits and achieving the desired Return on Investment (ROI).
2. **Project impact and risk management**
Participants pointed to the impact of the current project to justify the need for change management. They drew attention to the size, scope, impact, significance and importance of the project delivering intended results and risks associated with these elements were change management not applied. Risks included project delays, project restarts, being over budget and not meeting project objectives.
3. **Results of past projects**
Previous projects and their associated results were used to justify the need for change management on a current project. Historical project failures were attributed to a lack of change management. In cases in which change management was applied, projects were more successful.
4. **Employee reactions and resistance**
Participants justified change management by linking it to employee satisfaction and retention. They demonstrated the importance of change management when addressing and managing employee resistance and when supporting positive employee morale.
5. **Business performance improvement**
Participants associated effective change management with organizational performance in their justification to senior leaders. Improving productivity, increasing organizational efficiency, growing long-term sustainability, cultivating innovation, developing agility and increasing client satisfaction were organizational performance factors participants associated with effective change management.

In addition to the content of their justification, participants also identified tactics they used when engaging senior leaders including:

- Presenting a formal business case for change management
- Explaining the purpose of change management and educating senior leaders on the topic
- Familiarizing senior leaders with change management activities and intended outcomes
- Leveraging change management advocates to influence senior leaders
- Presenting research and best practices in change management

In cases where no justification was needed

Source date: 2013

Participants who did not have to justify change management explained that senior leaders and executives:

1. **Already valued change management**
Many participants identified change management as the organizational standard or accepted by the executive team.
2. **Associated outcomes of past projects**
Senior leaders had attributed the success of past projects to the application of change management or they associated the failure of past projects with a lack of change management and wanted to prevent similar failures on a current project.
3. **Originally initiated change management**
Individuals at the executive level were responsible for initiating change management on a project and were already convinced of the need, so there was no need to justify change management.
4. **Acknowledged project impact**
Executives acknowledged that due to the scope, impact and potential risks of a current project, change management was required.

Justifying change management to other groups

Participants identified other groups to which they had to justify change management (Figure 4.3). More than 60% reported having to justify change management to middle managers, and 70% to departmental leaders. There was an increase in justification needed for change management in the 2015 study compared to the previous study.

Figure 4.3 – Other groups that required justification

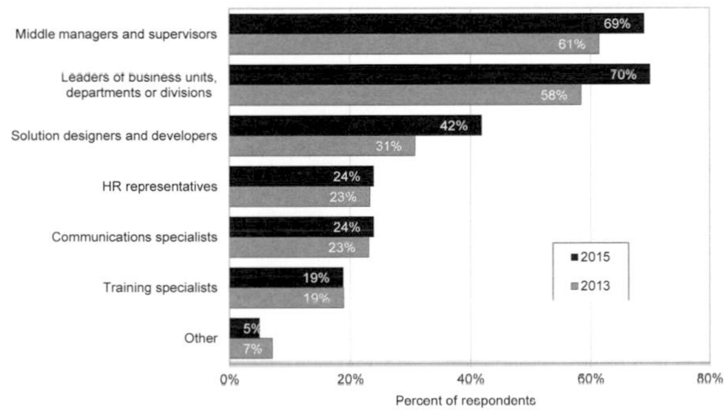

Editor's note: Participants were able to select multiple responses, resulting in a total of more than 100%.

Other groups to which participants had to justify change management included frontline employees, change agents, colleagues and employees within certain business units such as Information Technology (IT), process optimization and finance.

Using risk mitigation as justification for change management

Source date: 2013

Nearly two thirds of participants (62%) used risk mitigation as a means to justify change management (Figure 4.4).

Figure 4.4 – Used risk mitigation to justify change management

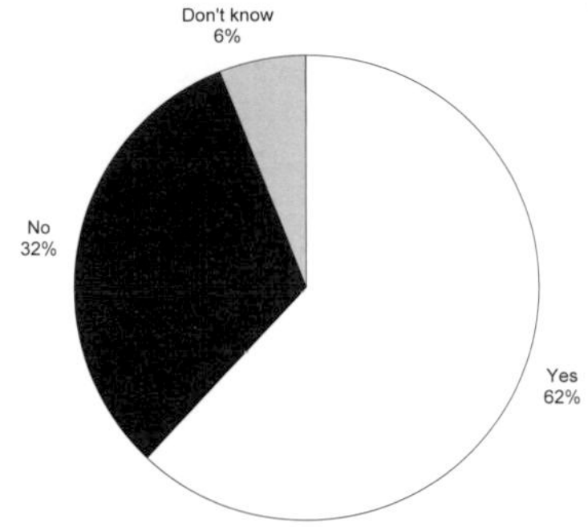

Participants presented the following risks that change management could mitigate:

1. **Lack of employee adoption**
   Participants presented the risk of low or slow adoption. Change management could build employee proficiencies, improve ultimate use and increase the speed of adoption. Participants drew special attention to adoption, use and proficiency rates being minimized if reinforcement was not present. Without change management, these factors would be compromised and the expected Return on Investment (ROI) of the project would not be met.

2. **Failure to meet project objectives**
   The risk of project failure was presented which included failed implementation, missing deadlines and over-spending. Participants also described the cost of REs (such as rework, redesign, re-scope, reschedule, etc.) that would be avoided were change management applied.

3. **Negative employee reactions**
   Negative employee reactions to change were presented as risks. High employee turnover and change fatigue due to the individual impacts of change saturation were cited. If change management was performed, the organization could better manage the impact on individual employees. If not, additional negative employee reactions could include demoralization, low motivation, disengagement and increased stress.

4. **Negative organizational impacts**
   High-level risks to the organization included the threat of an extended period of low productivity or operational delays. Participants also shared the risk of the impact on the organization's culture when change management was neglected.

5. **Indirect risks**
   Practitioners presented indirect risks unique to a project to justify change management. Noncompliance with government standards, higher likelihood of employee strikes and negative impacts to the organization's public image were presented as risks that would be mitigated by change management.

Using cost avoidance as justification for change management

Source date: 2013

Just over 30% of participants used cost avoidance as a means to justify change management (Figure 4.5).

Figure 4.5 – Used cost avoidance to justify change management

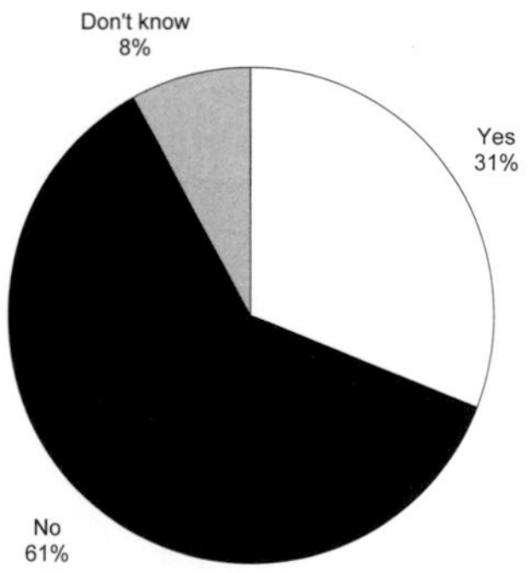

Participants referenced four costs that would be avoided were change management applied to projects.

1. **Operational and project costs**
   Costs presented that the use of change management would avoid included:
   - Employee overtime expenses
   - Expenses associated with missed milestones and deliverables
   - Additional resource allocations required were projects not completed on time
   - Consultant costs

2. **Costs of rework**
   The need to redo components of a project was one cost participants presented as avoidable through change management. Reworking large components of a project, if not the entire project, was the most common cost avoidance. Many participants referred to the cost of retraining employees when change was not managed well.

3. **Non-engaged employees**
   Participants drew attention to the costs of low use and adoption were change management neglected. They connected this to the need for project team members to work on the project longer than intended which added costs to the project.

4. **Opportunity costs**
   Participants expressed that through change management a project was more likely to meet or exceed objectives. "*We used previous projects that did not have change management as an example of the additional costs associated with extended benefit realization and the business objectives not being delivered on time.*"

EFFECTIVENESS AND MEASUREMENT

MEASURING CHANGE MANAGEMENT WORK AND OUTCOMES BASED ON RESEARCH

SUMMARY

The 2015 study further advances the body of knowledge around measurement and outcome accountability. This chapter reveals actionable criteria for measuring progress through the change management process and demonstrating the impact and effectiveness of change management activities. One of the simplest tools for demonstrating the value of change management is the strong correlation between change management effectiveness and project outcomes. Prove your value by tying your work to project results.

HIGHLIGHT

94% of projects with excellent change management met or exceeded objectives compared to 15% with poor change management.

Effectiveness

Correlation between project success and change management effectiveness

An analysis was conducted that correlated change management effectiveness with three dimensions of project success:

- Meeting objectives
- Staying on schedule
- Staying on budget

When evaluating change management effectiveness, participants were provided 12 factors that constituted effective change management (see Table 5.4), and evaluated their overall change management effectiveness on a scale of *poor*, *fair*, *good* or *excellent*.

The number of responses varies in the three correlational charts because participants were allowed to indicate *too early to tell* for each project success category. More participants indicated *too early to tell* for meeting project objectives than for schedule or budget adherence.

Figures 5.1, 5.2 and 5.3 show the percentage of projects performing at or above expectations, correlated with change management effectiveness using data from the 2007, 2009, 2011, 2013 and 2015 benchmarking studies. For each change management effectiveness category – poor, fair, good and excellent – the chart shows the percentage of participants performing at or above expectations (i.e., meeting or exceeding objectives, on or ahead of schedule, and on or under budget).

Projects with excellent change management effectiveness were more than six times more likely to achieve project objectives than teams with poor change management effectiveness, 94% to 15%, respectively. Excellent change management also correlated with staying on schedule and budget.

Figure 5.1 – Correlation with meeting objectives

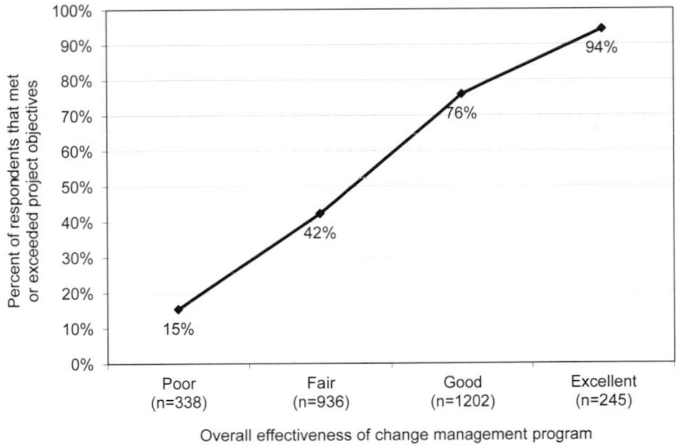

Figure 5.2 – Correlation with staying on or ahead of schedule

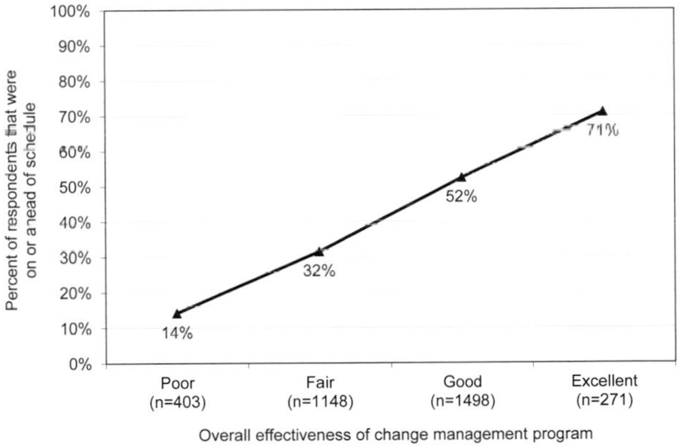

Figure 5.3 – Correlation with staying on or under budget

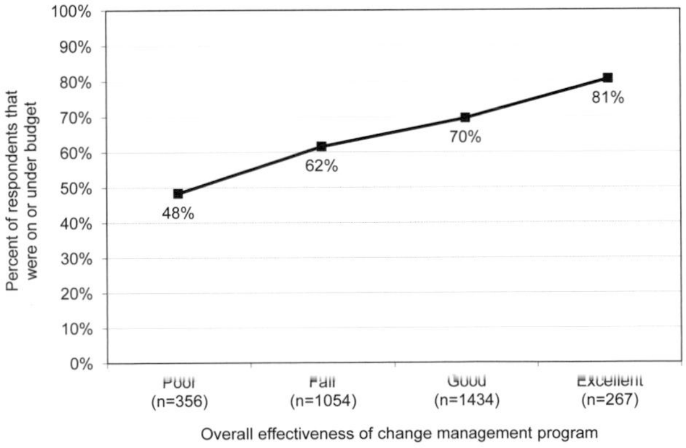

Change management effectiveness factors

Table 5.4 shows 12 change management effectiveness factors and the percentage of participants in the 2015 benchmarking study that indicated *strongly disagree*, *disagree*, *agree* or *strongly agree* for each factor. As in the 2009, 2011 and 2013 studies, the factors that received the most *strongly disagree* and *disagree* responses were 2, 6, 8, 10 and 12. Interestingly, these five factors fall outside of the direct control of the change management practitioner. More than 80% of participants *agreed* or *strongly agreed* with factors 1, 3 and 5. Values from the 2015 study largely paralleled those from 2013 and 2011.

Table 5.4 – Change management effectiveness factors

Factor	Strongly Disagree	Disagree	Agree	Strongly Agree
1. We applied a structured change management process.	3%	16%	51%	30%
2. We had sufficient resources on the team to implement change management.	10%	40%	41%	9%
3. Our change management activities were customized and scaled to fit the change and the organization being changed.	4%	14%	54%	28%
4. Our change management team had the necessary training and expertise in change management.	7%	29%	41%	23%
5. We integrated our change management activities into the project plan.	3%	15%	53%	29%
6. Our business leaders fulfilled their roles as effective change sponsors throughout the entire project.	13%	38%	40%	9%
7. We implemented an effective communications plan.	3%	20%	57%	20%
8. Managers and supervisors engaged in the change and effectively coached their employees through the change process.	9%	46%	41%	4%
9. We provided the necessary training to employees on new processes, systems and job roles.	3%	19%	57%	21%
10. Our senior leaders, mid-level managers and supervisors managed resistance to change effectively.	10%	45%	42%	3%
11. We measured compliance with the change and our overall performance in meeting project objectives.	8%	29%	53%	10%
12. We effectively reinforced the change with employees through recognition, performance measurement and celebrations.	8%	40%	42%	10%

Overall effectiveness of change management program

Participants indicated the overall effectiveness of their change management programs (Figure 5.5). Slightly fewer participants rated their change management programs as good in 2015 than in 2013, and slightly more rated them as excellent. The distribution remained consistent throughout the last three studies.

Figure 5.5 – Overall effectiveness of change management programs

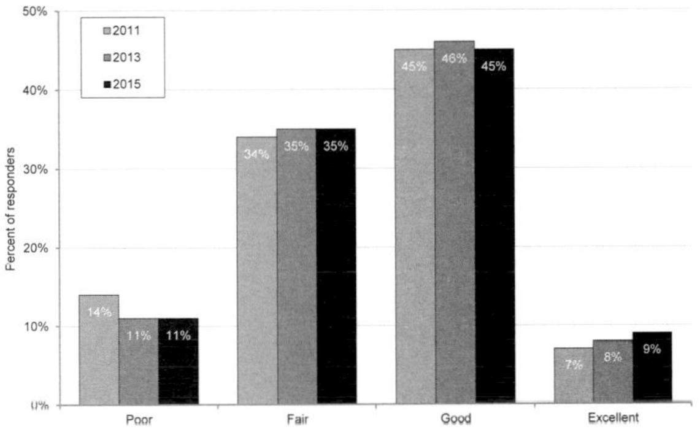

To whom change management effectiveness was reported

Participants in the 2015 study identified to whom the change management effectiveness was reported. Participants were able to select multiple responses when answering the question.

A direct sponsor was the most common response, with 78%, and project program personnel and general leadership both tallied 66%, as shown in Figure 5.6. For the *other* classification, participants were allowed to write in a response, and the most common replies were steering board or committee, project team and specific leadership positions.

Figure 5.6 – To whom effectiveness was reported

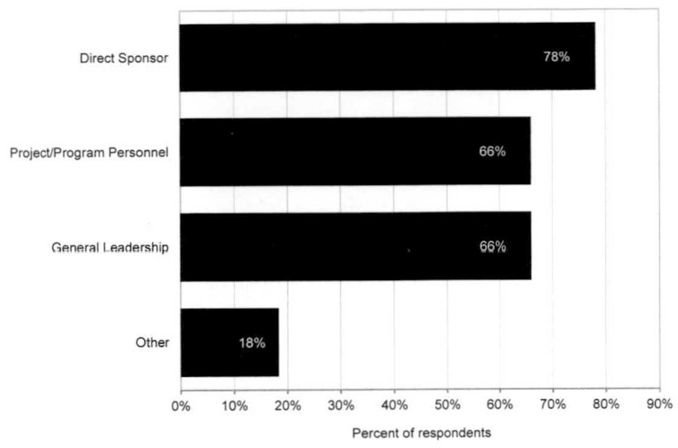

Editor's note: Participants were able to select multiple responses, resulting in a total of more than 100%.

The most common number of stakeholders to whom change management was reported was three, making up 38% of study participants (Figure 5.7).

Figure 5.7 – Number of stakeholders to whom change effectiveness information was reported

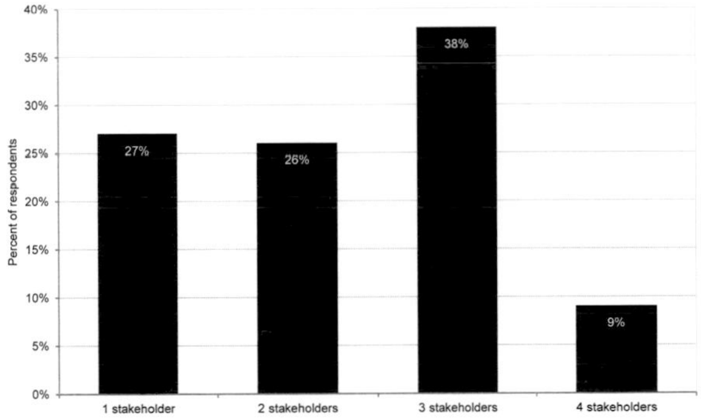

Organizational challenges while employing change management

Participants in the 2015 study identified organizational challenges while implementing change management. The top six barriers, in rank order, were:

1. **Leadership and sponsorship**
   Respondents frequently identified lack of buy-in from executives and lack of visible and effective leadership as challenges to implementing change management.

Other challenges included resistance from managers, lack of leadership capability and skill, lack of consistency and "*primary project sponsors not being visible.*"

2. **Appreciation for and commitment to change management**
Lack of understanding of change management and lack of commitment to the change constituted barriers to the success of the change. Frequently, lack of understanding of the value of change management contributed to a reluctance to commit dedicated resources including trained practitioners, financial resources and time.
3. **Organizational dynamics**
Dynamics and elements of organizations presented challenges to change management. The two most frequent responses were the presence of a "*silo-ed mentality*" and unreasonable expectations of the timeline for change implementation. Other examples included organizational hierarchy, culture of non-disclosure regarding change, organizational complexity and politics and power plays.
4. **Culture of change resistance**
Underlying factors and a culture of change resistance were barriers to change management. A pre-existing culture of resistance to change often manifested in an attitude of "we've always done it that way." Other elements of culture included "*preconceived ideas of change,*" lack of trust associated with working with third parties, such as change management consultants, and a history of success without change. The change history in a company was a significant factor; a history of "*previous poor implementation*" created enduring skepticism and resistance toward future change.
5. **Communication**
Respondents felt that lack of clear communication about the change among members of the organization created a barrier to the implementation of change. Respondents identified building awareness, clearly defining change success and the future state and bridging communication gaps between cultures and geographic locations as challenges to overcome.
6. **Competing initiatives and change saturation**
Lack of prioritization and an overload of change presented challenges when attempting to implement change. Many respondents felt that a large number of competing initiatives within their organizations diverted focus, resources and momentum from change, making them difficult to implement. Change saturation and fatigue affected employee attitudes toward change, making implementation difficult.

Impact of organizational goals and values on change management

Participants shared whether their organizations' goals and values impacted their change management work. Seventy-one percent answered affirmatively (Figure 5.8)

Figure 5.8 – Did organizational goals and values impact change management

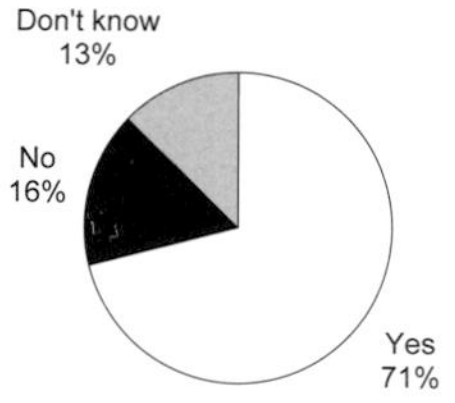

Participants identified how their understanding of their organizations' goals and values impacted their change management.

1. **Customization of change management plan**
Participants found that a clear understanding of the organization's goals and values allowed for a more customized and focused approach to developing a change management plan. Activities affected by this understanding included key message development, identification of impacted groups, determination of project scope, identification of resistance and creation of

stakeholder engagement tactics. Many participants mentioned using some form of assessment as an additional aid to determine how open the organization was to a change.

2. **Goal/value alignment**
   Participants found that aligning a project's initiatives with the organization's goals and values increased the likelihood of project adoption. Alignment with an organization's core mission statement aided with overall justification of a project, and participants noted a clear benefit to aligning a project with the long-term or "big picture" view of the organization. Regular checks throughout the lifecycle of the project helped ensure that alignment persisted and mitigate the potential loss of credibility.
3. **General project impact**
   Organizational goals and values impacted the technical and overall framework of the project. Projects that leveraged the organization's goals and values experienced an increased likelihood of meeting project objectives. Areas of the project framework that were specifically impacted by organizational goals included: assessment and mitigation of business risk, establishment of project milestones, resource allocation for change management and project prioritization. A higher degree of impact was noted for projects that were heavily people dependent.
4. **Negative impacts**
   Participants identified several common organizational situations that negatively affected project success and increased the need for change management. These situations included: lack of available and accessible leadership, lack of clear communication by the project team regarding goals/values and a lack of explicitly defined organizational goals. Participants noted that projects that were misaligned or contradictory to an organization's goals or values frequently suffered from a lack of adoption because impacted groups did not understand how the change related to the overall mission of the organization.

Change management effectiveness — regression analysis

For the first time, advanced statistical techniques were applied to identify relationships among factors that influence the effectiveness of change management programs. These results are not necessarily causal, but they are valuable nonetheless. In fact, research reported in the following section represents the most rigorous and robust analyses performed on the effectiveness of change management methodology to date. The strength of quantitative analysis stems from holding fixed the characteristics that could impact both the effectiveness of the change program and the factors which it is being analyzed against. Therefore, estimates are free from influence by other factors that could be explained. The controlled variables are listed in Appendix F and include organizational characteristics, project characteristics and individual characteristics. Although not every element can be controlled for, the purpose of the analysis is to show results in an understandable manner using the data available. The technical aspects of the analysis process, model, validation techniques and general information regarding the quantitative analysis are described in Appendix F.

Placing a quantitative value on qualitative aspects of change management allows for the relative value of change management methodological factors to be understood in a more transparent context. In combination, findings listed below increase the credibility of the research and construct a coherent and integrated foundation for further analysis.

Relationships analyzed include: having a dedicated change resource on the project team and its effectiveness, use of a particular change management methodology and its effectiveness, the level of a structured change management model used and its effectiveness, the level of sufficient resources used and its effectiveness, and the level of integration of change management methodology and its effectiveness.

The relationship between having a dedicated change resource on the project and effectiveness of the change program

Although it has been established that the presence of change management resources on the project correlates with more effective change management programs, the strength of the relationship had not been measured until the 2015 study. Using regression analysis, it was found that projects with a dedicated change management resource experienced a more effective change management program by 23%, on average, when compared to projects lacking a dedicated change resource. Individual, project and organizational factors were controlled. Results were significant; the t-value of 4.60 is beyond the 99% confidence level. In other words, there is less than a 1% chance that the results found are untrue. The estimate had a corrected standard error of 0.05. For more information regarding the analysis, model and validation tests, refer to Appendix F.

Use of a change management methodology and effectiveness of the change management program

Participants who used a change management methodology experienced a more effective change management program by 15%, on average. Individual, project and organizational factors were controlled. Results were significant at the 95% level, with a t-value of 2.45 and standard error of 0.04. For more information regarding the analysis, model and validation tests, refer to Appendix F.

Degree of a structured change management model used and effectiveness of the change management program

The relationship between the degree of structure a change management model had and the effectiveness of the change management program was measured. Participants rated the level of a structured methodology on a scale, with categories *strongly agree*, *agree*, *disagree* and *strongly disagree* as options. For every 1% increase in structure of methodology, effectiveness of the change program increases by 0.61%, on average; increasing the structure of a change management methodology by 10% was associated with an increase of the effectiveness of the change management program by 6.1%. Individual, project and organizational factors were controlled. Results were significant at the 99% confidence level, with a t-value of 11.81 and corrected standard error of 0.05. For more information regarding the analysis, model and validation tests, refer to Appendix F.

Level of sufficient resources and effectiveness of the change management program

The interaction between the level of sufficient resources and the overall effectiveness of the change management program was measured. Participants rated the level of a sufficient resources on a scale, with categories *strongly agree*, *agree*, *disagree* and *strongly disagree* as options. For every 1% increase in the level of sufficient resources on the project team, effectiveness of the overall change management program increased, on average, by 0.33%; increasing the level of sufficient resources by 10% was associated with a 3.3% increase in the effectiveness of the change management program. Individual, project and organizational factors were controlled. Results were significant at the 99% confidence level, with a t-value of 9.21 and corrected standard error of 0.04. For more information regarding the analysis, model and validation tests, refer to Appendix F.

Level of change management integration on the project team and effectiveness of the change management program

The relationship between the level of integration between change activities on the project team and effectiveness of the change management program was measured. Participants rated the level of change management integration on a scale, with categories *strongly agree*, *agree*, *disagree* and *strongly disagree* as options. For every 1% increase in the degree of integration between teams, effectiveness increased by 0.58%, or every 10% increase in the level of integration was associated with a 5.8% increase in effectiveness. Individual, project and organizational factors were controlled. Results were significant at the 99% confidence level, with a t-value of 10.31 and corrected standard error of 0.06. For more information regarding the analysis, model and validation tests, refer to Appendix F.

Measurements

Criteria used to measure change management effectiveness

Participants in the 2015 study identified criteria used to measure the effectiveness of change management. Analysis of results provided five categories of criteria: adoption metrics, communication metrics, employee performance, overall project performance and readiness assessments.

1. **Adoption metrics**
   Responses in this category focused on employee adoption and use of new processes. Employees were evaluated based on whether they were performing as required by the project or change initiative. Examples included:
   - Percent of user adoption
   - Rate of user adoption
   - Adherence to and proficiency in new processes
2. **Qualitative/feedback metrics**
   Responses were various forms of direct feedback given on the perceived effectiveness of change, whether from employees or clients as end users. Examples included:
   - Surveys and other forms of direct feedback
   - Informal and self-reported feedback
   - End-user satisfaction reports
3. **Employee performance**
   Responses focused on measurement of changes in employee performance as a result of change management. Examples included:
   - Changes in productivity/efficiency resulting from the change
   - Qualitative assessments of changes in culture and behavior of employees
4. **Overall project performance**
   Responses included measurements related to the performance of projects on a large scale, and with overall project goals in mind.
   - Benchmarking progress against goals
   - Project Return on Investment (ROI) and measurable benefits indicators
   - Project timeline progression and completion
5. **Readiness assessments**
   Responses identified assessments designed to measure readiness for change within parts of the organization. Readiness was then used as a criterion to determine the effectiveness of change management:
   - Readiness assessments based on Prosci methodology and ADKAR®
   - Assessments of executive/stakeholder engagement and readiness
   - Organizational awareness and resistance assessments

Data used to evaluate change management effectiveness

Participants identified what data they used to evaluate the effectiveness of change management. Responses revealed five categories of data and five categories of criteria used to measure adoption.

1. **Qualitative/feedback-based**
   Participants most frequently identified data that came in the form of direct feedback or qualitative observations as a way to evaluate change management effectiveness. Surveys were the most common type. Other forms of data included qualitative observations of changes in team members' behaviors, customer feedback and reports from leaders or supervisors.

2. **Change management metrics**
Participants identified data related to change management and its processes. Responses included data related to training such as attendance and percentage of employees trained, results of readiness assessments, sponsor engagement and assessments such as ADKAR®.

3. **Quantitative/business outcome metrics**
Participants identified metrics that were easily quantifiable and frequently related to business outcomes as an important source of data. Examples included adherence to overall project deadlines, external system audits, budget changes and Return on Investment (ROI) measured by "*comparing the financial benefit of old and new.*"

4. **Individual employee performance metrics**
Respondents identified changes to employee performance and behaviors, specifically proficiency with the system, as a key source of data to measure effectiveness. The most frequent response for this category dealt with the number of errors made and issues that arose in relation to the use of new systems or processes. Other employee performance metrics included results of competency assessments, changes to productivity and measures of engagement and awareness among employees.

5. **Adoption metrics**
Participants felt that metrics measuring adoption and compliance were some of the most important and straightforward ways of assessing change management effectiveness. Sources of data most frequently identified included use and compliance metrics, number of transactions completed with the new system, website visits and number of process deviations.

Tracking change management activities

Participants in the 2015 study indicated whether they tracked change management activities. Three quarters of participants indicated they measured change management activities.

Participants were asked to identify the methods by which they tracked change management activities. Participants identified six primary methods for tracking change management activities.

1. **Project plan**
The most commonly identified method of tracking change management was through the use of a pre-existing project plan into which change management was integrated. This method included the use of checklists of milestones and completed activities, as well as individual tasks within the project plan, as metrics for tracking change management.

2. **Feedback**
Participants identified the use of both direct and indirect feedback as the second most frequently utilized method of measuring change management activities. The various forms of reported feedback included: weekly meetings, surveys, the use of a communications plan, direct communication with stakeholders, and other forms of regular reporting.

3. **Tracking tools**
Participants identified tracking tools as important and widely used ways of tracking change management activities. Examples of tracking tools utilized by participants included: spreadsheets, Microsoft Project and other project tracking software programs, dashboards and external consultants.

4. **Change management plan**
Many participants identified the use of a specific change management plan as a method of tracking change management activities. This included monitoring activities specifically related to change management, either through a plan developed in-house by the organization or the use of Prosci templates including plans structured around the ADKAR® framework.

5. **Realization of change through employee behavior**
Participants identified specific employee behaviors or measures of employee attitudes as methods for tracking change management activities. Examples included: employee

attendance at trainings, use of training plans, adoption surveys and overall proficiency with the new system.

6. **Measures of output**
Participants identified measures of final output of the change initiative as a valuable method for tracking change management activities. These measures included measures of business success, such as profits, and output measurements, such as number of hits on the website.

Measuring the overall outcome of applying change management

Source date: 2013

Participants in the 2013 study explained how they measured the overall outcome of applying change management on a project. Responses revealed a tendency to evaluate overall outcome at the conclusion of the effort and into the sustainment phase. Participants used post-implementation reviews, lessons learned, sustainability measures and post go-live assessments as vehicles to evaluate and capture the overall outcome of applying change management. A number of participants also used a sponsor's overall evaluation of change as an indicator of an outcome. The following three categories summarize how participants measured the overall outcome of applying change management:

1. **Impacted employee responses**
Participants measured the overall impact of change management by how impacted employees responded to change. Common measurements focused on end-user adoption, uptake, use and compliance metrics. Participants used surveys and feedback to gauge how employees were responding based on a number of other factors including readiness, engagement, participation, willingness, acceptance and satisfaction.

2. **Project results**
Overall project results were used to evaluate the outcome of applying change management on a project. Project success and meeting objectives were commonly referenced when assessing the outcome, followed by benefit realization, performance against key performance indicators (KPIs) and Return on Investment (ROI). Project outcomes, such as revenue, cost, customer satisfaction and quality improvement, were also used to evaluate the outcome of applying change management.

3. **Project execution**
Participants considered how timely project deliverables were achieved when evaluating the overall outcome of applying change management. They evaluated how smoothly a change was implemented and the amount of disruption that occurred. Productivity measures and resistance measures through the duration of the change reflected the impact of change management. A number of participants indicated that lack of noise during implementation was a sign of positive impact of change management.

Demonstrating the value-add of applying change management

Source date: 2013

Participants used a number of approaches to demonstrate the value-add of applying change management for a project on which they were reporting. Evidence of the impact of change management on project performance and on employee adoption were the most common approaches used to demonstrate the value-add of change management. Practitioners focused on six areas when demonstrating value-add.

1. **Increased realization of project benefits**
The most common demonstration of the value-add of change management came through examination of overall project performance. Project success and meeting objectives were most common, with focus on factors and metrics the project aimed to improve. The value of change management was also demonstrated through sustainment

of benefits and evaluations of benefit realization. Project progress showed the value of change management including executing project deliverables and faster delivery of expected benefits.

2. **Improved adoption of the change**
Participants pointed to improved employee adoption, acceptance and compliance as evidence of the value-add of change management. A number of participants specified the speed of adoption, ultimate use and proficiency factors as measures of value-add.

3. **Increased engagement and involvement**
Participants showed that change management added value by increasing employee buy-in and engagement. Stakeholders were more involved and had greater participation and understanding. Employee confidence in the change was higher.

4. **Eliminated challenges**
The value-add of change management was demonstrated by presenting challenges and risks that were avoided. Resistance was low because change management helped to avoid or minimize it. Fewer issues needed to be resolved, and there were fewer support calls. Change was less disruptive and the organization experienced less of a productivity dip.

5. **Compared to other projects**
A number of participants used comparisons to other projects as a way to demonstrate the value-add of change management on a particular project. Comparisons were made to historical projects during which change management was not applied, highlighting the difference in project experiences and outcomes. Some participants compared current change to previous attempts at similar changes.

6. **Improved employee readiness**
Participants showed that with change management, employees were more prepared and ready for change.

Some participants identified channels used to demonstrate the value-add of applying change management, including:

- Employee surveys including interviews, engagement surveys and satisfaction surveys
- Anecdotal evidence and stories from impacted employees and managers
- Presentations and reporting to project teams and leaders
- Industry data
- Lessons-learned reporting

Change management effectiveness measurement

Forty percent of participants in the 2015 study reported measuring change management effectiveness (Figure 5.9).

Figure 5.9 – Measured change management effectiveness

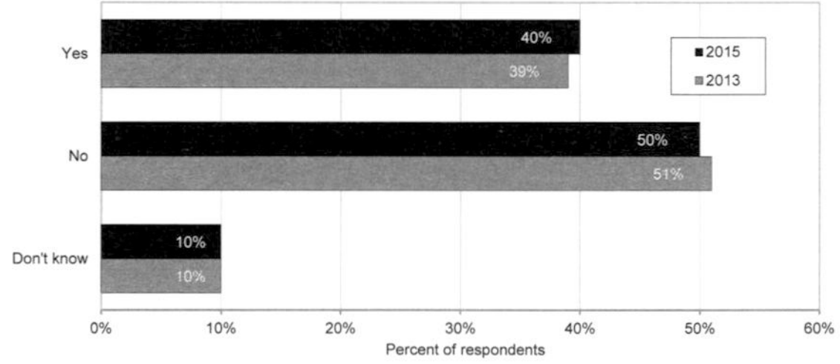

Methods

Participants in the 2015 study identified five methods for measuring change management effectiveness.

1. **Surveys**
Delivering surveys and questionnaires to employees was the most commonly reported method for gauging change management effectiveness. The surveys captured the effectiveness of change at the individual level. Participants used both in-person and online surveys, and both were effective.

2. **Level of adoption/observation**
   Participants monitored each employee's system use. Compliance rates were measured by each employee's ability to start and complete new processes and observed as the employees worked within the new process.
3. **Feedback**
   Many participants held one-on-one meetings with employees to garner feedback on how effective a change had been. Other participants used written feedback forms or group sessions during which they encouraged honest communication regarding a change.
4. **Assessments**
   Tests were given to employees to assess their abilities and skill levels. Assessments were a good indication of whether change management had adequately prepared employees for a change.
5. **Meetings**
   Both one-on-one and group meetings took place to evaluate individual and team performance. Group meetings often took place at several stages during the project and were conducted multiple times because participants felt that a one-time meeting would not be effective in gauging change management effectiveness.

Data sources

Participants in the 2013 study identified specific data sources for measuring change management. Although most measurement focused on end users, participants also collected data on change management effectiveness from others in the organization. Top sources of data included:

1. **End users** – those in the organization who had to change how they did their jobs and adopt a solution that was deployed by a project or initiative.
2. **Key stakeholders in the organization** – managers and leaders within affected parts of the organization.
3. **Project team** – the team leading the project and designing the change provided feedback on the effect of change management.
4. **Change agents** – including the primary change management resource or team and members of the extended change agent network within the organization.
5. **Senior leaders** – the primary sponsor and other sponsors heading the effort within their parts of the organization.

Timing

Participants in the 2013 study reported when measurement of change management effectiveness occurred at various points during the project lifecycle. The time frames for measurement included:

1. **Post** – after implementation
2. **Pre and post** – before a project began to create a baseline and after implementation to gauge changes in performance
3. **At key milestones** –at key points during a project's lifecycle, tied to major developments or milestones
4. **Continuous** –continuously throughout a project's lifecycle

Individual transition measures

Figure 5.10 shows that 44% of all participants measured whether change was occurring at the individual level.

Figure 5.10 – Measured if change was occurring at the individual level

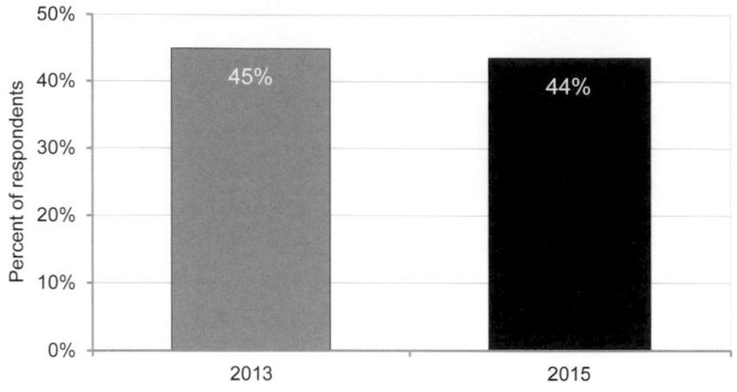

Participants used the following metrics and collection methods to measure changes at the individual level:

Metrics for individual change measurement

1. **Compliance and usage**
   Identified more than twice as often as any other finding, process compliance and system use statistics were the most commonly used metrics. Compliance rates were measured by tracking employees as they started and completed new processes. Participants measured system use through database queries and tracking logins to a new system.
2. **Attendance and engagement**
   Participants measured the number of individuals attending meetings and training regarding a change. They compared the number of attendees to the total number of employees being impacted by a change to gauge receptivity and engagement.
3. **Existing business metrics**
   Existing business metrics that related to a change were used. Metrics included response time, client-facing time, conversion time, cost reduction, sales, revenue and profit. Work output was also analyzed including product quantity and quality. Other business metrics included absenteeism, staff overtime and employee attrition and retention.
4. **Error rates and issues raised**
   Some participants tracked the number of errors made in a new state to measure progress at the individual level. Others tracked the number of calls and tickets submitted to a help desk, the rate of problems being reported and the types of queries that required support. Participants measured these values before and after implementation for comparison.

Methods for individual measurement

1. **Surveys**
   Delivering surveys or questionnaires to impacted groups was the most common method for measuring progress at the individual level. These tools were used to analyze individual behavior, determine satisfaction and acceptance levels and assess awareness of the need for change. Participants often administered surveys before implementation to establish a baseline and again after implementation to draw comparisons.
2. **Observation and communication**
   Participants relied on observation and communication to judge how individuals were progressing through change. Feedback, noted by participants as an important aspect of communication, was collected through interviews, meetings, informal conversations, focus groups and key informants including managers and change networks. Participants also observed the attitudes and behaviors of individuals throughout the change.
3. **Tests and assessments**
   Tests assessed individuals' skills, competencies and abilities with the goal of determining whether individuals were prepared and capable of performing in the new state. Tests and assessments were given before and after implementation, or after impacted groups received training. Readiness assessments were also conducted.
4. **Performance evaluations**
   Performance evaluations were used to measure individual change. Performance reports and documents were completed to define roles and analyze fulfillment. Participants also used key performance indicators (KPIs) as benchmarks.

Defining and measuring successful adoption and usage

Participants indicated whether they had defined what successful adoption and usage would be for their change initiative. Just over half did, as shown in Figure 5.11.

Figure 5.11 – Definition of successful adoption and usage

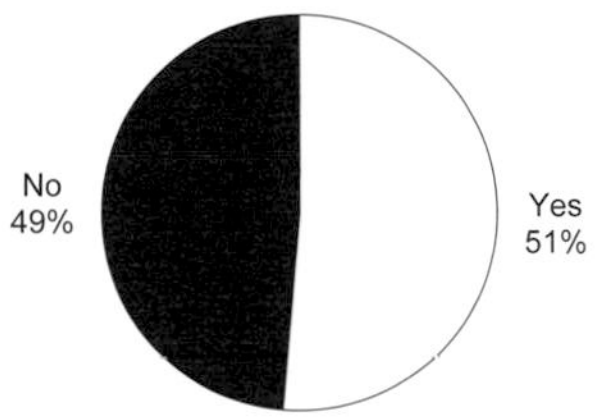

Speed of adoption, ultimate utilization and proficiency performance

Participants in the 2015 study indicated how the project was performing according to speed of adoption, ultimate utilization and proficiency. Speed of adoption represents how quickly employees adopt change. Ultimate utilization is the terminal adoption rate (or the converse of the opt-out rate). Proficiency is how effectively employees performed as required by a change.

Approximately 10% of participants indicated that performance was better than they expected, and just over one third of participants indicated that performance met expectations (Figures 5.12, 5.13 and 5.14).

Figure 5.12 – Speed of adoption performance

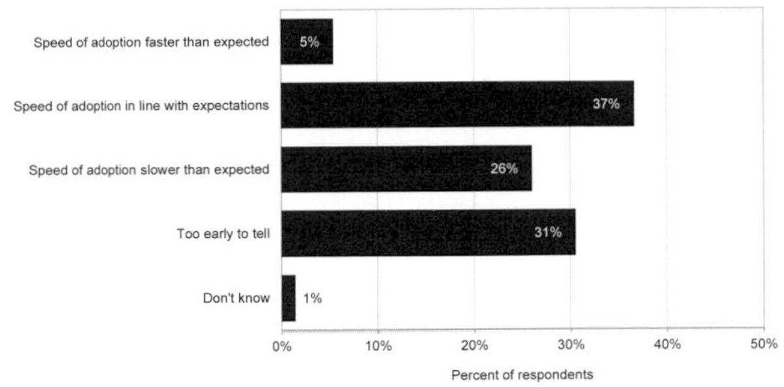

Figure 5.13 – Ultimate utilization performance

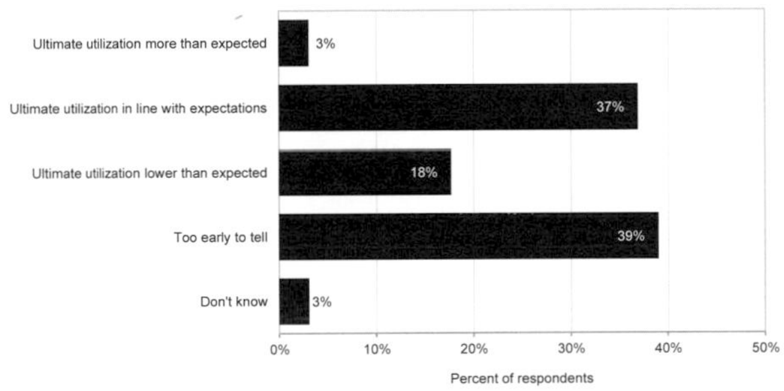

Figure 5.14 – Proficiency performance

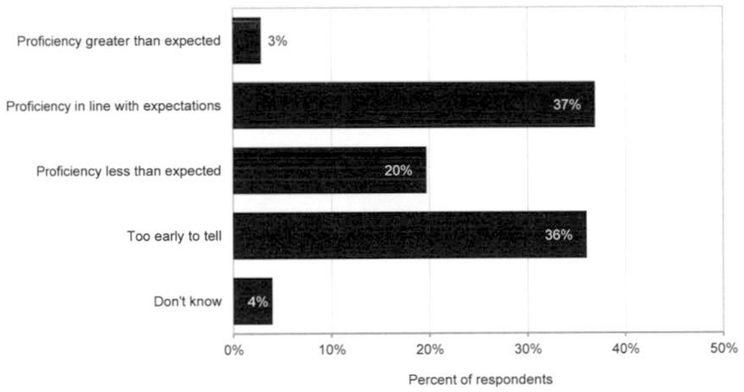

Correlating people-side ROI factors

2015 data on speed of adoption, ultimate utilization and proficiency were segmented by overall effectiveness of a change management program. Figures 5.15, 5.16 and 5.17 show the percentage of participants that performed in line or better than expected for each of the three variables segmented by overall change management effectiveness.

The data demonstrate that participants with more effective change management programs showed better performance in all three variables. Excellent change management programs resulted in better speed of adoption, ultimate utilization and proficiency. Poor change management resulted in fewer respondents meeting speed of adoption, ultimate utilization and proficiency targets.

Figure 5.15 – In line or better than expected speed of adoption versus change management effectiveness

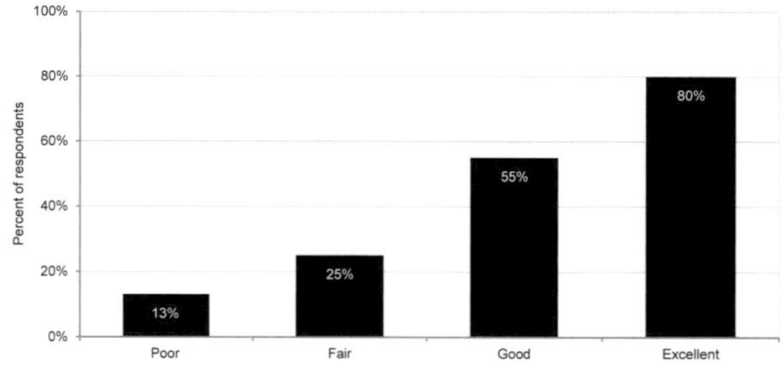

Figure 5.16 – In line or better than expected ultimate utilization versus change management effectiveness

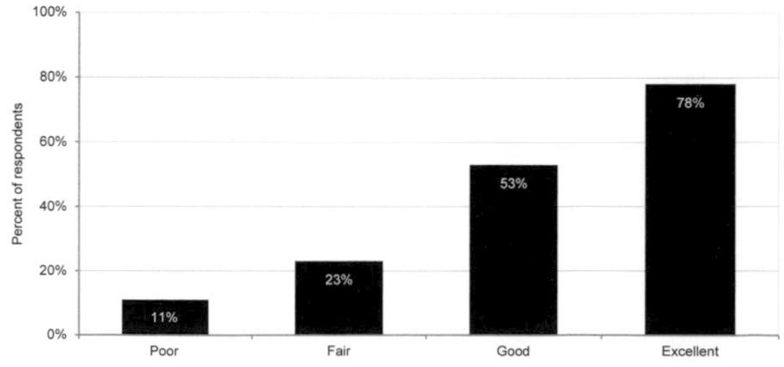

Figure 5.17 – In line or better than expected proficiency versus change management effectiveness

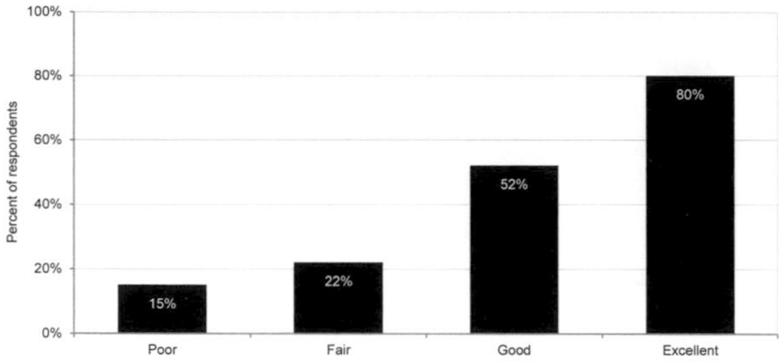

Measuring speed of adoption

Twenty-four percent of participants measured speed of adoption. The following metrics and methods were used to measure the speed at which impacted employees adopted change.

1. **Project timeline completion**
   Participants determined speed of adoption based on how quickly a project moved toward completion. Participants tracked the time it took to complete tasks, achieve milestones and meet deadlines. These measurements were compared to a timeline. The time it took employees to learn and apply new skills during and after training also indicated how quickly employees were adopting the change.

2. **Usage**
   Participants tracked use of new tools, systems and support sites to determine speed of adoption. Depending on the change, they looked at frequency of use, number of users, number of logins, number of site visits, amount of content contribution and number of document uploads and downloads. In some cases, participants tracked workarounds.

3. **Surveys and assessments**
   End-user surveys were frequently cited as a means for collecting information about speed of adoption. Participants also used assessments to determine skills and abilities. Assessments were completed before and after implementation and training for comparison.

4. **Observation and feedback**
   Participants observed employees to understand attitudes, behaviors and

willingness to adopt change. Special attention was given to demonstrated engagement. Sometimes managers were tasked with observing employees and reporting to change practitioners. Feedback was also collected from employees, managers, change agents, senior leaders and clients to gauge speed of adoption. Interviews, one-on-one conversations, focus groups and Question and Answer (Q&A) sessions were some of the feedback channels used.

Other methods or metrics included performance evaluations, compliance reports, audits, error tracking and issues raised to support groups or help desks.

Measuring ultimate utilization

The 39% of participants who measured ultimate utilization used the following methods and metrics:

1. **Compliance and use**
   Compliance was measured through process audits and compliance reporting. Participants also measured use based on the number of employees logging into new systems, completing new processes, and downloading and uploading new documents. Participants tracked use before and after implementation by comparing the number of employees using the new solution to the total impacted by the change. Others gauged use by monitoring workarounds, and how many employees were reverting to the old ways of doing things.
2. **Surveys and assessments**
   As a method to measure ultimate use, participants delivered surveys and assessments to impacted employees. These tools were aimed at revealing productivity, readiness, user acceptance and employee satisfaction. Participants also focused on surveying managers to collect information about their direct reports. Assessments were given to determine employees' knowledge and skills. Specific assessments included processes, post-implementation and staff capacity assessments.
3. **Feedback and observation**
   Participants collected feedback through interviews, focus groups and one-on-one conversations. Feedback was collected from key individuals including employees, managers, clients and change network members. Participants also gauged ultimate use by observing and monitoring employees in the new state.
4. **Work output and performance**
   Identified less than half as often as the previous finding, employee performance and output also determined ultimate use. Performance evaluations, project goals and updated key performance indicators (KPIs) were used. The quality and quantity of work output was also evaluated to determine how many employees were using the solution.
5. **Timeline and process completion**
   Participants tracked timeline, process and task completion often using checklists. Some said the time it took for employees to become efficient using a new solution contributed to ultimate use measurement.

Measuring proficiency

Participants who measured proficiency used the following methods and metrics.

1. **Work output and performance**
   Participants analyzed the quantity and quality of employees' work output to determine proficiency. Productivity and quality measures were taken before and after implementation for comparison. Participants tracked and rated employees' performance in the new state. Percent completion of specific job tasks and speed of execution were used as performance indicators. Performance evaluations were also used to measure proficiency. Work performance was compared with established key performance indicators (KPIs).
2. **Surveys and assessments**
   Surveys were used to gauge employee satisfaction and confidence in operating with a new solution. Assessments were given to

impacted groups to analyze skills and abilities, assess change readiness and determine training needs. Assessments were given before and after implementation for comparison.

3. **Error rates and issues raised**
Participants measured error rates and failure incidents daily, weekly or monthly. Some participants determined the amount of rework that took place due to errors. The number of issues presented to support groups and help desks also indicated proficiency. Participants analyzed the types of problems being reported and the most frequently asked questions to gauge proficiency.

4. **Feedback and observation**
Feedback was collected from employees, managers, clients, trainers, super users and change agents to determine proficiency. Participants engaged in interviews, focus groups, forums and one-on-one conversations with these groups to collect feedback. Impacted groups were also observed to determine whether they were meeting required proficiencies. Checklists were sometimes used to aid this work.

5. **Compliance and usage**
Compliance and process audits were used to measure proficiency. Use statistics were collected from systems reports and other channels to determine whether employees were using a new solution proficiently. Number of logins, downloads, uploads and time spent using the new system or support sites were also tracked.

Definition of project objectives

Participants in the 2011, 2013 and 2015 benchmarking studies commented on how well overall project goals and objectives were defined.

Forty-one percent of participants indicated that goals and objectives were defined *very well* or *well*, an increase from 38% in the 2011 study but a decrease from 43% in 2013 (Figure 5.18). Just less than one fifth of participants said that goals and objectives were defined *poorly* or *very poorly*.

Figure 5.18 – Definition of project goals and objectives

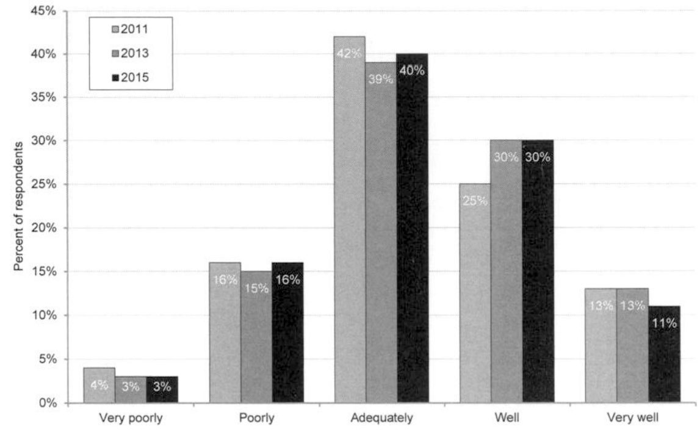

Project metrics and KPIs

Source date: 2011

Participants in the 2011 study identified key performance indicators (KPIs) that were tracked to evaluate project success. The two most frequently cited indicators were:

- The project adhered to the schedule and was completed on time
- The project was delivered on budget

In addition to delivering on time and on budget, the following indicators were mentioned by participants:

1. **Achievement of intended outcomes**
Participants measured the degree to which the project met objectives, achieved intended improvement in performance and realized expected benefits. A number of indicators that were tracked related to project outcomes. The most commonly cited indicators included customer satisfaction, cost savings, process time, sales or revenue, productivity, quality, efficiency gains, functionality, data integrity, service targets and accuracy.

2. **Use by employees**
These indicators focused on adoption of a change as demonstrated by employee usage. Indicators related to employee use included system use, process adherence, adoption, usability, behavioral indicators, proficiency and acceptance.

3. **User response**
Similar to use, these indicators evaluated end users' satisfaction with and readiness to adopt a change. Indicators included direct feedback, satisfaction levels, training attendance, knowledge evaluation, communication effectiveness measures, participation at events, training feedback and training effectiveness.
4. **Achievement of interim milestones**
Indicators related to monitoring project progress were tracked including milestone achievement, completion of deliverables and percent completion.
5. **Error tracking**
Instead of tracking positive adoption and metrics, some respondents tracked metrics that indicated a change was not occurring. These negative indicators included support calls, calls to the help desk, error rates, problem and issue tracking, complaints and disruptions.
6. **Engagement measures**
These metrics measured user perceptions and attitudes toward a change including engagement, awareness, morale, buy-in and understanding.

If your project failed or only partially met objectives, what obstacles did you encounter?

Source date: 2009

Participants in the 2009 benchmarking study whose projects failed or only partially met objectives reported obstacles in one or more of the following areas:

1. Leadership and sponsorship
2. Project management
3. Change management

1. **Leadership and sponsorship obstacles**
   - Slow decision-making by a sponsor
   - Lack of involvement of key business leaders; difficulty getting all key stakeholders on board to build the necessary sponsor coalition
   - Wavering support for the change; shifting or conflicting priorities of business leaders and managers
   - Competing initiatives (too many projects going on at the same time)
   - Insufficient resources or funding allocated to the project
   - Insufficient visibility and communication from a sponsor
   - Sponsor changed mid-project; lack of consistent leadership for the change
2. **Project management obstacles**
   - Project changed or expanded in scope (scope creep)
   - Poor estimation of the project's magnitude; insufficient details to plan properly
   - Unrealistic schedule from the planning process
   - Poor project management throughout the project; failure to report progress honestly
   - Inadequate management of vendors; development was behind schedule or vendors did not meet commitments
   - Insufficient resources or lack of the correct resources for a project
   - Poor-quality deliverables from vendors, specifically regarding release of new technology
   - Poor assumptions about project's impact on the organization
   - Lack of a solid business case for change

3. **Change management obstacles**
    - Employee resistance to the change; lacked buy-in and involvement
    - Middle managers resisted the change
    - Insufficient change management resources for the size of the change
    - Underestimated the impact this change would have on employees
    - Did not provide sufficient training to employees
    - Poor communication about the project
    - Lacked a formal change management process

METHODOLOGY

INCREASE CHANGE MANAGEMENT EFFECTIVENESS WITH A STRUCTURED METHODOLOGY

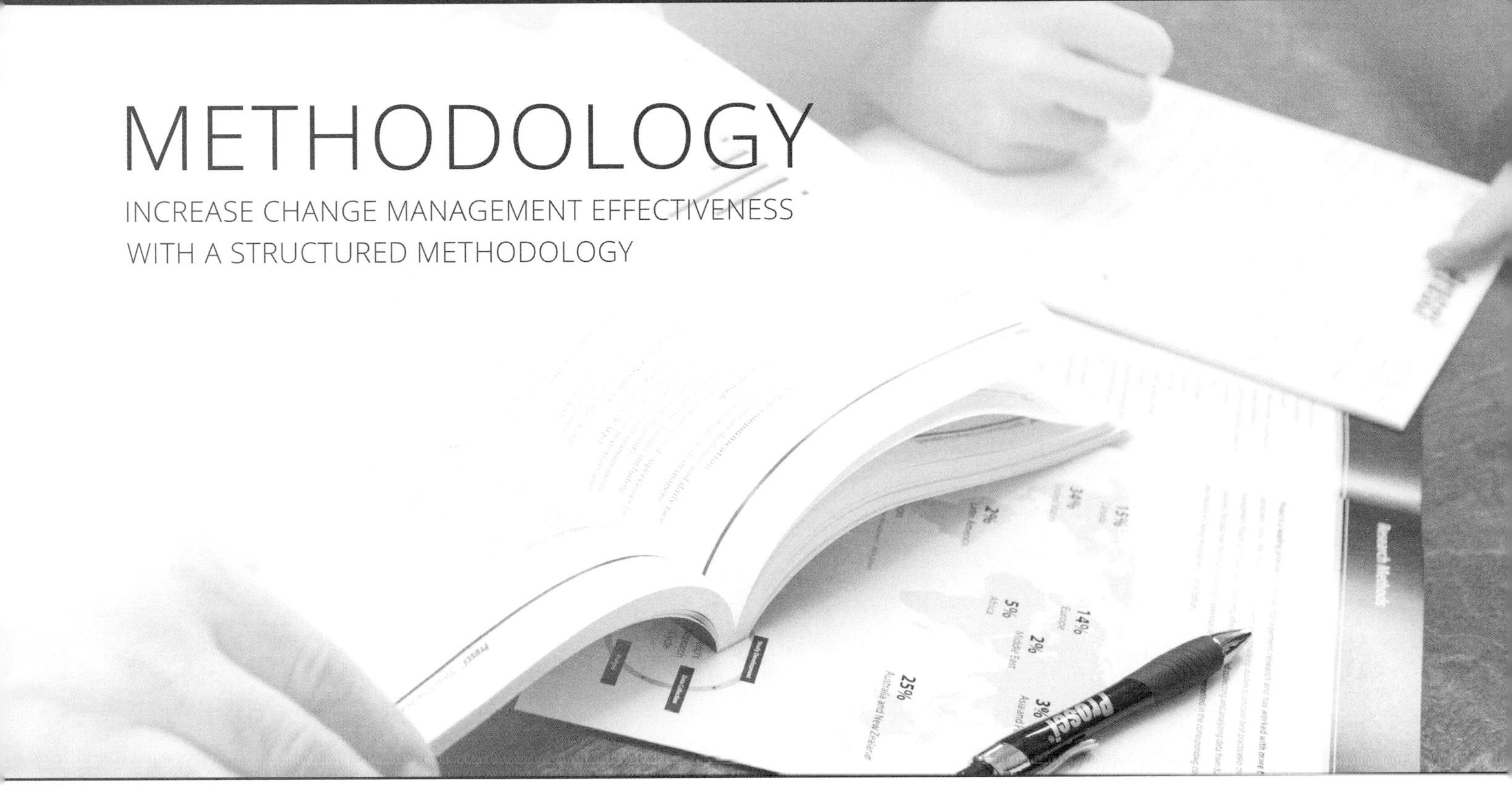

SUMMARY

Applying a structured change management methodology and starting application early in the project lifecycle are both top contributors to success as well as growing trends in the discipline. Learn best practices for selecting a methodology and applying it for maximum effectiveness. See the direct correlation between starting change management early and delivering project results, and learn what factors influenced starting change management early.

HIGHLIGHT

The earlier change management started on the project, the more likely the project was to meet or exceed objectives.

Initiating change management

When to start change management

Participants in the 2015 study indicated when change management began on the project on which they were reporting and when they would recommend starting change management (Figure 6.1). More than 85% of participants recommended beginning change management at project initiation, though only 40% started this early. Ninety-eight percent would start change management during either the initiation or planning stages.

Figure 6.1 – When to start change management

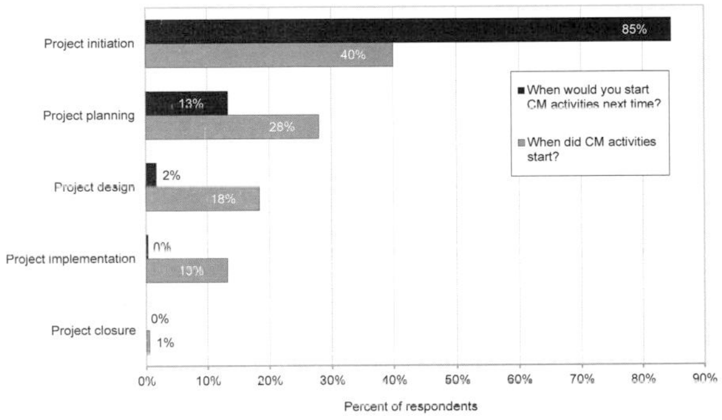

Data show a direct correlation between when change management was started on the project and the likelihood that the project met or exceeded objectives (Figure 6.2). Sixty-four percent of respondents who started change management during project initiation met or exceeded project objectives, compared to only 37% who started change management during implementation.

Figure 6.2 – Impact of starting change management early on effectiveness

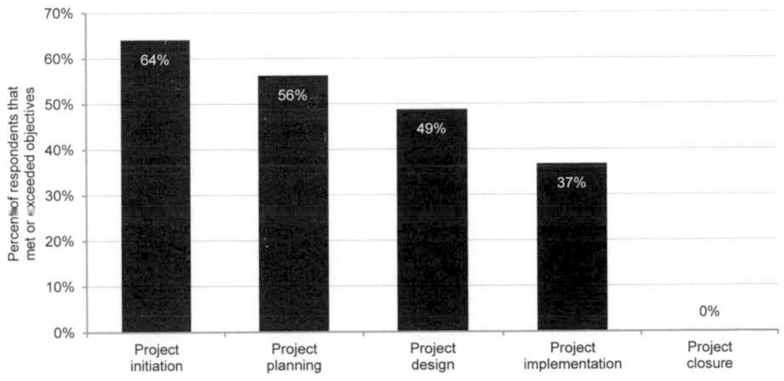

Contributors to starting change management early in the project

For the first time, participants in the 2015 study identified factors that contributed to having change management begin at the onset of a change project. Having previous experience with change management and senior leadership directive were the top two contributors to starting change management early, as shown in Figure 6.3.

Figure 6.3 – Contributors to starting change management early in the project

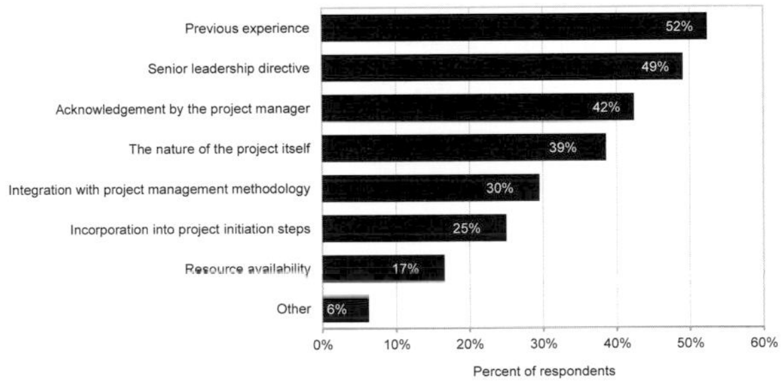

Editor's note: Participants were able to select multiple responses, resulting in a total of more than 100%.

As seen in Figure 6.4, participants cited a single factor (34%) as the most common number of contributors to starting change management early in the project, with three factors as the next most frequent response (27%).

Figure 6.4 – Number of contributors to starting change management early in the project

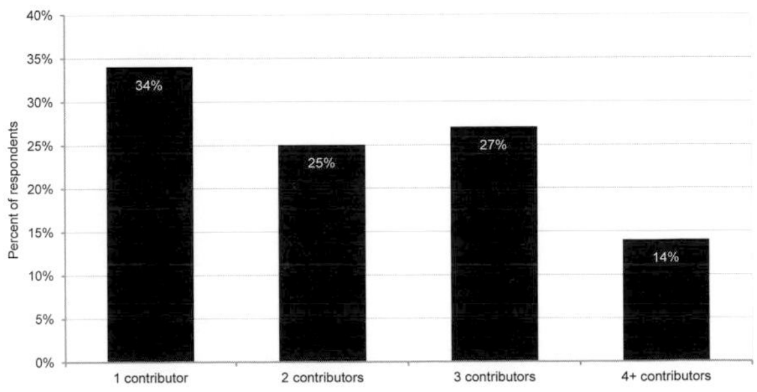

What you can do at initiation when there is incomplete information

Source date: 2011

Participants in the 2011 benchmarking study provided change management actions that can be taken when change management begins and there is incomplete information regarding the project or solution design. Top suggestions included:

1. **Create a communications plan to describe the desired results of and need for change**
   Communicate details of the change openly and often to increase transparency and awareness of the change, including desired results, the need for change and current information gaps. Establish expectations for communication surrounding the change by designating structured channels.
2. **Analyze the organizational climate and its reaction to change, and document common risks and areas of resistance**
   Use systematic, measurable assessments to analyze the organizational climate and its reaction to change. Common measures include change impact analyses, change readiness assessments, organizational culture assessments and change saturation assessments. Identify common or historical risks, areas of resistance and pain points for both the organization and the project.
3. **Identify stakeholders and involve them in the design of the solution**
   Perform a stakeholder analysis to identify and categorize stakeholders by the extent that the change will affect them. Involve stakeholders and end users in the design of the solution corresponding with their proximity to the change to encourage engagement.
4. **Develop a flexible, high-level change management plan that includes key deliverables and required resources**
   Create a high-level change management plan that identifies deliverables of the change management function, timing of those deliverables and required resources. Design this plan flexibly, allowing for adjustment according to future insights and information.
5. **Coordinate change management and project management plans**
   Incorporate change management actions into project management plans from the beginning of the project to establish change management as a valuable component. Express the need for change management in a business case and document tangible benefits, Return on Investment (ROI) and statistics on change management success. Logically relate change management activities to the project plan and deliverables in the project schedule.
6. **Identify and solicit support from sponsors of change**
   Identify change sponsors at the initiation of the project to identify and remedy resistance within leadership. Establishing support from change sponsors clearly and coherently guides the change in a manner consistent with the project's goals and timeline.
7. **Designate and educate a change management team**
   Designate members of a change management team and educate them fully on the change management methodology chosen for the project. The change management team should build a fundamental understanding of the process to be used across stakeholder groups by explaining the basic roles and steps of the methodology.

Consequences of starting late

Participants in the 2015 study identified consequences that resulted from implementing change management late in the project lifecycle. Shown in Figure 6.5, the most commonly cited consequence, by nearly three-quarters of participants, was spending time playing catch up.

Figure 6.5 – Consequences of starting late

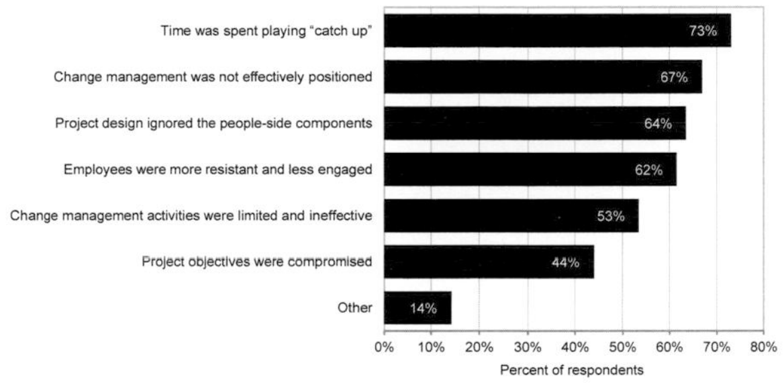

Action steps if change management is started late during a project

Source date: 2013

Participants in the 2013 study who reported that change management was brought on late in the project lifecycle shared steps that were taken in response to the late addition.

1. **Identify and engage sponsors**
   Participants identified sponsors who should be involved with the project. Sponsor analysis was performed and steps were taken to educate sponsors on their roles in change to get them engaged and participating.
2. **Build a communication plan or increase communications**
   Participants focused on building awareness of the change and the need for change management. They created a communication plan, or if one already existed, communications were increased when change management was a late addition to the project. Tactics for increasing communications included more frequent town halls, increased status calls, deliberate efforts to ensure key messages were understood, more frequent project updates and more time scheduled for open discussions, and Question and Answer (Q&A) sessions.
3. **Engage with project management**
   Participants leveraged project management when change management was brought into the project late. The current project was reviewed and analyzed, meetings with the project team were held and change management was incorporated into the project plan. In many cases, the project team itself became responsible for change management, or a change management resource was added to the project team. Participants also supported the project team publicly.
4. **Develop a change management plan**
   Participants focused on building a change management plan in response to the late addition of change management. This involved assessing the current state which was compared to the defined future state. The change plan included roadmaps and action steps supported by basic tools to increase change capability. Many participants requested an increase in change management resources and budgets.
5. **Shorten or condense change management activities and backtrack**
   Tactics identified to shorten or condense change management included scaling the amount of activities that could be used, re-scoping the project, eliminating steps or adding steps into later stages that would normally be completed during initiation or planning. Participants emphasized preparing, increasing or compressing training to focus on continuing support and building knowledge. Another important activity was identifying and managing resistance.

Application of methodology

Benefits of using a structured approach

Source date: 2011

Participants identified six primary benefits of using a structured approach to change management.

1. **Definition of activities, roles, language, processes, tools and assessments**
   Structured approaches designated and defined key activities and roles, common language and documentation practices to guide the process. Templates, tools and assessments provided by a structured methodology visibly outlined procedures for steps. Best practices reports were used as a reference for issues unaddressed in the structured approach and toolset.
2. **Systematic structure resulting in a consistent and repeatable approach**
   Structured approaches directed change systematically fostering consistent practices, generating more rapid familiarity with the system and allowing for repetition of activities and results.
3. **Logical, detailed progression of stages**
   Structured approaches presented steps logically. Communicating the motives behind each step gave clarity to the methodology's direction and reasoning and contributed transparency to the approach itself.
4. **Easier to understand and explain**
   The organized and documented framework of structured approaches made them easier to learn, understand and explain to others. Training supplemented the ease of understanding and explaining.
5. **Support for the value of change management**
   Structured approaches contributed credibility to change management as a practice. Presenting a legitimate, controlled and structured approach helped to dispel the notion that change management is soft and vague. This credibility bolstered confidence in the initiative and encouraged buy-in.
6. **Identification of gaps and common mistakes**
   Structured approaches addressed change management thoroughly and fostered anticipation of gaps and resistance. Common mistakes were avoided, reducing risk and ensuring no components of the process were overlooked.

Use of a methodology

The percentage of participants using a change management methodology has continued to grow since 2003 when only 34% of participants applied a methodology. In 2005, use of a methodology increased to 55% and grew slightly through 2009. The number of participants applying a methodology jumped in 2011 to 72% and again in 2013 to 79%. The number dropped slightly in the 2015 study to 73% (Figure 6.6).

Figure 6.6 – Use of methodology

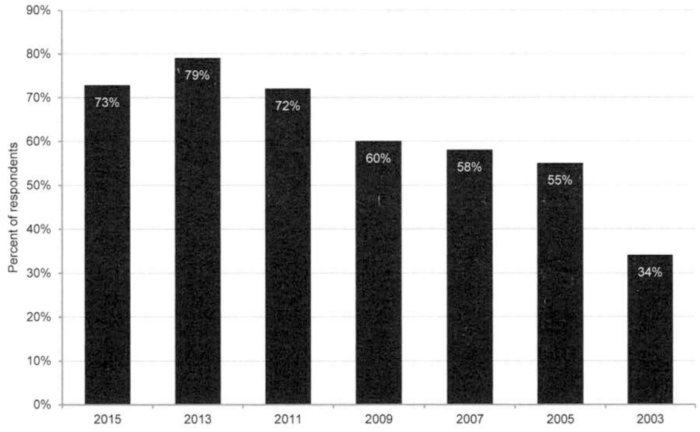

Figures 6.7, 6.8, 6.9 and 6.10 present further segmentation on the use of a methodology by region, industry and size of the organization. Results are shown relative to the entire study population average of 73%.

Figure 6.7 – Use of methodology by region

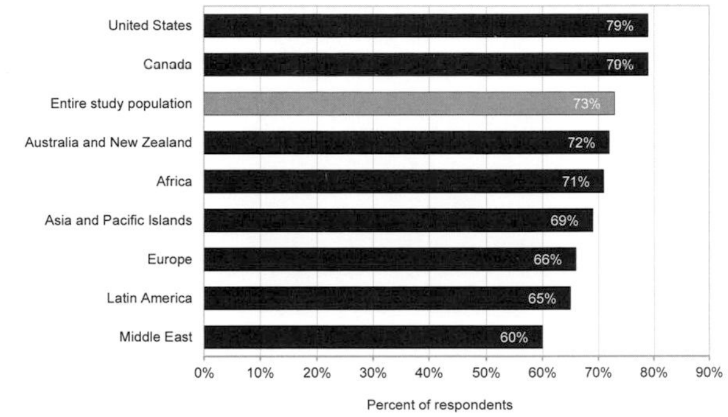

Figure 6.8 – Use of methodology by industry

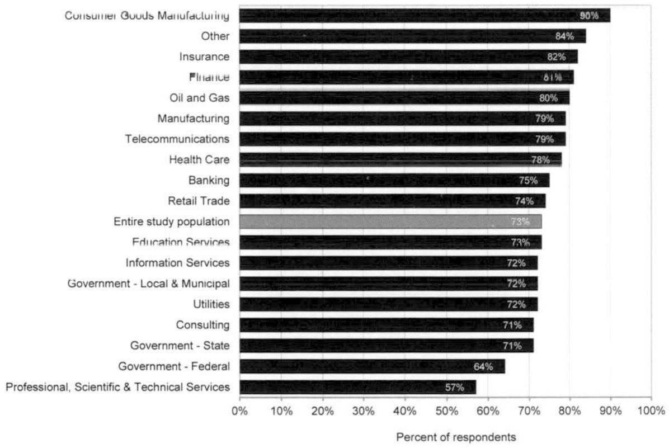

Figure 6.9 – Use of methodology by annual revenue

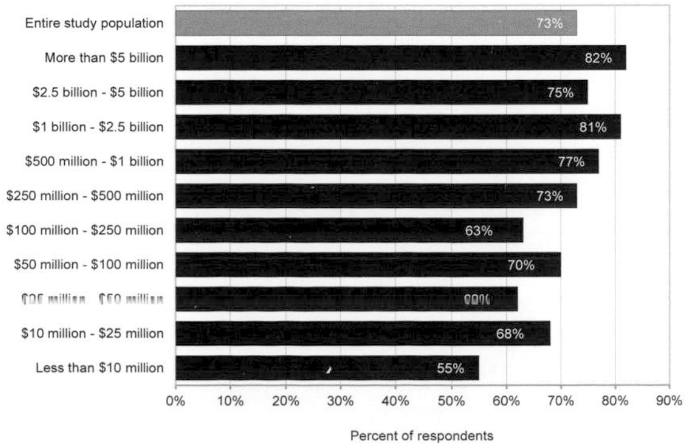

Figure 6.10 – Use of methodology by number of employees

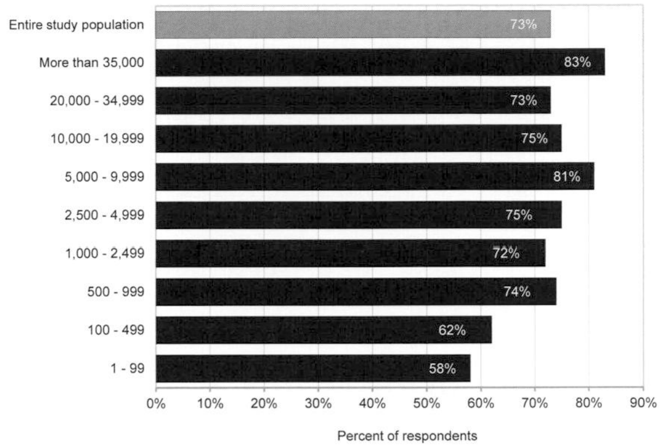

Figure 6.11 compares use of a methodology to the organization's level of change management maturity (refer to Appendix C for more information on the Prosci Change Management Maturity Model).

Figure 6.11 – Use of methodology by level of maturity

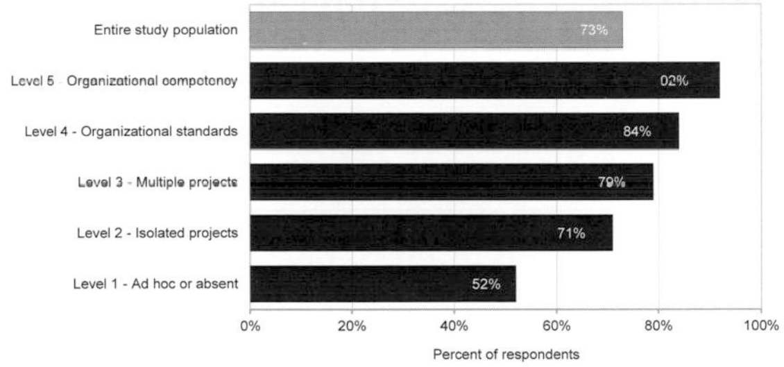

Impact of methodology on effectiveness

Participants who used a methodology reported higher overall change management effectiveness (Figure 6.12). Forty-one percent of participants who did not use a methodology reported *good* or *excellent* overall effectiveness compared to 57% who did.

Figure 6.12 – Impact of use of a methodology on overall change management effectiveness

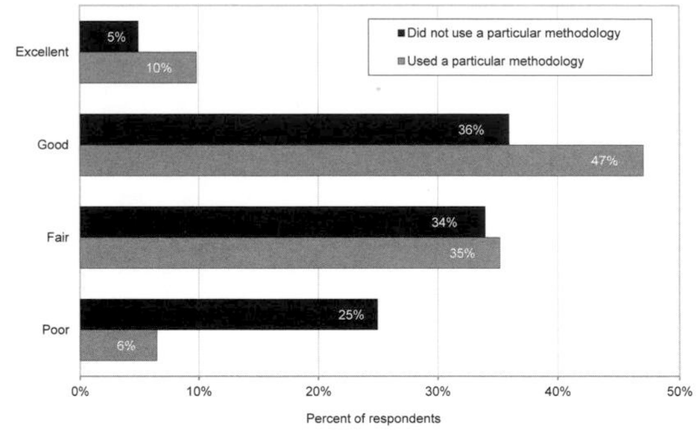

How the methodology was used

Participants using a methodology indicated whether it was used to provide general guidance, as an activities checklist, to monitor or track progress, or as a step-by-step process that was executed precisely. Eighty-one percent of participants used the methodology for general guidance. Figure 6.13 presents how participants used the methodology.

Figure 6.13 – How a methodology was used

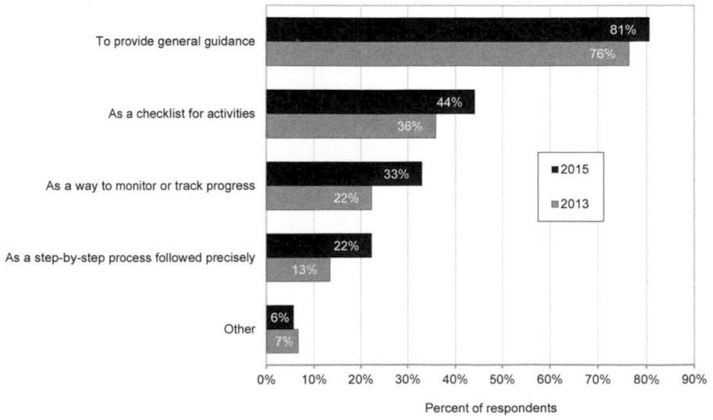

Editor's note: Participants were able to select multiple responses, resulting in a total of more than 100%.

Accommodating for organizational culture in the change management approach

Source date: 2013

Participants in the 2013 study described how the culture of their organization was accommodated for in their change management approach. Approximately 10% indicated that the approach did not accommodate for organizational culture. Reasons included lack of resources, the regulatory nature of their project or barriers from senior leadership. Those who did accommodate for their organization's culture used the following tactics:

1. **Tailor change management to each impacted group**
   Participants created unique transition plans for each business area. Plans varied in type and number of activities based on the needs and culture of the group. The length, content and style of training were adjusted. Resistance management tactics and reinforcement mechanisms were adjusted to appeal to each group's unique motivators. When possible, participants tailored the pace or time frame for implementation.
2. **Adapt communications to the culture of the organization**
   To align with organizational culture, participants adjusted the tone, style, frequency and formality of change management communications. They used existing channels and vehicles with which impacted groups were familiar. Preferred senders were leveraged to deliver messages.
3. **Seek input and engagement from impacted groups**
   Input and engagement resulted in a greater ability to adjust to unique needs of various groups. Participants gleaned valuable insights from subject matter experts and end users. They also solicited feedback through focus groups, Question and Answer (Q&A) sessions and direct communication with impacted individuals. Representatives from impacted business units were invited to collaborate with the change team.

4. **Secure early involvement of senior leaders in change management**
   Getting senior leaders involved and committed to the change, so they could lead others, helped participants accommodate for culture. Participants focused on engaging senior leaders before engaging all impacted groups. Early and frequent communication was emphasized to gain buy-in. Executives were trained and coached to ensure they fulfilled their roles and responsibilities with change such as cascading messages and demonstrating commitment to change.
5. **Research and assess the unique culture of each group**
   Participants studied impacted groups to understand issues unique to geographic location, job roles and change histories. They used assessments, surveys and focus groups to identify cultural customs, risk factors and anticipated points of resistance. To support these efforts, participants sought lessons learned from similar past projects.

Two additional tactics participants used to accommodate for organizational culture during change management were:

- **Leverage networks of key influencers**
  Participants identified individuals to whom impacted employees looked for guidance such as managers or change champions. These influencers were enlisted as advocates, message senders and sources of feedback.
- **Demonstrate alignment of the change with organizational priorities**
  Participants provided a clear case for change linked to the organization's vision, values, objectives and strategic priorities.

Methodologies used

Key factors in choosing a methodology

Participants identified the key factors that led them to choose the methodology they ultimately selected.

1. **Previously used, organizational standard or external advice**
   Participants based decisions on experience with a methodology, advice from external consultants, a methodology's status as an industry standard or a methodology's basis in research/data.
2. **Credible structured approach**
   A methodology that was credible, well-known and specifically structured was favored over unknown or new methodologies. Methodologies with a clear, structured and tested approach were favored. Examples of methodologies included the Prosci/ADKAR® and Kotter.
3. **Compatibility with project, company, culture or industry**
   Participants reported that they were likely to select a methodology if it offered special compatibility with an ongoing project, the culture of the organization and the industry, or if it offered benefits or traits valuable to the organization. Participants sought a methodology that was compatible with the needs of the organization, the needs of a particular project, budgetary requirements or a specific Return on Investment (ROI).
4. **Ease of use and scalability**
   Participants favored a methodology that was easy to use and could be scaled to meet the change being managed. Additional characteristics in this category included simplicity, ease of use, familiarity, practicality, consistency and flexibility.
5. **Certified or trained in methodology**
   Participants were more likely to select a methodology if change management resources were already present in the organization that had been trained or certified in the methodology. The degree of familiarity and amount of previous success with the model by practitioners contributed to confidence expressed toward the methodology.

Which type of methodology was used

Participants in the 2015 study who used a methodology shared which approaches they used. Figure 6.14 shows overall findings.

Figure 6.14 – Methodology used

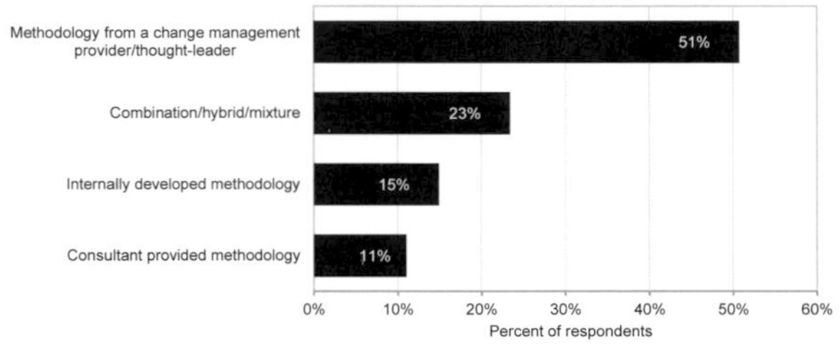

For the 51% of participants who selected the provider/thought leader methodology, 86% indicated they used Prosci, 3% stated they used Kotter – 8 Steps, 1% used Change Guides and the remaining 10% indicated other methodologies.

Editor's note: The change management study invitation was sent to nearly 85,000 members of Prosci's Change Management Learning Center and announced through thousands of online media outlets unaffiliated with Prosci. Due to how participation was solicited, the rank order of these methodologies might not be representative of a random sample.

Methodology type and change management effectiveness

Figure 6.15 compares which type of methodology was used to the overall effectiveness of participants' change management. Participants who employed combination/hybrid/mixture or consultant-provided methodologies experienced the highest change management effectiveness, with more than 60% reporting good or excellent effectiveness.

Figure 6.15 – Methodology used and change management effectiveness

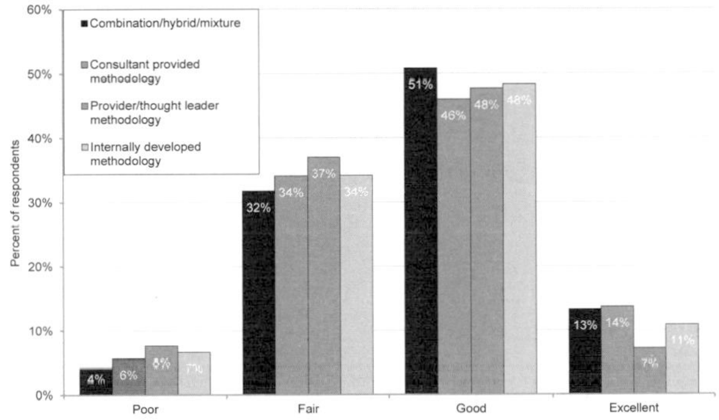

Internally developed methodology

Source date: 2013

Participants in 2013 who indicated using an internally developed methodology provided insights on the rationale, steps and sources for creating their approaches.

Rationale for internally developed

Participants identified motivating factors for creating an internal change management methodology. Participants identified factors similar to those mentioned in the overall criteria for selecting a change management methodology in the 2011 study including:

1. **Ability to customize**
   Participants revealed the need to customize a change management methodology to meet unique requirements. There were three motivating factors driving the need for customization:

   - **Cultural acceptance**
     Those who created an internal methodology needed to brand it as their own to encourage buy-in, acceptance and ownership across the organization. Commitment to the methodology arose from being built by internal resources with insight into the organization. Developers accounted for cultural norms and other environmental factors.
   - **Alignment with various functions**
     The second reason for customization included aligning the change management methodology with other functions to add structure and create cohesiveness in the approach. Developing an internal approach allowed for alignment with project management, Human Resources (HR) and Information Technology (IT).
   - **Scalability and flexibility to meet project needs**
     Similar to the top factor for choosing a methodology from the 2011 study, an internal methodology was developed to make it flexible and scalable. Organizations that created an internal methodology did so to have an adaptable approach that could be tailored to projects and would include transferable tools.

2. **Need for standardization**
   The second motivating factor was the need to have a standardized approach that was applicable to all types of projects. These organizations set out to find consistency by building a common language and standard process that could be used across the organization.

3. **Desire to combine best practices**
Participants reported a desire to combine best practices as a motivating factor for creating their own change management methodology. Organizations that built their own methodology were able to combine select components from various thought leaders' approaches to blend with their own successful practices.

Steps for internally developed

Participants who developed an internal methodology identified steps taken to create it. The most common steps are listed below. Steps are listed by how frequently participants mentioned them but do not represent a sequential order.

- **Establish the change management team**
Organizations that developed an internal methodology established a formal team of dedicated resources. Developing a central change team or committee enabled input from various divisions, subject matter experts and practitioners.
- **Initiate planning and engagement**
Treating development of an internal methodology as a project of its own, participants focused on communicating the need for an internal change management methodology and began developing plans that incorporated change and project management. The list of activities included creating training plans, delivering workshops, securing sponsorship, engaging stakeholders and executing formal communications.
- **Assess the current state**
Evaluation of existing processes, tools and methods was often the initial step in developing an internal methodology. Participants collected feedback from business units and reviewed strategic plans, barriers and challenges for building an internal methodology.
- **Review and refine**
Participants identified continuous, ongoing efforts to review and evaluate the internally developed methodology. Trial and error was a common technique. Organizations continued to refine and enhance their approach based on the latest review.

Sources for internally developed

Participants who developed an internal methodology also identified the sources used. The most common included:

- Internal change management experience
- Research publications and best practices
- Consultant input
- Prosci
- The organization's own mission, vision and standards
- John Kotter

Combination/hybrid methodology
Source date: 2013

Participants in the 2013 study who used a combination or hybrid approach identified the sources and rationale for their approach.

Rationale for combo/hybrid

In addition to providing the sources used, participants explained motivations for using a hybrid change management methodology. The top four were:

1. **Alignment with organization and culture**
Participants reported that a hybrid methodology allowed them to account for unique cultures and norms, particularly if the organization had a geographic span. When evaluating and experimenting with methodologies, participants concluded that using one methodology created limitations.

Participants considered the experiences of individuals who would be applying the tools. Participants reported that a hybrid methodology allowed for use of a greater variety of tools and focus on human behavior or emotion.

2. **Combine the thinking of change management thought leaders**
   Although similar to the first finding, participants identified a desire to leverage components from change management thought leaders. Organizations with this motive were not trying to improve a single approach; they were starting with a blank slate and adding attractive components from a selection of recognized methodologies.
3. **Project focus**
   Of those who used a hybrid approach, a focus on developing a methodology specific to the current change was cited as the third most common motive. Participants set out to develop a hybrid approach that aligned with the type of change and unique project needs.
4. **Leverage internal resources**
   Organizations desired to capitalize on the knowledge of internal resources and build a methodology supported by the experiences and knowledge of their team. Saving time and keeping costs low were two core factors for using what was internally available.

Sources for combo/hybrid

Participants using a combination or hybrid approach identified the following top four sources.

1. The Prosci® ADKAR® Model and 3-Phase Process
2. Internally developed methodology
3. Consultant-provided methodology
4. John Kotter

Other notable sources included:

- William Bridges
- Daryl Conner
- *Switch* by Chip Heath and Dan Heath
- Denison Model
- GE's Change Acceleration Process
- Accenture
- Deloitte
- Kurt Lewin

Editor's note: Many change management approaches and tools are proprietary. Practitioners leveraging these as sources for internal or hybrid development should take necessary steps to avoid infringing on intellectual properties.

Scaling and customizing the methodology

Source date: 2013

Participants in the 2013 study indicated how they scaled or customized the methodology to their projects. Responses focused on inputs for scaling and outputs of customization.

Inputs for scaling

Participants reported on factors considered when deciding how to scale or customize a methodology.

1. **Project characteristics**
   Participants considered factors, such as scope, size, type, complexity, objectives and timing of the project, as inputs when deciding how to scale a change management methodology. Project timing was emphasized more than other project characteristics because it determined how much scaling was practical given the project timeline.
2. **Change management assessments**
   Several types of assessments were identified as mechanisms for determining how to scale a methodology. Participants applied

assessments at different stages of the project, from pre-implementation analysis to intervals after go-live. Assessments included current state assessments, impact assessments, change readiness assessments, organizational assessments, change characteristics assessments, risk assessments and gap analyses.

3. **Organizational attributes**
   Participants considered unique attributes of the organization that would impact deployment of the project and change management. The organization's culture was the most significant factor considered when determining what aspects of the approach to customize. Additional factors included size of the organization, industry, strategic initiatives and organizational structure. Participants considered the organization's capacity for change management, what activities were most manageable and how much change management the organization could support considering its maturity.
4. **Resource availability**
   The number of resources available for change management was considered when scaling the approach because it impacted the degree to which the approach could be customized.
5. **Experience**
   Final input for customizing a change management methodology was the experiences of those performing the work. Experience deploying change management offered further insights and judgments regarding the amount of scaling necessary and how best to achieve it.

Outputs of customization

Participants explained steps taken to tailor the approach including:

1. **Focus change management**
   The most common step taken to scale a methodology was engaging only in activities considered most valuable. By starting with a comprehensive methodology and scaling back activities, participants leveraged input factors when determining which activities were most critical to a project.
2. **Focus on audiences**
   By considering, addressing and targeting audiences with each change management activity, participants customized a plan to address the needs of each group. The groups were often divided by business unit, location, job type or degree of impact. Participants customized the change management strategy with an awareness of and sensitivity to the unique needs of each impacted group.
3. **Customize tools**
   Participants focused on tools used with the change management strategy as a way to scale the approach to a project. They added tools, combined multiple assessments and adjusted existing templates to make the toolbox of the change management approach most effective and applicable to a project.
4. **Integrate change management and project management**
   To customize a methodology, participants added change management activities to their project management plan. Participants leveraged one succinct plan by embedding change management milestones into the project lifecycle. Many components in the plan then served a dual purpose of focusing on the people side of change and project deliverables.
5. **Combine change management methodologies**
   Participants combined components of multiple change management methodologies when scaling effort to a project. Some participants added to an internal approach or combined several well-known methodologies to customize their change management approach.

CM BUDGET, RESOURCES AND TEAM STRUCTURE

SIZE AND SECURE THE RIGHT RESOURCES FOR OPTIMIZING YOUR CHANGE MANAGEMENT EFFORTS

SUMMARY

Where do you start when you are tasked with creating a change management deployment budget? Increasing budgets and resources for change management is a top industry trend. This chapter introduces a data-driven foundation for evaluating and scaling the people, financial and structural aspects of a change management approach. Explore concrete data on the elements to include in a change management budget and the factors that influence how many resources are needed on a change management team. Whether you find yourself creating a change management budget or petitioning for additional resources, customize your resourcing plan with a research-based evaluation of your project's specific needs.

HIGHLIGHT

86% of respondents indicated that change management budgets came from the project budget; 43% of respondents influenced the change management budget.

Change management budget

Use of dedicated budget

Although nearly three quarters of participants had a dedicated resource, only 33% reported having a budget dedicated to change management for their projects (Figure 7.1). Participants without a dedicated budget had to look for creative and resourceful ways to fulfill the needs of their change management teams.

Figure 7.1 – Project had dedicated change management budget

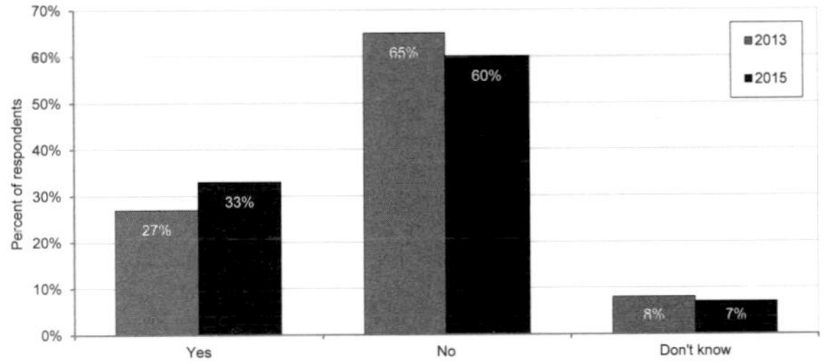

Change management budget

Participants in the 2015 study reported the total dollar amount of the budget allocated to change management and the percentage of the budget designated to change management. The most common amount allocated to change management was $500,000 with a median of $250,000 and the largest budget being $25 million. The overall average value was $1,183,486. The most common percentage of the budget dedicated to change management was 10% with the largest being 100% of the project budget. The average percentage of project budget allocated to change management was 16%.

Figure 7.2 shows the average percentage of project budget dedicated to change management. Forty-seven percent of participants indicated that less than 10% of the project budget was allocated to change management.

Figure 7.2 – Percent of project budget dedicated to change management

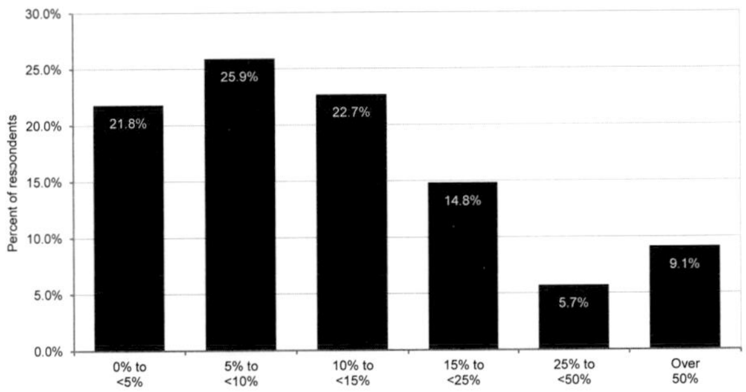

Source of change management budget

For the first time, participants in the 2015 study identified the source of the change management budget. Overwhelmingly, the most common source of the change management budget was from the project budget, as shown in Figure 7.3.

Figure 7.3 – Source of change budget

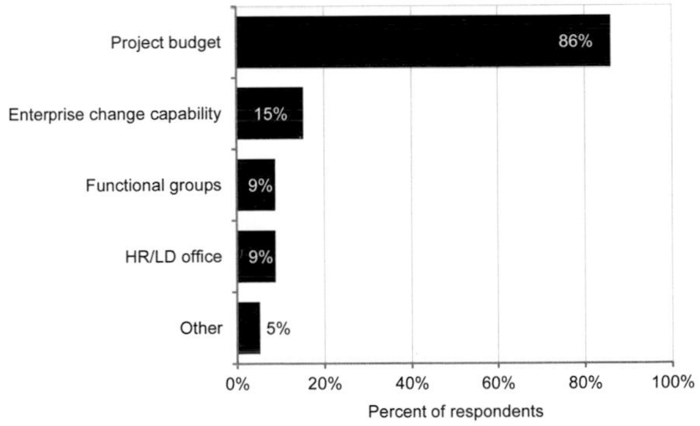

Editor's note: Participants were able to select multiple responses, resulting in a total of more than 100%.

Sufficient change management budget

Source date: 2013

Participants in the 2013 study indicated whether they had sufficient budget for their project. Forty percent reported that the amount of budget was slightly or significantly less than sufficient (Figure 7.4).

Figure 7.4 – Sufficiency of budget allocated to change management

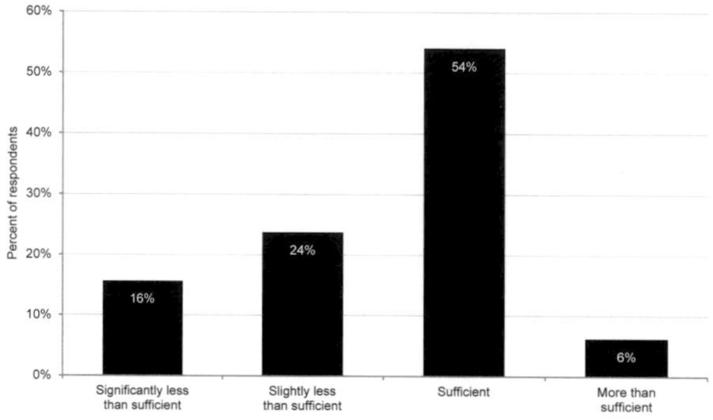

Participants also indicated the sufficiency of budget during each project phase (Figure 7.5). During implementation, 39% of participants reported having insufficient budget.

Figure 7.5 – Insufficient change management budget available at each phase

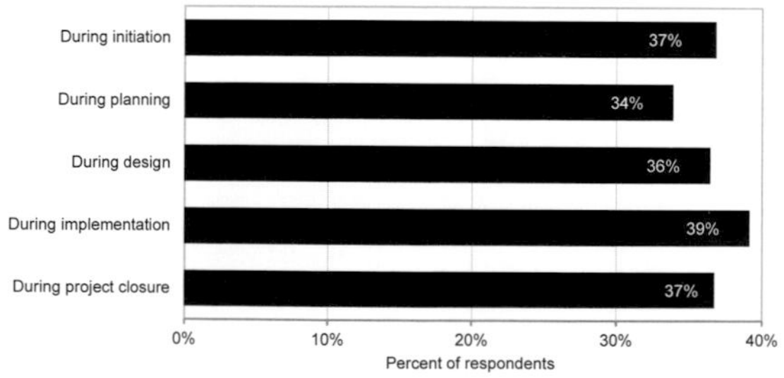

Estimating the change management budget

In the 2015 study participants listed factors used to estimate the change management budget. Responses were nearly identical to the 2013 study findings. The top responses were:

1. **Change resource costs**
   Participants assessed costs associated with change management in the development of the budget estimate. In rank order, the following costs were assessed:
   - Resource costs – adjusted based on availability
   - Training costs – adjusted based on skill gaps and amount of training expected
   - Communication costs – adjusted based on effectiveness of past efforts
   - Time – determined by number of hours and wages
   - Travel costs
   - Change management material costs
2. **Timeline and objectives**
   Factors specific to the project were considered when estimating the change management budget. The project timeline and activities to determine the impact were most influential, though project objectives were also considered.
3. **Scale and complexity of the change**
   Participants identified factors, such as scale and complexity of the change and organizational restrictions, when determining budget needs for change management.
4. **Informal estimation strategy**
   Participants considered the overall project budget when estimating budget needs for change management. A number of participants reported using funds and resources that were already available to the project to support change management budget requirements.
5. **Experiences**
   A number of participants relied on experience to estimate the change management budget. Characteristics of the change were compared to similar projects from the past. Budgets and outcomes of previous projects were assessed to estimate budget needs for the current project.

Average budget for change management

Participants provided the amount that was budgeted for change management for the project on which they were reporting. The following four graphs (Figures 7.6, 7.7, 7.8 and 7.9) show the average change management budget based on project investment, project scope, number of employees impacted and duration of the project.

Figure 7.6 – Average budget versus project investment

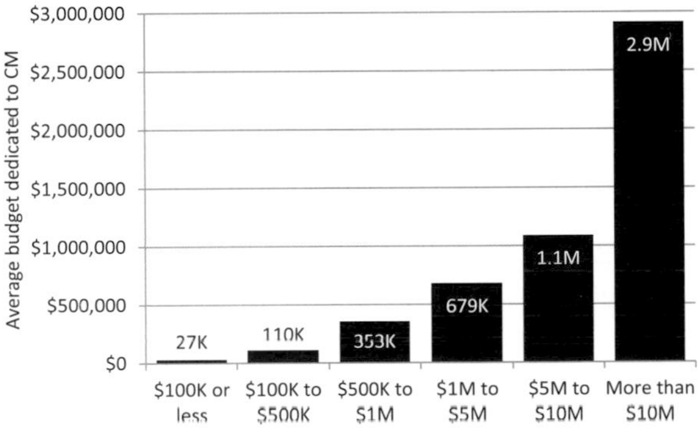

Figure 7.7 – Average budget versus project scope

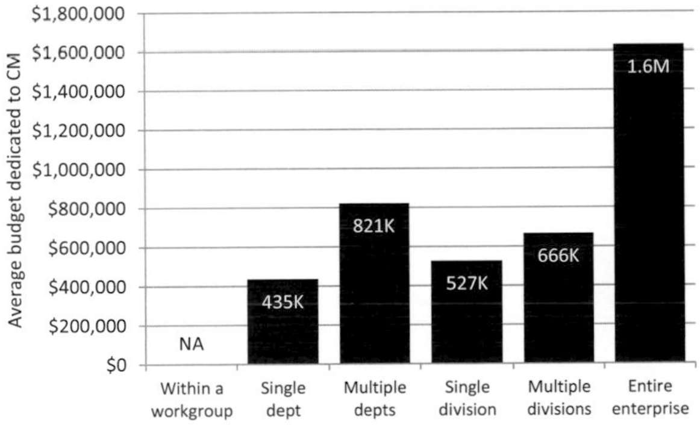

Figure 7.8 – Average budget versus employees impacted

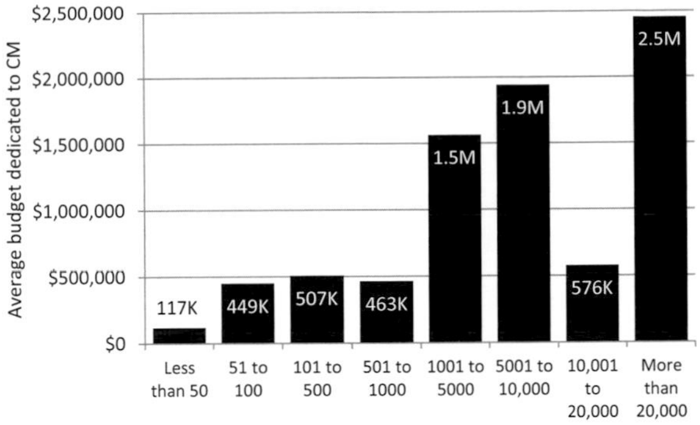

Figure 7.9 – Average budget versus duration

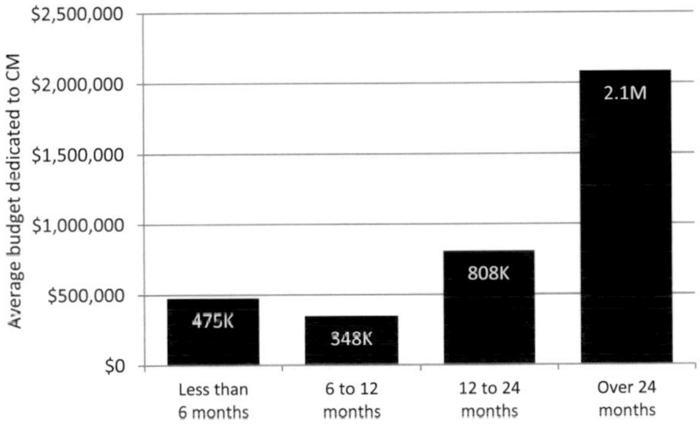

Editor's note: Data on this question include some variability because there is no common standard specifying which line items are considered part of the change management budget.

Percent of project budget allocated to change management

Figures 7.10, 7.11, 7.12 and 7.13 show the percent of total project budget allocated to change management based on project investment, project scope, number of employees impacted and duration of the project. The average percent of project budget allocated to change management was 16.3%.

Figure 7.10 – Percent of project budget versus project investment

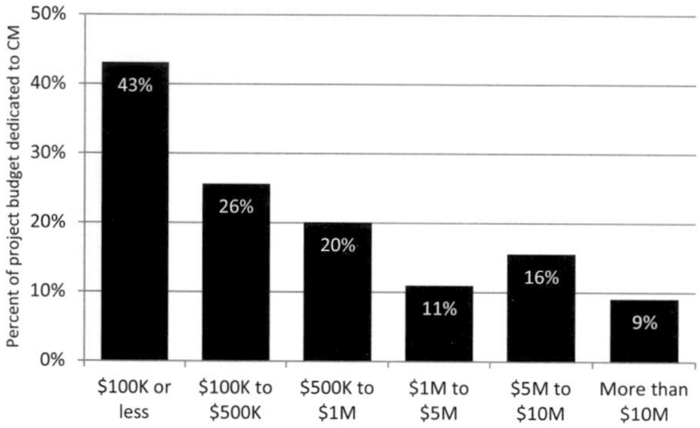

Figure 7.11 – Percent of project budget versus project scope

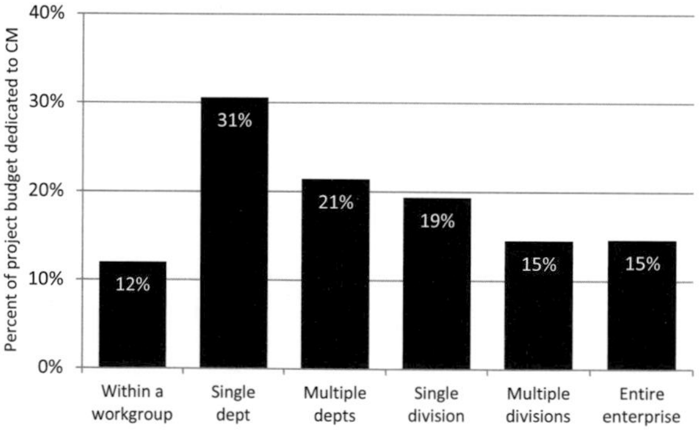

Figure 7.12 – Percent of project budget versus employees impacted

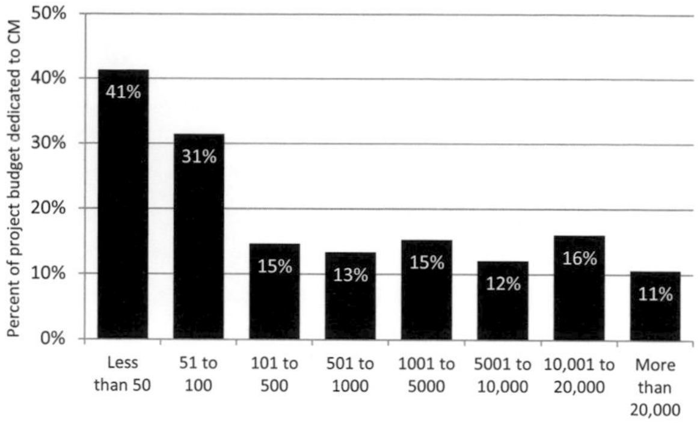

Figure 7.13 – Percent of project budget versus duration

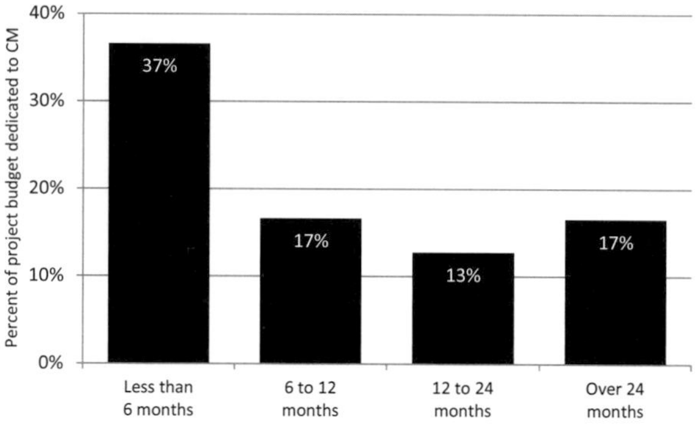

Change management budget components

In the 2011 study, participants provided details on elements included in the change management budget. The top elements were:

1. **Change management resource costs**
   Compensation and salary for change management practitioners or resources supporting the effort.
2. **Training costs**
   Design, development, delivery and materials for training, including costs for training specialists.
3. **Communications costs**
   Development and delivery of the communications approach including costs for communications specialists and communications collateral including printed materials, brochures, posters, videos, promotional marketing materials, websites and intranet sites.

Secondary budget components were:

- **Consultant costs** – fees for consultant support
- **General expenses** – travel, food and refreshments
- **Event costs** – workshops, group meetings, lunch-and-learn events, road shows and town-hall meetings
- **Change management materials** – change management training, plan development, supplies and licensing of materials
- **Reinforcement and recognition costs** – celebration costs, rewards, gifts and team-recognition events

In the 2015 study, participants provided details on how the change management budget was allocated to each of these components. Figure 7.14 shows the percentage of participants that reported allocating budgets to resources, training, communications, change management materials, consulting, events, general expenses and reinforcement and recognition costs.

The greatest number of participants (between 75% and 62%) reported allocating budgets to communications, training or resource costs.

Figure 7.14 – Allocated budget to cost components

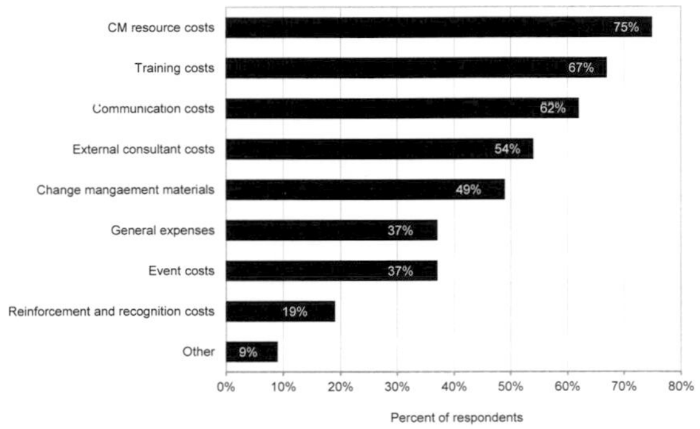

Figure 7.15 shows the average percentage of the budget that was allocated to each cost component. The averages include only participants who reported an allocation greater than 0% for a given cost component.

Figure 7.15 – Average percentage of budget allocated to each cost component

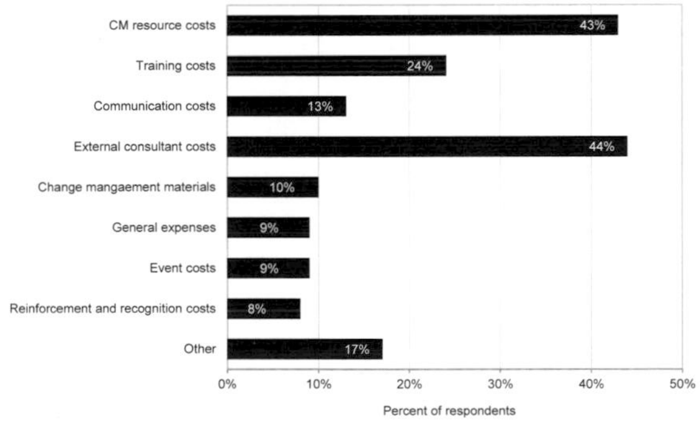

Budget profiles

Participants revealed a series of budget profiles when explaining how a change management budget was allocated. Figure 7.16 shows the percentage of budgets that were comprised of one to nine components. Forty-one percent of budgets were allocated to one, two or three costs, 45% to four to six, and 14% to seven, eight or nine.

Figure 7.16 – Number of budget components

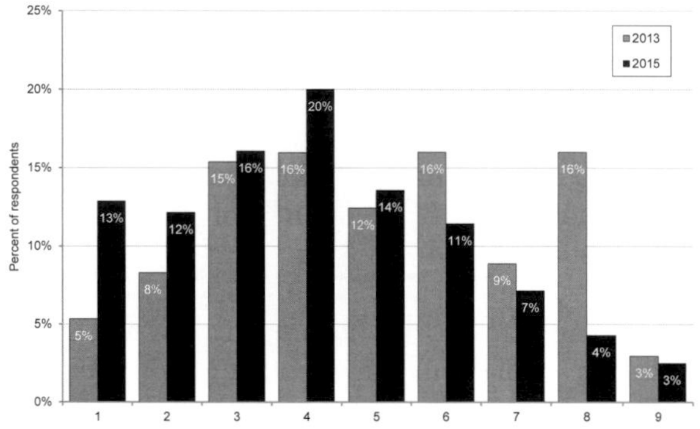

Table 7.17 below shows the most common budget profile combinations from participants who allocated change management budget to more than one cost component. The top row shows the percent of participant with that particular budget profile combination and the columns below indicate which line items were included in their change management budget.

Table 7.17 – Common budget profiles

	5.0%	4.3%	4.0%	3.7%	3.7%	3.3%	3.3%	3.3%	3.3%	2.7%
CM Resources Costs	●	●	●	●	●	●	●	●	●	●
Training Costs	●	●		●	●	●	●	●	●	●
Communications Costs	●	●		●	●		●	●	●	●
CM Materials Costs	●	●			●		●	●	●	●
Consultant Costs	●	●	●		●			●	●	
Event Costs	●	●			●				●	●
General Expenses	●	●			●					●
Reinforcement Costs		●			●					●
Other					●					

Change management resources

Use of dedicated resources

Over three quarters of participants (76%) indicated having dedicated change management resources for a project on which they were reporting, a slight increase from 2013 (Figure 7.18).

Figure 7.18 – Project with dedicated change management resources

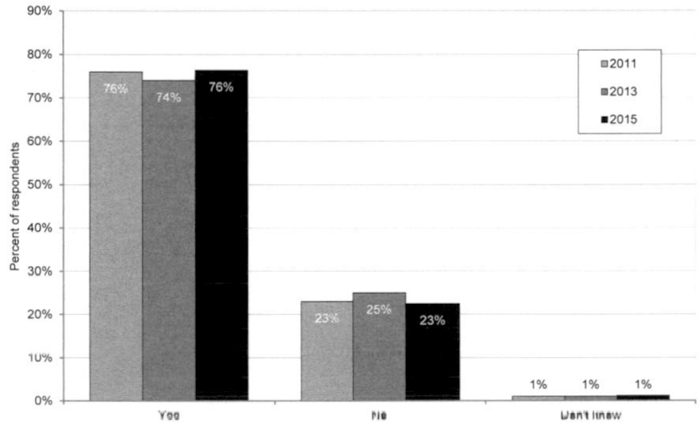

Use of dedicated resources by region

Figure 7.19 shows these data segmented by region. Latin America, the United States, and Australia and New Zealand had greater numbers of projects with dedicated change management resources. Participants from the Middle East had the fewest number of projects with dedicated change management resources.

Figure 7.19 – Dedicated resources by region

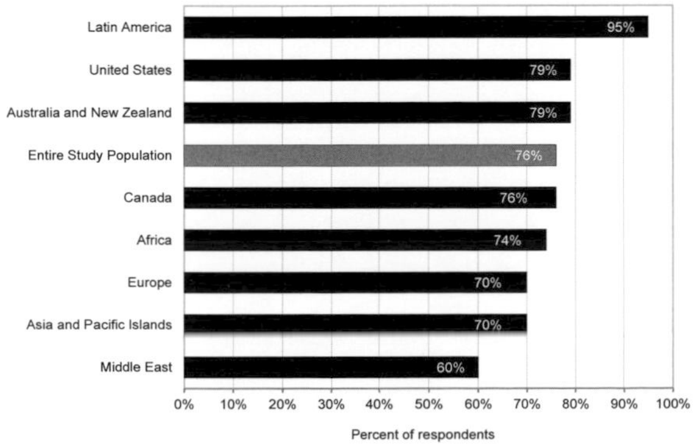

Use of dedicated resources by industry

Figure 7.20 shows dedicated resources segmented by industry.

Figure 7.20 – Dedicated resources by industry

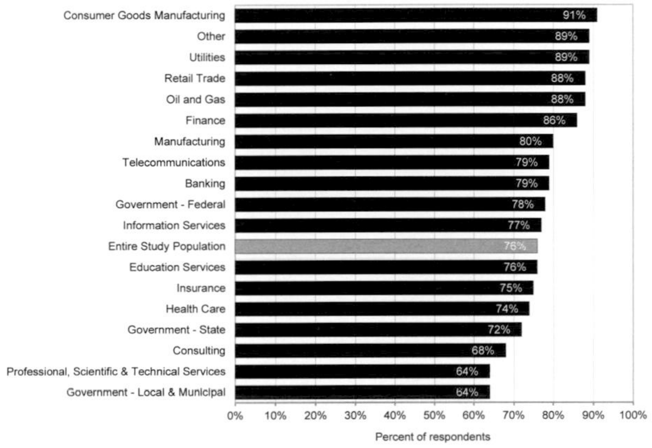

Use of dedicated resources by organization size (revenue and employees)

Figures 7.21 and 7.22 show the results for having a dedicated change management resource according to organization size (both annual revenue and number of employees).

Figure 7.21 – Dedicated resources by annual revenue

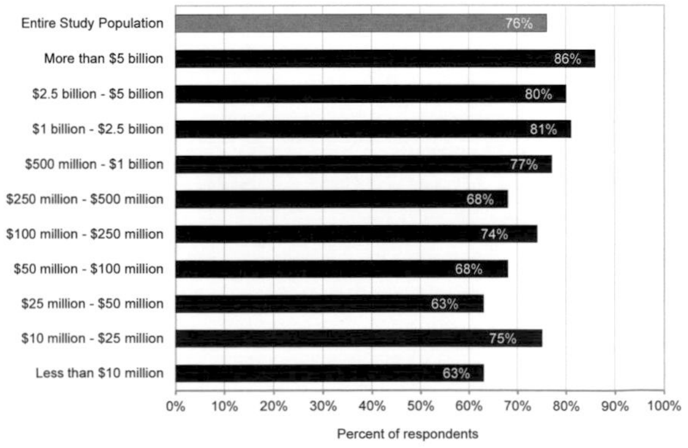

Figure 7.22 – Dedicated resources by number of employees

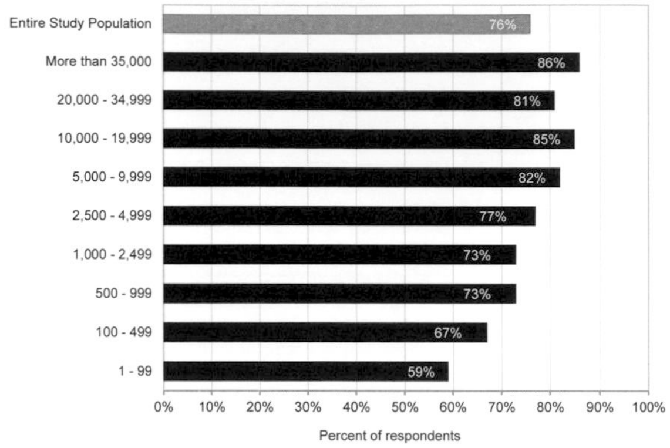

Use of dedicated resources by change management maturity

Organizations that reported high change management maturity also had higher instances of resources dedicated to change management (Figure 2.23).

Figure 7.23 – Dedicated resources by change management maturity

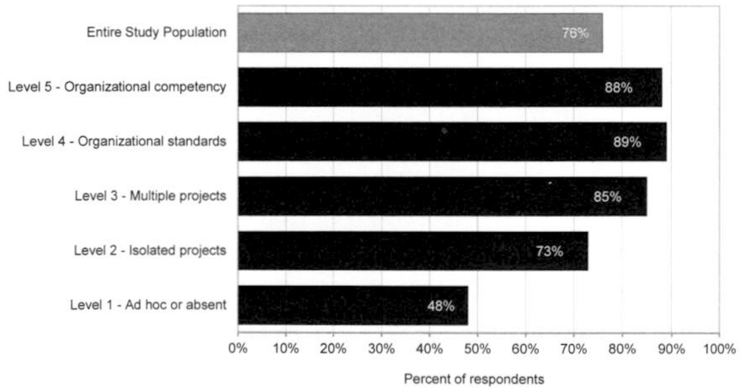

Correlating dedicated resources to effectiveness

Use of a dedicated resource for change management influenced the effectiveness of a change management program. Figure 7.24 shows the relationship between having a dedicated change management resource and the effectiveness of the program.

Figure 7.24 – Relationship between dedicated resources and change management effectiveness

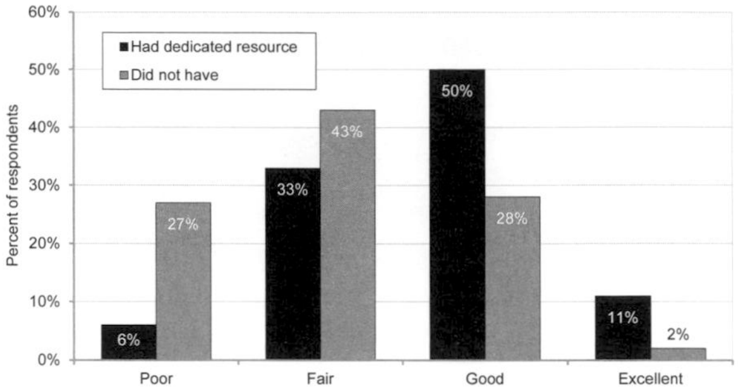

Sufficient resources

Source date: 2013

Participants in the 2013 study reported whether they had sufficient resources for their projects. Fifty-seven percent said that resources were slightly or significantly less than sufficient (Figure 7.25).

Figure 7.25 – Sufficiency of resources

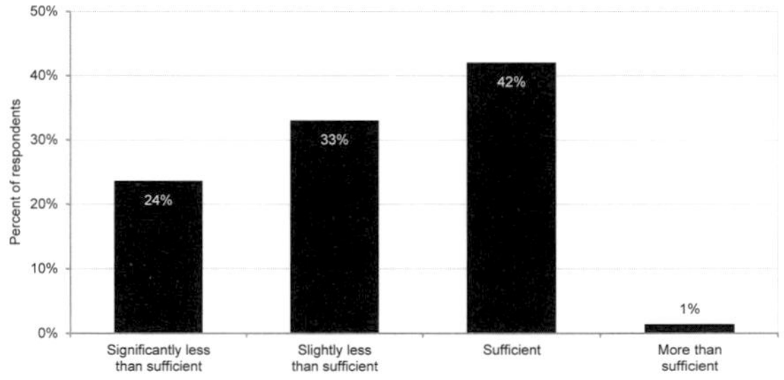

Participants then reported whether they had sufficient resources during each project phase. Although half of participants reported insufficient resources at each project phase (Figure 7.26), the greatest number of participants had insufficient resources during implementation (57%).

Figure 7.26 – Insufficient resources available by project phase

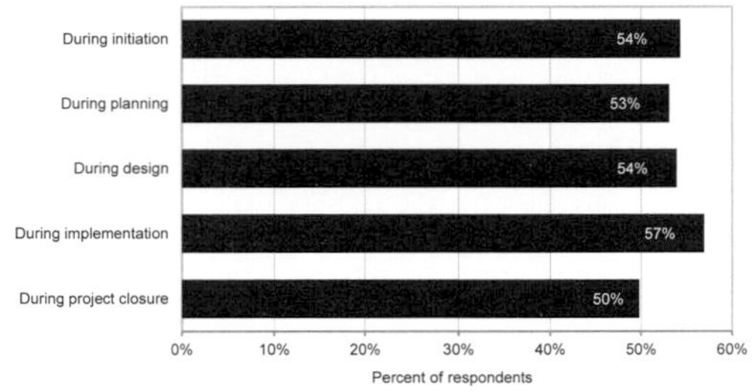

Figure 7.27 compares change management effectiveness to whether there were sufficient resources on the project. Seventy-five percent of participants with sufficient resources reported *good* or *excellent* change management effectiveness, while less than 40% who had insufficient resources reported *good* or *excellent* change management effectiveness.

Figure 7.27 – Relationship between sufficient resources and change management effectiveness

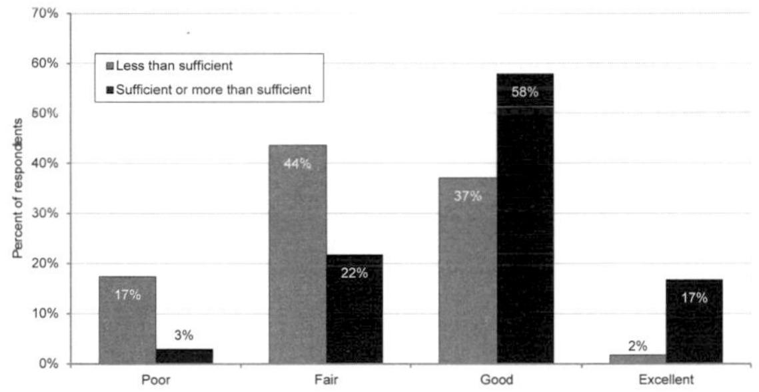

Estimating the amount of resources needed for the project

Participants specified which factors were used when estimating the number of resources needed on a change project (Figure 7.28). Scale and complexity was the most cited factor (73%).

Figure 7.28 – Decision variables on change management resources needs

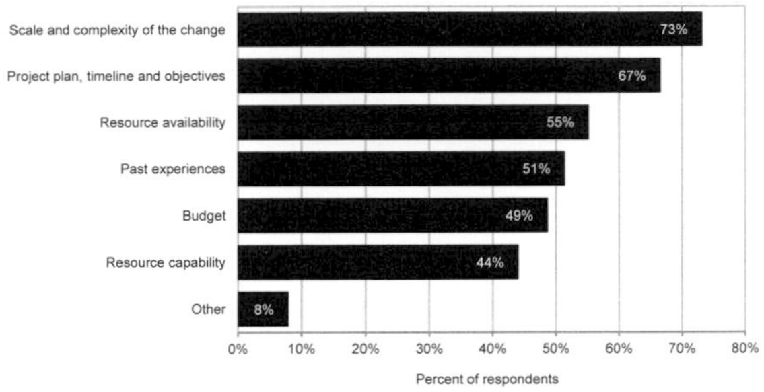

Editor's note: Participants were able to select multiple responses, resulting in a total of more than 100%.

Advantages of a dedicated resource

Source date: 2011

Participants in the 2011 study identified four main advantages to having resources dedicated to change management on the project. The most common response, providing focus and keeping track of change management activities, was cited more than twice as often as the second most common response.

1. **Provides focus and keeps track of change management activities**
   The primary advantage of having a dedicated resource was the focus that the resource could commit to the people side of change including being responsible for change management activities and ensuring that the focus on change management was sustained. In addition, this person or group developed plans, prioritized activities and helped manage resistance.

2. **Acts as a single point of contact with clear responsibility and accountability**
   Participants indicated that having one person or group dedicated to change management was advantageous because they could offer credible and consistent communications regarding the change. Additionally, this person or group maintained ownership and accountability over the change management activities; "*One source for all change questions.*"

3. **Has the required knowledge, skills and experience**
   A dedicated change management individual or team had the necessary skills, experience, training and motivation to provide guidance throughout the change and to educate others on effective change management processes. These individuals understood all of the key issues involved with the change, could see the change holistically and had a unique perspective on the change.
4. **Focuses solely on the change without distractions or other commitments**
   Distinct from the first response, the fourth advantage identified was having a dedicated resource without competing priorities and with fewer distractions. This resource could more effectively focus on and pursue change management activities; "*If it's not someone's job, it's no one's job.*"

Consequences of not having a dedicated resource

Source date: 2011

Although participants indicated four primary consequences of not having a dedicated change management resource, neglected change management was cited nearly three times as often as other responses.

1. **Neglected change management activities**
   Without a dedicated change management resource, key change management activities were neglected or not prioritized. Consequences included:
   - Change management diluted and disjointed
   - People not engaged
   - End user not considered
   - Low staff morale
   - Project poorly supported
   - People unprepared for change
   - Conflicting priorities
   - Project management resources spread too thin
   - Change management did not receive adequate resources
   - Project driven by non-change-management-oriented objectives
2. **Increased risk of project failure**
   Participants reported increased risk of not meeting objectives, inadequate project outcomes or project failure as a consequence of not having a dedicated change management resource.
3. **Lack of coordination**
   Without a dedicated change management resource, there was lack of direction, continuity and overall coordination of change management.
4. **Lack of ownership or accountability**
   Lack of ownership or accountability over change management aspects of the project was identified due to not having a dedicated resource. Participants cited further consequences such as lack of plan, scope, structure and definition regarding change management.

Decisions on the number of change management resources

Source date: 2009

Participants identified factors that influenced the number of change management resources on a project and the constraining factors that limited the number of resources used. The top factors were:

- Nature of the change
- Scope of required change management efforts
- Number of impacted groups
- Organizational capacity for change
- Benchmarking
- Geographical distribution
- Phase of project

- Established organizational guidelines
- Strategic importance of the project
- Project team's change management experience

Top constraining factors were:

- Budget
- Availability
- Skill sets
- Organizational maturity in change management
- Confidentiality

Influencing factors

1. **Nature of the change**
   Participants reported that the change itself was a major factor in determining change management resource requirements. Change characteristics cited most frequently were type of change (process, systems, reorganization, etc.), complexity of the project, number of people impacted and pace of implementation.
2. **Scope of required change management efforts**
   Resourcing decisions were determined by the amount of change management to be completed. The scale of communications plans, training requirements, coaching needs and assessments was a key factor in calculating resource needs. Participants asked themselves if they had enough people to do all of the work.
3. **Number of impacted groups**
   The number of business units, work streams or levels involved in a change affected the number of change management resources required. Responses underscored the importance of involving key representatives from each impacted group to answer questions and allow cross-organizational input.
4. **Organizational capacity for change**
   An organization's cultural acceptance of change and change capacity impacted change management resourcing decisions. Factors, such as higher volumes of ongoing change and larger amounts of anticipated resistance, resulted in higher resource needs.
5. **Benchmarking**
   Change management resources were allocated based on best-practices research, consultants' recommendations and lessons learned from project experiences.
6. **Geographical distribution**
   Projects with global or widely distributed regional implementation required more change management resources.
7. **Phase of project**
   Participants reported that the number of resources needed for change management varied throughout the project lifecycle. Many noted fewer requirements during early stages and increasing needs as a project neared implementation. Additional resources were added to projects that fell behind or experienced a lack of progress.
8. **Established organizational guidelines**
   Organizations established enterprise-wide guidelines for making resourcing decisions, based on in-house change management methodologies or mandated by a central Project Management Office (PMO), Change Management Office (CMO) or Human Resources (HR) group.
9. **Strategic importance of the project**
   Participants responded that a project's impact to the business was considered when allocating resources. More resources were used on critical or urgent projects, and projects with a high risk of failure.
10. **Project team's change management experience**
    The level of change management skills and expertise on the project team, coupled with the team's level of awareness of the importance of change management, was factored into resourcing decisions.

Constraining factors

1. **Budget**
   Participants cited budget constraints as a primary factor that limited their ability to obtain change management resources. Sponsors and project team leaders were unwilling or unable to pay for change management resources, and many organizations had no formal budget for change management.
2. **Availability**
   Participants indicated resource availability as a limiting factor during change management resource decisions. Time and workload constraints on employees, ongoing commitments and conflicting priorities limited the pool of resources available for change management.
3. **Skill set**
   Participants reported lack of trained and experienced change management resources within their organizations. To be effective in a change management role, practitioners must have not only technical skills but also skills such as teamwork, flexibility and the ability to engage a sponsor.
4. **Organizational maturity during change management**
   Resourcing decisions were impacted by the level of awareness of change management within the organization. Lack of buy-in and a low perceived value of change management, particularly at the sponsorship level, resulted in fewer resources.
5. **Confidentiality**
   In several cases, the sensitivity of a project inhibited the number of change management resources.

Average FTE dedicated to change management

Participants in the 2015 study provided data on the number of full-time equivalents (FTE) for the entire project team and the number of FTE dedicated to change management. Figure 7.29 shows the distribution of FTE dedicated to change management.

Figure 7.29 – FTE dedicated to change management

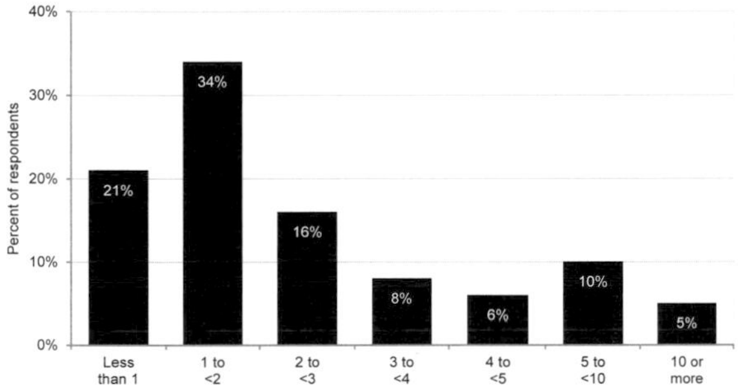

The following four graphs (Figures 7.30, 7.31, 7.32 and 7.33) show the average FTE dedicated to change management based on project investment, project scope, number of employees impacted and duration of the project.

Figure 7.30 – Average FTE dedicated to change management versus project investment

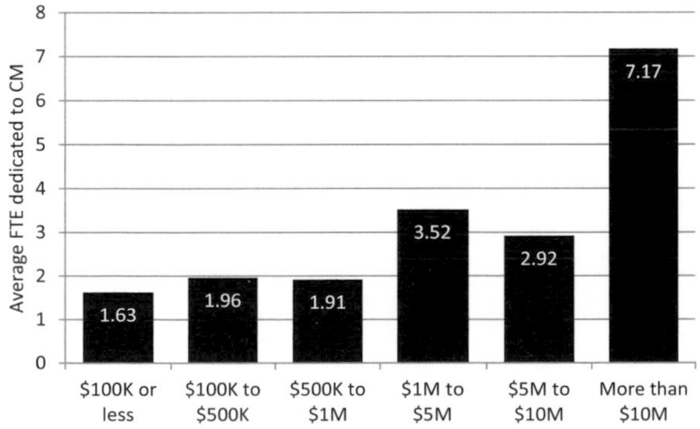

Figure 7.31 – Average FTE dedicated to change management versus project scope

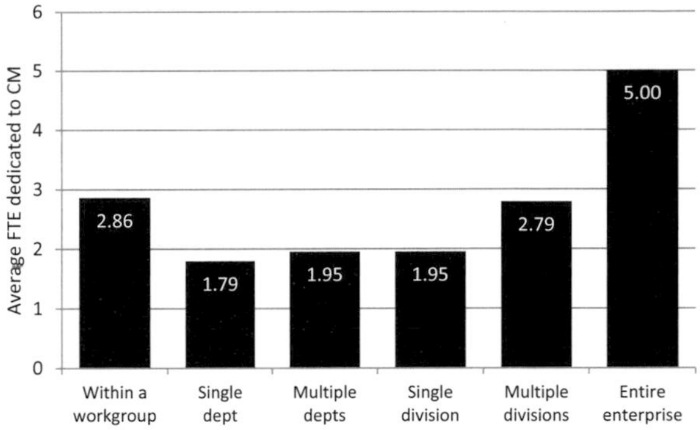

Figure 7.32 – Average FTE dedicated to change management versus number of employees impacted

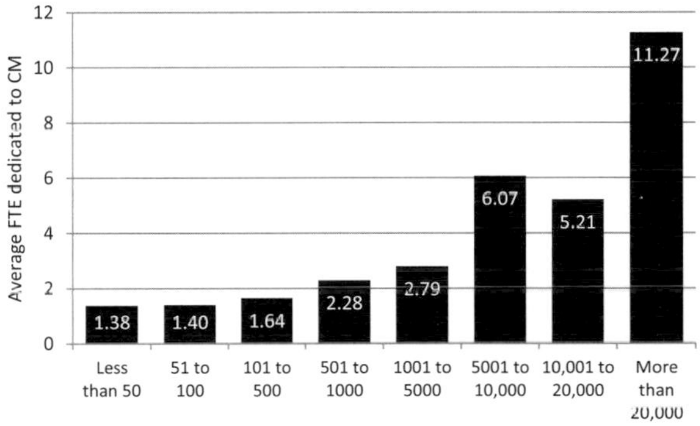

Figure 7.33 – Average FTE dedicated to change management versus duration

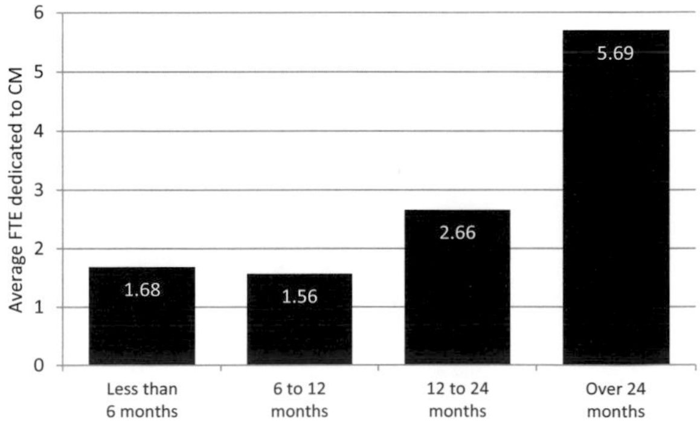

Percent of project FTE dedicated to change management

Figure 7.34 shows the distribution of the percentage of project FTE that was dedicated to change management. The average percentage of project FTE allocated to change management was 22%. The most common percent of project budget allocated to change management was 10% with a median of 10%.

Figure 7.34 – Average percent of project FTE dedicated to change management

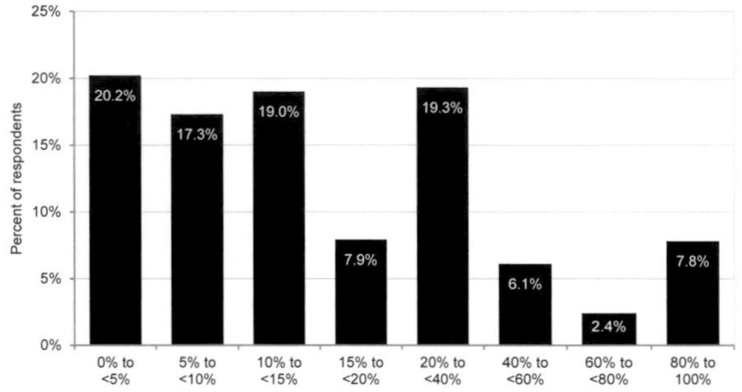

Figures 7.35, 7.36, 7.37 and 7.38 show the percentage of total project FTE dedicated to change management based on project investment, project scope, number of employees impacted and duration of the project.

Figure 7.35 – Percent of project FTE dedicated to change management versus project investment

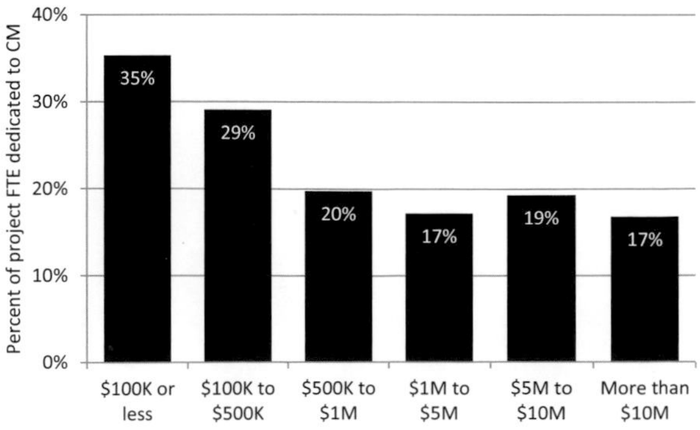

Figure 7.36 – Percent of project FTE dedicated to change management versus project scope

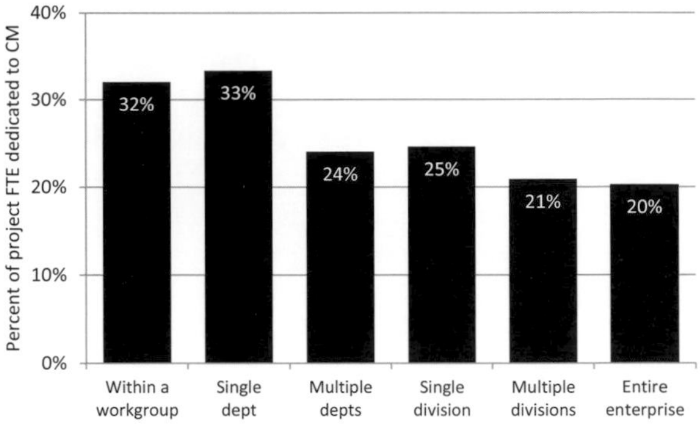

Figure 7.37 – Percent of project FTE dedicated to change management versus employees impacted

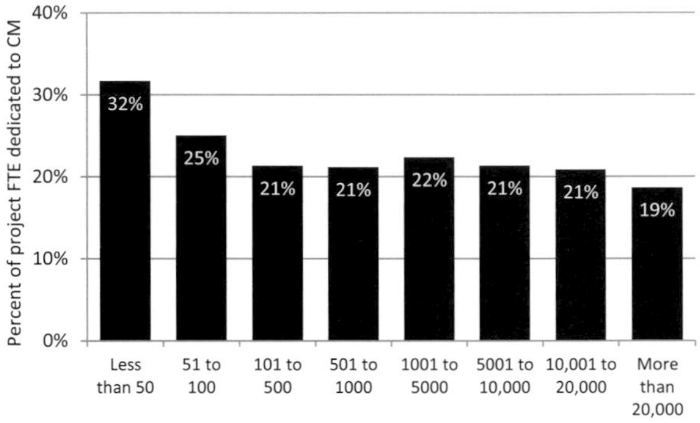

Figure 7.38 – Percent of project FTE dedicated to change management versus duration

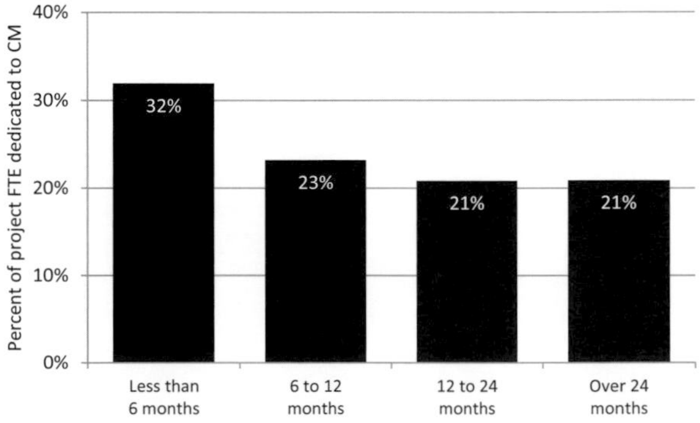

Had influence on change management resources and budget

Participants in the 2015 study indicated whether they had influence on the amount of resources and budget for change management. Less than half, 43%, reported they did have influence on the budget and resources.

Why participants had influence on the change management budget and resources

Participants who had influence on their change management budget and resources described why they had influence.

1. **They controlled the budget**
   The majority of participants who had influence on the budget were already directly in control of it. Whether on steering committees, leadership boards, acting as advisors or in charge of their organization's change management, participants could directly influence the change management budget.
2. **Planned for the budget**
   Effective planning for an event allowed most participants to secure budgets far in advance of change. Participants reported having an easier time securing a budget during the planning stage than later in the change cycle.
3. **Presented a business case**
   Participants presented a business case for change management that included goals, outcomes and a well-defined Return on Investment (ROI) for their change projects. Participants reported higher success with influencing the budget when they could lay out the business reasons for implementing change management.

Adaptations when not having influence on the change management resources or budget

Participants listed several approaches that aided the project success when they had no direct influence on the budget or resources. The following methods were used most often:

1. **Use a strategized approach**
   Participants advised scaling down and scoping the change management plan to match the budget available to help ensure the success of the project. Providing a clear plan up front had a positive impact. They identified the costs of necessary training, printed materials, time, labor and other activities and presented data before the project began. Clarifying the risks of not having a proper budget and the trade-offs that would be needed proved helpful to start a change management budget conversation.
2. **Be creative with existing resources**
   Participants used other departments and employees to be informal change agents. It was important to find well-liked, charismatic employees who were early adopters of change and coach them on how to influence their work groups. Participants recommended linking change management to other funded projects. An example included using small segments of established meetings to educate and excite groups affected by change. They also used free or low costs resources, such as coffee chats, general conversations during lunches, fliers and informational pieces that were posted around the workplace, to keep employees involved.
3. **Reaching out to people with influence**
   Participants reported that, as a last resort, they reached out to anyone who could influence resource allocation whether on their change initiatives or not. This was the least preferred method of gaining resources as many participants viewed it as begging.

Team structure used

Team structure

Data was collected on the change management team structure during the 2015 study. Participants chose among the four structures shown in Table 7.39 or selected *other structure*. Table 7.39 provides descriptions for each team structure and presents each structure as a diagram.

Table 7.39 – Change management team structure descriptions

Team Structure	Description
Team Structure A 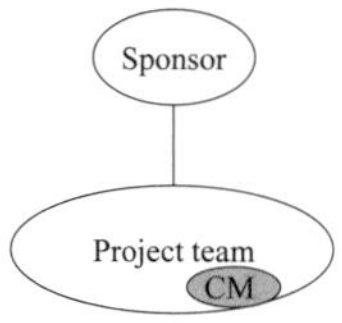	Change management resources are in the project team
Team Structure B 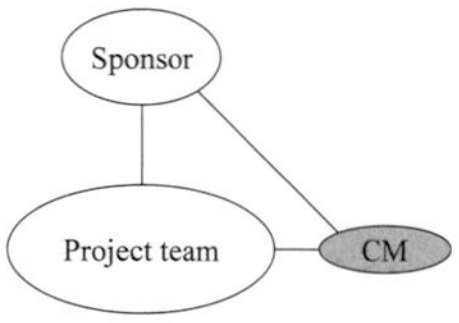	Change management resources are external to but support the project team
Team Structure C 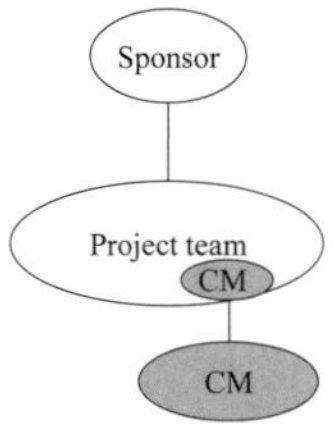	Change management resources are on the project team and are supported by an external change management team
Team Structure D 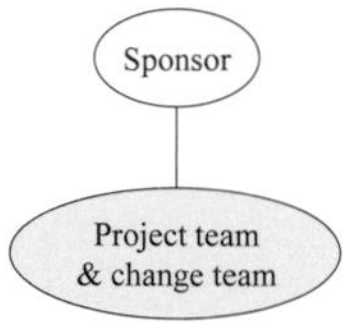	Project team and change management resources are the same

When participants were asked to describe the team structure they used, the most common answer given was incorporating change management resources into the project team (Figure 7.40). Responses were similar to those from the 2013 study and the ranking was unchanged.

Figure 7.40 – Team structure used

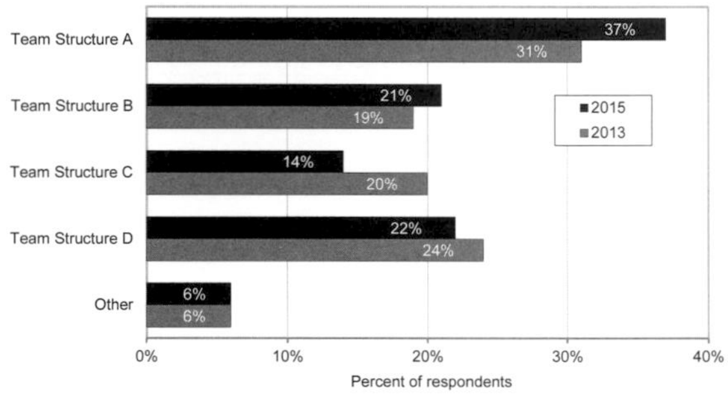

The team structures described below are in rank order based on frequency of use.

1. **Change management in the project — Team Structure A (37%)**
   As with the 2013 findings, the most common team structure was to have change management incorporated into the project team itself (37%). Change management resources were typically a management role, team member or key person in the business. Within the project team, these individuals were responsible for enacting change plans and activities.

2. **Change management and project team are the same — Team Structure D (22%)**
   Respondents also frequently used a structure in which a change management practitioner also held the position of project manager (22%). The change manager was responsible for driving change policies and development of the project. The number of respondents who used this type of team structure decreased by 2% from the previous study.

3. **Change management and project teams are separate — Team Structure B (21%)**
The third most prevalent response was that the external change management resource supported the project team, increasing from 19% in 2013 to 21% in the 2015 study. Participants explained that the two teams worked in tandem.

4. **External and internal change management teams — Team Structure C (14%)**
Team structure C was cited as having the largest decrease of use between the 2013 and 2015 study, with a change from 20% to 14%. Participants described that a change management member was present on the project team and was supported by an outside change management team. The external change management team was either an internal department or a third-party consulting firm.

Participants from previous studies who did not use one of the structures presented described their structure. The most commonly identified structures were:

1. **Unstructured**
Study participants indicated that change management was "*something one of us did on the side,*" "*the responsibility of everyone and no one*" or "*nothing more than formal communication.*" Other characteristics included working on an informal project and not having a dedicated project manager or change manager.

2. **Reported to another department or individual**
Change management reported directly to another department or individual, which included:
    - Finance
    - Program director, manager or team
    - Project Management
    - Human Resources (HR)
    - Center of Excellence

Other unique responses explained that change management was practiced only as part of an executive's role or change champions were used.

Advantages of having the change management resource on the project team

Participants identified six advantages of having change management resources on the project team (Team Structure A).

1. **More effective teamwork**
When change resources were integrated into the project team, the project manager and change manager developed a strong, cohesive relationship. They achieved better buy-in from team members, became aligned in project goals and vision, and had increased dedication to the project with overall cohesiveness and cooperation.

2. **Responsiveness and dedication to project**
When change management was embedded into project management, change management became a dedicated resource to the project team. The project team became more aware of the reason for the change and gained a greater knowledge of the change. Further, change management resources were able to respond more quickly and effectively to issues arising from the people side of change.

3. **Effective communication**
Dedicated change resources aided in uniform and aligned communication, an easier flow of information and created a collaborative environment. When the change manager and project manager were aligned, they were able to clearly communicate both project and change-related information to the team.

4. **Enhanced project management**
Change managers on the project team were identified as key to effective project management. Dedicated change resources were associated with more effective problem solving, allowed for faster response times,

more efficient resource utilization and allowed project managers to better understand user responses and risks.

5. **Increased project knowledge**
   Change resources within the project team gained a deeper understanding of the project, its vision, goals, scope and deliverables. Change management resources were used more effectively due to the knowledge and understanding gained by being integrated into the project team.
6. **Increased influence of change manager**
   Presence of a change management resource allowed for the change manager to have an increased influence in the day-to-day activities of the project. The change resource became an integral part of the team and was able to provide direction to the team members.

Advantages of having the change management resource separate from but supporting the project team

Participants described the advantages of having a change management resource that was separate from but that supported the project team (Team Structure B). The top response related to having an objective viewpoint. Top responses were:

1. **Objectivity**
   Resources outside of the project team offered neutrality and an independent viewpoint. They provided objective feedback, more accurately assessed the people impacts of the project and were cited as having greater credibility.
2. **Autonomy and independence**
   Change management resources outside of the project team had autonomy to maintain the priority of their change work without being constrained by project boundaries or being pulled into the "*day to day aspects of the project.*"
3. **Direct access to leadership**
   Change management resources were in a better position to manage sponsorship when they were external to the project team. The flow of communications between sponsor and change manager was direct and not filtered through a project manager.
4. **Flexibility**
   External change management resources allowed them to be allocated efficiently across projects. This flexibility resulted in cost reductions and better use of time.
5. **Enabled specialization**
   Members of both the project and change management teams were able to focus on their own tasks.
6. **Provide support**
   Participants with a change management resource outside of the project team expressed that the project was provided with additional guidance and tools.

Additional structure considerations when separate but supporting the project team
A number of participants indicated that there were disadvantages to having a change management resource that was separate from but supporting the project team. The largest reason in this category was that change resources were too far removed from the project to have an effect. Responses included:

- Too far removed from the project
- The change resource and project manager could not stay in sync
- The project management team engulfed the change management resource
- The project was too complex for efficient use of a change management resource

Team structure and change management effectiveness

Figure 7.41 compares team structures to overall effectiveness of change management. Participants who used Team Structures A and C reported the highest rates of *good* and *excellent* change management effectiveness.

Figure 7.41 – Change management effectiveness of team structures used

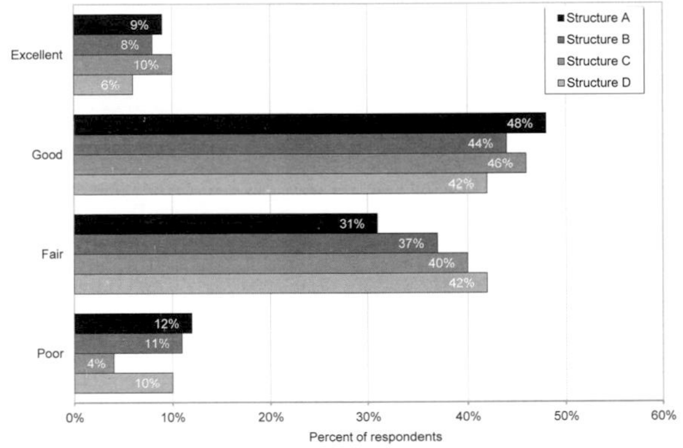

Reasons for using the team structure

Participants indicated why they used a team structure by selecting one of the following responses:

- The structure was used as a deliberate decision specific for the project
- The structure was given to the practitioner
- The structure was the default option considering the resources available
- The structure was the organizational standard

Over one third of participants reported that the structure was selected deliberately for the specific project (Figure 7.42).

Figure 7.42 – Reason for using the team structure

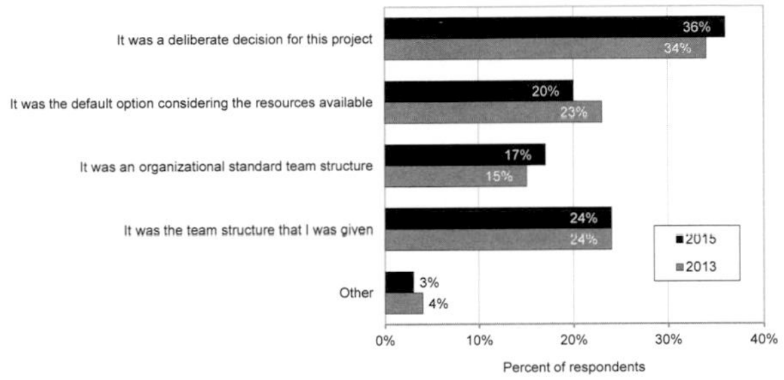

Table 7.43 shows the rationale for using each team structure. The majority of participants who used Team Structure A selected it deliberately for the project (37%), or used it because it was given to them (28%). These were also the top two reasons participants used Team Structures B and C. However, for participants who used Team Structure D, the majority of participants either used it because it was the default option considering resources available (35%) or selected it deliberately for the project (34%).

Table 7.43 – Reasons for using a particular team structure

Team structure	It was a deliberate decision for this project	It is an organizational standard team structure	It was the team structure that I was given	It was the default option considering the resources available	Other
Team Structure A 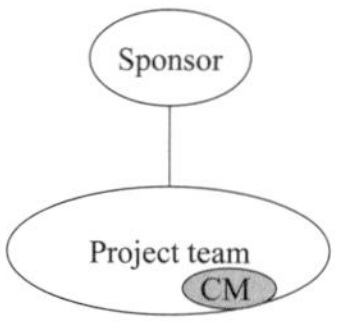	37%	18%	28%	15%	2%
Team Structure B 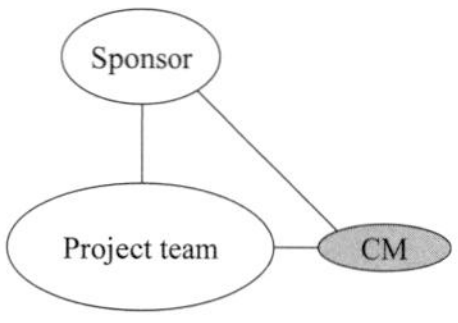	29%	16%	28%	21%	6%
Team Structure C 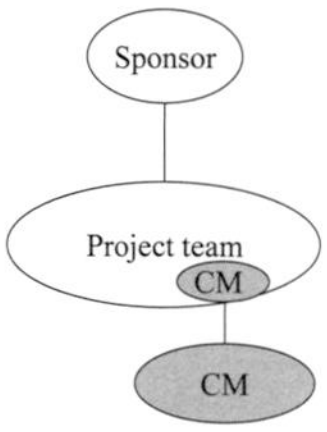	48%	17%	20%	12%	3%
Team Structure D 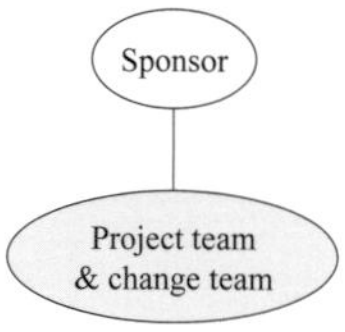	34%	13%	16%	35%	2%

Additional team structure considerations

Source date: 2009

A number of participants did not indicate a preference between a team structure in which the change management resource was integrated into the project team or in which the resource was outside of the project team. Instead, they responded with alternative ideas about the most effective change management team structures.

1. The most effective team structure varied from project to project depending on:
    - The nature of the project including size, scope, complexity, impact on people, risk or geographic distribution; responses were equally divided regarding which structure was best for the size of the change
    - Cultural factors within an organization such as employee response to outside help and fragmentation of groups
    - Resource considerations such as availability of change management skills and experience within the project team and sponsorship coalition
2. Participants proposed hybrid structures that combined resources both internal and external to the project team. These hybrid structures offered benefits including:
    - Balancing project knowledge with outside perspective
    - Having support and expertise from a center of excellence as needed, particularly during busy project stages
    - Allowing business unit representation while building change skills within the organization
3. Unique team structures included:
    - Change management owned by all impacted groups with involvement from all levels, "*everyone in the change circle*"
    - Sponsor included in the change management team bubble

Building change management knowledge

Source date: 2009

Participants from the 2009 study identified how they overcame or addressed lack of change management experience or knowledge during their projects. They described the following top five tactics and methods:

1. **Training in change management**
Change leaders, project team members, managers and sponsors participated in training to learn about change management methodologies and strategies. Some attended formal training programs, and others received less formal training through internally developed programs, train-the-trainer programs or ongoing training during regular team meetings.
2. **Coaching and mentoring**
Coaching and mentoring relationships allowed more experienced change management leaders to provide direction and support to counterparts with less change management experience. Some organizations created a formal mentoring program or shadowing opportunities to allow inexperienced individuals to work alongside experienced team members. Experienced team members took the lead on projects by setting a personal example and offering one-on-one advice and guidance.
3. **Self-study**
Many participants sought change management knowledge on their own through independent study and research which included reviewing training materials, books, published materials and benchmarking information. Internet-based resources, such as online tutorials and webinars, were referenced frequently. Participants also cited learning on the job through trial and error and addressing issues as they arose as a self-study tactic.

4. **Engaging consultants and external resources**
Hiring external resources or consultants helped fill gaps in expertise and supplement full-time employee knowledge. External resources provided support through delivery of training programs that emphasized competency building. Consultants worked to provide knowledge transfer through coaching and strategic advice, and in some cases, even built a change management methodology for the project.

5. **Peer-to-peer networking**
Support groups and communities of practice provided avenues to communicate with other professionals in the field. These networking opportunities allowed for knowledge sharing, collecting of lessons learned and liaising with leaders of similar projects. More informally, asking questions and fostering open dialogues with other departments that had relevant expertise (communications, training, etc.) addressed gaps in change management knowledge.

Attributes of a great team member

Source date: 2011

Participants identified the most important attributes of a great change management team member. The top four attributes were:

1. **Communication skills**
Able to communicate effectively with all levels of the organization; being an effective communicator includes listening to others, accepting feedback and demonstrating competencies in both written and oral communication

2. **Change management competency**
Has attended change management training and has experience applying a structured methodology; has experience managing resistance and coaching employees throughout the change

3. **Flexibility**
Has an open mind and is flexible during times of change; demonstrates resilience throughout the change and is able to adapt and be creative with what is available

4. **Interpersonal skills**
Demonstrates strong interpersonal skills with coworkers and has respect from employees within the organization; is people-oriented, trusted and honest in all situations

CHANGE MANAGEMENT ACTIVITIES

THE SPECIFIC STEPS EFFECTIVE CHANGE MANAGERS TAKE TO INFLUENCE PROJECT SUCCESS

SUMMARY

Best practices in communications, training, resistance management and reinforcement define the concrete activities and actions at the core of your work as a change professional. This chapter outlines comprehensive guidance from seasoned practitioners to shape the planning and execution of change management. Learn how social media is being used during change, what steps to take to avoid resistance and what attributes constitute exceptional training. Ensure your change management planning and implementations are aligned with best practices and drive results.

HIGHLIGHT

Once again, senior leaders were the preferred senders of business messages (74%) and frontline supervisors were the preferred senders of personal messages (78%).

Change management activities grid

Participants described their change management approaches by listing actions and steps they completed. Data were divided into three major project phases: start-up (i.e., planning), design and implementation. The activities and steps were further categorized according to target audiences:

- Project team
- Managers (including business leaders)
- Employees

The activities and steps can be shown in a 3 x 3 matrix, with rows representing project timing (start-up, design and implementation) and columns representing the audience or group (Figure 8.1).

For each box in this grid, detailed lists of corresponding activities are provided. The labels for each box are general descriptions of the categories, and are not intended to stand alone from the activity lists in Tables 8.2, 8.3 and 8.4.

The lists (List A, List B, etc.) referred to in Tables 8.2, 8.3 and 8.4 can be found in the section titled "Supplemental change management activities lists" following the tables.

Editor's note: The Change Management Activity Model shown in Figure 8.1 was developed in 2003 and now includes data from the 2003, 2005, 2007, 2009, 2011 and 2013 studies to create a comprehensive view of change management activities across multiple studies.

Figure 8.1 – Change Management Activity Model

	Project team	Managers	Employees
Start-up	**Select and prepare the team**	**Create sponsorship model**	**Create awareness**
Design	**Execute work plans**	**Involve sponsors**	**Engage employees**
Implementation	**Transfer ownership**	**Coach sponsors**	**Train employees**

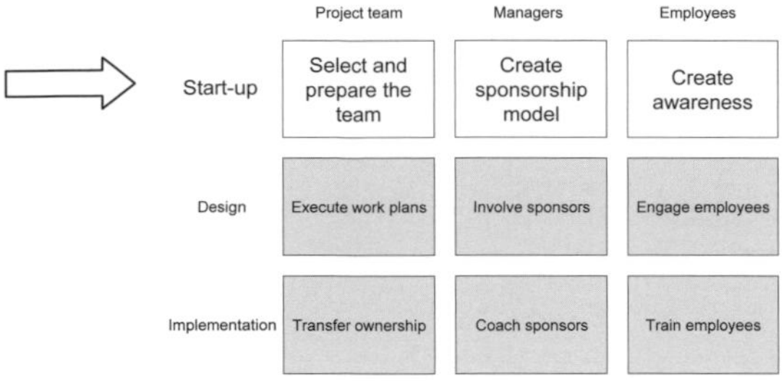

Table 8.2 – Change management start-up activities

	with the project team	with managers	with employees
	Select and prepare the team	**Create sponsorship model**	**Create awareness**
Start-up	• Identify the right change management team members; consider representation by location or function; use outside expertise when necessary • Establish a team structure • Train the team on change management methods and develop team principles and rules; secure the needed resources and budget for change management • Understand the nature of the change and the future state (see List A); assess the timing of the change; ensure clarity concerning why the change is being made • Define the impact of the change on specific groups; conduct a gap analysis • Assess and analyze the current organization (see List B), climate and culture (readiness for change) • Create a sponsorship model (see adjacent column) • Complete change management readiness assessments (assess culture, barriers and risks) • Create change strategies and plans (see List C); develop a schedule and budget; review these plans and get approval from the steering committee • Develop change management training for managers and supervisors • Integrate change management plans into project management plans; be a part of the project team • Use a structured, proven change management methodology; customize or scale to fit the organization and the change • Identify critical success factors and potential obstacles	• Identify required primary sponsor (at the right level in the organization); directly engage his/her support • Identify key senior managers and stakeholders throughout the organization who are needed to sponsor the change; assess their support of the change and competency to manage change • With the direct involvement of the primary sponsor, begin building support among all key managers; engage them as active and visible sponsors of the change and ensure alignment with project objectives • Form a steering committee for the project (dependent on overall project size) • Show managers the current state versus the future state; create a common view of the nature of the change, why the change is being made and the organization's readiness for change • Train senior and mid-level managers on change management and their roles as sponsors of change • Help create key messages for managers to communicate to the organization (presentations and elevator conversations) • Create identifiable actions that senior managers can do to begin supporting the change (see Sponsorship section of this report) • Customize the change management strategy to address potential resistance from managers • Train managers and supervisors on change management and their role as coaches, including how to use change management tools, manage resistance and support employees through the transition • Provide managers with the tools and information needed to manage change with their employees	• Begin initial communications with employees to create awareness of the need for change and to share the nature of the change (see List D)

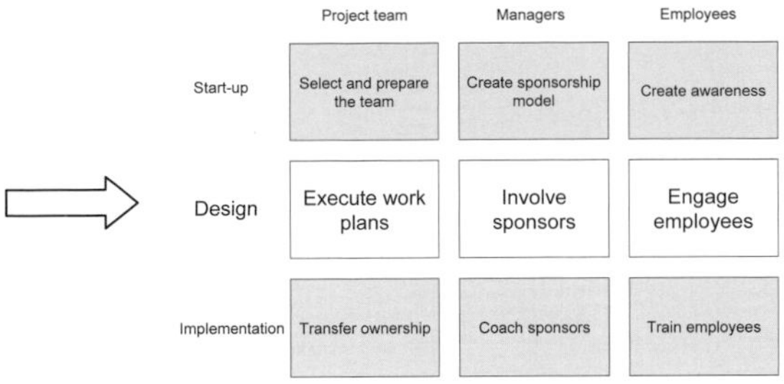

Table 8.3 – Change management design activities

	with the project team	with managers	with employees
	Execute work plans	**Involve sponsors**	**Engage employees**
Design	• Implement change management strategies (from start-up phase) including plans for communications, sponsorship, coaching and training • Conduct regular workshops with change agents • Identify pockets of resistance and develop special tactics with groups to counter it • Identify job roles impacted; begin to define future skills and competencies for employees; use as input for training requirements and curriculum design • Develop coaching and mentoring strategies for frontline supervisors, including development of change management competencies • Train the trainers; begin developing internal competencies regarding managing change throughout the organization • Hire external resources if necessary to support the change • Collect input from customers on how this change will impact them • Define measurable objectives and key performance indicators (KPIs)	• Interview all critical senior managers to determine their expectations and desired outcomes; gather input on the change strategy and understand their concerns • Maintain regular contact with all senior managers; schedule and conduct frequent and regular meetings; seek their input on critical decisions • Conduct steering committee meetings regularly (dependent on project size) • Work to develop sponsor capabilities: What do they need to be doing to support the change? How can they best accomplish those goals? • Coach sponsors; provide sponsors with a roadmap of sponsor activities and help them prepare key messages; provide coaching on how to share the business vision and the change with employees • Identify resistant managers; engage the primary sponsor and other senior managers to address this resistance • Seek approval from senior managers at key milestones during the process • Engage managers in the design process; gather input from managers and understand their concerns; ensure that key stakeholders are involved in the solution design • Create a close relationship between the change team and sponsors • Collect feedback from managers about how employees are embracing the change, areas of resistance and potential issues with the change	• Build awareness concerning the overall change and why the change is being made (see change messages in List D) • Engage employees during design; gather input from employees on the design and understand their concerns • Use pilots or models to test ideas with employees, and share the future state • Use face-to-face meetings to share the vision and strategy • Gather employee feedback on the vision and strategy using focus groups and interviews • Use Question and Answer (Q&A) sessions, interviews and memos to address employee concerns and share information regularly • Demonstrate successes and early wins to employees • Share ongoing progress of the design team, including updates to the schedule, so employees know what to expect and when • Continue to answer questions about the personal impact to employees: How will this impact me? How will this change my daily work? How will I benefit from this change?

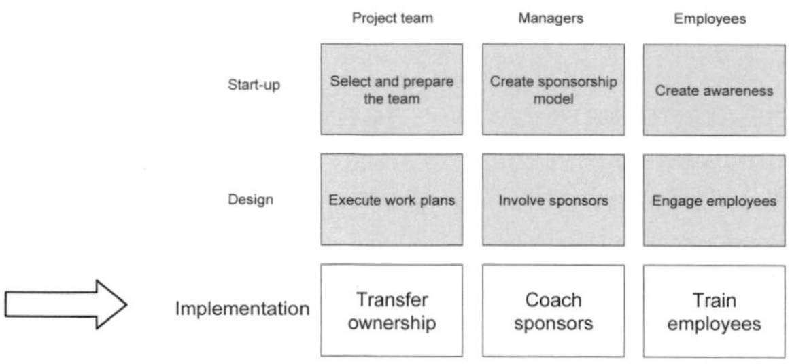

Table 8.4 – Change management implementation activities

	with the project team	with managers	with employees
	Transfer ownership	**Coach sponsors**	**Train employees**
Implementation	• Review project progress; monitor activities and measure performance (e.g., KPIs); identify successes and demonstrate short-term wins • Adapt change management plans as necessary to address gaps in performance • Develop ways to celebrate successes with both managers and employees • Create feedback mechanisms • Create coaching aids for supervisors to enable them to help employees through the transition (see List E for Coaching Aids) • Begin to migrate change leadership to operational managers • Extend team structure to involve local groups in change activities • Support local trainers within the organization to implement education and training about the new processes and systems • Identify lessons learned and update change management approach and tools	• Engage sponsors in managing resistance (encourage one-on-one intervention) • Continue regular and frequent meetings to review progress and performance; update business leaders and senior managers on the solution and implementation progress • Increase the level of senior manager communications with employees (e.g., leadership must stay active and visible throughout implementation) • Provide managers with concrete activities they can perform to support implementation (provide upward coaching) • Report roadblocks to senior managers promptly; resolve critical issues quickly through steering committee • Use senior managers to manage resistance • Maintain frequent and honest communications with managers • Provide opportunities to voice resistance • Collect data from employees about the change (issues, concerns, resistance areas), and share with managers • Evaluate manager effectiveness at managing the change; create corrective action plans where needed	• Implement training on the new processes, systems and job roles; align this training with gap analysis completed by frontline supervisors for their employees (include one-on-one training) • Listen to employees and value their feedback; move quickly to adjust the design or resolve issues that surface during implementation • Provide one-on-one follow-up and coaching • Share critical success factors with employees; audit compliance with the new processes and implement corrective action when needed • Assess employees (where are they in the change process?); measure effectiveness of the change management plans and adjust as necessary • Quickly identify and address pockets of resistance • Celebrate successes and achievement of milestones • Implement reward and incentive systems for employees • Continue ongoing communications about project outcomes and progress, including specifics about what will happen, when and why • When appropriate, tie compensation to performance

Supplemental change management activities lists

List A – Understanding the future state

- Nature and scope of the change
- Overall time frame
- Alignment with the business strategy
- Goals of the change
- Reasons for changing
- Risk assessment (risk of not changing)
- The gap between the future state and today
- Who is impacted and how? Who is impacted most adversely?
- Future state design (if available at this phase) including sample models or scenarios
- What will change? What will stay the same?

List B – Organizational assessment

- Change capacity (How much change has the organization made recently, and how much more change can the organization absorb?)
- Change history (What was the effectiveness of past changes, and what perceptions do employees have of past change projects?)
- Culture assessment (To what degree does the values and norms of the organization support or oppose change?)
- Change competency (What are the change management skills and abilities within the organization?)
- Authority and capability of primary sponsor (Does the primary sponsor have sufficient power to lead the change?)
- Strengths and weaknesses of the organization related to this change (What is working in favor of the change, and what is working against it?)

List C – Strategies and plans

- Change management plan (overall strategy)
- Communications plan
- Sponsor roadmap
- Training plan (including change management training)
- Coaching plan
- Resistance management plan

List D – Employee messages

- The current situation and the rationale for the change (why the change is needed)
- A vision of the organization after the change takes place (alignment with business strategy)
- The basics of what is changing, the nature of the change and when it will happen
- The goals or objectives for the change
- The expectation that change will happen and is not a choice (risk of not changing)
- The impact of change on daily activities of the employee; "what's in it for me?" (WIIFM)
- Implications of the change on job security (Will I have a job?)
- Behaviors and activities expected from the employee during the change
- Status updates on the performance of the change, including success stories
- Procedures for getting help and assistance during change

List E – Coaching aids

- Concrete activities frontline managers and supervisors can perform to support the change with their employees
- Tools to communicate new roles and responsibilities to employees
- Self-assessment guides for employees to assess skill and knowledge gaps
- Resistance assessments and mechanisms to collect feedback from employees during early implementation phases
- Tools to create individual development plans

Communications

Preferred sender

Participants in the 2015 study indicated preferred senders of communications for both personal- and organization-level messages. Figure 8.5 shows preferences for senders of change messages. Overwhelmingly, the employee's supervisor was the preferred sender of personal messages, and executives and senior leaders were preferred senders of business messages. These findings reinforce findings from previous studies.

Figure 8.5 – Preferred sender for business and personal messages

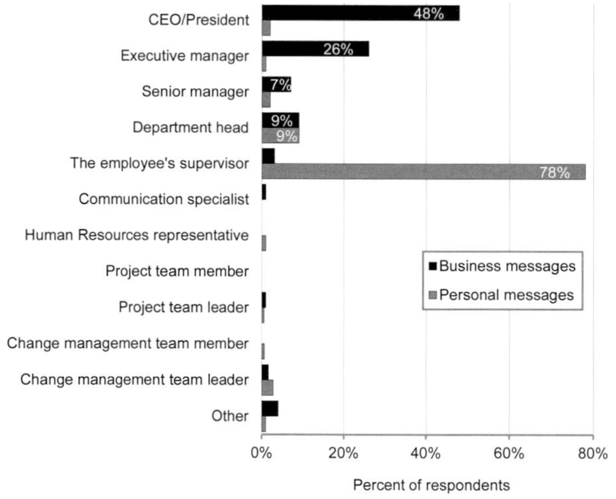

Most important messages for employees

Source date: 2011

Participants identified the most important messages to communicate to employees regarding the change. Although participants identified five important messages communicated to employees regarding the change, responses surrounding the business reasons for the change were stated twice as often as the next most frequent response.

1. **Business reasons for the change**
   Messages communicated to employees conveyed the reasons the organization was changing including:
   - The necessity of the change to ensure organizational success and sustainability in the future
   - The benefits of the change including strategic objectives, potential Return on Investment (ROI), improved performance and increase in business value
   - The risks of not changing and the negative consequences if the change was not pursued
   - The necessity of the change to remain competitive in the market
   - Improvements to processes, operations and design enhancements
   - The role of the change in support of business initiatives and business strategy
2. **Why the employees should want to participate**
   Messages communicated to employees built desire to participate in the change, or answered "what's in it for me?" (WIIFM), from the employee's perspective including:
   - Demonstrating how the change will make their jobs easier, more efficient, more productive, more rewarding and less redundant
   - Normalizing the change or the occurrence of change
   - Indicating potential opportunities for new jobs or advancements
   - Explaining how the change aligns with employee priorities
   - Sharing how the change would increase the quality of their work lives and environment

- Transferring ownership of the change to employees with phrases such as "*this is your change*" or "*innovation is the right and fun thing to do*"
- Providing testimonials and examples of where the change was successful elsewhere

3. **Impact of the change on employees**
These messages identified how the change would impact employees including:
    - Changes to the way employees did work or changes to their job roles
    - Behavior changes that would be required
    - Who specifically was impacted
    - The tradeoffs and downsides of the change
    - Employees' new roles and what needs to be done
    - What the change meant for the employees including what they could expect, what their new roles would entail and how the change applied to them
    - How they were expected to perform
    - What was needed from employees in terms of involvement, commitment, support and contribution
    - Emphasis that the employees' support of the had a direct impact on the success of the project
    - Potential for job loss
4. **How the change was happening**
These messages included information regarding the specifics of how the change was occurring within the organization including:
    - The dates of implementation, the rollout schedule or timeline, the time frame for adoption and the go-live date
    - Project status including progress updates and milestones
    - The change plan or phases of the change
    - The next steps of the change
    - Who was leading or managing the change
    - Where the change was happening
    - Celebration of short-term successes
5. **Details about the change**
These messages explained the specifics of the change including:
    - What the change was and the accompanying project objectives
    - The new processes, activities or procedures
    - What was not changing (e.g., ensuring job security)
    - Specifics about the difference between the future and current states (i.e., how tomorrow will be different from today)
    - Acknowledgement that not all the answers were available, "*what we don't know*"
    - The scope of the change
    - The challenges of the change
    - What the change meant for the organization

Additional key messages to employees included:

- How employees would be supported through the change
- To whom or where they could go for more information such as training resources, updates, job aids or requests for additional support
- Information pertaining to how and when employees would be trained and the necessity and importance of training
- For what they would need to be prepared and how they could best prepare
- The resources that would be made available to them to help with the transition
- Encouraging statements that emphasized the importance of the individual or reassurances that the transition would be made as a group such as "*the change is a journey we will accomplish as a team from the start to the end*," or "*this will be tough but together we'll get through it*"

Most important messages for managers and supervisors

Source date: 2011

Participants identified six important messages to communicate to managers and supervisors regarding the change.

1. **Roles and expectations for managers and supervisors**
   Most messages regarding roles and expectations emphasized the importance of the roles, responsibilities and the expectations of managers and supervisors during change. These messages conveyed how imperative their roles were as change advocates, ambassadors and role models of the change. For example, "*your participation in the change as an adopter/champion increases the likelihood of the change's success.*" Expectations of managers also included:
   - How to communicate change to staff members
   - How to answer questions
   - Key messages to pass to employees
   - How often communication should take place and the importance of keeping employees informed about the change
   - Identifying and managing resistance including identifying areas of potential resistance
   - Helping staff members adapt to change through coaching, preparation and guidance
   - Managing questions and facilitating a smooth transition
2. **Business reasons for change**
   Similar to messages communicated to employees, participants listed the business reasons for the change as one of the most important messages communicated to managers and supervisors including:
   - The need for change
   - Alignment of the change with the direction of the organization
   - Risks of not changing
   - Benefits to the organization
3. **Impact of the change on managers and supervisors**
   Participants identified the importance of communicating the impacts of the change on managers and supervisors including:
   - Impacts to their job roles and behaviors in the work place
   - Impacts to employees in terms of the type of work employees were expected to perform, employee behaviors in the work place and new job roles for their employees
   - Impacts to their team or line of business
   - Potential or expected delays or disturbances to their work area
4. **Details about the change**
   These messages explained the change in terms of the change objectives and the specifics of the change. Other points included:
   - The change vision
   - What was not changing
   - Challenges of the change
   - Today versus tomorrow
5. **How the change was being implemented**
   Participants communicated how the change was happening within the organization to managers and supervisors including:
   - Timelines for change implementation
   - How employees were being trained and prepared for the change
   - Progress, status and updates
   - Project plans and next steps
   - What was being done to minimize risk

6. **How managers and supervisors would be prepared and supported**
   These messages included details pertaining to the ways the organization was supporting managers and supervisors and also how managers and supervisors were being prepared to support their employees. Main points included:
   - Where to go for support
   - How support would be provided
   - Who to contact with concerns
   - Where to get more information
   - Which managers and supervisors needed to be prepared
   - How to lead people through change; how to be "*the mirror of change*"
   - How to manage change

Most important messages for senior managers and executives

Source date: 2011

Participants identified five messages to communicate to senior managers and executives regarding the change.

1. **Roles and responsibilities of senior managers and executives**
   The primary message communicated to senior managers and executives regarding the change emphasized their roles and responsibilities as sponsors of change such as:
   - The necessity of their help in preparing for, leading and supporting the change; "*your leadership, wisdom and active support are vital to success*"
   - The expectations of them in terms of what they need to do and their responsibilities such as staying up-to-date on the project and managing change with their direct reports
   - Their roles in communicating with staff members in an open and timely manner including messages that reflected the reasons for the change and messages that "*sell the vision*" of the change
   - The need for them to be active, visible and engaged in the change
2. **Business reasons for the change**
   The second most important message communicated to senior managers and executives included the reasons the change was occurring including:
   - The necessity of the change from the organization's perspective
   - The benefits to the organization on completion of a successful change such as increased competitiveness and proficiency
   - Alignment with other business objectives, priorities, organizational strategies or long-term goals
   - The change drivers
3. **How the change was happening and progressing**
   These messages included information regarding how the change was taking place and how well the change was being adopted within the organization including:
   - Status updates and milestones reached
   - Timelines of the project including project schedules and deadlines
   - The planned approach for the change, implementation and next steps
   - Challenges that arose during the change process such as unforeseen issues, problems, increased workloads and strain on resources
   - How change management was being used and applied during the change
   - Reactions from staff

4. **The impacts of the change**
   These messages identified the impacts of the change including:
   - Impacts to the organization in terms of who would be impacted, the costs of the change, performance dips and potential declines in productivity during change
   - Impacts to senior managers and executives specifically such as what they could expect from the change and its impacts to their area or group
   - Impacts to employees in terms of job role changes, required behavioral changes and new expectations
5. **Details about the change**
   These messages identified the specifics of the change by addressing what was changing such as:
   - The change objectives, expected results and scope of the change
   - The change vision and desired outcomes
   - What would not be changing, what would be new and what would be different

Attributes of a successful change message

Source date: 2009

Participants in the 2009 study identified three attributes of a successful change message when communicating with employees.

1. **Shares what the change will mean to the employee**
   Employees want to hear about how the change will impact them personally including:
   - How will this change impact me?
   - What will I do differently?
   - What's in it for me? (WIIFM)

   Employees want to know how the change will affect their jobs including the impact on daily job duties, reporting responsibilities and changes in compensation.
2. **Explain business reasons for why the change is happening**
   Employees want to know why the change is important and necessary for the success of the business and the benefits to the business as a whole. Employees need to understand the business reasons for the change and how the change aligns with the organization's goals, vision and strategy. Employees also want to know what would happen to the business were the change not made, the consequences of inaction.
3. **Is honest and clear**
   Employees want to hear a message that is sincere, truthful and accurate. The message should include the good and bad, and honest answers about what the communicator does and does not know. "*Say what you know and admit what you don't know.*"

Additional attributes of an effective change message from the 2007 study include:

- **Shares what is changing**
  The message should define the nature of the change and what specifically is changing in the organization. Information about the transition from the current to future state should be included along with what is expected of employees during this transition period.
- **Conveys the impact on the organization**
  Employees should know how the organization and departments will be affected by the change and benefits or negative impacts that might result.
- **Prepares employees for the change**
  Employees should be assured that they are not alone when moving into the future state. They should have a clear picture of the training and support they will receive to enable them to make the transition. This might include help desks, ongoing training or online resources.

Attributes of successful communicators

Source date: 2009

In addition to commenting on effective messages, participants in the 2009 study also shared feedback on effective communicators. The most successful and effective communicators demonstrated the following ten attributes in rank order:

1. **Committed, engaged and passionate about the change**
   Successful communicators were positive, enthusiastic and passionate about the change; they believed in it. They were committed to and engaged in the change, and showed their support visibly. They were champions of the change and led by example.
2. **Credible**
   Effective communicators were trusted and respected, and had the ability to influence all levels in the organization. They had experience and authority.
3. **Able to deliver a clear message**
   Clear message were simple, focused and concise. Effective and successful communicators delivered clear messages in non-technical language that could be understood by all receivers.
4. **Knowledgeable about the change and its impact on the organization**
   Successful communicators understood why the change was needed, the purpose and benefits of the change and its impacts on the people. They were also knowledgeable about the organization's internal processes and history. They connected this knowledge with their ability to see the big picture and future state. Their communications shared this perspective and context. "*Explained clearly the organizational reason for the change and the personal impact on the individual; did this in an informative and respectful way.*"
5. **Consistent and timely in their messages**
   Communicators delivered frequent messages, which remained consistent and were repeated often.
6. **Open and honest**
   Communicators and their messages were genuine and delivered with truth and transparency.
7. **Two-way communicators**
   The most important element for communicators during two-way communication was the ability to listen. Two-way communicators were open to conversations and feedback.
8. **Fluent in the language of their audience**
   Effective communicators created a message that was tailored and relevant to their receivers. They always included the answer to "what's in it for me?" (WIIFM) for the intended audience. "*Taking the broad message and making it meaningful for the group being communicated with.*"
9. **Personable**
   Personable communicators were patient, confident and compassionate. They had excellent interpersonal skills, communicated with empathy and were approachable.
10. **Choosing the right channel**
   Choosing the right channel meant the ability to offer communications in a variety of ways while ensuring that face-to-face communication was one of those channels.

Tactics for correcting misinformation and misunderstanding

Source date: 2009

Participants in the 2009 study identified six tactics used for correcting misunderstandings resulting from background conversations or the rumor mill.

1. **Enabling open discussion time**
   Open discussion time included events that allowed people to exchange information freely, present questions and provide feedback. Open discussions happened in many formats including town halls, brownbag lunches, roadshow presentations, conference calls, site visits, forums, small group meetings and focus groups.

2. **Identifying current rumors and addressing them immediately**
   It was important that the identification of current rumors be conducted anonymously. Participants cited the following ways to collect rumors anonymously: telephone hotlines, designated email addresses, help desks and collection boxes. Participants also noted that it was best to address those rumors, when possible, in a face-to-face format.
3. **Engaging sponsors**
   Participants cited many methods of engaging leadership. No matter how sponsors were engaged, they were recognized as the most effective group to address and correct background conversations resulting from misinformation. "*National leadership team traveled to each location and allowed an opportunity for Q&A.*"
4. **Providing regular communications**
   Regular communications were a source of consistency and provided updated information on the change. The most common interval of regular communications among participants was weekly followed by monthly.
5. **Updating Frequently Asked Questions**
   Frequently Asked Questions (FAQs) answered common inquiries and addressed misinformation spreading through background conversations. Frequently Asked Questions (FAQs) were updated regularly and circulated among employees in various ways including newsletters, electronic postings and written documents.
6. **Providing information electronically**
   A source of information that could be accessed electronically at any time by employees and could be updated by the team was a useful tool for keeping employees updated. This source of information was available to everyone in the organization to provide transparency and openness. Participants also cited the value of interactions through an electronic source including blogs, discussion boards and postings. "*Set up a 'rumor busters' website and fed it with both real and manufactured rumors and corrections.*"

What would you do differently regarding communications?

Source date: 2011

Participants in the 2011 study provided five suggestions for what they would have done differently regarding communications. The most commonly cited response, more communication, was cited twice as often as the next response.

1. **More communication**
   Participant responses indicated that they would communicate more, to more people, more often and to all levels within the organization. Responses also indicated that these communications should be more targeted, more face-to-face, more interactive and more relevant to the audience.
2. **Better communication strategy**
   The second most common response reflected the need for a more detailed communication strategy including a succinct, consistent and accurate set of core messages. A strategy would also include a more robust implementation timeline for communication activities.
3. **Communicate earlier**
   Participants indicated they would begin communication earlier. These efforts included syncing with other communication networks, connecting to the project sooner and beginning in-person meetings earlier, even if only partial information was available.
4. **More attention to senior leadership**
   The fourth recommendation from participants involved more attention, interaction and involvement with senior leadership. Participants reported they would evoke more support and ownership from senior leadership.
5. **More dedicated people working on communication**
   Study results revealed that communication efforts needed to have more people dedicated to them, including having more dedicated and expert resources assigned to producing and implementing communications.

Use of social media in communications

Twenty-eight percent of participants used social media to support their change management communication, a slight increase from 26% of participants in the 2013 study, but continuing the trend of growth from 2011 (Figure 8.6).

Figure 8.6 – Use of social media

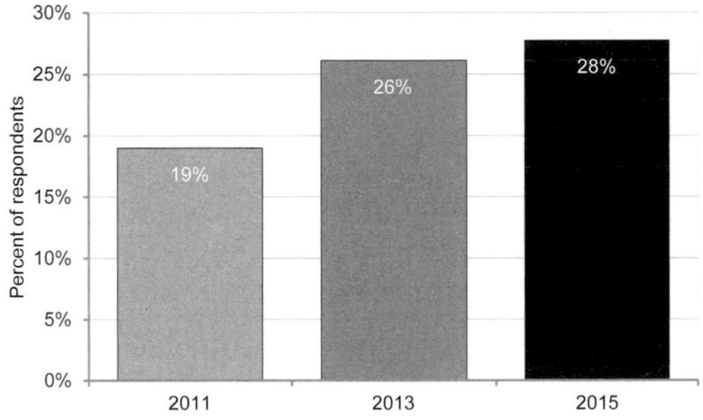

Why social media was used in change management communications

Participants cited the following drivers for using social media in their communications:

1. **Wide reach**
   The top driver for using social media was its wide message reach. Participants considered social media to be highly accessible to both message senders and receivers. It also allowed some participants to overcome communication challenges presented by geographically dispersed organizations.
2. **Communication channel variety**
   Participants indicated that use of social media aligned with organizational standards or objectives, allowing multiple communication formats and avoidance of email which was overused. Participants also reported that informal communication channels were beneficial.
3. **Efficient channel**
   Participants used social media because of its cost effectiveness and efficiency in supporting change management communication.

Other participants reported that social media provided an ability to support collaboration and aligned with the organization's culture.

Benefits of social media in communications

Source date: 2011

Three primary benefits were identified by participants who used social media during communications.

1. **Get messages out**
   The most commonly cited reason for using social media was to communicate messages to a broader audience faster and more efficiently.
2. **Engage the organization**
   Participants reported that social media tools were used to create a more inclusive and supportive work environment by encouraging open dialogue within the organization. These newer methods of communication were used to engage all generations.
3. **Informal feedback and tracking**
   A third benefit was the availability of informal feedback and monitoring of staff member's perceptions regarding change. This helped identify and manage resistance or potential resistance, and solve misconceptions or problems early during change.

Social media's impact on change management

Participants explained how they used social media in support of their change management initiatives.

1. **Platform for additional communications**
   Social media was used to support internal communication to reinforce key messages of change and as an informal communication vehicle for sending updates and encouraging networking.

2. **Create a space for feedback**
   Social media was used as a space for impacted groups to give feedback that could then be addressed, actively discuss the change with other impacted groups and ask questions.
3. **Support training initiatives**
   Participants used social media to support training on change, including using social media as a repository of information such as training materials and related change documents. Social media spaces were places where impacted groups could share best practices for implementing change management and allow a change team to evaluate and gather data on employee training.
4. **Reinforce the change work**
   Participants used social media to celebrate successes, raise awareness about the need for change, mark and communicate milestones and engage impacted group through interactive experiences.
5. **Gamification**
   Participants used social media as a vehicle for introducing gamification into the change process including creating and running educational games through the social media platform and promoting fun and engaging activities related to the change.

Frequency of social media usage

Source date: 2013

Participants who used social media indicated how frequently they used it during change. Figure 8.7 shows that the majority of participants (53%) used social media infrequently (once or twice, or occasionally) during a project. Another 22% used social media weekly and 25% for constant, ongoing messages.

Figure 8.7 – Frequency of social media use

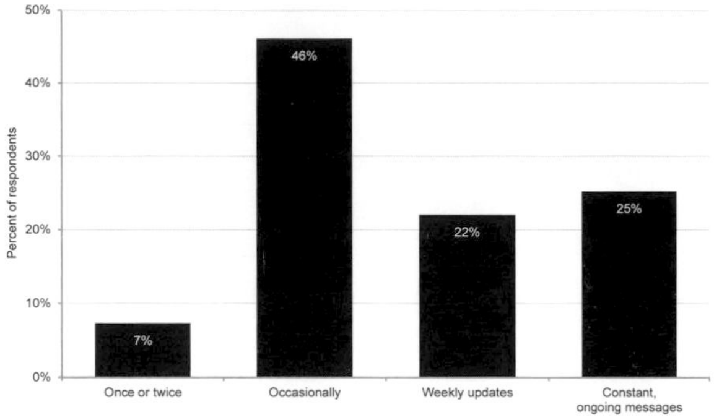

Social media tools used

Source date: 2013

Participants in the 2013 study used the following social media tools, applications or services:

1. **Internal collaboration platform**
   Participants used intranet sites or collaboration sites like SharePoint to create a single location for posting announcements and updates and creating a transparent and collaborative environment.
2. **Social media sites**
   Participants used sites like Facebook, Twitter or Yammer, in addition to YouTube, LinkedIn and Google+, for sharing change messages or as vehicles for collecting data related to change.

The remaining participants identified a wide variety of tools including multiple message formats, blogs, webinars, wikis, videos, custom websites and internal tools in addition to mobile and instant messaging and applications for collecting feedback.

Social media effectiveness

Source date: 2013

Participants rated how effective social media was in supporting change management communications (Figure 8.8). Nearly 45% of participants considered social media to be *effective* or *extremely effective*. Only 9% considered it *ineffective* or *extremely ineffective*.

Figure 8.8 – Social media effectiveness

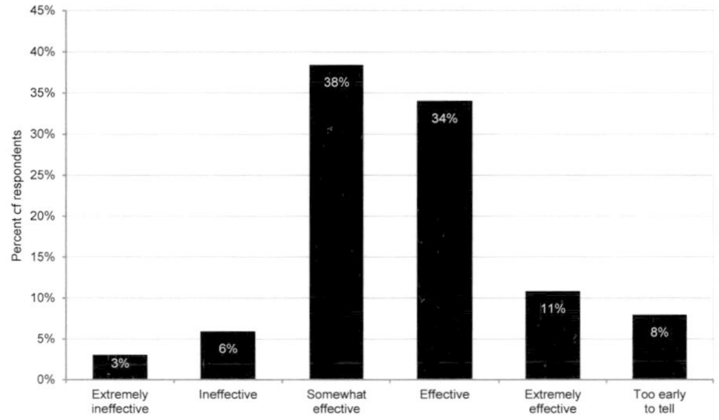

Participants emphasized the importance of face-to-face communication, but they identified the most effective social media tools based on functionality.

1. **Tools that support or encourage collaboration**
   Most commonly, participants found tools that enabled collaboration to be most effective, including intranet platforms, wikis, document repositories and shared calendars.
2. **Web media tools**
   Participants considered web media tools that supported media uploads and downloads to be effective such as blogs, bulletins, newsletters, forums and discussion boards.
3. **Messaging tools**
   The third group of most effective tools included messaging tools such as eblasts, SMS or chat.

Other common responses for most effective tools included social media sites like Twitter and Facebook and feedback collection tools like surveys and polls.

Recommendations regarding social media

Source date: 2011

Participants who used social media provided five primary recommendations.

1. "*If it works for you, use it*"
2. Consider the culture of your company and the audience you are trying to reach before considering the use of Web 2.0 and social networking tools
3. Dedicate someone to be responsible for monitoring and responding to postings, emails or other communications
4. Determine how you want to use the application before using it
5. Use a variety of tools and methods

Communication vehicles

Participants used a variety of communication methods during their change projects. Below is a comprehensive list of communication vehicles identified by participants in the 2003, 2005, 2007 and 2011 benchmarking studies.

Articles in industry journals

Banners

Billboards

Blogs

Booklets

Branded promotional materials

Briefings

Brochures

Brown bag meetings

Bulletin boards

Bulletins

Café meetings

Cafeteria postings

Calendar of events

Cascading communications

Celebration events

Change agent networks

Charts/graphs to show progress

Circulars

Coffee mornings

Communication toolkits

Conversations

Demonstrations

Department meetings

Desk drops

Documents

Electronic billboards/plasma screens

Email

Executive messages

Executive presentations

Face-to-face interactions

Fact sheets

Faxes

Fliers

Focus groups

Forums

Frequently Asked Questions (FAQs)

Gallery walks

Giveaways

Group meetings

Hallway conversations

Help desk

Industrial theater

Information fairs

Informational meetings

Internal messaging systems

Interviews

Intranet sites

Intranet pop-ups

Kickoff events

Leadership meetings

Leaflets

Lectures

Letters

Lunch and learns

Magazines

Mailers

Memos

Networks

Newsletters (corporate)
Newsletters (project)
One-on-one meetings
Online content management systems
Online training
Organizational meetings
Pamphlets
Pay stub inserts
Performance reviews
Physical mailings
Podcasts
Posters
Presentation aids and outlines
Presentations
Project fairs
Question and Answer (Q&A) sessions
Rallies
Reader boards
Recognition packages
Road shows
Roundtables
Site visits
Skits
Social media
Stakeholder meetings
Status reports
Storyboards
Success stories
Surveys
Targeted emails
Team meetings
Teleconferences
Testimonials
Text messages
Town hall meetings
Tradeshows
Training courses
TV displays
Video conferences
Videos
Virtual meetings
Voicemail messages
Walk-arounds
Webcasts
Webinars
Websites
Wikis
Word of mouth
Workshops

Training

Role of change management team in project-specific training

Source date: 2013

Participants in the 2013 study described the role of the change management resource or team regarding project-specific training.

1. **Design**
   The change management resource was either the chief designer or a member of the team that designed necessary training for the project. This role included everything from leading the team to advising training consultants brought in to deploy training.
2. **Training providers and support**
   As trainers and facilitators, the change management team was responsible for delivery of a training program. The team also served as post-training coaches and provided support.
3. **Start-to-end accountability**
   The change management resource was responsible for all aspects of design, development and deployment of project training, including identifying necessary audiences for training, doing training-needs analyses, delivering training and monitoring the effectiveness of a program.
4. **Needs analysis**
   Change management resources were responsible for identifying impacted groups and required skills that needed to be addressed. They were also responsible for identifying gaps in current employee skills in comparison to the skills that would be required during implementation.
5. **Logistics**
   Participants responded that the change management resource was responsible for the logistics of training sessions. Tasks included scheduling and organizing training sessions and locations.

Other roles included:

- **Communicating about the training session**
  The change management resource was responsible for crafting messages to build awareness and desire ahead of training. These messages were commonly handed to sponsors and managers who then delivered messages to impacted groups.
- **Developing training guides**
  Change management resources created training guides for the course and job aids as references for employees before and after training.

Attributes of top tier project-specific training

Participants identified attributes of top-tier, project-specific training.

1. **Program design**
   Participants identified a variety of factors that should be addressed when designing training programs. The majority of responses cited role-specific training as the most important factor. Other factors included use of multiple training mediums, high-quality materials, clearly defined outcomes and approaches, a focus on process and measurable success.
2. **Program delivery**
   Participants also indicated that delivery of training programs contributed to the quality of programs. Timing of programs, both in terms of when programs were delivered and how long they lasted, was mentioned nearly twice as often as other elements of delivery. Additional elements included having quality instructors or facilitators, engaging delivery and use of adult learning methods.

3. **Accessibility**
   Participants specified the way programs were accessed. The majority of responses cited hands-on, practical applications as the most effective method of access to training. Managers and supervisors had to be supportive of training to be successful. Online, on-demand tools were also prominent among responses.

Primary vehicles used to train employees

Source date: 2013

Participants in the 2013 study specified which of the following vehicles were used to deliver project-specific training:

- Face-to-face training
- Web-based or online training
- On-the-job training
- Self-paced training

Figure 8.9 shows the percentage of participants that reported on project-specific training that used each of the vehicles. Face-to-face training was the most prevalent, reported by more than 90% of participants.

Figure 8.9 – Training vehicles used

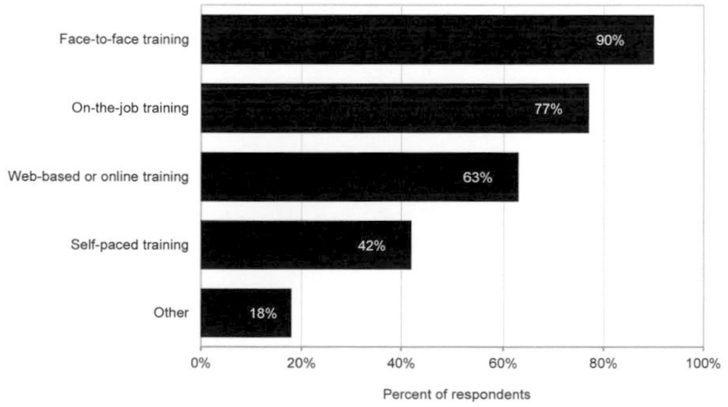

Editor's note: Participants were able to select multiple responses, resulting in a total of more than 100%.

Other vehicles for delivering project-specific training included:

- Handouts, reference materials, Frequently Asked Questions (FAQ) sheets and job aids
- Online support, videos, help screens and desktop tools
- Coaching, mentoring and super-user support
- Workshops, meetings and conferences
- Simulation

Participants estimated the percentage of total training that was delivered through each of the vehicles (Figure 8.10). On average, 45% of training was delivered face-to-face, and self-paced training comprised the smallest percentage at 9%.

Figure 8.10 – Average of total training delivered through each vehicle

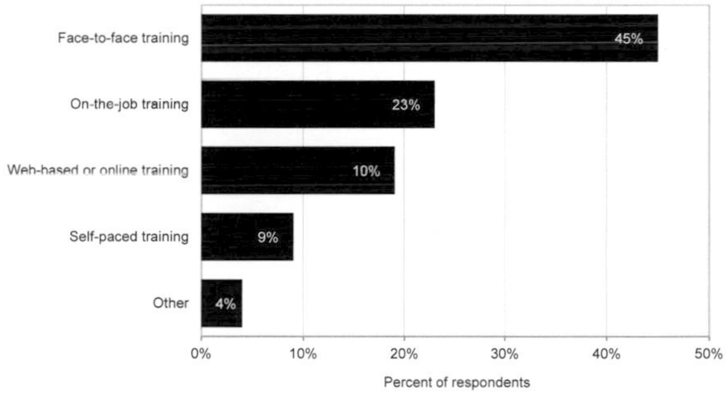

Percentage of impacted employees that received project-specific training

Participants reported on the percentage of impacted employees that received project-specific training. Nearly half of participants said that 75% or more of impacted employees received training (Figure 8.11).

Figure 8.11 – Percentage of impacted employees that received training

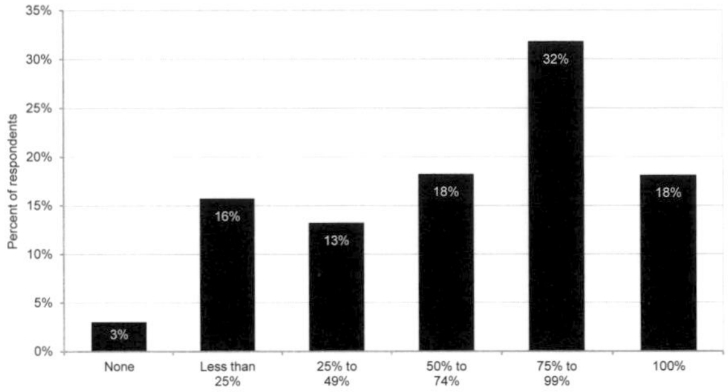

When training was delivered

Participants identified the point during the project lifecycle at which training was delivered. Figure 8.12 shows the overall percentage of participants that reported delivering training at project initiation, planning, design, implementation and closure. Overwhelmingly, project implementation was the most common stage for delivering training.

Figure 8.12 – Stages at which project training was delivered

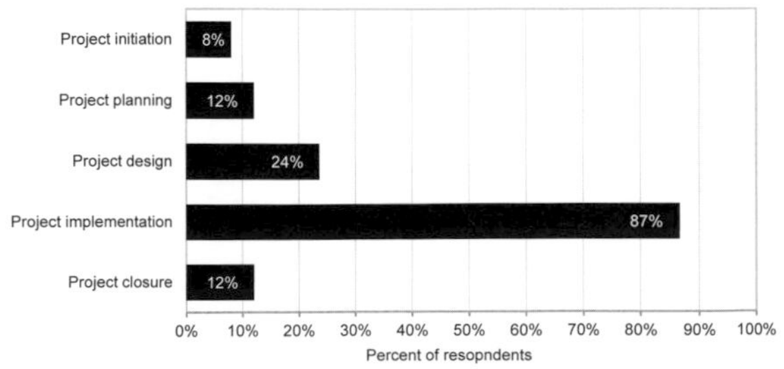

Editor's note: Participants were able to select multiple responses, resulting in a total of more than 100%.

Figure 8.13 shows the number of stages during which participants reported delivering training. Seventy-three percent of participants reported delivering training during only one stage in the project lifecycle.

Figure 8.13 – Number of stages at which project training was delivered

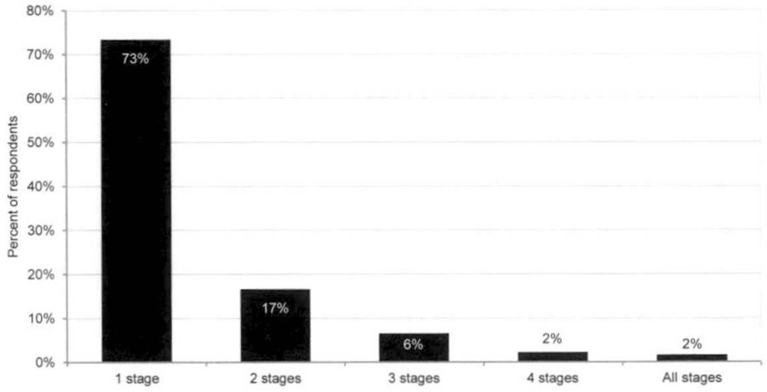

For those who delivered training during only one stage, 83% delivered training during implementation, followed by 7% during design and 5% during planning.

The remaining 27% of participants reported delivering project-specific training at more than one point during a project's lifecycle.

Table 8.14 shows the most common stages at which training was delivered when it was delivered two, three and four times throughout a project's lifecycle. Fewer than 2% of participants reported that training was delivered during all five stages of the project lifecycle.

Table 8.14 – Project stage combinations when training was delivered at more than one stage

	Of the 17% that delivered training at two stages:		Of the 6% that delivered training at three stages:		Of the 2% that delivered training at four stages:
	50%	34%	46%	32%	76%
Initiation					●
Planning				●	●
Design	●		●	●	●
Implementation	●	●	●	●	●
Closure		●	●		

Critical success factors on project-specific training

Participants identified critical success factors for project-specific training. Six factors were noted. The top factor was noted more than twice as often as the other five.

1. **Planning/design**
   Participants found that preparation and design was a primary contributor to successful training, including incorporation of training needs assessments, audience customization and proactive resistance management. Participants also identified that involvement of the impacted audience during development of training was also an important success factor.
2. **Timing**
   The second most frequent factor was timing, timeliness or delivering training just-in-time as key contributors to the success of a training session. Adding the availability of training resources and flexibility into the training schedule had a direct impact on the effectiveness of project-specific training.
3. **Ability and measurement**
   Participants determined success by measuring the demonstration of adoption and usage. They cited management observation, post-training surveys, exams, monitoring support sites and team usage.
4. **Awareness and desire**
   Participants also identified the importance of pre-training approaches. Participants noted higher audience engagement when information was provided ahead of time regarding training requirements, how it related to a change and what was expected of them during training. Additional information was mentioned concerning training schedules, locations and durations.
5. **Trainee support**
   Forms of support were noted at the leadership, management, peer and project team levels. Support was conducted through various modes such as intranet, peer-to-peer coaching, consistent leadership messaging, one-on-one discussions and Questions and Answers (Q&As).
6. **Training approach**
   Having an engaging or hands-on approach to training was an additional factor participants identified. Providing trainees an immediate opportunity to practice and apply what they learned aided in the success of training. Although a blended approach to training was mentioned, many emphasized incorporating hands-on activities for the immediate reinforcement of training.

Evaluating effectiveness of project-specific training

Participants in the 2015 study shared how they evaluated the effectiveness of project-specific training.

1. **Surveys**
   Participants cited giving surveys to employees and sponsors as a way to gauge training effectiveness. These surveys came in the form of training and competency questionnaires and end-user surveys.
2. **Level of adoption**
   Employees were monitored to assess whether new processes had been learned and implemented. The number of errors and help calls were recorded to check if metrics indicating lack of adoption or proficiency decreased after training.
3. **Assessments**
   Many participants reported giving their employees readiness assessments before and after training to gauge how effective project training had been and how prepared employees were for the change.
4. **Overall project feedback**
   Participants cited a need to gather feedback from employees, sponsors and end users on the project as a whole. Feedback was gathered using company forums, one-on-one meetings and group discussions.

Resistance management

Identifying resistance

Participants in the 2015 study indicated how they identified change resistance.

1. **Measurement tools**
   Participants used a number of measurement tools designed to identify resistance. These included surveys, assessments, impact indexes, impact maps, interviews and others. Participants employed these tools continuously throughout the change initiative.
2. **Soft measurement**
   Participants reported a number of soft skill measurements. These included face-to-face communication, feedback forums, asking questions and engaging in dialogue. Participants stressed the importance of speaking directly with impacted groups about their experience of the change, as assumptions could be wrong.
3. **Building in resistance measures**
   Participants reported planning for times and methods of measuring resistance throughout the change project. Participants planned when they would employ their resistance measure and observe resistance throughout the project.
4. **Observation**
   Participants consistently reported the need to observe impacted groups throughout the process. Participants expected resistance to the change and were on the lookout for indictors in impacted groups.

When resistance was encountered by project stage

Source date: 2013

Participants reported stages during which they experienced resistance. Figure 8.15 shows that very few participants (between 2% and 17%) experienced no resistance at any given stage. At least half of participants experienced little or some resistance during each point in the project's lifecycle. The most significant resistance arose during implementation, when nearly 40% of participants reported experiencing much or significant resistance.

Figure 8.15 – Resistance during each stage of the project lifecycle

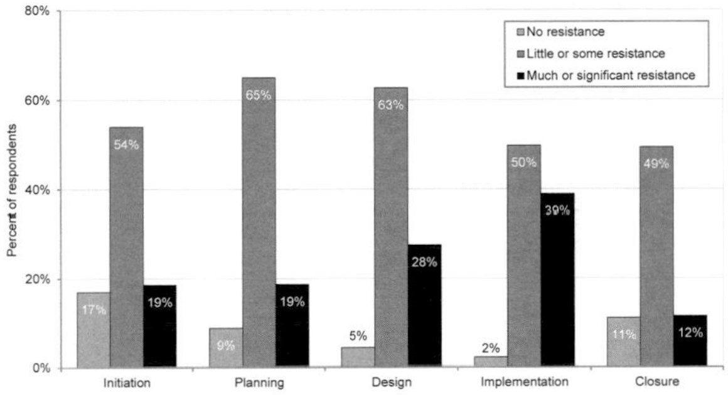

Editor's note: Phase totals do not equal 100% because "N/A" responses were not included.

When resistance was encountered by project event and timing

Source date: 2013

Participants identified events and times during the project that caused the most resistance. Participants who identified an event or instance that resulted in the most resistance commonly said it occurred after communicating about the change and delivering training sessions. Other events that caused resistance were:

- Project teams moving forward without input from impacted groups
- When impacted groups realized the degree of impact
- When restructuring of impacted groups was announced

Most resistant group

Participants in the 2015 study identified groups from which they experienced the most resistance (Figure 8.16). As in previous studies, middle-level managers were identified as the most resistant group by nearly half of participants, followed by frontline employees and senior supervisors.

Figure 8.16 – Most resistant groups

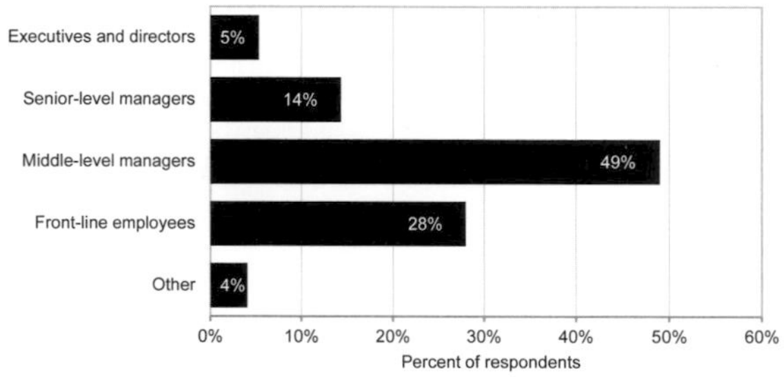

Primary reasons employees resisted change

Participants in the 2015 study identified primary reasons employees resisted change. Five primary reasons were cited as the source of resistance from frontline employees.

1. **Lack of awareness**
   Participants cited lack of awareness of the reason for the change as the primary source of employee resistance. This lack was caused by failure to communicate details of a change to employees. Participants stated that resistance occurred when employees could not answer the question "what's in it for me?" (WIIFM)
2. **Change specific resistance**
   Participants noted many sources of resistance that came from change. The most common responses included an increase in workload by added process steps, changes to job roles and deployment of technology. Other notable sources included lack of involvement by employees, lack of incentives and increases to accountability. It was common that frontline employees simply did not like the change or did not agree with the solution that was deployed.
3. **Resistance due to change saturation**
   Change saturation was reported by participants as a major source of resistance among employees. Many participants cited an overwhelming number of current changes, along with previous failures during project implementation as sources of resistance among frontline employees.
4. **Fear**
   Participants indicated that fear was a significant source of resistance. Although fear of job loss remained the most significant concern for frontline employees, other responses included fear of uncertainty in the future and of losing power, status, influence or compensation.
5. **Lack of support from management or leadership**
   Participants indicated that managers and direct supervisors impacted resistance. Responses included concerns that leadership would not be good role models for the change or that direct supervisors did not support the change. Lack of trust in the executive leadership by employees created resistance to change, citing flavor-of-the-month projects as disconnected with the needs of employees and organization.

Participants indicated that some changes caused resistance simply because something was changing. Comfort with the status quo was frequently cited as a contributing factor to resistance. Regardless of the change or how it was managed, organizations with a culture of resistance would experience resistance to change.

Avoidable employee resistance

Participants in the 2015 study indicated how much they felt that the employee resistance they experienced could have been avoided with effective change management (Figure 8.17). Results from the 2015 study are similar to findings from the 2013 and 2011 studies. A slight jump in resistance that was identified as avoidable occurred when compared to the 2013 findings; 52% of participants indicated that more than half of the resistance they experienced could have been avoided, in comparison to 44% in the 2013 study.

Figure 8.17 – Percentage of employee resistance seen as avoidable

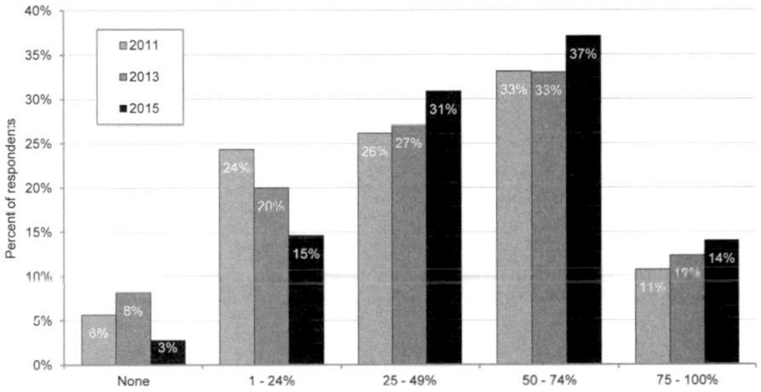

Proactive steps for avoiding or preventing resistance from employees

Participants provided the most effective steps for proactively avoiding or preventing employee resistance. Participants identified three courses of action as the most successful tactics for preventing resistance.

1. **Communications**
   Participants most frequently stated that communication was required to avoid or prevent employee resistance. Responses highlighted two key elements of communication:
   - **Content**
     Participants specified content areas including "what's in it for me?" (WIIFM), setting clear expectations, solicitation of feedback and consistent messaging. Participants also indicated communication should start early, be multi-directional and come through a variety of media from appropriate senders.
   - **Honesty**
     Communication must be honest, genuine, transparent and trustworthy to be effective at avoiding or preventing resistance.
2. **Engagement**
   Participants reported that engaging employees in development of solutions and strategies was effective at avoiding resistance. Participants also identified sponsors, managers, change champions and key influencers as important audiences for engagement that should be leveraged to sponsor change initiatives or coach employees.
3. **Application of a methodology**
   Participants also stated that use of change management practices aided in avoiding or preventing employee resistance. These practices included anticipating resistance and planning accordingly, developing quality training programs and use of formal change management strategies such as ADKAR®. Participants specified that these strategies are best executed face-to-face supported by reinforcement activities.

Advice for dealing with employee resistance

Participants in the 2015 study shared the advice they would give to a new change management practitioner for dealing with employee resistance.

1. **Communicate**
   Communication was identified more than three times more frequently than other responses. Respondents emphasized the importance of listening, avoiding responding in an overly defensive manner, personalizing both the content and style of communications and communicating honestly and transparently.

2. **Develop a plan to address resistance**
Expecting resistance and preparing for it by developing a well-thought out plan aids in dealing with resistance. Elements of an appropriate plan include early deployment, demonstrating the benefits of change, training and education plans and attention to technology issues associated with change.
3. **Understand both the change and the resistance fully**
Respondents emphasized the importance of understanding the root cause of resistance; resistance frequently grew out of legitimate and important problems/concerns that were not necessarily visible from the perspective of a change management practitioner. Tactics for gaining understanding of change or resistance included conducting readiness or adoption assessments, creating the time and space necessary for change and setting realistic expectations about change.
4. **Engage and support leadership**
Participants frequently identified leadership as a key element and necessary resource during change; engaging and supporting leadership was important for dealing with employee resistance. Many participants felt it was the job of leadership, not change management practitioners, to set an example for employees and deal with resistance. Engaging managers, supervisors and executives in change accomplished this. These efforts were supplemented by providing support for leadership in the form of training and guidance regarding change management.
5. **Encourage individual stakeholder engagement**
Techniques used to further this goal included studying stakeholder groups to understand them and selling individual benefits of change, particularly by emphasizing "what's in it for me?" (WIIFM). Encouraging stakeholder engagement at the individual level was a valuable tool for addressing resistance because engaging with change on a person-by-person basis allowed for direct input by employees and personalized approaches to change.

Several other important pieces of advice were:

1. **Be patient**
Participants noted the importance of patience when dealing with resistance. Employees need an appropriate amount of time to adjust to changes, and initially giving them this time decreases resistance.
2. **Convert strongest resisters, make them leaders**
Several participants explained that targeting the strongest resisters for conversion could be a valuable technique for addressing wide-spread resistance. Once converted, these former resistance leaders could be seen as change champions and an endorsement of a change by the rest of the organization.
3. **Focus on early adopters, not hardcore resisters**
Conversely, other participants recommended concentrating on early adopters instead of the hardcore resisters. In some situations, strong and enthusiastic early adopters could be seen as a quick win and immediate proof of the viability of a change; focusing on hardcore resisters was a waste of time and energy when there were already people in a position to act as change champions within the organization.

Primary reasons managers resisted change

Participants identified five primary reasons managers resisted change.

1. **Organizational culture**
Participants reported that organizational culture was a primary cause of resistance. Specifics included risk-averse cultures, past negative experience with change, groupism versus organizational dedication and issues such as mistrust between departments and reporting levels. In cultures devoid of sponsorship in which leaders and direct supervisors failed to support them, managers felt undermined.

2. **Lack of awareness and knowledge about change**
Lack of knowledge about what a change entailed, lack of information and understanding regarding Return on Investment (ROI) and reasons for change, and lack of knowledge for personal reasons for a change ("what's in it for me?" or WIIFM) were cited as reasons managers resisted change. "*They didn't understand it and/or they didn't get the support they needed. Managers have the greatest challenge as they are in charge of translating the change message from the top to their employees. If they don't understand the change or don't have the support to do it, it makes them more resistant.*"

3. **Lack of buy-in**
There were multiple reasons participants felt that managers did not buy-in to change. Managers:
    - Believed the change would fail or was a bad solution
    - Were comfortable with the status quo
    - Believed it was out of line with company goals as they knew them
    - Did not like what the change entailed or required of them
    - Feared losing control, power or status
    - Did not want increased visibility or accountability

4. **Misalignment of project goals and personal incentives**
Issues on the project management side were consistent reasons for manager resistance including pace of the change, lack of metrics, metrics that did not align with promotion parameters or pay/bonus scales and misaligned incentives. Participants acknowledged that these deterrents or lack of incentives made change unappealing to managers.

5. **Lack of confidence in their own ability to manage people side of change**
A recurring reason cited for managers' resistance had to do with their inability to be a leader of change and facilitate its adoption. They lacked the skills to manage resistance and communicate difficult messages to direct reports.

Avoidable manager resistance

Participants in the 2015 study indicated how much they felt resistance from managers could have been avoided with effective change management (Figure 8.18). Fifty-two percent indicated that more than half of the resistance they experienced could have been avoided. Generally, participants indicated an overall increase in avoidable resistance, as shown in Figure 8.18.

Figure 8.18 – Percentage of manager resistance seen as avoidable

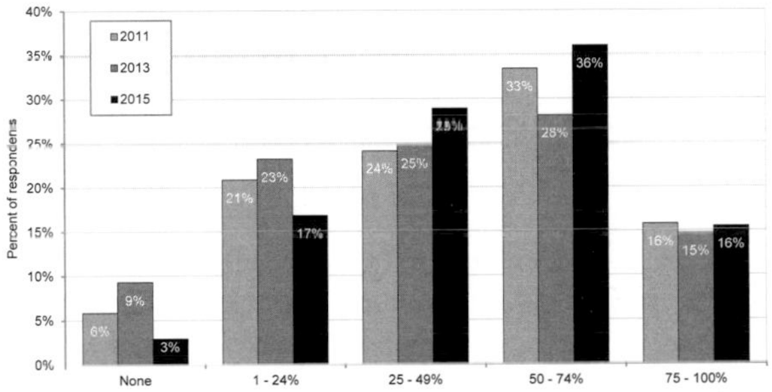

Effective steps for avoiding or preventing manager/supervisor resistance

Participants in the 2015 study identified the steps they took to avoid resistance from managers and supervisors. They specifically indicated which steps were the most effective in mitigating resistance before it surfaced. Participants overwhelmingly reported that communicating with employees was most effective.

1. **Communicate**
Participants said that communicating with managers and supervisors was the most effective way to mitigate resistance before it surfaced. By more than a 2:1 margin,

communicating openly, honestly and timely was the best way to avoid or prevent resistance. Participants stated it was important to ensure that communications were tailored to the audience and to set up feedback mechanisms for managers and supervisors to share their thoughts and feelings about change.

2. **Involve impacted groups**
Engaging impacted groups early in the process helped create a sense of ownership in the project and thus lessened resistance.

3. **Address ADKAR® barriers**
Participants used the Prosci® ADKAR® Model to focus on avoiding resistance. Specific actions for addressing ADKAR® barriers included coaching and training managers and supervisors to use the new solution, having a highly credible sponsor and setting up reinforcement methods throughout the project.

4. **Share the need for change**
An executive sharing the need for change also addressed resistance. Recommendations from participants included explaining why the change was necessary, sharing a vision for the organization's future state and informing people of business drivers.

5. **Engage senior leaders**
Participants recommended engaging direct senior leaders and getting them on board early to advocate change with their direct reports and leveraging senior leaders to meet one-on-one with and influence their direct reports.

Participants also said that showing the benefits of change from the onset helped. They recommended identifying and planning for resistance rather than just letting it surface. In doing so, they had actions in place to address resistance quickly when it occurred. A critical success factor in their proactive resistance management approach was having an active and visible sponsor that employees trusted to lead change.

Ineffective methods of managing resistance

Participants in the 2015 study identified the methods they used to manage resistance that they found to be ineffective.

1. **Ignoring resistance**
Participants said that executives ignoring resistance or pretending it was not a real issue were the most ineffective methods. Participants reported that resistance had negative consequences and leaving any potential resistance unchecked compounded those consequences.

2. **Broadcasting one-way communications**
Having executives send mass emails to the organization highlighting change had little effect on managing resistance. These messages included sending messages that did not target a group or individual but that blanketed the organization as one group. Newsletters, memos and speeches to large groups were also ineffective ways to manage resistance.

3. **Using threats, fear or coercion**
Creating fear around consequences of not adopting the change, putting additional pressures on employees or outright threatening employees if they were resisting change caused resistance to go underground and did little to address it. Problems associated with resistance were still present, but the source of resistance was much harder to identify.

4. **Dictating, mandating or telling people to change**
When executives assumed that telling people to change was sufficient, more resistance to change emerged.

Impacts of using pain and/or fear to manage change

Participants reported on the impact that using of pain and/or fear had on managing resistance. Although some participants reported that they had never used this method, the majority said that using pain and/or fear to manage resistance had an overall negative impact, though a small percentage said it served a valuable purpose during some scenarios.

1. **Negative impact**
   Participants identified four negative outcomes of using pain and/or fear to manage resistance. Firstly, using pain and/or masked resistance, forcing resistance to go underground where it went unaddressed. Secondly, using pain and/or fear led to an increase in absenteeism and lack of employee effectiveness. Thirdly, using pain and/or fear created distrust between employees and change leaders and often led to a decline in morale. Finally, participants cited that using pain and/or fear led to an increase in attrition among impacted groups. As one participant reported, "*The best and brightest are the first to go.*"
2. **Short-term results**
   Participants felt that use of pain and/or fear to manage resistance often got short-term compliance but did not have positive, long-term effects on managing resistance. Pain and/or fear also reduced employee trust and made future projects much less likely to succeed.
3. **Increased resistance**
   The third most common response was that pain and/or fear increased resistance. Participants described lack of employee engagement and a culture of change resistance that stemmed from use of pain and/or fear as a tactic to manage initial resistance.

Participants cited some instances in which using pain and/or fear was useful or effective.

1. **If used to highlight deficiencies of the current state**
   Some participants felt that using pain and/or fear could be an effective technique when it was used to illustrate the pain caused by the current state which could be alleviated by undergoing and participating in change. One participant called it "*the pain or fear of not changing.*"
2. **If applied in a conducive culture**
   Some participants felt that using pain and/or fear could be successful in the right organization and environment. If use of pain and/or fear is the norm for that organization or if that organization's culture embraces tactics of this nature, then the tactics can be effective.
3. **If used as a last resort**
   Participants who felt that using pain and/or fear did not aid with managing resistance in the long-term did not dismiss these tactics. Pain and/or fear could be used as a last resort, employed when the failure of change would bring about worse consequences.

Reinforcement and feedback

Determining whether employees are engaging in change

Source date: 2011

Participants in the 2011 study shared the most effective methods they used to determine whether employees were engaging in change. The top methods were:

1. **Using surveys, assessments and feedback systems to measure engagement**
   Participants used a number of vehicles to collect direct feedback from impacted employees to monitor engagement, including surveys, engagement assessments and formal feedback mechanisms such as dedicated email inboxes, comment drop-boxes and Frequently Asked Question (FAQ) forums.
2. **Observing and interacting informally with change recipients**
   Participants suggested observing change recipients' reactions and responses to change through informal interaction to determine engagement. The informal nature of this method encourages an open, honest view of change engagement.
3. **Monitoring engagement through feedback channels and networks**
   Participants used communication networks and organizational channels including managers, change agents, trainers and Human Resources (HR) to determine overall employee engagement throughout the organization.
4. **Soliciting feedback by creating deliberate opportunities**
   Allotting dedicated opportunities for input and questions from change recipients during events and meetings related to change motivated open, continuous feedback on employee engagement.
5. **Tracking fluctuations in performance**
   Defining and tracking key performance indicators (KPIs) offered evidence of productive engagement regarding change and comparisons with benchmarks and projected outcomes.
6. **Tracking general use of and proficiency with implemented changes**
   Monitoring use of changes and associated procedures indicated engagement in a concrete, evident manner. Including metrics for proficient use of change systems in tracking and documentation clarified the extent of engagement.

Planning for reinforcement and sustainment activities

Those who planned for reinforcement and sustainment reported greater success with projects. Figure 8.19 shows that 68% of participants who planned for reinforcement or sustainment met or exceeded project objectives, in comparison with 42% who did not.

Figure 8.19 – Impact of planning for reinforcement on project success

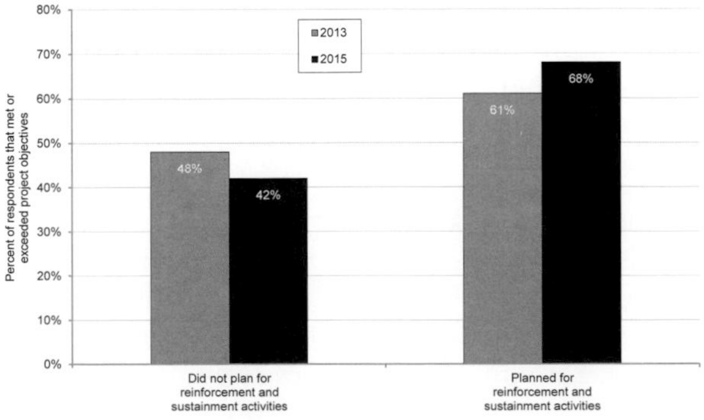

Resourcing for reinforcement and sustainment

Participants indicated whether project resources were allocated to reinforcement and sustainment. Forty-four percent reported that resources were so allocated (Figure 8.20).

Figure 8.20 – Allocated resources to reinforcement and sustainment

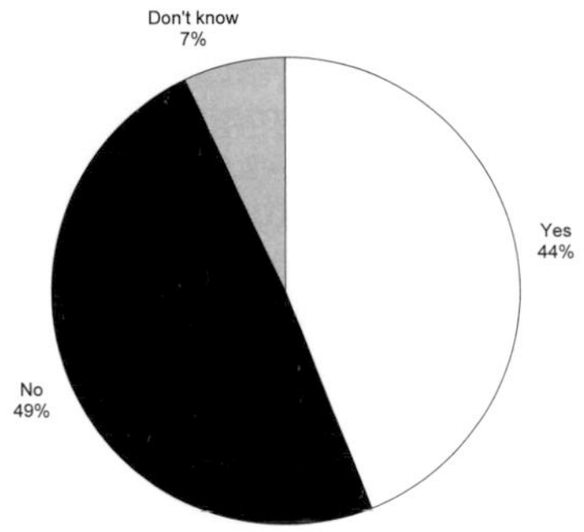

Participants who allocated resources to reinforcement and sustainment reported greater success with projects. Figure 8.21 shows that 60% of participants who allocated resources to reinforcement and sustainment met or exceeded project objectives compared to 53% who did not.

Figure 8.21 – Impact of allocating resources to reinforcement on project success

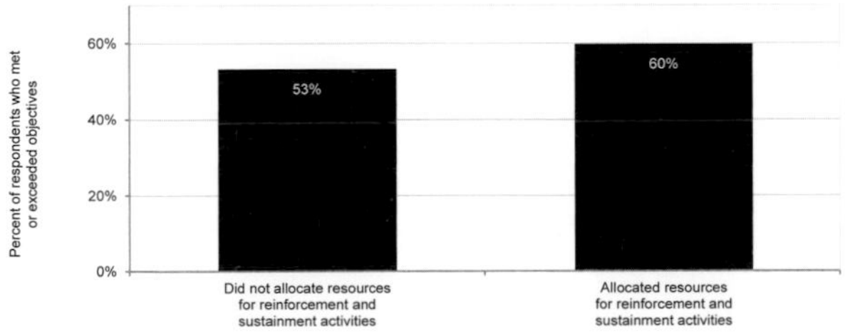

Tactics to reinforce and sustain change

Source date: 2013

Participants identified four tactics used to reinforce and sustain change.

1. **Ongoing and consistent communication**
   Participants highlighted the need for consistent and continuous communication. Communication included updates about project progress, employee follow-ups, benefit realization reports and other messages about change. Participants emphasized the importance of messages delivered by senior leaders.

2. **Support mechanisms**
   Participants identified use of support mechanisms to reinforce and sustain change. Support mechanisms included visible support from leaders, change champions and super users. Participants identified that support mechanisms contributed most to reinforcement when they were available during each stage of change. Participants underscored one-on-one coaching as a way to sustain engagement from impacted groups throughout the project. In some cases, a team created to sustain a project after the go-live date provided support.

3. **Tracking**
   Participants highlighted use of tracking to reinforce and sustain change. Tracking measures included surveys, assessments, progress reports and performance monitoring. Participants used key performance indicators (KPIs) and other performance measures to gauge use of new systems or processes.

4. **Rewards and recognition**
   Participants highlighted use of rewards and recognition as a tactic when reinforcing and sustaining change. Rewards and recognition included celebrating successes (both large and small), rewarding employee buy-in and recognizing individuals impacted by or managing change. Participants underscored the importance of not only rewarding employees for success and project adoption but also showing appreciation for effort from individuals.

Roles in reinforcement and sustainment
Source date: 2013

Participants in the 2013 study identified who was responsible for reinforcement and sustainment activities on their change initiative (Figure 8.22). Half of participants said it was the leader or manager of an impacted group. Just less than 40% reported that the change management resource or team was responsible for this effort.

Figure 8.22 – Role responsible for reinforcement and sustainment

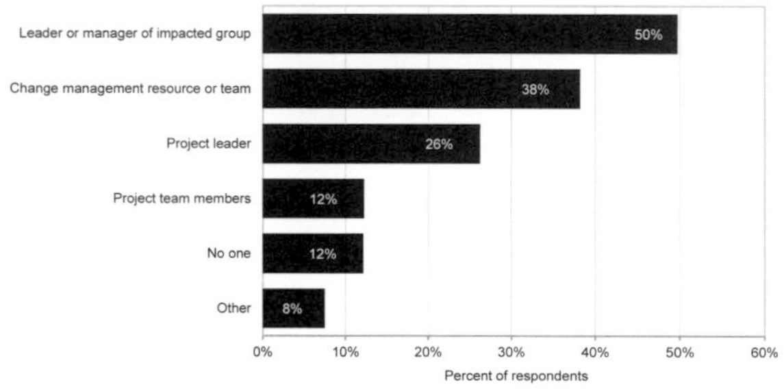

Editor's note: Participants were able to select multiple responses, resulting in a total of more than 100%.

In the 2011 study, participants identified who would be the best provider of reinforcement and recognition. Figure 8.23 shows the groups participants identified as the best providers at both the individual and group levels. Although participants leaned toward the direct supervisor for individual recognition, the primary sponsor or mid-level manager was identified as the best provider of group recognition.

Figure 8.23 – Best provider of reinforcement and recognition

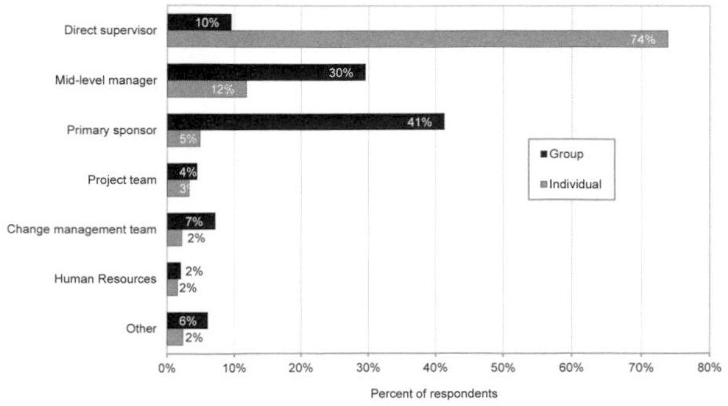

Individual reinforcement
Source date: 2011

2011 study participants identified the most effective ways to reinforce and sustain change at the individual level citing four tactics.

1. **Communicating success**
   Communicate consistently and continuously, including progress updates and short-term successes. Use positive and consistent communications in both one-on-one situations between a supervisor and direct report and with peers in informal settings. Communicate through post-implementation of the project to drive sustained change.
2. **Providing and collecting feedback**
   Ensure that feedback is collected at all levels, and demonstrate that feedback was heard. Address both positive and negative feedback using one-on-one and team meeting settings. Provide honest and helpful feedback to end users during implementation and post-implementation.
3. **Recognizing and rewarding adoption**
   Provide a variety of channels for recognition through both one-on-one and team meetings with direct reports. Acknowledge success of both short-term wins and long-term goal achievement. Show appreciation for effort made by individuals. Celebrate success and offer incentives throughout each phase of change.
4. **Providing on-the-job support**
   Make support mechanisms available during each phase of change. Provide technical and moral support from super users, change champions, leaders and early adopters. Allow for practicing and trial experiences with the future state. Provide job aids, help desks and updated process documentation.

Group reinforcement

Source date: 2011

Participants identified the five most effective ways to reinforce and sustain change at the group level.

1. **Communication**
   Communicate key messages consistently with each group to share status updates and success stories. Share lessons learned, frequently asked questions and success within the team. Make multiple forms of communication available to each group or division.
2. **Recognition**
   Recognize wins at the group level in public, informally and face-to-face. Acknowledge the effort of each team and celebrate positive outcomes. Include recognition and acknowledgement from leadership.
3. **Workshops**
   Deliver workshops, training and group activities that provide a strong, fun learning environment in which individuals can learn from each other while supporting the team as a whole. Offer pre- and post-implementation workshops providing support and follow-ups. Allow groups to participate, share successes, voice opinions and improve collective efforts.
4. **Key performance indicators (KPIs)**
   Use key performance indicators (KPIs) to track and report progress. Record metrics and publish organizational results. Include accountability in job descriptions and create ownership.
5. **Sponsorship**
   Encourage sponsors to share the bigger picture and strategy of the company and to be visible at the group level. Get executive leaders and steering committees to share status updates and offer feedback.

Mistakes to avoid when reinforcing change

When participants were asked to identify which mistakes should be avoided when reinforcing change, the four primary responses were:

1. **Do not forget to plan for reinforcement**
   The top mistake to avoid when reinforcing change was not planning for reinforcement at the beginning of a project. This can be done by ensuring there is a budget and time allotted for reinforcement activities. Do not ignore the importance of reinforcement for project success.
2. **Avoid making decisions based on assumptions**
   Participants also voiced that assumptions should be avoided, including that the work is completed when the project is launched, that employees know their roles and that there is a reinforcement leader.
3. **Avoid unclear communication**
   Provide clear and consistent communication that encourages honest feedback. Take the time to listen to valid concerns from employees. Ensure project managers are on the same page before messages are sent.
4. **Do not forget to follow through**
   Participants reported that it was important to follow a clear plan that leaves no room for backsliding. Follow-through can occur by acknowledging milestones and rewarding demonstrated ability at the individual level.

How reinforcement was handled after project closure

Source date: 2013

Participants reported on the challenge of reinforcing change after project closure. The following elements for reinforcing and sustaining change after project closure were identified.

1. **Ongoing communication**
   Continuous and ongoing communication was the top-cited tactic for reinforcing and sustaining change after a project closed.

Participants stressed the importance of communicating through various avenues and highlighting the benefits and positive effects of change to impacted employees. Encouraging and supporting two-way communication by gathering feedback and following up with employees was critical.

2. **Support systems**
   Participants noted that creating an environment of support was instrumental to reinforcing and sustaining change after project closure. Support systems included help desks, management support systems and tailored support activities. Some tailored activities included post-implementation workshops and targeted events that encouraged impacted groups to participate, share success stories and voice opinions on how a project went. Management support systems involved one-on-one coaching from supervisors, help centers and super user communities.

3. **Transition plan**
   Participants highlighted the importance of having a transition plan. For some projects, a team established after a project closed executed the transition plan. Key responsibilities of the team included following up with impacted groups, creating documentation processes for employees and assigning clear and consistent staff responsibilities after a project closed.

Using performance appraisals and measures to encourage adoption

Source date: 2013

Participants in the 2013 study shared how they used performance appraisals and measures to encourage change adoption. The top three methods were:

1. **Embedded new behaviors in performance appraisals**
   Participants tied desired behaviors to employees' individual performance goals and evaluations. Integrating the two provided greater incentives for employees to carry out new behaviors required by change.

2. **Aligned to project goals**
   Participants also embedded project goals into performance appraisals and measures. Goals specific to change were embedded in overarching annual goals and existing key performance indicators (KPIs). KPIs specific to change were incorporated into performance plans for managers and supervisors.

3. **Established incentive programs**
   Rewards and recognition were presented as possibilities if performance appraisals were positive allowing participants to incentivize employees to adopt change.

Participants in the 2007 study indicated that performance appraisals, which link business goals to individual performance, enhance change adoption by:

- **Clarifying roles and expectations for every employee**
  Goals specific to and focused on individual contributions remove uncertainty and provide the necessary structure for employees to support new business objectives. "*Structure drives behavior, so make sure how people are measured and rewarded supports the strategy and expected behaviors of the company.*"

- **Rewarding change adopters in an equitable manner**
  Employees quickly recognize value placed on change when tied to pay. Incentives that go hand-in-hand with performance increase the likelihood of positive outcomes.

- **Creating an accountability model**
  Goals tied to performance and business objectives allow managers to check, correct and celebrate wins along the way.

- **Identifying and managing resistance**
  Performance appraisals address and offer consequences for non-compliance.

In addition to using performance appraisals to reinforce change, more than half of 2007 participants cited using new job descriptions as an additional mechanism to reinforce change.

Change readiness

Defining change readiness

Participants in the 2015 study identified how they defined change readiness within their organization. The top five responses were:

1. **Organizational preparedness**
   Respondents identified various facets of organizational preparedness as criteria for defining change readiness. Examples included change infrastructure in place, training completed, resources for change readily available, sponsor committed to change and clear objectives/plans in place for the change.
2. **Open attitudes toward change from the organization**
   The definition of change readiness also included attitudes the organization held toward change. Change readiness was defined by an attitude of receptiveness toward change and willingness to change and successful management of employee resistance.
3. **Individual preparedness**
   Respondents identified individual preparedness as a factor used to define change readiness. Individual preparedness was frequently defined as individuals being ready, willing and able to implement change. A number of respondents noted that the Prosci® ADKAR® criteria were helpful tools to define and measure individual preparedness for change.
4. **Effective communication regarding the upcoming change**
   Effective communication regarding change was noted as an important factor to define change readiness. Communication ideally results in a high degree of understanding of both the nature of and the need for change and change management generally. One participant reported, "*Change readiness is the extent to which an individual is likely to understand, accept and implement a particular set of changes.*"
5. **Smooth implementation of change**
   Some respondents identified success or ease of implementation as criteria for defining change readiness. This was characterized by adoption of change resulting in minimal business impacts, high competency when implementing change or the technical readiness of the system.

Readiness evaluation

Source date: 2013

Forty-three percent of participants reported that their organizations evaluated general readiness for change (Figure 8.24).

Figure 8.24 – Organization evaluated general readiness for change

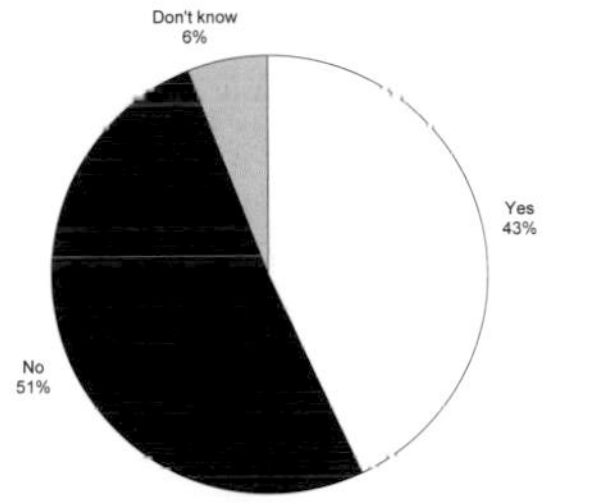

However, more than 50% evaluated organizational readiness for their specific change (Figure 8.25).

Figure 8.25 – Evaluated change readiness on particular projects

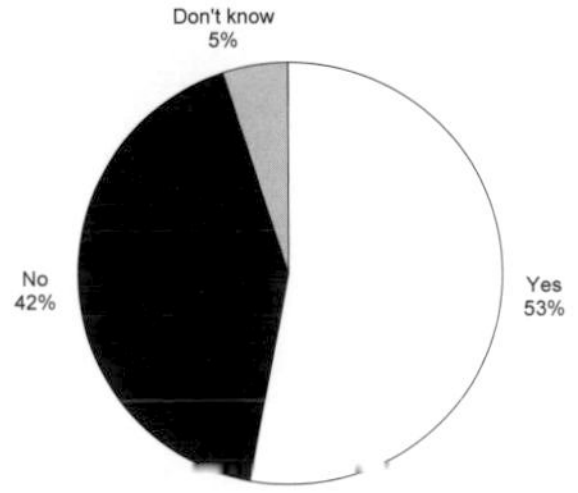

Assessing change readiness

Participants in the 2015 study described the primary methods used to assess their organization's change readiness. The top responses were similar to findings from the 2011 study.

1. **Written assessments and surveys**
   Participants favored using written assessments and surveys to identify change readiness. Participants used a variety of tools to gather information on the change readiness of their organization including readiness assessment, business impact assessment, change characteristics assessment, organizational attributes assessment, gap analysis, perception survey, stakeholder analysis and change portfolio assessment.
2. **Meetings and trainings**
   Participants cited meetings and trainings as means of identifying their organization's change readiness. At these events, key stakeholders were communicated with to ensure change goals were aligned and to address issues from different levels of the organization.
3. **Interviews**
   Participants reported that interviews with senior leaders, managers and end users were an effective way to gauge their organization's change readiness. Interviews also had the benefit of allowing one-on-one interactions with these groups. Informal, confidential discussions provided insights on the readiness of the change and surfaced potential obstacles or resistance.

Additional means of readiness identification included:

- **Sponsor determination** – Executives and senior leaders solely determined the change readiness in the organization
- **Previous change experience** – Participants identified change readiness based on previous change management experience
- **Nothing** – A few participants indicated that their organization did not perform any actions to identify the level of change readiness

Evaluating readiness at individual and group levels

Source date: 2013

In comparison to more than half of participants in the 2013 study who evaluated organizational readiness for their change initiatives, only one in three participants evaluated readiness at the individual level (Figure 8.26).

Figure 8.26 – Evaluated change readiness at the individual level

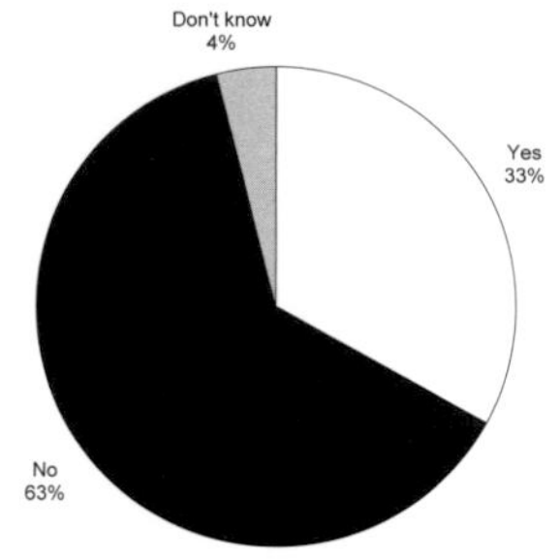

The 33% of participants who evaluated individual readiness explained their considerations and methods for evaluating an individual's readiness for change.

1. **Assessed individual drivers**
   Mentioned over three times more frequently than other factors, individual drivers of change included:
   - Individual awareness of the need for change
   - Individual understanding of what change was occurring and how the change was going to affect them and their role in the organization
   - Individual knowledge and skills required to operate in the new environment and the gap between skills and knowledge used in the current environment

- Individual desire to participate in and embrace change
- Personal circumstances that might influence change readiness

2. **Assessed the support network**
Participants evaluated employees' support networks to ensure employees could approach their managers with questions and concerns regarding change. Participants evaluated sponsorship to ensure sponsors were prepared to help with questions and concerns.

Additional factors included:

- Communication effectiveness
- Personality of the individual
- Training needs
- Individual change history

Participants also shared methods used to evaluate individual readiness factors. The majority of participants identified the Prosci® ADKAR® Model as a foundation for evaluation. Participants employed a variety of general end-user readiness assessments. Other methods included:

- Stakeholder analysis
- One-on-one meetings with managers
- Individual feedback
- A change agent network
- Surveys
- Personality assessments

PM AND CM INTEGRATION

THE POWER OF COMPLEMENTARY DISCIPLINES WORKING IN PARTNERSHIP TOWARD A COMMON OBJECTIVE

SUMMARY

Leading organizations are effectively executing an intentional integration of change management and project management. This chapter includes benchmarking data on the prevalence and degree of integration, segmented by region and organization size. Learn how practitioners are integrating change management and project management along the dimensions of people, processes and tools. Together with your counterparts in project management, tailor a research-based integration plan to leverage the power of these two crucial disciplines working in tandem to produce results and outcomes.

HIGHLIGHT

Over three-quarters of participants (77%) integrated change management and project management in some way.

Project and change management integration on projects

Seventy-seven percent of participants in the 2015 study integrated change management and project management (Figure 9.1).

Figure 9.1 – Integrated change management and project management

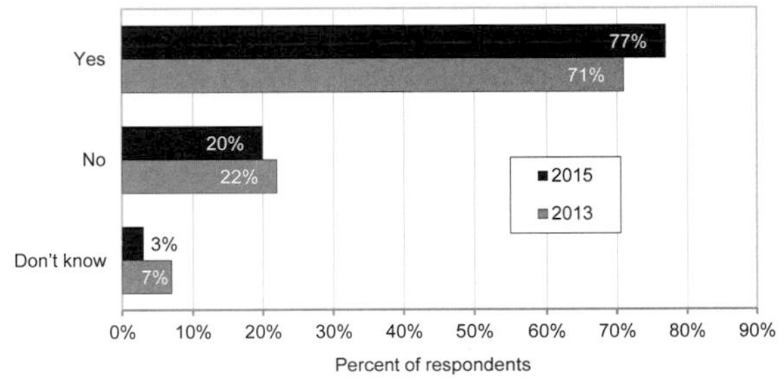

Figure 9.3 shows segmentation on integration by industry. Results are shown relative to the sample average of 77%.

Figure 9.3 – Integrated change management and project management by industry

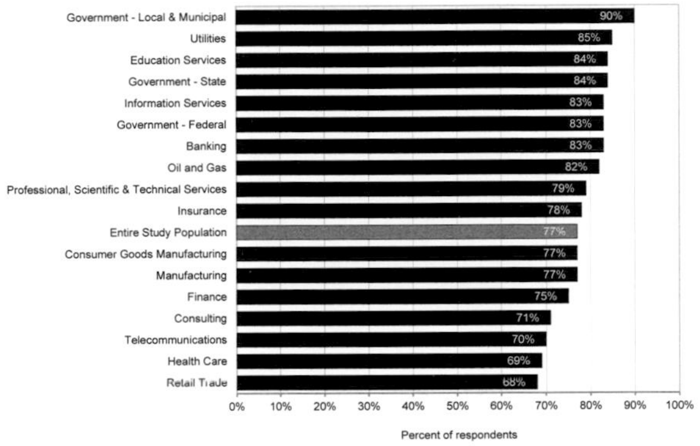

Prevalence of integration

Figure 9.2 presents segmentation on integration by region. Results are shown relative to the entire sample average of 77%. Respondents from Africa, Canada, Australia and New Zealand, the Middle East and the United States reported levels of integration higher than the overall average.

Figure 9.2 – Integrated change management and project management by region

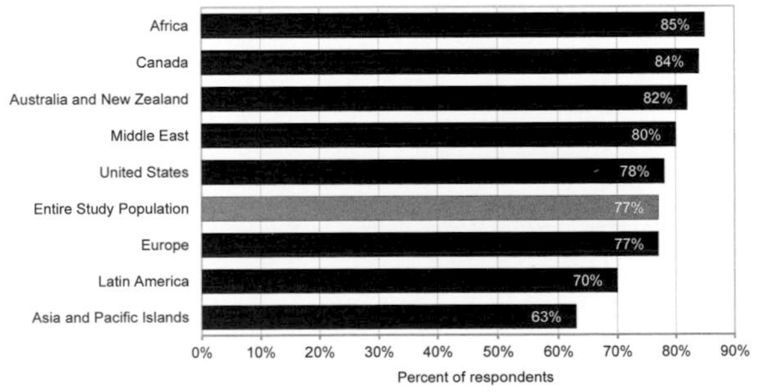

Figures 9.4 and 9.5 present further segmentation on integration by organization size, both annual revenue and number of employees.

Figure 9.4 – Integrated change management and project management by annual revenue

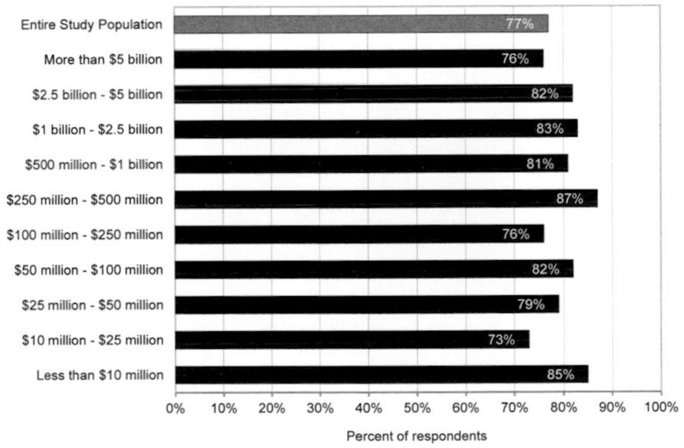

Figure 9.5 – Integrated change management and project management by number of employees

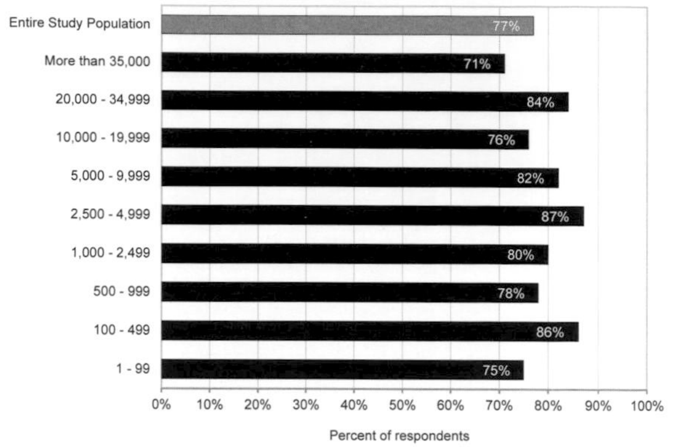

Impact of integration

Participants who integrated project and change management reported meeting or exceeding project objectives more than those who did not. Figure 9.6 shows that 58% of participants who integrated project and change management met or exceeded project objectives compared to only 42% who did not.

Figure 9.6 – Impact of integration on meeting objectives

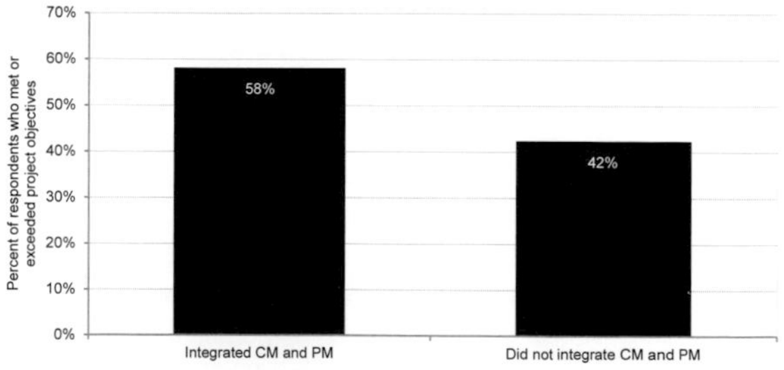

Participants who integrated project management and change management reported higher change management effectiveness compared to participants who did not integrate. Figure 9.7 shows that 60% of participants who integrated also rated the effectiveness of their change management as *good* or *excellent* compared to only 33% of participants who did not.

Figure 9.7 – Impact of integration on change management effectiveness

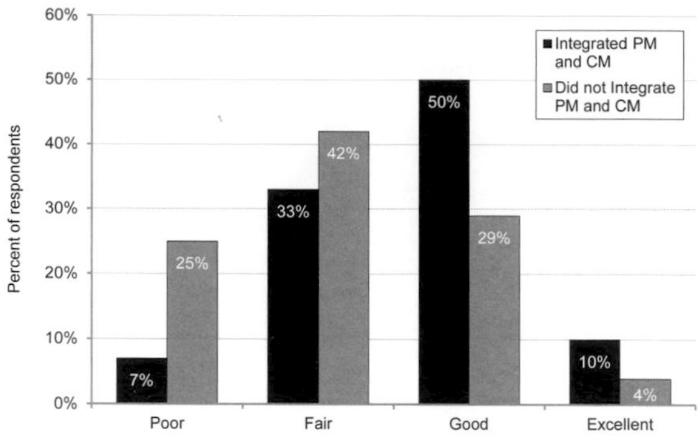

Steps to integrate project and change management

Source date: 2013

Participants who integrated project and change management explained general steps they took to do so.

1. **Add change management to the project plan** Integration occurred by augmenting a project plan with change management and including change management milestones. Activities that were added included building communication plans, designing reinforcement plans, gaining sponsor support and conducting employee interviews.
2. **Work collaboratively with the project team** Project and change management teams shared progress reports and project updates and communicated regularly with team leaders to carry out collaboration. Tasks, such as conducting impact analyses and creating work breakdown structures, were conducted collaboratively between teams. Change practitioners also participated in meetings that were traditionally specific to project management including project team, status and decision-making meetings. Informal and ad hoc meetings also encouraged collaboration.
3. **Align change plans with project plans** Change plans were aligned with existing project plans. Participants coordinated change management timelines, work streams and critical project milestones with project

management requirements. Plans were aligned at team meetings or to accord with work breakdown structures.

4. **Combine or assign responsibilities and roles**
Change management responsibilities were added to the project team. Similarly, participants assigned change management activities to project team members. Participants combined leader roles, assigning accountability for both functions to a single resource. Others assigned a dedicated change practitioner to the project team to facilitate integration.

5. **Provide change management training to project team**
Project teams were trained in change management principles and concepts. Key project management resources were certified in change management, not only to build their own capabilities in integration, but also to encourage knowledge dissemination across their teams.

Advice on integrating change and project management

Participants in the 2015 study identified what advice they would give to a change practitioner working to integrate project and change management.

1. **Use a structured plan**
Participants identified use of clearly structured integration plans as crucial when integrating project and change management. Examples include using a simple and consistent plan, engaging early at the initiation of the project, conducting impact assessments and incorporating adequate time and other resources into the integration plan.

2. **Communicate**
Respondents frequently noted the importance of clear and frequent communication during an integration project. The most commonly identified communication strategy involved clear and explicit role definition. Many participants felt this was necessary for successful integration. Respondents also identified face-to-face communication as a highly effective technique and "[using] *data to back up your activities,*" particularly when communicating the benefits of integration to leadership within the organization.

3. **Build a relationship**
Participants identified a patient and persistent attitude as key to building these relationships. Techniques included leveraging existing or planned activities as opportunities to integrate, highlighting the co-dependent "two-sides-of-the-same-coin" nature of the relationship between project and change management, and integrating change management practitioners into the project management team and activities.

4. **Emphasize the benefits of change management**
Participants noted that emphasizing and explaining the benefits of both change management and integration was helpful to increasing support for the project and reducing resistance to integration. Participants suggested explaining the necessity of change management and using data-backed arguments to prove these points.

5. **Educate and train**
Participants identified education and training as crucial tools when working on a project that integrates project and change management. Education was needed for both change and project management teams regarding each other's techniques and objectives.

6. **Secure sponsorship**
Respondents noted the importance of executive support and support from influential adopters and leaders of project management teams.

Reasons for integrating project and change management

Source date: 2013

The participants who integrated change and project management provided their reasons for doing so.

1. **Viewed integration as critical to success**
   The largest group of participants who integrated change and project management did so because the organization viewed it as necessary and critical to success.
2. **Requested by project managers or other influential individuals**
   Project and change management were integrated at the request of a project manager or another influential leader. Project managers who supported change management involvement, or who were experienced in change management themselves, was the most common group to make this request. Senior executives, external consultants and clients also pushed for integration.
3. **Experience with or without integration**
   The success of past projects that integrated project and change management encouraged participants to integrate again. Failure of projects that lacked integration also motivated participants to integrate. Past project plans that were focused only technically and did not consider employee adoption were linked to project failures. As a reaction, change management was integrated to address adoption, coordinate communications and manage resistance. Integration also made it easier for work teams to assign accountability.
4. **Organizational preferences for integration**
   Some participants cited that integration was a common practice for the organization. Many were applying internally developed methodologies with built-in integration of project and change management. Organizations preferred integrating the functions to prevent project and change teams from working in isolation. Others integrated to reduce resource costs by combining role responsibilities.
5. **Nature of the project called for integration**
   The nature of some projects supported the case for integration of change and project management. Integration seemed natural when "*the change affected everyone in the organization,*" and it "*just made sense.*"

Reasons for not integrating project and change management

Source date: 2013

The participants who kept change and project management separate explained the reasons for doing so.

1. **Integration was not considered**
   The largest group of those who did not integrate either did not consider integrating or did not consider it until after project initiation. Time constraints on a project made integration after initial planning appear impractical.
2. **Separation of functions was preferred**
   Organizational preference or the preference of a project leader led to separation. This intentional separation prevented overlapping of responsibilities and accountability.
3. **Experienced resources were unavailable**
   Some organizations lacked experienced change management resources. Without support from a dedicated resource, the idea of integrating was considered only briefly and not acted upon. Additionally, project sponsors who "*wanted to save money*" did not see the value in appointing a change management resource to a project.
4. **Nature of project prevented integration**
   The nature of some projects prevented integration. Separation was considered more effective for large-scale projects with a widespread impact. Functions were not integrated when a project was informal or when a formalized project plan did not exist.

5. **Lack of buy-in from project manager or organization**
Integration was hindered by project managers who did not buy into the need for change management. A general lack of organizational awareness of the need for change management also created a barrier to integration.

Dimensions of integration

Participants who integrated project and change management did so on various aspects or dimensions (Figure 9.8). Most commonly, integration occurred at the people level; 86% of participants integrated teams, resources or roles and responsibilities. Seventy-eight percent integrated project management and change management processes, 56% integrated around results and outcomes and 51% integrated tools.

Figure 9.8 – Dimensions of integration

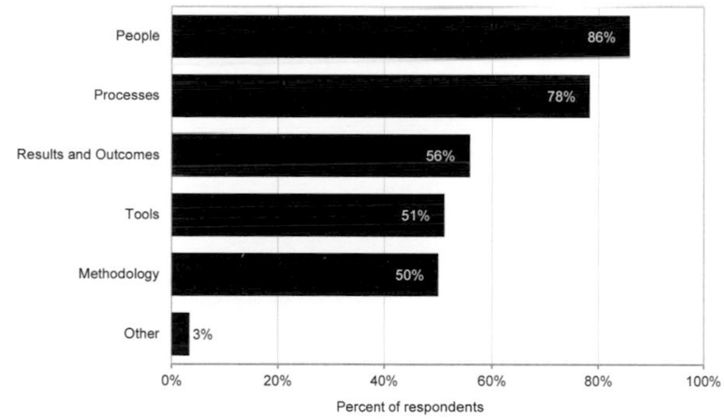

Tool integration

Source date: 2013

The participants who integrated project and change management tools identified which tools were integrated (Figure 9.9). Communication plans were integrated the most (91%), followed by project (81%) and training plans (79%). Tools that were integrated by the fewest number of participants included sustainability plans (18%), and statements of work (28%).

Figure 9.9 – Project and change management tools that were integrated

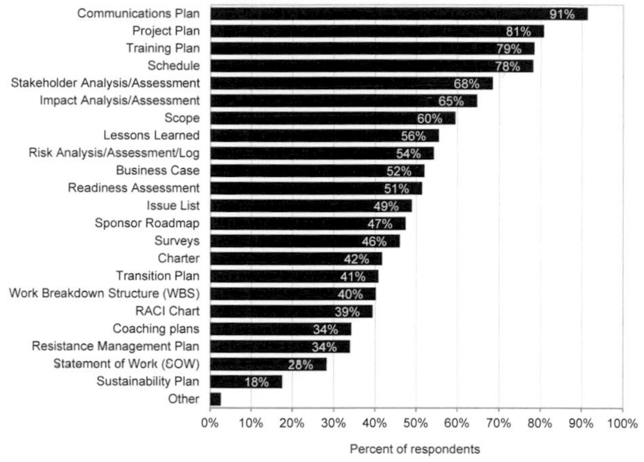

Process integration

Source date: 2013

Participants who integrated at the process level explained the steps taken to bring activities of project and change management together during the lifecycle of a project.

1. **Aligning or integrating plans, activities and teams**
Some participants aligned change deliverables and timelines with project plans. To ensure alignment, change plans were built with input from a project team during planning phases. Project plans were integrated to include tasks and activities from both disciplines. Integrated teams worked together on documentation and activities such as current state analyses and creating work breakdown structures. Integrated teams also consolidated role responsibilities and merged content from toolkits.

2. **Training project teams in change management**
Participants trained entire project teams in change management practices or a single team member who was encouraged to disseminate knowledge to the rest of the team. Other training methods included group workshops or distribution of job aids and educational materials.

3. **Adding change management tasks to the project plan**
Change management tasks were added to the project plan, and some practitioners redesigned project plans to accommodate these tasks. Tasks included impact assessments, risk mitigation plans and reinforcement plans. Many participants added tasks focused on building adoption. Examples included involving end users to gain buy-in, forming performance metrics for adoption rates, interviewing impacted individuals or gathering feedback to monitor adoption.
4. **Collaborating with key departments or individuals**
Collaboration occurred with training departments, business analysts, functional leaders, project managers or project teams. Frequent meetings facilitated interaction between these groups. In some cases, change teams acted in a support role for project teams. In others, project teams formed their own change plans to be executed by a separate change management team.

Integration across the project lifecycle

Source date: 2013

Participants who integrated project and change management explained the stages during the project lifecycle in which the disciplines were integrated (Figure 9.10). Ninety-nine percent of participants integrated the two functions during the implementation phase. Only 62% of participants integrated at project initiation.

Figure 9.10 – Integration at stages of the project lifecycle

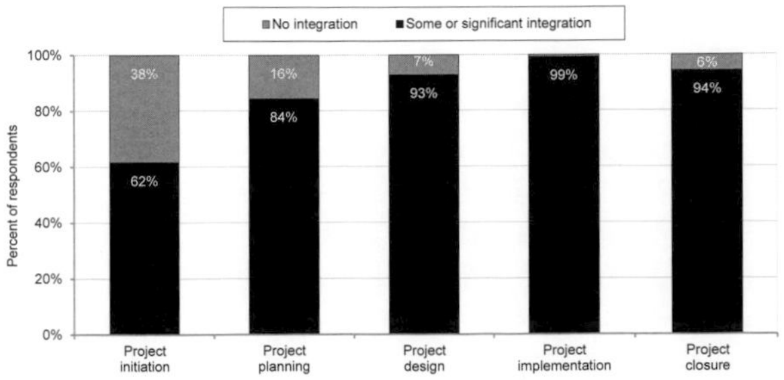

Perception of change management by project teams

Seventy-two percent of participants in the 2015 study reported that their project teams considered change management either critical or necessary (Figure 9.11), an increase from 71% in 2013.

Figure 9.11 – Project team view of the role of change management

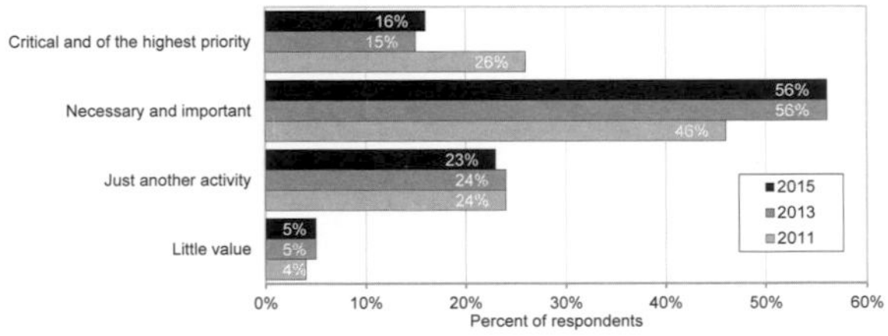

Participants shared how their project team's perceptions of change management had changed within the past several years (Figure 9.12). Over one third (36%) said perceptions had increased significantly, and 49% said it had increased slightly. Fewer than 4% felt that perceptions had decreased.

Figure 9.12 – Change in project team perception

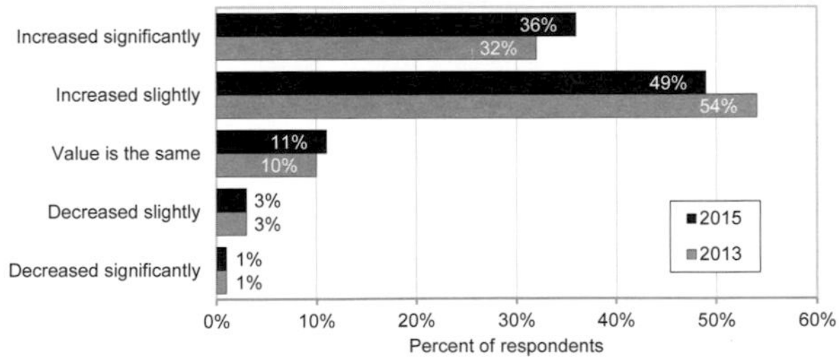

Effective steps for engaging the project team

Participants described the techniques they found to be effective in engaging with project teams to ensure that change management principles were applied successfully. For each of the techniques listed, participants frequently cited the need to conduct these activities early in the project lifecycle and to engage the project team early on.

1. **Describe the value of change management to the project team**
   Participants cited several techniques for describing the value of change management which began with ensuring the project's business objectives were clearly defined. These techniques included the project sponsor conducting a kickoff meeting to coach project team members on describing the business objectives of the project, not just the technical criteria; working with the project leaders to collaboratively define the outcomes needed to achieve the overall project goals; holding a workshop early in the project to demonstrate the importance of people adopting and using the solution in order to achieve the goals and objectives of the project; and jointly conducting a Return on Investment (ROI) calculation for change management.
2. **Educate the project team on change management**
   Providing education on change management was cited as an effective way to engage the project team. Educational topics frequently cited included how change management work is performed, how change management work is integrated with project management and the value of change management.
3. **Integration of change management and project management**
   Research participants described various forms of integration to be of value including integrating project and change management methodologies, integrating change activities into project plans, and integrating change management and project management teams.

Obstacles with project team

For the first time, participants identified obstacles with project teams when integrating change management (Figure 9.13). The largest obstacle identified was lack of knowledge and understanding of change management (69%) followed by role confusion (50%).

Figure 9.13 – Obstacles when introducing change management to a project team

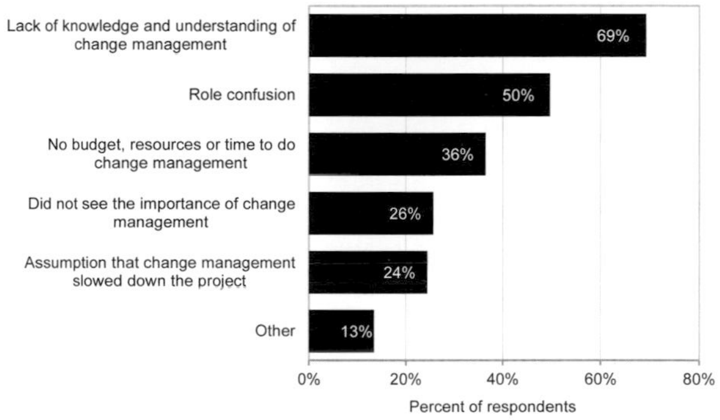

Editor's note: Participants were able to select multiple responses, resulting in a total of more than 100%.

What would you do differently on the next project regarding integrating change management into project activities?

Source date: 2009

Participants in the 2009 study provided a number of suggestions regarding what they would do differently in terms of change management and project activity integration. The top five suggestions were:

1. **Begin change management earlier**
   By a two-to-one margin, participants suggested starting change management at the onset of a project. By starting change management earlier, at the initiation of a project, change management and project activities were integrated more easily. "*Have a CM person in the initiating phase of the program to have enough time to design a proper program instead of having to retro-fit and catch up.*"

2. **Provide training on change management**
More change management training and educational workshops for project team members allowed for better partnerships and integration. When project team members understood change management, they were in a better position to use and integrate change management into their work.

3. **Ensure adequate resources for change management**
There were several suggestions regarding resources. The first was designation of a change management resource for a project, including the option of hiring a change manager. Participants also commented on the importance of having qualified, experienced practitioners doing change management work. In addition to the human resource component, participants mentioned ensuring that time and budgets were available for change management work.

4. **Engage senior leaders**
Senior leaders were important for two reasons. The first was engaging senior leaders in the importance and necessity of change management so they could support it during a project. The second was ensuring adequate sponsorship and leadership involvement during the project itself. A number of participants indicated they would have the change management resource report directly to senior leaders.

5. **Engage with project members**
Engaging the project team involved both building a case for change management and working together on a project. Participants indicated they had to sell the story of change management to project managers to ensure they understood the need for effectively managing the people side of change. Participants also provided tactical suggestions including having the project team work in partnership on change management issues, sitting in with the project team, being more involved in the technical side of change and ensuring that the project leader takes accountability and ownership of change management issues like user adoption and acceptance.

Additional suggestions included:

- Fully integrating plans into a holistic, single project plan that included all change and project management deliverables
- Clarifying responsibilities for the change management group and project team members regarding change management
- Using a formal change management approach and methodology

Impact of project management maturity on change management

Source date: 2013

Participants in the 2013 study described their organization's project management maturity. Most participants (70%) reported a moderate to extremely high level of project management maturity (Figure 9.14).

Figure 9.14 – Project management maturity level

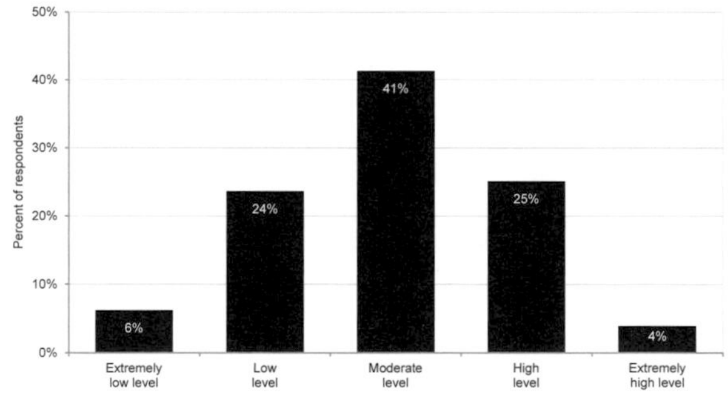

Participants then described how the maturity of project management influenced change management. The following were reported as impacts of both high and low project management maturity:

- **High maturity contributed to change management success**
Greater maturity led to greater change management success for the majority of participants who reported high project management maturity. Awareness and acceptance were high in these organizations especially if change management had been applied successfully in the past. Practitioners

also piggy-backed change plans onto an established project framework, expediting the planning process and moving quickly to execution.

- **High maturity undervalued change management**
  A small group of participants reported that high maturity caused change management to be undervalued. Project management was viewed as an action-oriented function and change management as unnecessary. This was exacerbated when organizations perceived a history of success without change management application. As a result, there was "*a tendency to override change management.*"
- **Low maturity delayed change management execution**
  Of those participants who reported low project management maturity, a majority said it reduced change management effectiveness. Practitioners had to define change management and focus primarily on raising awareness. When maturity was nonexistent, "*aspects of change were ad hoc, uncoordinated and fragmented.*" Similarly, if "*maturity was low, it made it difficult to apply structured change activities.*" In this situation, change practitioners had to prioritize basic project management principles such as project planning and scope definition.
- **Low maturity facilitated engagement and integration**
  Participants said that low maturity facilitated engagement and integration of change management. Sponsors, managers and employees were interested and readily engaged when no preconceived ideas about the relationship between project and change management existed. Integration of change management into project management was simplified in this situation versus "*a mature process which might have been more resistant.*"

Impact of project management maturity on integration

Figure 9.15 shows the relationship between project management maturity and whether participants integrated project and change management. Organizations with higher project management maturity were more likely to integrate project and change management than those reporting low maturity.

Figure 9.15 – Integration versus project management maturity

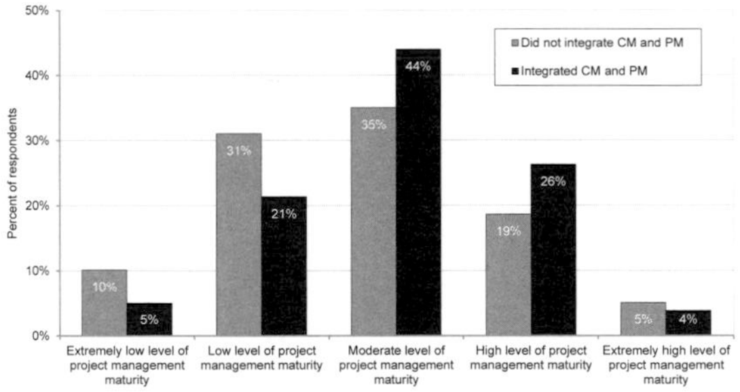

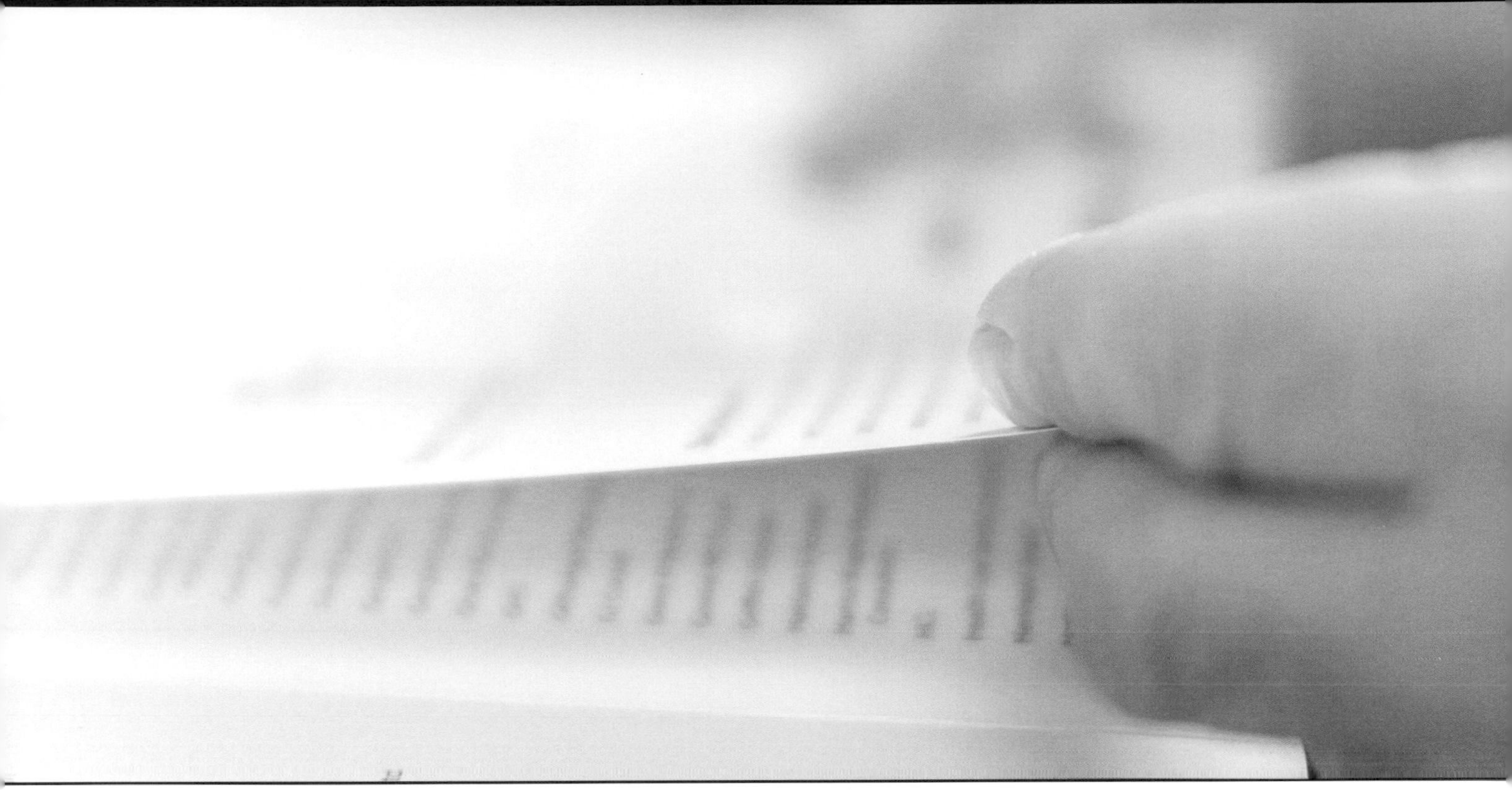

PART 3

ROLES IN CHANGE MANAGEMENT

SPONSORSHIP

ACTIVE AND VISIBLE SPONSORSHIP IS THE SINGLE GREATEST CONTRIBUTOR TO THE SUCCESS OF A CHANGE INITIATIVE

SUMMARY

Take leadership of change from a nebulous concept to a concrete set of actions and activities aligned with best practices. Decades of research have demonstrated the pivotal role leaders play in ensuring the successful outcomes of a change initiative. Leaders can consult this chapter to understand what it takes to be an effective sponsor of change, including traits of an effective sponsor, the most critical sponsorship activities and common mistakes to avoid. Change professionals can use this chapter to guide effective engagement of senior leaders and learn how to support leaders in their role.

HIGHLIGHT

72% of respondents with extremely effective sponsors met or exceeded objectives compared to 29% with extremely ineffective sponsors.

Most critical activities

Participants identified three sponsor roles required for the success of a change project or initiative and cited activities that characterize each role. A complete list of sponsor activities to support these three roles is included in the Sponsor Activity Model at the end of this section.

1. **Participate visibly throughout the project**
   Participants overwhelmingly identified the need for sponsors to be active and visible throughout a project as a critical activity. Participant responses fell into two categories of active and visible participation.

   Support the team

   - Proactively remove obstacles for the change management team
   - Provide resources and control the budget
   - Understand the change process, its impact and the desired future state

   Champion the change

   - Actively support the change management work, methodology and practices
   - Participate in change activities and messages
   - Own the change
   - Build excitement and enthusiasm for the project
   - Be the first adopter

2. **Communicate support and promote the change to impacted groups**
   - Communicate the end vision
   - Create awareness about the specifics and the need for change
   - Advocate the change to impacted groups that might be resistant
   - Vocally support the change
   - Clearly and succinctly explain the "what's in it for me?" (WIIFM) of the change to impacted groups

3. **Build a coalition of sponsorship**
   - Engage across the organization
   - Create, work and maintain a network of change agents
   - Encourage senior leaders to participate and support the change
   - Cultivate management support of the project
   - Clarify roles and establish expectations with mid-level and frontline managers
   - Solicit and listen to management feedback

Participants also felt that the level of the sponsor impacted success with a preference toward senior leaders being sponsors.

Sponsor effectiveness and meeting objectives

Sponsor effectiveness had a direct impact on whether projects met objectives (Figure 10.1). Projects with extremely effective sponsors met or exceeded objectives more than thrice as often as those with very ineffective sponsors.

Figure 10.1 – Correlation of sponsor effectiveness with meeting objectives

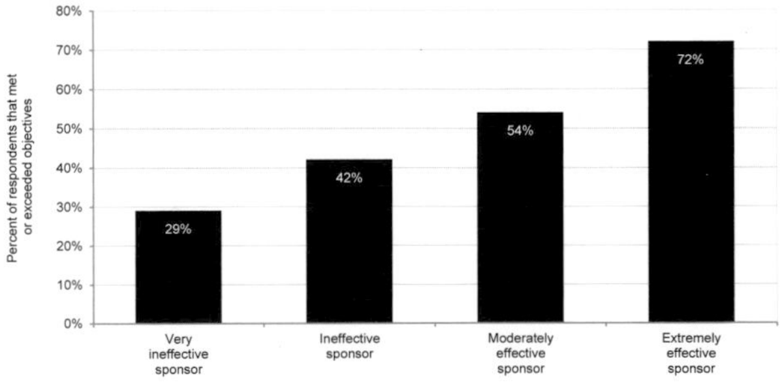

Creating active and visible sponsorship

In 2015, participants identified activities that created active and visible sponsorship.

1. **Presence at public events**
   Sponsor presence at large employee project events was identified as one of the easiest ways to create active and visible sponsorship. These meetings included town hall meetings, project kickoff meetings, roadshows, training session kickoffs and formal and informal Question and Answer (Q&A) sessions. The presence of the sponsor at these events was critical. In absentia, a video message from the sponsor provided an alternative way to demonstrate support.
2. **Actions with employees**
   Engaging employees outside of scheduled public forums was identified as an effective way to create sponsorship. Some actions included communicating the need for change across all levels of the organization, management by walking around or "*being on the shop floor where the change is happening,*" having personal discussions about the change with impacted employees and sharing what the change meant from an organizational perspective.
3. **Communicating about the change**
   Important communication tactics included sending messages with clear and regular cadence, providing face-to-face messages that focused on progress and gave employees the opportunity to provide feedback. Participants also identified that having the sponsor present on social media that related to the change created visible sponsorship.
4. **Embracing the change**
   It was important for sponsors to embrace the change. Participants shared that the best way for this to happen was to support the change publicly by modeling change behaviors. Ensuring sponsors were doing what they say, or "walking the walk," was a critical point regarding creating active and visible sponsorship.

Biggest mistakes

Participants identified the biggest mistakes top-level sponsors made during major changes.

1. **Failed to remain active and visible throughout the life of the project**
   The disappearing sponsor was cited as the most common sponsor mistake. Participants felt that, too often, sponsors would attend the opening kickoff or send out the announcement email and then never be heard from or seen again. Participants called this "*launch and leave.*" Sponsors would then move on to the next initiative without realizing the benefits of the original change.
2. **Underestimated or misunderstood the people side of change**
   Participants stated that sponsors made incorrect assumptions about the degree of impact a change would have on employees. Sponsors underestimated the time and resources needed to conduct change management. Many sponsors believed that all that was required to get people to adopt the change was telling employees the change was going to happen.
3. **Failed to communicate messages about the need for change**
   Lack of frequent communication from a sponsor concerning impacts of the change on employees was a common mistake. Sponsors did not provide consistent messaging on business drivers and did not communicate the value of change.
4. **Delegated the sponsorship role and responsibilities**
   A major cause of sponsors not communicating and not being visible was that they had delegated that role to the project team or lower managers thus becoming sponsor in name only.
5. **Failed to demonstrate support for the project in words and actions**
   Sponsors did not walk the talk when it came to supporting change. Sponsors failed to lead by example, or promote or champion the

change. They instead viewed change as the "flavor-of-the-month" and did not hold people accountable for a project's success.

Ideal sponsor traits

Participants identified a variety of traits that made for an ideal sponsor, though six were cited more often than others.

1. **Strong communication skills**
   Participants stated that sponsors should be vocal, articulate, comfortable communicating with all levels in the organization and able to provide awareness by explaining the reasons behind change.
2. **Create engagement through passion and enthusiasm**
   Energy, enthusiasm and a passion for change that created engagement were highlighted as necessary when sponsoring change.
3. **Engaged and involved**
   Involvement and engagement throughout the project was highlighted, including engagement with change and project teams.
4. **Visible and supportive**
   Participants stated that sponsors must be willing to be the visible face of change within the organization and support change through actions including providing necessary resources.
5. **Approachable and available**
   Participants revealed that the ideal sponsor is accessible and approachable regarding change, has the time to dedicate, attends meetings when needed and allots time for sponsorship.
6. **Recognized leader with sponsorship experience**
   Ideal sponsors were credible and recognized leaders within the organization. They were experienced, capable and had a strong understanding of the sponsor role.

Additional traits included:

- Knowledgeable about and believes in change management
- Knowledgeable about the business and change
- Personable and people-focused
- Trustworthy and respected
- Sets a clear vision regarding change
- Committed to and advocates change
- Sincere and compassionate
- High level within the organization
- Proactive and decisive
- Excellent listener
- Honest and has integrity
- Removes barriers and manages resistance
- Builds a coalition of sponsors and has a strong organizational network
- Accountable and holds others accountable
- Self-aware and emotionally intelligent

Sponsor role understanding and fulfillment

Figure 10.2 shows participants' evaluations of how well their sponsors understood their sponsorship roles and responsibilities. In each of the 2015, 2013 and 2009 studies, more than half of participants reported that their sponsors had less than adequate understanding of the role of an effective sponsor.

Figure 10.2 – Sponsor role understanding

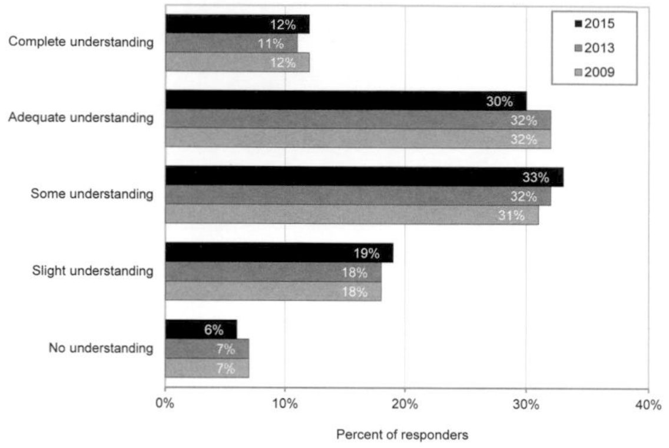

Participants also evaluated how effective their sponsors were at fulfilling each of the three primary roles.

Figure 10.3 shows the percentage of participants that indicated that their sponsors were ineffective or extremely ineffective at fulfilling each role.

One fifth of participants reported that their sponsors were ineffective at being active and visible throughout the project, and about one fourth indicated that their sponsors were not communicating effectively and directly with employees. Participants also reported that nearly one third of sponsors failed to build a coalition of Sponsorship, an increase from previous studies.

Figure 10.3 – Ineffective or extremely ineffective sponsor role fulfillment

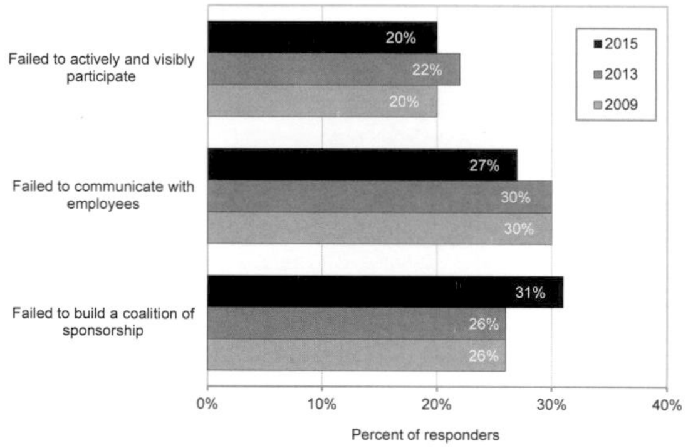

Sponsor effectiveness at specific activities

Participants in the 2015 study rated their sponsor's effectiveness at participating actively and visibly in the change, communicating directly with employees and building a coalition of sponsors on a scale. Nearly half (47%) of participants reported that their sponsors were effective at being active and visible throughout the change, 43% reported that their sponsors were effective at communicating with employees and 36% reported that their sponsors were effective at building a coalition of sponsors (Table 10.4).

Table 10.4 – Sponsor effectiveness at specific activities

	Extremely effective	Effective	Somewhat effective	Ineffective	Extremely Ineffective
Participated actively and visibly	16%	31%	33%	15%	5%
Communicated	14%	29%	31%	20%	6%
Built a coalition	12%	24%	33%	22%	9%

Formal evaluation of sponsor role fulfillment

Source date: 2013

Seventeen percent of participants in the 2013 study formally evaluated the effectiveness of sponsors fulfilling their change management role (Figure 10.5).

Figure 10.5 – Formally evaluated sponsor role fulfillment

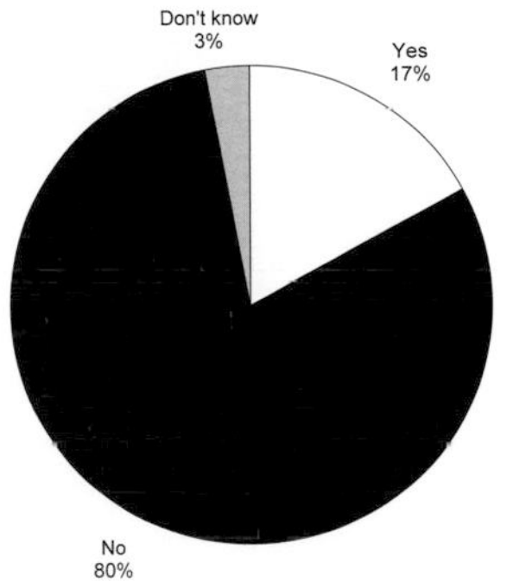

Participants noted three methods of evaluating the degree to which a project sponsor was fulfilling the role.

1. **Clearly outlined objectives**
Participants consistently noted outlining and defining activities and responsibilities expected of the sponsor early during the project. A roadmap or checklist was used to evaluate sponsor role fulfillment. Once a sponsor's role and activities were outlined, participants were able to measure and track the sponsor's adherence to defined activities. In some cases, project impact assessments completed by the project and/or change team assisted with outlining sponsor activities and responsibilities.
2. **Observation and feedback**
Participants reported that informal and formal feedback loops and observation tactics were used to evaluate role fulfillment among sponsors. Methods for observing and gathering feedback included surveys, group discussions and one-on-one interviews. Feedback and observations were based on pre-defined role descriptions. "*Informally we evaluated effectiveness of our program sponsors. Evaluation was done secretly as this type of information is very sensitive for leaders. Several action points came out of these meetings to ensure a better understanding of change management with sponsors.*" and "*We conducted interviews, collected survey feedback from employees, managers and customers. Also,* [we] *conducted some onsite observations.*"
3. **Use of formal tools or methodologies**
Participants also reported using a formal scorecard, assessment or methodology template to evaluate role fulfillment. Tools included sponsor assessments, project and role impact assessments, internal methodologies and engagement tracking methods. These tools and tracking measures were completed by the sponsors themselves, the change management team or project team members. "*Using the Prosci sponsor assessment tool, I completed the assessment and also had the sponsor perform a self-assessment.*"

Engaging the sponsor

Source date: 2013

Participants used several tactics to ensure project sponsors remained involved throughout the duration of a project.

1. **Deliver regular meetings and updates**
Meeting with sponsors regularly to provide them with project updates and progress briefings was reported as the number-one tactic to maintain sponsor involvement throughout a project. Participants hosted regular meetings at varying intervals; some held daily or weekly meetings, and others held them quarterly. Meetings were conducted in both one-on-one and group settings. "*We continued engagement at regularly scheduled staff meetings—asking for 15 minutes of their agenda—to keep them all engaged. This did not add another meeting to their calendar and kept the project in the forefront of their brains.*"

2. **Outline objectives**
Participants reported outlining objectives early and continuing to focus on those objectives as the second most common tactic to ensure project sponsors remained involved. Tactics included inviting sponsors to key events, highlighting the success and impact their participation was having on a project, creating a sponsor roadmap and tracking adherence, making them the project owner and going to them for key decisions throughout the project lifecycle.

3. **Communicate directly with sponsor**
Participants noted that staying in constant communication with sponsors was a common tactic to maintain involvement. Communicating directly with sponsors helped keep them accountable for and excited about project progress. Communication should be two-way to ensure that the change manager was available and ready to provide project communication for the sponsor at all times. "*We were very flexible and approachable and developed a close trust-based relationship so that we could criticize without holding punches and our support was not patronizing.*"

4. **Provide sponsor with coaching and support**
The fourth most common tactic was to provide the sponsor with coaching and support in their role. Coaching provided focus on the sponsor's role and demonstrated how to execute responsibilities effectively. Steps for providing support included writing key communication messages, preparing them with messages prior to events, sharing success stories and providing tools.

A notable portion of participants also involved steering committees, when necessary, as a tactic to influence and ensure that sponsors remained engaged throughout change.

Sponsor access

Participants who reported having adequate or more than adequate access to sponsors also experienced higher rates of meeting project objectives than those with inadequate sponsor access (Figure 10.6). Nearly two thirds of participants with adequate sponsor access met or exceeded project objectives compared to 40% of those with inadequate access.

Figure 10.6 – Correlation of sponsor access with meeting/exceeding objectives

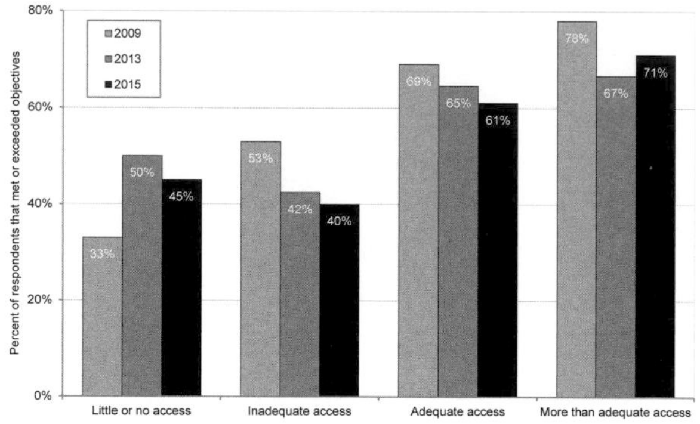

A similar trend regarding sponsor access and change management effectiveness is shown in Figure 10.7. Nearly two-thirds of participants with adequate or more than adequate access to sponsors reported good or excellent change management effectiveness (represented by the black bars). Fewer than 6% of participants who reported adequate access experienced poor change management effectiveness compared to 26% of participants who had little or no access to sponsors.

Figure 10.7 – Correlation of sponsor access with change management effectiveness

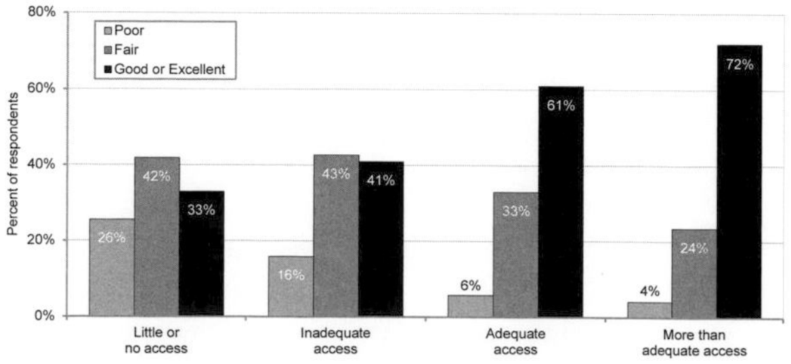

Securing sponsor access

Source date: 2013

Participants reported tactics used to secure access to sponsors.

1. **Meet with the sponsor**
   Participants reported scheduling meetings prior to a project kickoff or at project initiation. Participants noted that scheduling meetings far in advance and during key points in the project ensured that sponsors were available and reduced the chances of schedule conflicts. Both informal and formal meetings were used. Participants also identified opportunistic and chance meetings to access project sponsors. "*We used informal channels such as scheduling breakfast or lunch rather than formal meetings with agendas.*"
2. **Establish expectations**
   By establishing expectations of sponsors early, participants secured better access to sponsors. Participants outlined the positive project impact that continued access would have and requested that sponsors agree to be accessible. The project impact was illustrated by sharing best practices and highlighting the correlation between sponsor access and project success, which they also tied to sponsors' professional goals and expectations for a project.
3. **Leverage individuals with access to sponsors**
   Participants with little to no access to sponsors reported leveraging others within the organization who did have access. Participants were able to schedule appointments and be present at meetings they knew the sponsor would be attending. A common example was getting steering committees' agendas from an executive assistant.
4. **Communicate consistently with sponsor**
   Consistent communication at key points in the project was a tactic participants used to establish credibility and access sponsors. Participants also reported that communicating quick-wins and success stories to sponsors increased longer-term accessibility.
5. **Work through the project manager**
   Participants reported establishing a relationship with project managers and having them communicate key change management messages to sponsors at project meetings. By having an established relationship with the project manager, participants received more invitations to meetings with the project team and sponsor.
6. **Leverage the sponsor coalition**
   Participants leveraged other leaders within the organization who had business influence and worked closely with project sponsors. "*We accessed other executive level stakeholders who had a strong commitment to change management and showed their support and guidance to engage the sponsor.*"

A notable number of participants reported relationship development as a way to gain and maintain access to sponsors. Relationship development included working with sponsors in a number of capacities to gain trust, networking with sponsors during informal events and directing conversations with sponsors to become a credible source of information on projects.

Frequency of change management meetings with sponsor

Source date: 2009

In the 2009 study, participants indicated how frequently they met with sponsors during a project (Figure 10.8). More than half of participants reported meeting only monthly or quarterly with sponsors. More than half recommended weekly meetings with sponsors.

Figure 10.8 – Frequency of meeting with sponsors

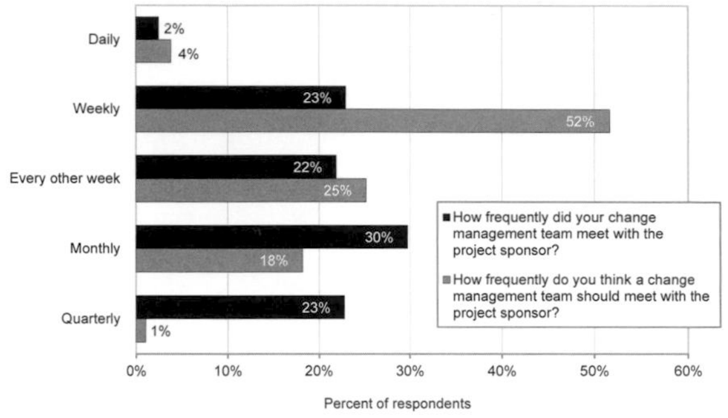

Sponsor communication frequency

Source date: 2009

Participants in the 2009 study identified how many times per month their sponsors communicated with employees regarding change. Figure 10.9 shows data for direct communication frequency. More than half of participants said that their sponsors communicated directly with employees only once per month or less.

Figure 10.9 – Sponsor communication frequency

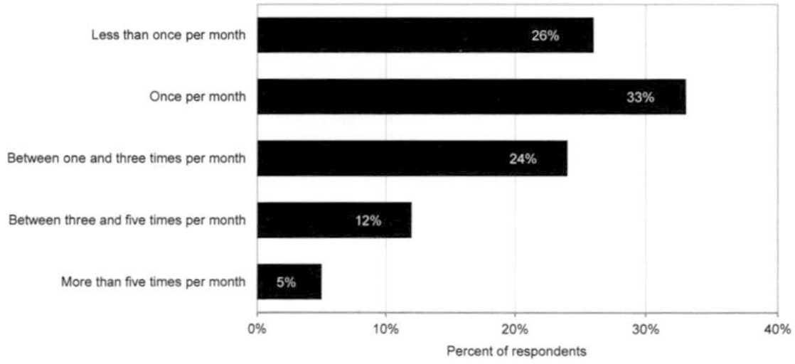

Symptoms of ineffective sponsorship

Source date: 2011

Participants indicated the symptoms of ineffective sponsorship they experienced (Figure 10.10). Inactive or invisible sponsorship was the most cited symptom followed by poor alignment among key stakeholders.

Figure 10.10 – Sponsor symptoms

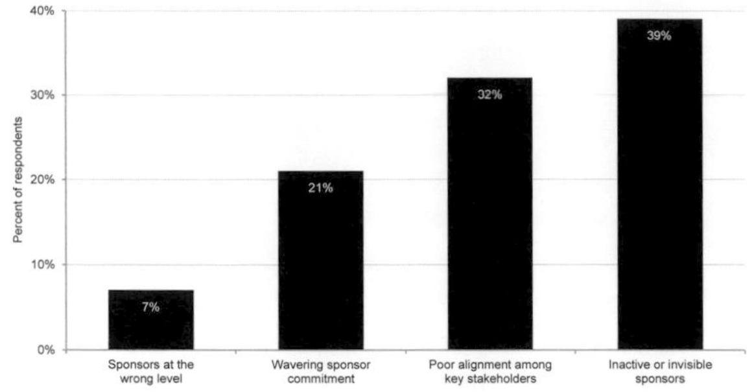

How would you characterize your sponsor at the beginning of the project?

Source date: 2009

Participants in the 2009 study characterized their sponsors at the beginning of the project (Figure 10.11).

Figure 10.11 – Sponsor characterization at beginning of the project

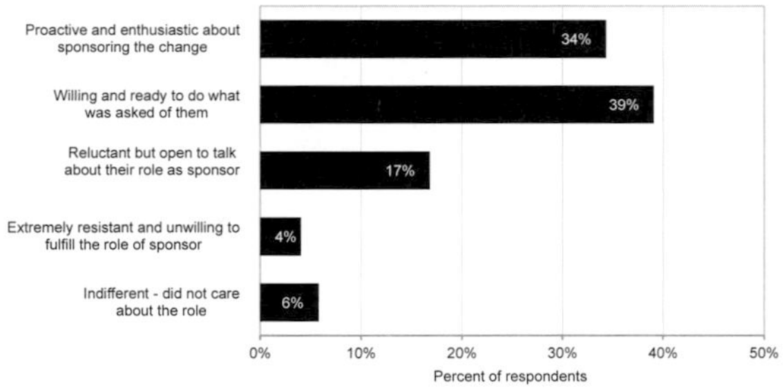

Nearly three quarters of participants in the 2009 study characterized sponsors positively at the beginning of a project, with 34% indicating that sponsors were proactive and enthusiastic, and 39% indicating sponsors were willing and ready to do what was asked of them. Only 4% reported that their sponsors were extremely resistant and unwilling to be a sponsor of change.

Engaging reluctant senior leaders

Respondents in the 2015 study identified the most effective techniques they employed to engage resistant or reluctant senior leaders. Results indicate similar trends to research conducted in 2007 and 2009.

1. **Engage in one-on-one interactions**
   Participants cited face-to-face, one-on-one interactions with sponsors as the most effective technique when accompanied with honesty and openness. Participants recommended offline, interpersonal relationship-building meetings as the most impactful which included walking the halls, carparks, walkways between buildings and watercoolers. Two-way communication, genuinely listening to concerns, flattery and being perceived as a trusted advisor were characteristic of high-value interactions. "*Real empathy—actually 'hearing' their reluctance and then addressing this as far as possible.*"
2. **Provide coaching on their role as a sponsor**
   Participants cited coaching as a highly successful method for engaging reluctant or resistant leaders. Types of coaching included informal and formal sponsor education on their roles, drafting their communications and emails and explaining the risk of ineffective sponsorship. Special tactics included use of a sponsor roadmap, building awareness, sharing tools and techniques, to-do lists, sharing best practices and modeling the outcomes of their decisions.
3. **Demonstrate the benefits of the change**
   Highlighting the business reason, objective and benefit of change was a frequently cited tactic. Often, this was accompanied with presenting personal benefit to the executive ("what's in it for me?" or WIIFM), the Return on Investment (ROI) of change management or a briefing of possible negative impacts were their roles unfulfilled. Participants reported sharing case studies of successful and failed past changes to support these conversations. Other strategies included aligning change with their strategies, appealing to their specific goals and desires and contextualizing change.
4. **Use of peer pressure by leveraging other sponsors**
   Leveraging another peer sponsor or influencer to talk to a sponsor and demonstrate support for change was commonly cited to influence reluctant executives. If a peer leader was chosen to work with a resistant leader, participants recommended they be credible, authoritative colleagues. Participants reported focusing on creating buy-in from a larger sponsor coalition and encouraging friendly competition among teams and between peer sponsors from different departments.
5. **Increase involvement of resistant senior leaders**
   Participants suggested increasing the involvement and decision-making of resistant senior leaders. Scheduling regular meetings with sponsors to inform and gather input was a key success factor. Sponsors' involvement occurred in a variety of ways including invitations to initial project design sessions, invitations to change champion or change agent network meetings and presentations in existing forums. Participants also experienced success by publicly recognizing their help, providing them with hands-on experience with change, early and regular involvement in the project and sending follow-ups from meetings they did not attend.
6. **Provide regular communication**
   Participants associated regular communication with listening and understanding a sponsor's objections. Two-way communication, tailored messages and arranging small group meetings with sponsors were frequently cited.
7. **Arrange meetings and feedback loops**
   Participants recommended providing opportunities for interactions between impacted groups and sponsors. Engaging with direct reports and stakeholders to provide direct feedback was cited often.

Establishing formal feedback loops, communicating observations from the field and sharing survey results from impacted groups were also used.

8. **Apply special tactics**
Many participants noted special tactics they used to engage resistant leaders, including requesting a liaison from CM and PM teams to meet with sponsors, encouraging or convincing to delegate, providing clear choices, creating urgency or "a burning platform," storytelling, playing devil's advocate, allowing time to work through things, booking time on their schedules early or late in the day, obtaining sign-off documenting responsibility, using blogs or social media sites, treating leaders as stakeholders and creating support structures for executive assistants.

9. **Intervene with primary sponsor**
Occasionally, participants reported success appealing to a higher authority. Participants mentioned strategically using the CEO to outline expectations with a sponsor coalition or to tie individual compensation to realizing results from change. Participants also mentioned recommending sanctions on sponsors for non-compliance or having them pay for the cost of old equipment.

Losing a sponsor
Source date: 2011

Only 14% of participants from the 2011 study were involved in a project during which a sponsor left before completion (Figure 10.12).

Figure 10.12 – Sponsor left before completion of a project

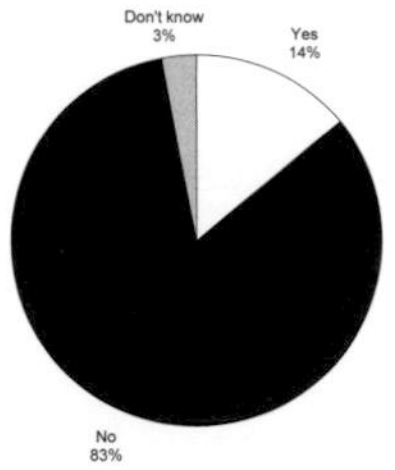

Consequences of losing a sponsor
Source date: 2013

Participants commented on the most common consequences of losing a sponsor during the course of a project.

1. **Loss of or shift in direction**
The loss of a sponsor impacted direction, objectives, vision and expectations. These elements had to be reevaluated, and decisions had to be made regarding the direction of the change.
2. **Employee disengagement**
The loss of a sponsor resulted in confusion, disillusionment and disengagement at the employee level.
3. **Loss of momentum**
The project fell into stagnation and lost continuity.
4. **Time spent getting new sponsor up to speed**
The team had to invest time in getting a new sponsor up to speed about project details and developments that had occurred.
5. **Project time frames altered**
The project was delayed or in some cases restarted.
6. **Instability**
The loss of a sponsor resulted in turbulence, disruption and general instability.

Tactics for dealing with losing a sponsor
Source date: 2013

Participants who had a sponsor leave during the course of the project commented on tactics they used to address losing a sponsor. The top four were:

1. **Get the new sponsor up to speed quickly**
Meet face-to-face with the new sponsor regularly. Provide briefings and background on the project, and updates on the status of the project.
2. **Secure commitment**
Ensure the new sponsor is supportive of the change and their role in sponsorship.

3. **Maintain communications**
   Continue to communicate about the change and keep the dialogue open. In some cases, communicate about the reasons for a change in sponsorship.
4. **Focus on and work with the coalition**
   When the top sponsor moved, the members of the coalition of managers and supervisors at lower levels were important allies. Effort focused on this group to keep them engaged and supporting the change with their employees.

Correct level of sponsor

Source date: 2013

Participants identified whether the sponsor for their change was at the *right level*, *too high* or *too low* in the organization (Figure 10.13). Over three quarters of respondents indicated that their sponsor was at the right level.

Figure 10.13 – Sponsor at right level in the organization

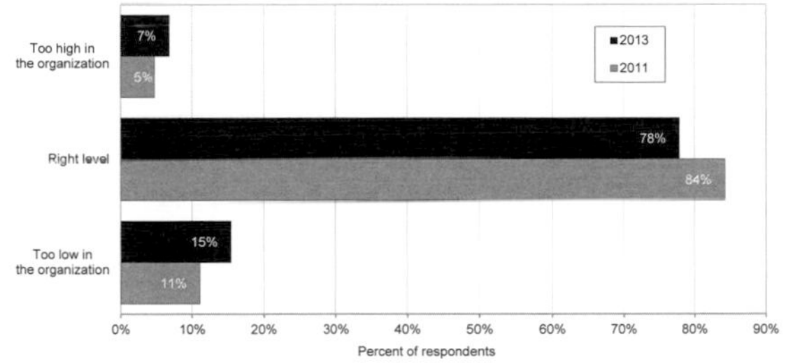

Ideal sponsor level

For the first time in 2015, participants were asked about the ideal level for a sponsor. Responses were relative given the subjective and loosely-defined responsibilities and roles provided across organizations. The most common responses were:

- **Senior management:** The majority of participants identified the senior management level as a primary source for sponsorship. Titles for this parallel of sponsorship included vice president, director and general manager.
- **Executive management:** The second most common response was executive management. Examples were senior manager and senior vice president.
- **CEO and CIO**: Participants identified the CEO or CIO as the third most common sponsorship position within an organization.

Recommendations for dealing with a sponsor at the wrong level

Source date: 2011

Participants who provided recommendations for practitioners supporting change that had the wrong level of sponsor identified two primary tactics: work with the current sponsor or engage the correct level sponsor. Participants who either recommended or had to work with the current sponsor identified four tactics.

1. **Build and leverage the coalition**
   Of the four tactics proposed by participants, building a coalition of change leaders throughout the organization was the most common. Participants recommended creating a layer of change leadership with multiple sponsors from various levels to support change.
2. **Enter open and honest dialogues with the current sponsor regarding his/her role**
   Participants proposed having a candid conversation with the current sponsor to address questions and concerns regarding the level of sponsorship, including raising awareness about his/her responsibilities. This conversation should include topics such as the impacts of change to the current sponsor, the impacts of proper sponsorship on project success and how resistance will be managed and barriers removed.

3. **Offer coaching to the current sponsor**
   Participants recommended coaching the current sponsor on how to be effective. Topics for coaching included helping the sponsor network and build coalitions, offering training, providing recommendations on effective sponsorship and developing messages for the sponsor.
4. **Re-scope the project**
   If the level of sponsorship provided was inadequate, participants recommended restructuring or re-scoping the project to accommodate the level of the current sponsor.

Participants who recommended engaging the correct level of sponsor provided three tactics for implementing a change in sponsorship.

1. **Elevate the issue and engage senior leadership to initiate a change**
   Participants recommended escalating the issue to an executive steering committee, senior management or senior sponsor or making the situation known and having a senior leader advocate for a change in sponsorship.
2. **Show the impacts of proper sponsorship on project success and how the current sponsor is inappropriate**
   Participants who proposed engaging a different level of sponsor suggested showing the impacts of appropriate sponsorship on project results and explaining criteria of effective sponsorship. Participants recommended including reasons the current sponsor was not a good fit for the role.
3. **Conduct a stakeholder analysis or sponsor assessment to indicate proper sponsor**
   Participants suggested using a sponsor assessment diagram or stakeholder analysis to explain the need for change in sponsorship or to show who is better suited for the role.

Traits for sponsorship of large-scale change

Participants identified traits necessary for a sponsor who leads large-scale change.

1. **Excellent communication skills**
   Overwhelmingly, participants identified having excellent communicative and rhetorical skills as crucial skills for a sponsor leading large-scale change. Participants felt that during large-scale changes, communicating with large groups of stakeholders and impacted employees was required. A sponsor should be comfortable speaking before large groups, able to persuade or sell change to others and craft and tell the story of a change.
2. **Leadership capability**
   Participants reported that the sponsor must have above-average leadership ability. As a leader, sponsors must have a vision of what the goal of change will look like and be able to communicate that vision to others. A sponsor must be influential within the organization and peer groups. A sponsor must be a visible and present part of the change to respond to issues as they arise and available to change managers as a resource. A sponsor must be credible, either having experience with the specific change type or with leading change.
3. **Knowledgeable**
   Participants found that sponsors should be knowledgeable about several areas. They need to have an understanding of their organization and organization's culture to best maneuver and work within it. The sponsor should be knowledgeable about the change, its impact on employees and its desired deliverables. The sponsor should be fluent in both change and project management.

4. **Availability**
   A sponsor must devote and prioritize the time required to see change through to completion. This involves being present and accessible to the change management team, project management team and employees impacted by change. Having a sponsor only physically present is insufficient; a sponsor must be engaged, energetic and active/interactive.

5. **Influential**
   Participants stressed that a sponsor of a large change needed to wield influence within the organization. This included the ability to build a coalition of peers and executives to support change. He/she must have, build and maintain relationships with top-level executives, have an understanding of the political climate of the organization and be able to negotiate it with minimal backlash on the change team. The ideal sponsor was a skilled networker, was well known throughout the organization and has experience leading and sponsoring this type of change.

Ideal traits for a sponsor managing a small-scale change

For the first time, participants also specified the traits a sponsor of a small-scale change should have.

1. **Correct level within the organization**
   Sponsor should be close to the change. When small-scale changes were being managed, high-level sponsors often had little involvement or knowledge about the change. Sponsors should be high enough in level to influence change but not so high that they are disconnected.

2. **Ability to prioritize**
   Participants reported that small-scale change often occurred simultaneously with other change projects or daily work and required the ability to prioritize. Small-scale projects risked being placed on the back burner because of their size and required diligent care to ensure that timetables and deadlines were not missed.

3. **Leadership traits**
   Participants reported numerous leadership qualities necessary for a sponsor including trustworthiness, passion, high emotional intelligence, influence and dedication.

Sponsor Activity Model

Participants described the most important sponsor activities for managing change. Data were broken into three major project phases: start-up (planning), design and implementation. Activities and steps were further categorized by target audiences:

- Project team
- Managers (including business leaders)
- Employees

Figure 10.14 is a 3 x 3 diagram that illustrates responsibilities of the sponsor during each project phase (start-up, design and implementation). Activities required for each box are described on the following pages.

Note: The labels for each box in Figure 10.14 are intended to be general descriptions for the category and are not intended to stand alone from the activity lists in Tables 10.15, 10.16 and 10.17.

Editor's note: The Sponsor Activity Model shown in Figure 10.14 was developed in 2003 and now includes data from the 2003, 2005, 2007, 2009 and 2011 reports to create a comprehensive view of sponsor activities across multiple studies.

Figure 10.14 – Sponsor Activity Model

	Project team	Managers	Employees
Start-up	**Acquire project resources**	**Build management support**	**Create awareness**
Design	**Provide direct support**	**Develop sponsorship**	**Educate**
Implementation	**Maintain momentum**	**Align leadership and manage resistance**	**Reinforce and reward**

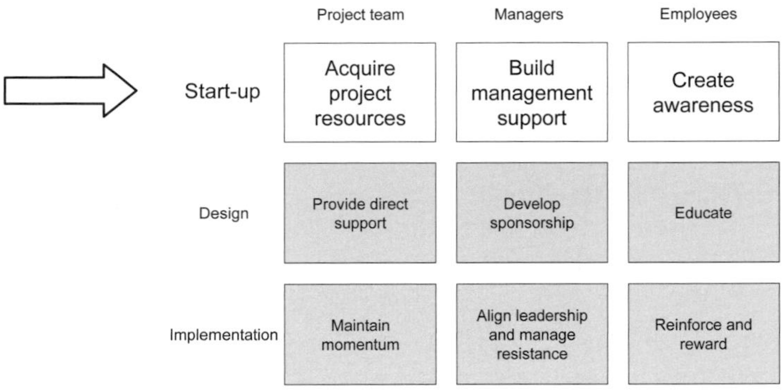

Table 10.15 – Sponsor start-up activities

	with the project team	with managers	with employees
	Acquire project resources	**Build management support**	**Create awareness**
Start-up	• Select the best project leader and team members; include resources with change management expertise • Provide necessary funding for the team, including training for all team members on change management • Set priorities related to daily work versus project work to allow adequate team member participation • Help the team understand critical business issues or opportunities that must be addressed • Provide clear direction and objectives for the project; describe what success will look like • Jointly develop a high-level view of the future and link change to the business strategy • Be directly involved with the project team; set expectations; review key deliverables and remove obstacles • Take ownership for success of the project and hold the team accountable for results • Establish a commitment to change management; talk about change management and ensure required roles are filled	• Enlist the support of executive managers and create a support network (coalition of managers needed to support change) • Create a steering committee of key managers to monitor progress (depends on project size) • Educate senior managers about the business drivers of change and the risks of not changing • Work directly with managers who show early signs of resistance • Create change advocates within the leadership team; build support and enthusiasm for change • Provide training on change management for senior managers • Establish change activities that the leadership group is responsible for completing • Define accountabilities for mid-level managers • Determine and communicate priorities between this change and other change initiatives • Resolve conflicting operational objectives with other senior leaders • Solicit and listen to management feedback • Connect project to the organization's strategy and goals	• Describe the current state of the business and share business issues or opportunities • Explain why a change is needed now; share the risks of not changing • Share a vision for the future; explain the nature of the change and show how change will address business problems or opportunities • Answer "How will this change affect me?" and "What's in it for me?" (WIIFM) • Be proactive, vocal and visible; communicate frequently, including face-to-face conversations • Listen and be open to dialogue and resistance • Tell employees what they can expect to happen and when • Understand the organizational culture and beliefs • Repeat key messages • Share plans with customers and suppliers • Show project milestones and provide progress updates • Communicate clearly and honestly about aspects of the project that are still unknown

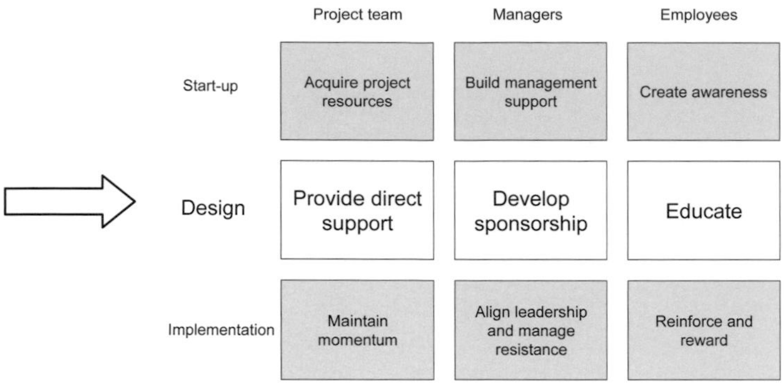

Table 10.16 – Sponsor design activities

	with the project team	with managers	with employees
Design	**Provide direct support**	**Develop sponsorship**	**Educate**
	• Stay involved: attend key project meetings, review project status and hold the team accountable for results • Provide necessary resources and funding, including ensuring that the right people are made available to support the design work • Be accessible to the team; be a sounding board; provide ideas and constructive criticism to the team; ask "What if?" • Remove roadblocks; make timely decisions on project issues and help manage conflicts and political issues • Communicate expectations and feedback from other managers • Keep the team on track and manage "scope creep" • Reward success and achievements • Take the time to understand the solution • Identify conflicts with other projects that might impact this team • Make sure the project team knows that your door is open and you are available to support their work • Play a role in all critical decisions	• Continue to build support and sponsorship among senior managers; reinforce key messages; resolve differences in perception; address areas of resistance • Let senior managers know how they can support change; provide them with a clear roadmap for sponsoring change with their direct reports • Conduct steering committee meetings; keep managers informed; use this forum to resolve critical issues • Use public and private conversations to reinforce leadership support; recognize outstanding managers • Communicate project progress to all executive managers • Hold mid-level managers accountable • Do not tolerate resistance from mid-level managers or allow managers to opt out of change; be clear on expectations • Ensure that a consistent message is being sent by managers to impacted employees	• Communicate frequently with employees; make your personal commitment visible, including face-to-face conversations • Reinforce the reason for change, the risk of not changing and evolving details about the future state • Show employees how the change aligns with the direction and strategy of the business • Answer "What will this change mean to me?" • Listen to what employees have to say; take the pulse of the organization and collect feedback • Share project progress and provide updates regularly; update employees on "what you can expect to happen and when" • Enable employee participation and involvement • Recognize good work employees have done • Involve customers and suppliers • Ensure adequate time is allocated for training and skill-building prior to implementation

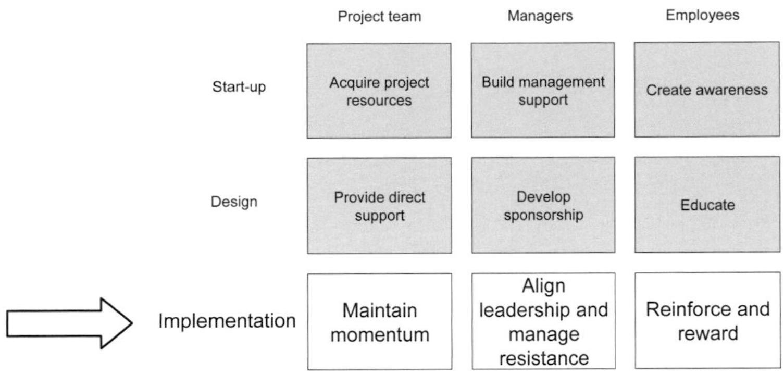

Table 10.17 – Sponsor implementation activities

	with the project team	with managers	with employees
Implementation	**Maintain momentum**	**Align leadership and manage resistance**	**Reinforce and reward**
	• Secure resources necessary for implementation • Stay engaged with the team: attend meetings, reward successes, hold them accountable for results and build enthusiasm • Remove roadblocks and help the team overcome obstacles • Stay on course; avoid shifting priorities too early • Attend frequent project status meetings and track progress • Resolve issues and conflicts; respond to escalations	• Continue to meet in public and private with business leaders and senior managers; align sponsorship; provide progress updates; resolve issues • Communicate expectations to senior managers for their support of change; provide activities they can do and messages they can communicate to the organization • Manage resistance from middle managers; correct or remove managers who will not support change • Model change through personal examples and hands-on involvement • Stay involved throughout the entire project; stay visible • Hold managers accountable for support	• Reinforce key messages; align business strategy with project objectives; increase personal communications • Reinforce why change is being made and the risk of not changing (some employees might be ready to hear this message only when change is near implementation) • Listen to employees and encourage feedback; be willing to answer tough questions • Set expectations for employees; clearly communicate consequences of not changing • Identify with the additional work and difficulties that might be experienced during implementation • Enforce application of new processes and behaviors • Look for quick wins; share successes and build enthusiasm for change • Celebrate success stories in person; be present and visible • Acknowledge challenges and obstacles honestly

MANAGERS & SUPERVISORS

MANAGERS AND SUPERVISORS LEGITIMIZE THE CHANGES IMPACTING THE TEAMS THEY LEAD

SUMMARY

Managers and supervisors play a key role in producing change outcomes. Employees look to their manager for overt instructions and subtle cues about how a coming change will impact them. Leveraging the power and influence of managers to support team members through their individual change will ultimately increase adoption and improve the outcomes of your change project. Best practices data in this chapter concretely defines what people managers must do to effectively lead their team during times of change. Learn tactics for engaging and enabling managers to be successful leaders of change.

HIGHLIGHT

Only 32% of participants indicated that they adequately prepared managers and supervisors for their role in change.

Most critical roles for managers and supervisors

Participants identified the most critical roles for managers and supervisors during change. The key roles reinforced the 2011 study findings.

1. **Communicate with direct reports about change**
   Communicating the need for change, the vision and the impact of change was the most critical activity identified for managers and supervisors to perform during change. Employees required a consistent message from leadership and direct managers and wanted to know why the change was occurring, what was in it for them and what the expected benefits for the organization were. Listening and allowing discussion and two-way communication were critical success factors concerning employees' ability to receive and internalize messaging from managers.
2. **Advocate and champion change**
   Managers needed to support change and played a visible role during the transition by attending training and project events and leading by example. This required a manager to be proactive in obtaining timely information and complete details about the change. Most importantly, managers needed to speak positively about change and be engaged.
3. **Coach employees through change**
   Participants identified the need for managers to be available for coaching throughout change, to listen to concerns, to answer questions and to be respectful of the impact change had on employees. They also identified helping employees understand required behaviors, articulating how their contributions support the initiative, removing barriers as needed and identifying corrective actions.
4. **Engage and liaise with the project team**
   Providing input to the project team and engaging in discovery and design phases were critical roles for managers, allowing employee needs and feedback to be incorporated in the solution. Having a close working relationship with a project team also enabled managers to be in tune with the project details and milestones of which their employees needed to be aware.
5. **Identify and manage resistance**
   Managers were reported as being in the best position to identify resistance and fulfill the role of mitigating resistance throughout the life of a project. Managers were able to report resistance. Their roles included understanding the root cause of resistance, removing barriers and having difficult conversations with employees to help increase desire to participate in change.
6. **Continuing managerial responsibilities**
   In addition to the roles noted above, participants emphasized the importance of managers continuing their normal roles in daily team operations and in operationalizing new ways of working. This included maintaining reporting functions and team engagement tactics, such as huddles and meetings, and providing structure and accountability for the new way of working. This included adjusting schedules and responsibilities as needed to attend training events and engaging in preparation and reinforcement.

Most common mistakes for managers and supervisors

Participants identified some of the biggest mistakes managers and supervisors make when managing change.

1. **Role abdication**
   Either intentionally or as a result of a lack of understanding, managers abdicated their roles during change or did not take responsibility for change.

- **Not accepting responsibility**
  The largest factor was supervisors not understanding their role as change champions. They often saw change management duties as extra work and not a normal function of their role, but rather the role of a change manager or project team.
- **Ignoring change**
  Managers felt they could ignore or hide from change and focus on business as usual, adopting the mindset that the change would either go away or happen on its own regardless of their efforts.
- **Not seeking better understanding**
  One of the most common mistakes participants pointed out was managers not seeking to understand the change and its impact – operating in ignorance. They struggled to ask for support during change management and did not acknowledge their personal journeys through change.

2. **Communication mistakes**
   Many participants stated that managers felt that a single communication was sufficient and communicated *to* rather than *with* employees. Rather than admitting their own knowledge gaps, managers would communicate what they knew at the time causing communications to be late or inaccurate. Supervisors often did not understand how to filter messages appropriately, or what messages to filter, often oversharing or adding personal bias.
3. **Failing to support staff**
   Many managers felt that employees would change if told to do so and did not need additional support. This led to unrealistic expectations because supervisors did not acknowledge that individuals accept change at different paces. Supervisors also struggled to manage resistance appropriately due to fear, empathy or a general misunderstanding of the root cause of resistance. Supervisors got caught up in their own journeys and how the change impacted them, keeping them from addressing their teams' needs.
4. **Ill prepared**
   Managers underestimated the impact change had on their teams or overestimated their teams' ability to handle change. Either due to false assumptions about change or not knowing how to prioritize change among daily operations, supervisors were ill prepared when it was time for change.
5. **Resisting the change**
   Participants reported that supervisors often would talk the talk but not walk the walk. Managers would take sides, usually with their direct reports, causing us-versus-them mentalities.

Role fulfillment by managers and supervisors

Participants rated the effectiveness of their organizations' managers and supervisors in five categories: communicator, advocate, coach, resistance manager and liaison (Figure 11.1). Managers and supervisors were more effective as advocates (28%), liaisons (28%) and communicators (24%), in comparison to coaches (12%) and resistance managers (11%).

Figure 11.1 – Effectiveness of managers and supervisors in roles

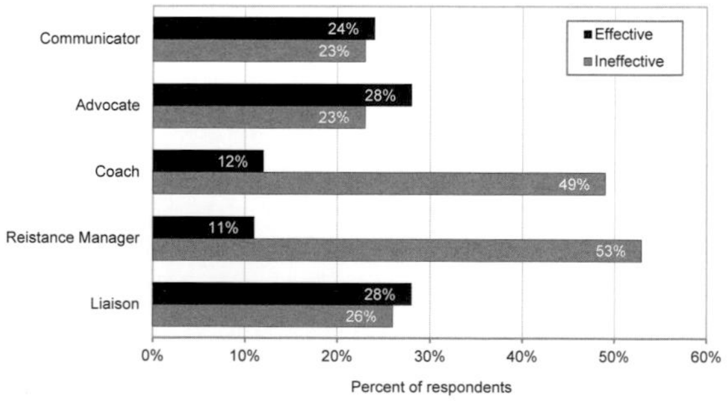

Table 11.2 shows that participants most commonly viewed managers and supervisors as somewhat effective with communicating, advocating and liaising, and ineffective at coaching and resistance managing.

Table 11.2 – Manager role fulfillment

	Communicating	Advocating	Coaching	Resistance Managing	Liaising
Extremely effective	3%	5%	2%	2%	4%
Effective	21%	23%	10%	9%	24%
Somewhat effective	53%	49%	39%	36%	46%
Ineffective	20%	20%	40%	42%	22%
Extremely ineffective	3%	3%	9%	11%	4%

Evaluating manager and supervisor change management role fulfillment

Thirty-five percent of participants in the 2015 study reported formally evaluating manager and supervisor effectiveness (Figure 11.3).

Figure 11.3 – Formally evaluated manager and supervisor role effectiveness

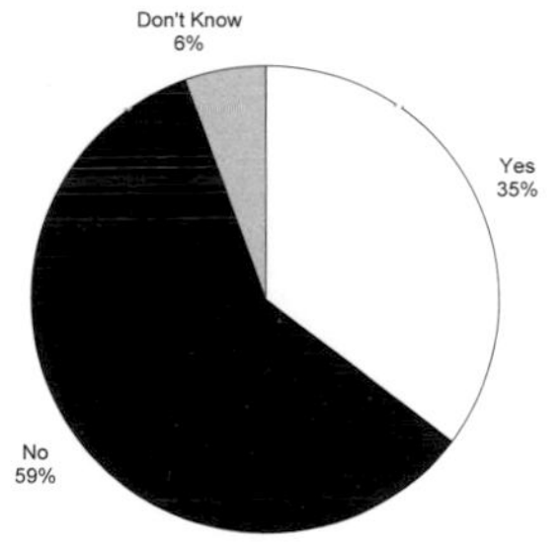

Methods to evaluate manager and supervisor change management role fulfillment

Participants who measured manager and supervisor role effectiveness identified the methods they used. Observation (67%), interviews (64%), and surveys and assessments (57%) were the most common responses, as shown in Figure 11.4.

Figure 11.4 – Techniques to evaluate manager and supervisor role effectiveness

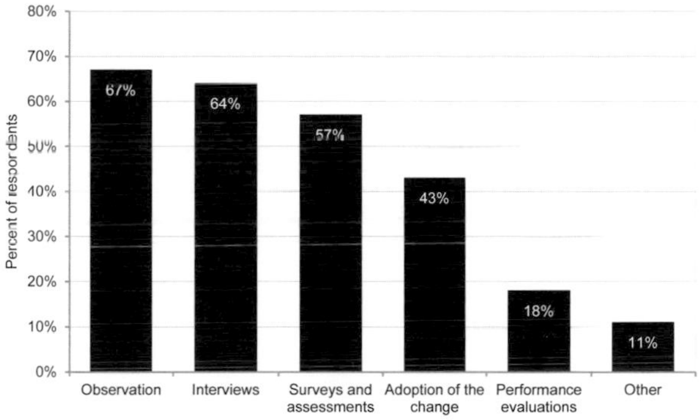

Editor's note: Participants were able to select multiple responses, resulting in a total of more than 100%.

Largest skill, competency or tool gap

Participants identified the largest gaps in skill, competency or use of tools that prevented managers from being great leaders of change with direct reports. Five gaps were identified most prominently.

1. **Communication skills**
   Effective communication was cited as the number-one shortcoming at the manager level. Managers struggled with knowing when, how and what to communicate.

Identifying appropriate communication channels, having the ability to speak face-to-face confidently and tailoring messages for audiences were notable responses.

2. **Lack of change management training**
   Lack of training in change management was the second most frequently identified gap. Training ideally includes focus on theory, principles, supporting tools and models and application. Managers were described as unaware of the nature of change management and its applications. Participants also recommended consistency in the selected methodology, stating that managers should be trained in the framework being applied on a project to allow effective collaboration between roles.
3. **Time management and saturation**
   Participants identified challenges with competing priorities and change saturation. Time management skills and the ability to prioritize change management were key skills, a lack of which inhibited a manager's ability to lead change. Participants reported that managers frequently claimed to be too busy or overworked and often underestimated the time needed by employees during rollout.
4. **Understanding the role of a manager during change**
   Managers frequently viewed change management as an activity performed by others and did not understand its impact on their role with direct reports. Managers struggled to engage with change management practices and did not take responsibility for their role in leading change.
5. **Buy-in for change**
   Participants identified a lack of buy-in and commitment for change and a lack of information as gaps for managers when leading change with direct reports. Managers were unaware of the business reasons for change and lacked understanding of the nature of the change, the impact to their team and the definition of success.

Other gaps included:

- **Resistance management**
  Managers lacked the ability to identify and manage resistance to change and often avoided conflict.
- **Coaching skills**
  Managers lacked the ability to recognize individual barriers or observe actions and to deliver constructive coaching.
- **Leadership skills**
  Participants identified lack of leadership, strategy, vision and influence as skill gaps at the manager level.
- **Change management buy-in**
  Participants identified managers as lacking buy-in for the discipline of change management.
- **Lack of sponsorship from senior leaders**
  Executive sponsorship for change management was missing, and senior leaders often did not account for the time and effort required to get managers on board and able to fulfill their roles.

Managing resistance

Source date: 2011

Eighty-nine percent of participants in the 2015 study indicated that managers and supervisors were ineffective or somewhat effective at managing employee resistance.

Participants from the 2011 study identified steps taken to help managers and supervisors become better at managing resistance. The top six steps were:

1. **Training on resistance management**
   Training that focused on managing resistance was provided to managers and supervisors. Training included targeted tactics in resistance management, identifying resistance and overcoming individual resistance. Additional training topics included human reactions and behavioral aspects of change.

2. **Change management training that included resistance management**
   Change management training was provided to managers and supervisors that included components on resistance management. Change management training varied in focus, including comprehensive change management courses, lessons targeted at leading personal change and sessions educating participants about roles and expectations during change.
3. **Provide toolkits and templates focused on resistance management**
   Participants provided managers with tools and templates to assist with resistance management. Commonly noted tools included best practices, case studies, shared success stories, Frequently Asked Questions (FAQs) and toolkits for managing resistance.
4. **Solicit feedback to understand resistance further**
   Soliciting feedback from employees to identify and understand resistance helped managers and supervisors become more effective at managing resistance. Multiple feedback channels were identified including forums, focus groups, surveys, involvement in design phases, direct feedback from prime resisters and historical reactions to change.
5. **Providing information, briefings and messaging about change**
   Providing information, briefings and messaging about change to managers and supervisors helped them preemptively identify possible resistance and answer resisters' queries in a prepared, coherent and consistent manner.
6. **Increased communication**
   Participants modified communication plans to increase communication. Proactive communication tailored to stakeholder groups and addressing possible objections was emphasized. Several participants noted training for managers and supervisors on communication.

Coaching

Source date: 2011

Eighty-eight percent of participants in the 2015 study indicated that managers and supervisors were not effective or only somewhat effective at coaching employees through personal transitions.

Participants in the 2011 study identified specific steps taken to help managers and supervisors become more effective at coaching employees through the personal transitions associated with change. The top five activities identified were:

1. **Training on coaching**
   Participants provided managers and supervisors with training specifically focused on coaching employees through the change process. Training programs varied from group workshops to individual training.
2. **General training in various competencies that included coaching**
   Managers and supervisors received some instruction on coaching during workshops and training for other competencies.
3. **Coaching tools and templates**
   Participants provided managers and supervisors with tools and templates specific to coaching for reference. Common tools cited included toolkits, best practices, Frequently Asked Questions (FAQs), shared successes and experiences with coaching.
4. **Feedback to target coaching activities**
   Participants utilized feedback collected from surveys, forums, performance reviews and informal channels to identify where coaching efforts were needed. This focused support and aided managers and supervisors in coaching their direct reports.
5. **Complete and timely information**
   To enable effective coaching, participants presented managers and supervisors with comprehensive information about the change. Information addressed why the change was needed, descriptions of the change, impact on employees, expectations of employees, goals, schedule, benefits and possible challenges. Talking point documents and communication aids ensured consistent messaging.

Tactics for ensuring managers spent adequate time managing change

Source date: 2013

Managers and supervisors are often already busy with daily responsibilities. Participants identified tactics employed to ensure managers and supervisors dedicated adequate time to managing change with employees.

1. **Support structured communications**
   Reported two times more frequently than other tactics, structured communications included using multiple communication avenues with high frequency, facilitating open discussions and one-on-one contact, creating deliberate communication plans for managers and allowing for two-way feedback.
2. **Integrate change management into existing activities**
   Change management was built into the project plan and project management reporting structures. Change management messages were added to daily briefings. Existing lunch-and-learns and meetings were used to address change topics. Change managers acted as liaisons at meetings and events that focused on a variety of topics not specific to change management.
3. **Schedule meetings**
   Participants held change management-specific meetings or briefings to keep managers and supervisors updated and informed about change. Participants used various channels to report the progress of a change initiative and address change management concepts, including webinars, focus groups, town halls and teleconferences.
4. **Provide training**
   Training was provided and workshops were delivered that focused on specific changes, change management concepts and the roles of managers and supervisors during change. Engagement sessions built awareness of change and got managers and supervisors involved.
5. **Involve other roles to champion change**
   Participants used sponsors to communicate the importance of change to managers and supervisors and advocate actively and visibly. The organization's change agents and change champions were leveraged, and a change leader was assigned to lead managers and supervisors.
6. **Administer tools**
   Managers and supervisors were provided tools to use with employees including talking points about change, toolkits, checklists, research findings and resistance management plans.
7. **Provide coaching**
   Coaching sessions, monitoring, mentoring, continued support and encouragement were provided to managers and supervisors throughout change.

Participants also emphasized building awareness of the need for change and the importance of managers' roles during change. Other tactics included clearly defining roles, getting early and active engagement, measuring performance and tying change management to managers' objectives.

Steps to get managers and supervisors on board with change

Source date: 2013

Participants identified the following steps that were taken to get managers and supervisors on board with change, so they could engage their direct reports.

1. **Emphasize communications**
   The most common step was creating structured, targeted and frequent communications about change and managers' roles during change. Participants engaged in face-to-face communications and reinforced messages with managers. Participants also created opportunities for managers and supervisors to give feedback.
2. **Hold meetings**
   Participants involved managers and supervisors in one-on-one meetings, team meetings, alignment sessions, briefings, town halls and web meetings. Participants also

noted the value of having a project or change management leader attend regularly scheduled meetings for managers and supervisors.

3. **Focus on awareness**
Information was provided to managers and supervisors to address how change would affect them and the business reasons for the change including risks of not changing. Awareness of the importance of change management and the manager's roles were also addressed.

4. **Provide materials, tools and support**
Managers and supervisors were provided with adequate tools to understand and navigate change including talking points, toolkits, action plans and key message outlines. Continued support was also provided to managers and supervisors.

5. **Engage managers**
Engaging managers during early phases of a project got managers on board with change, and holding engagement sessions was one tactic for doing so.

Other steps participants identified included delivering training and workshops, providing coaching, sharing project updates, leveraging sponsorship, clearly defining roles, using surveys and assessments, and leveraging change agents and change champions.

Preparation

Participants evaluated the following statement on a strongly agree to strongly disagree scale: "*My organization adequately prepares managers/supervisors with the skills, training and tools they need to lead during change.*" In 2015, 65% of participants either disagreed or strongly disagreed with the statement, a slight increase from 2013 when 61% of participants disagreed or strongly disagreed (Figure 11.5).

Figure 11.5 – Adequately prepared managers and supervisors

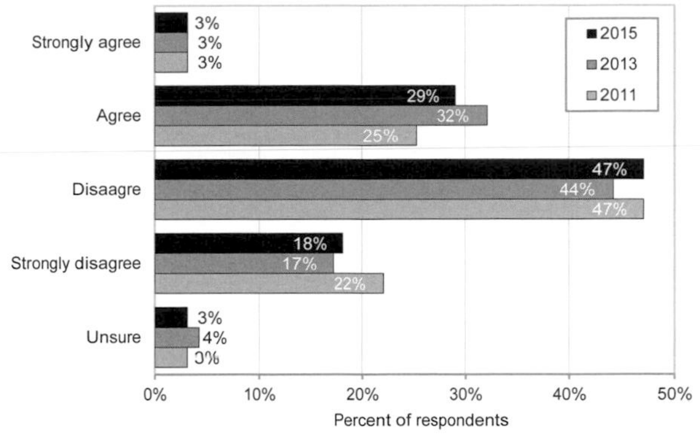

How to support managers and supervisors during change

Source date: 2009

Participants from the 2009 study offered a variety of suggestions on how to support managers and supervisors during change.

1. **Designate coaches, mentors and experts**
Designate a change champion or change team to coach and mentor managers. These subject matter experts provide expertise and moral support while working through issues with managers. Some organizations established a help desk to put managers in touch with resources quickly.

2. **Schedule communication**
Engage in constant dialogue and daily face-to-face communications with managers.

3. **Provide tools**
Provide tools for managers and supervisors to use while rolling out change including media kits, job aids, talking points, communication scripts, change management articles, case studies, reference materials and Frequently Asked Questions (FAQs).

4. **Share employee feedback**
Collect information related to change from employees through electronic or paper surveys, and share feedback with managers and supervisors.

5. **Provide continuous updates**
   Share progress updates. Keep managers and supervisors updated and recognize when milestones have been achieved.

Other tactics to support managers and supervisors included:

- Offering formal change management training
- Creating awareness for change among all departments
- Conducting process/technology training
- Setting goals

Additional learning opportunities

Source date: 2009

In addition to formal classroom training, participants offered the following approaches for building change management skills and knowledge with managers and supervisors:

1. **One-on-one discussions and coaching**
   These sessions provided safe interactions to help managers and supervisors lead change with direct reports. Participants mentioned peer coaching, mentoring by senior leaders and support from change management specialists as useful skill-building methods.
2. **Formal and regular communications**
   One-to-many communications included emails, pamphlets, newsletters, bulletin boards and electronic forum messages.
3. **Meetings**
   In some cases, change management was added as an agenda item to normal meetings. Meetings focusing on change management included short presentations, road shows, lunch-and-learn opportunities and forums covering a change management issue.
4. **Workshops and seminars**
   The most effective sessions were interactive, and included problem solving, Question and Answer (Q&A) facilitation and role playing.
5. **Tools**
   Managers and supervisors were provided tip sheets, quick reference guides, workbooks and toolkits to support change management.
6. **Articles and books**
   Managers and supervisors were provided additional literature on leading change.

Content addressed in these additional training methods included:

- Roles and responsibilities of a manager or supervisor to support change management
- Project-related information including details of the project plan, business case, key messages for communications and progress updates
- Stories and experiences including success stories from previous changes and examples of issues or concerns from the current change

CHANGE AGENT NETWORK

EXTEND PROJECT SUPPORT AND BUILD CREDIBILITY THROUGH AN ENGAGED GROUP OF ADVOCATES

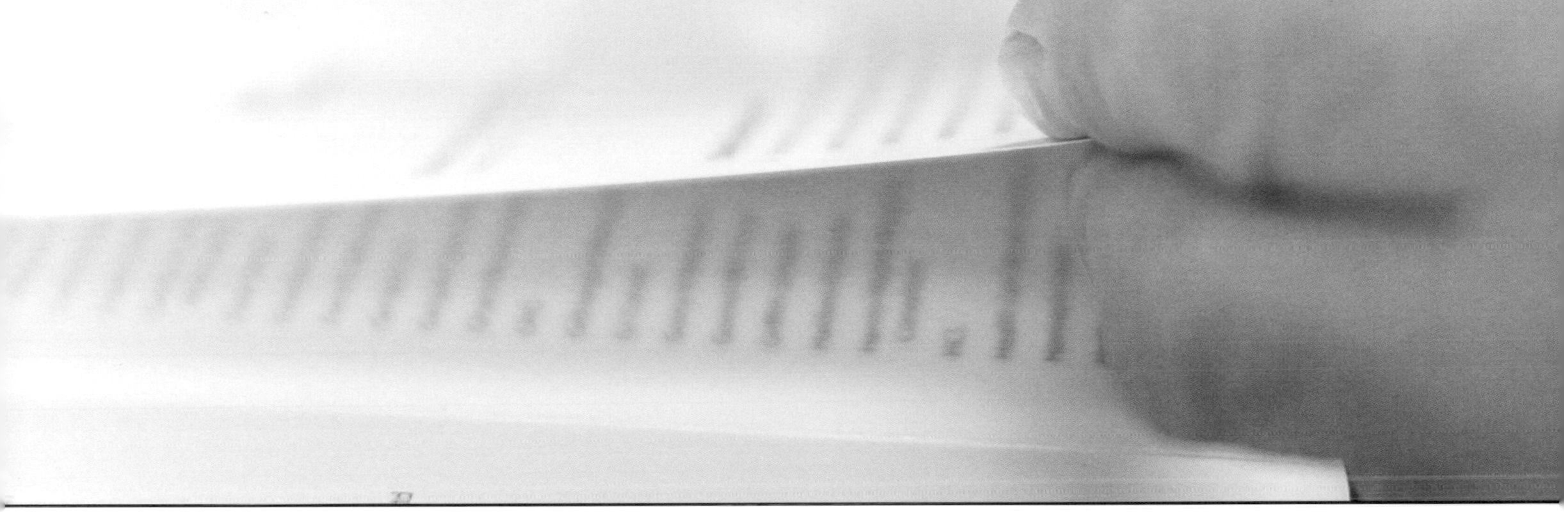

SUMMARY

Change Agent Networks are becoming an increasingly used mechanism for building momentum and broad support for change. New to this edition of the report, this chapter builds structure behind the concept by asking change professionals how they define Change Agent Networks and are leveraging these advocates across their organizations. Increase your change success by applying best practices for how you build a Change Agent Network and how you enable it to effectively support your project.

HIGHLIGHT

39% of participants leveraged a Change Agent Network and provided insights on the definition, construction, rationale and expectations of these networks.

Change agent network

Participants in the 2015 study indicated whether they leveraged formal change agent networks to support change implementation in their organization (Figure 12.1).

Figure 12.1 – Leveraged a change agent network

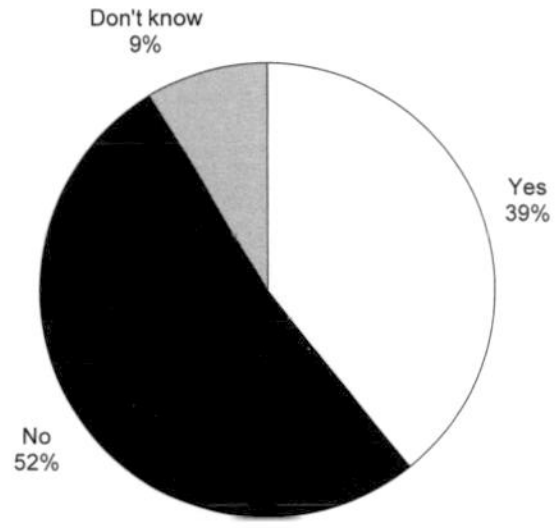

Definition

For the first time, participants described how they define a change agent network. The top four responses were:

1. **Body of change champions**
   Participants defined change agent networks as a body of change champions who are formally trained in change management methodologies. These people acted as liaisons between the project and business. These individuals were placed locally on the project team or in strategic positions within the organization to provide support and awareness of change.
2. **Impacted individuals**
   Participants defined change agent networks as comprised of individuals who were impacted first by the change. These individuals usually held positions as either managers or local agents and were impacted directly by change.
3. **Hierarchy structure**
   A hierarchy structure of individuals across multiple levels of the organization made up change agent networks. This system ensured alignment and consistency of change objectives.
4. **Influential leaders**
   A number of participants expressed that their change agent networks constituted groups of leaders who influenced and drove change. By providing guidance and direction, leaders with influence set an example of the importance of change.

Less frequent responses included:

- Change agent networks were defined by the project and changed for each project
- Respondents used a virtual platform that members accessed as a more literal change agent network
- Users stated they took advantage of and built off existing networks

Reasons to use a change agent network

Participants identified the reasons for using a change agent network. The most frequent responses were:

1. **Extend project support**
   The primary response was to provide additional support to the project, often from peers, which expedited change with fewer obstacles and greater focus.
2. **Use resources efficiently**
   By using change agent networks, participants readily allocated resources to necessary points of need. A large portion of participants indicated that they were also able to extend the scope and reach of change to geographical regions across organizations.
3. **Enhance communication**
   Change agent networks allowed participants to increase the flow of information across the organization. Barriers to communication were reduced because leaders and impacted employees had a more direct line to one another.

4. **Align consistent objectives**
A number of participants expressed that the purpose of their change agent network was to align change objectives with various levels of the organization and ensure consistency among impacted individuals.
5. **Increase knowledge**
Individuals expanded their skills and tools with a change agent network. Participants stated that they could exchange ideas and experiences which allowed increased growth of change abilities.
6. **Build credibility**
Credibility of the project was enhanced through change agent networks because impacted employees trusted their peers.
7. **Boost ownership**
Participants also used a change agent network to increase ownership because impacted individuals felt more connected with and united to the change.

Building a change agent network

The majority of participants indicated that they strategically selected impacted and influential individuals for change agent network positions when asked how they constructed their change agent networks. The top responses were:

1. **Strategic selection**
Over half of respondents stated that they formed change agent networks by leveraging individuals within impacted business areas using a formal approach. Leaders commonly nominated influential individuals as ideal change agents.
2. **Change management activities and exercises**
Change activities, such as education, training and constant communication, were common responses for how to build change agent networks. Participants emphasized the usefulness of frequent meetings to ensure alignment with change practices.
3. **Organic growth**
Change agent networks were created through natural business growth. Themes in this category included growing the network with preexisting networks, personal networking and ordinary business operations.
4. **Individual self-selection**
Participants built change agent networks by using informal strategies to identify influential individuals. Volunteers and communities of employees who shared an interest in change objectives constituted informal change agent structures.
5. **Virtual platforms**
Participants built change agent networks through virtual platforms which included training, content sharing and community building.

Criteria for selecting members of a change agent network

Participants provided the criteria they used to select members for change agent networks.

1. **Willingness**
Willingness to participate in and to promote change through the change agent network was a common theme. Participants identified the need to find those who wanted to be part of the change on a change-agent level, because change agents have a lot of potential impact on change and could cause damage through lack of support if they did not.
2. **Credibility**
Members of a change agent network should be credible, respected and influential within the organization. Participants felt that change agents should be limited to those who could positively impact the outcome of the change and not those who were simply passionate about change.
3. **Knowledgeable**
Participants reported that change was complex enough to require a leader familiar with the inner workings of the organization. Agents needed to be experienced in change

management, in some cases participants recommended certification in change management for change agents.

4. **Nominated**
   Participants reported that they often did not know who in the organization met their criteria to become members of a change agent network. Therefore, participants asked for and took nominations from impacted groups on who would be a good member of the change agent network; they provided criteria for selection but left it up to stakeholders to identify the individuals.

Change agent network roles

Participants in the 2015 study identified the roles played by a change agent network. Analysis revealed four primary roles.

1. **Communication role**
   The role most commonly identified by respondents was communication liaison. Members of the change agent network were used to disseminate communications to their respective departments, sites or regions to share information about the change project with a greater audience and provide various forms of feedback to the change project team, such as employee concerns.
2. **Leadership role**
   Respondents frequently identified various leadership roles for the change agent network. Examples included acting as the change leader for their department or region, coordinating regular meetings and leading events, acting as a role model for change in terms of adoption and use and promoting change internally by acting as change champions and selling the change.
3. **Training and support roles**
   Participants identified training and support roles as important for the change agent network. These were similar to leadership roles in that members of the change agent network guided others through the change, but these roles dealt with training others and providing support for implementing change. Examples included piloting training programs and techniques, coaching other change leaders or supervisors, managing change from the business side and deciding on strategies appropriate for the organization.
4. **Managing change internally**
   Participants identified roles change agent networks played to assist the change management team with managing change internally. Examples included conducting impact and change readiness assessments, identifying and managing resistance and tracking and reinforcing adoption. Respondents reported that members of the change agent network were held "*accountable for adoption within their organization.*"

Expectations of the change agent network

Participants in the 2015 study identified expectations they held for change agent networks. Participants highlighted the following five expectations most frequently.

1. **Advocate for and represent the change**
   Participants stated that change agent network members were informal representatives for the change in their areas. The network was intended to champion change, increase buy-in and adoption, and be a positive force regarding change to influence peers.
2. **Knowledgeable engagement and participation**
   Participants highlighted that members of change agent networks were expected to have a strong knowledge base of the change project, be early adopters, demonstrate a commitment to change and serve as subject experts.
3. **Identify resistance and report issues**
   Change agent networks were expected to assist in identification of resistance by serving as the eyes and ears of change. Participants expected members of the change agent network to report issues they encountered.

4. **Communicate messages regarding change**
   Participants said that change agents were leveraged to assist in the delivery of communication messages concerning change.

5. **Provide training and coaching on change**
   Participants stated that the change agent network was expected to provide coaching and training to employees on change and change management elements.

Additional expectations of change agent networks included:

- Develop a community of practice to share best practices
- Liaise between impacted teams
- Conduct change management on projects
- Serve as honest feedback channels
- Assist project teams

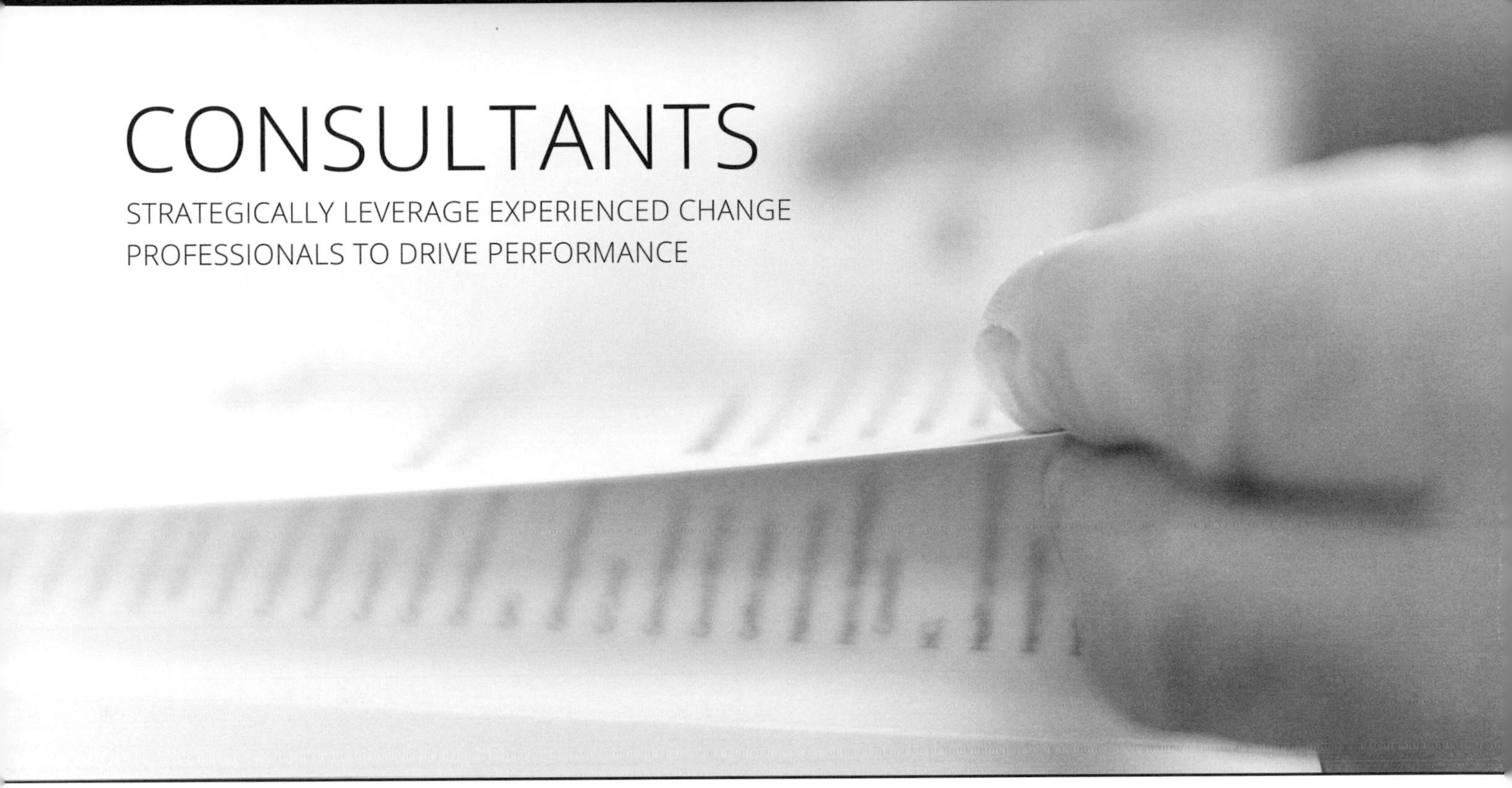

CONSULTANTS

STRATEGICALLY LEVERAGE EXPERIENCED CHANGE PROFESSIONALS TO DRIVE PERFORMANCE

SUMMARY

Engaging the right consultants can add credibility, critical knowledge and proven outcomes to your change effort. Increase your own ability to deliver project outcomes by identifying and effectively partnering with the right change management professionals. Explore how frequently consultants are used on change projects, the primary benefits and drivers for engaging outside experts and the most effective ways to leverage consultants in change efforts. If your project requires an external advisor, use the measurable criteria your peers have used in evaluating the right partner.

HIGHLIGHT

50% of participants used an external consultant to support their change project, a slight increase from previous studies.

Did you use an external consultant?

Half of participants from the 2015 study used an external consultant for change projects (Figure 13.1). This was a slight increase from 46% in the 2013 study.

Figure 13.1 – Used an external consultant for the change project

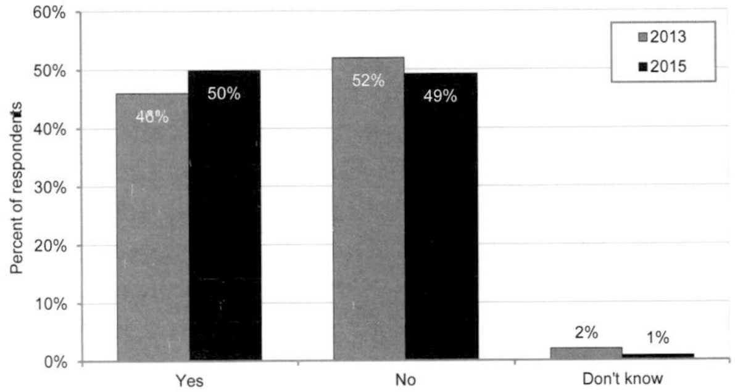

Why did you use a consultant?

Source date: 2011

Participants who used an external consultant to support change management identified six reasons for hiring one.

1. **Lack of internal competency or resources**
   Participants hired a consultant based on a lack of internal change management knowledge or competency. A number of participants also cited lack of resources and dedicated positions within their organizations.
2. **Knowledge, expertise and experience provided by consultants**
   Participants valued the knowledge, expertise and experience with change management that consultants provided.
3. **Support for the change management or project team**
   Consultants were chosen to provide support to internal change management resources and project management teams, particularly supporting duties such as daily tasks and work resulting from large changes.
4. **Proven results**
   Consultants were chosen because of a proven record of success, outside recommendations or certifications in a desired change management methodology or process.
5. **Part of project proposal or contract**
   In some cases, change management consulting was a condition or element of a project plan or was contracted as part of the change.
6. **Training to increase internal change management capacity**
   Consultants were chosen to train internal employees on change management and increase the organization's internal change management capability.

Why did you choose not to use a consultant?

Source date: 2011

Participants who did not hire a consultant provided four reasons. Sufficient existing internal capability and resources was the top reason by a two-to-one margin.

1. **Sufficient existing internal capability and resources**
   The organization had existing capabilities in change management including dedicated change management positions and certifications, trained practitioners or training available for internal resources.
2. **Budgetary constraints**
   Due to limitations in the project budget, an external consultant could not be hired.
3. **Need for change management was not identified or addressed on the project**
   The need for change management itself was not acknowledged, so no external support was sought.
4. **Lack of support from management**
   Senior management did not support use of external consultants for change management.

Primary role played by consultants

Participants in the 2015 study specified which roles their consultants played in the change. The largest decrease in consultant roles occurred in the category *mentor* which fell from 33% in 2013 to 21% in 2015 (Figure 13.2).

Figure 13.2 – Role of a change management consultant

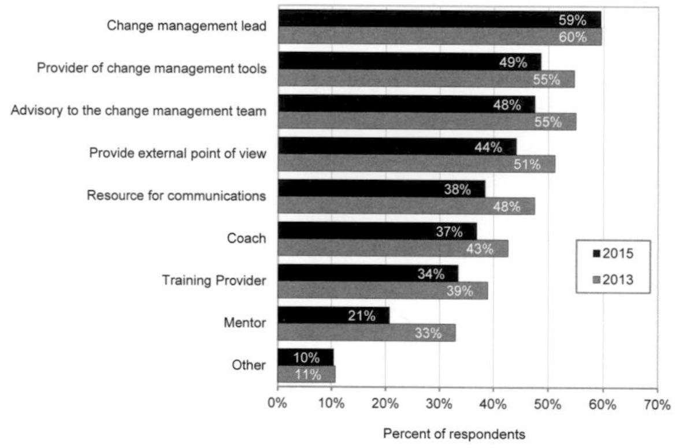

Editor's note: Participants were able to select multiple responses, resulting in a total of more than 100%.

Participants in the 2009 study originally provided a description of the following five roles fulfilled by consultants.

- **Change management lead**
  Consultants were asked to fill the role of change management lead. They created change management plans and took responsibility for all change management.
- **Advisor to a change management team**
  A number of consultants acted as advisors during change. Participants relied on these consultants to apply readiness and present-state assessments, long-term assessments and recommendations during change. A few scheduled only weekly visits with an organization. Although less connected to the people involved in change, these consultants were aware of what was going on and knowledgeable in change management.
- **Resource for communications regarding change and change management**
  Consultants were relied upon for creating and disseminating communication regarding change. They assisted with communication between executives, managers and employees.
- **Mentor and coach**
  A number of consultants filled the role of mentor or coach. Responses implied a close connection with the people involved with change. During planning and execution, consultants provided support and feedback, often at what seemed to be a more emotional level such as being a cheerleader or "*keeping fire under their toes.*" Other aspects of these consultants' roles were sponsor alignment and coaching, mediation and conflict resolution.
- **Training provider**
  Consultants provided change management training and imparted change management expertise. They educated employees, management and executives on topics such as change management methodologies, change strategies, resistance management and changing an organization's state of mind.

Participants from the 2013 study who reported other roles fulfilled by change management consultants identified:

- **Change management team member**
  As part of the change management team, consultants supported development and execution of change management. Participants reported that consultants in this role facilitated adoption, executed post go-live activities and supported creation of a Change Management Office (CMO) using their experience for guidance.
- **Project management support**
  In addition to supporting the design and release of a technical solution, change management consultants leveraged their role within the project team through transition planning and alignment with a change management team.

- **Business analyst**
  A number of change management consultants provided measurement and documentation for a project including impact analyses, training documentation, stakeholder engagement reports and overall project success updates.

Criteria for choosing a change management consultant

Source date: 2013

Participants from the 2013 and 2009 studies identified criteria for selecting change management consultants.

1. **Change management experience**
   Experience with change management was the top criterion cited by participants in the 2013 study. A change management consultant was selected based on experience with a particular change management methodology or experience with multiple methodologies. Experience with deploying change management from beginning to end, using a variety of tools and integrating change management with a project plan flexibly were core factors during selection.
2. **Existing relationship**
   A consultant's relationship and experience with the organization was the second most common criterion. Previous success with a project was also noted as an important factor. Knowledge of the company's culture and history enabled more fluent engagement with the organization. An existing relationship implied a sense of trustworthiness and resulted in operational consistency for the organization.
3. **Experience with a type of project**
   Participants prioritized consultants' experiences with their specific type of change as the third most common criterion. Having successfully worked through a similar project in the past left the organization feeling confident in the consultant's ability to manage this type of change again. Participants were in search of subject matter experts who were familiar with the current change, the impact to the organization and unique success factors.
4. **Consulting company qualifications**
   Participants considered the company's longevity, experience and references. Other qualities included a consulting firm's ability to work as part of a team in the existing company culture, interpersonal skills, work ethic and being judged a good fit for the organization.

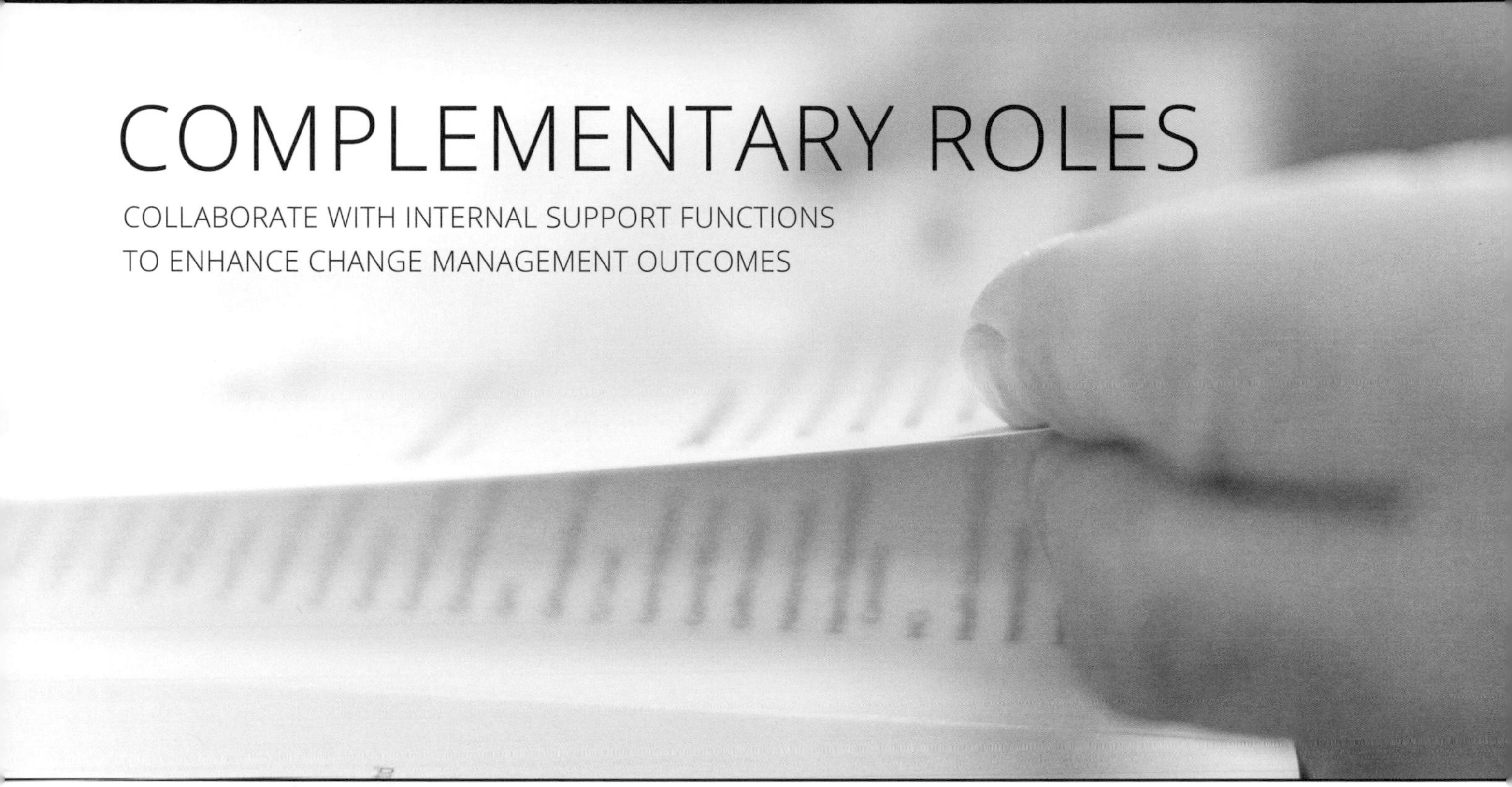

COMPLEMENTARY ROLES

COLLABORATE WITH INTERNAL SUPPORT FUNCTIONS TO ENHANCE CHANGE MANAGEMENT OUTCOMES

SUMMARY

Corporate communications departments, Organization Development, Human Resources business partners, business analysts and other business support functions can each contribute to the effective adoption of change. For the first time, research data provides insight from the change management perspective into which functional roles impact and support change deployment. Learn how to best engage with these roles and seek opportunities to leverage and collaborate with internal support functions to improve results.

HIGHLIGHT

67% of participants said their internal communications groups supported or impacted their change management work.

Use of a complementary role

For the first time, participants in the 2015 study were asked whether roles and positions within their organizations complemented or impacted change management. Participants were asked about various roles including Human Resources Business Partners, internal consultants, Organization Development, internal communications and Business Analysts. Figure 14.1 shows a breakdown of complementary role use by participants.

Figure 14.1 – Use of complementary roles

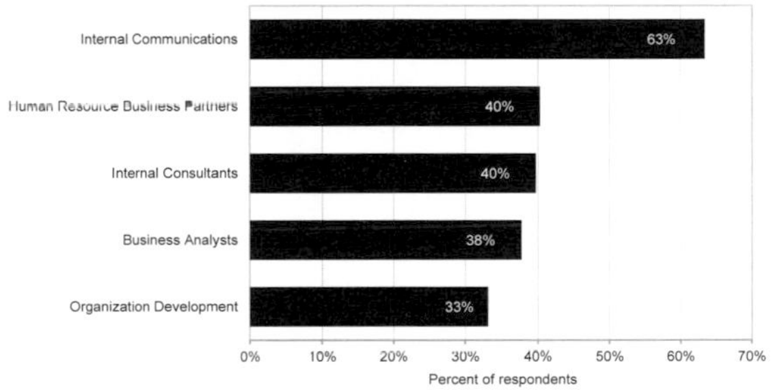

Internal Communications Group

Participants identified the roles internal communications played in change management. The top two roles were noted more than twice as often as the other three.

1. **Key messaging**
   More than any other role, participants found that key message drafting and delivery expertise were primary roles of internal communications regarding change management, including messaging concerning project impact, awareness building, coaching and training expectations, personal impact and change milestones. Messages were most commonly generated through posters, newsletters, live events, an intranet and social media.
2. **Project team member**
   More than half of respondents saw internal communications as a key contributor to the design and validation of a project communication plan. More general forms of team membership were identified such as having a direct relationship/collaboration with a change management team or integration of internal communications and the change manager role.
3. **Compliance review and approval**
   Participants felt that the internal communications group was a gatekeeper for all internal communications. They cited functions such as auditing for compliance, content review, message consistency and alignment with project/company initiatives.
4. **Advisory support**
   Internal communications served an as-needed approach to supporting the change management team. Internal communications was seen as a subject matter expert or resource available to advise and provide suggestions for appropriate messaging and delivery methods for messages produced by the project team.
5. **Strategic support**
   Internal communications created strategic corporate messages and supported communications delivered by executives. This form of support was used in largescale and/or organization-wide projects.

Human Resources Business Partners

Participants identified the roles Human Resources Business Partners played in change management. The top five responses included:

1. **Act as coaches and provide support**
   Participants highlighted that Human Resources Business Partners played a large role in coaching managers and senior leaders in their roles during change. They supported teams by providing training and development opportunities to all layers of the organization, assigning resources to the change teams and offering support when needed.
2. **Advisors to a project**
   Human Resources Business Partners served as advisors to change projects by offering advice and guidance regarding job role impacts, labor regulations, training requirements and legal matters.
3. **Oversee human resources impacts**
   Human Resources Business Partners were involved in elements of a project that impacted employee job roles, staffing modifications, recruitment, scheduling and employee well-being.
4. **Own change management within the business**
   Change management was often housed within Human Resources (HR), and Human Resources Business Partners often owned and oversaw the majority of change management.
5. **Be involved with communications**
   Human Resources Business Partners were often brought in to communicate change, conduct one-on-one meetings and assist with writing communications for the organization.

Internal Consultants

Participants identified the roles internal consultants played in change management.

1. **Change management experts**
   Internal consultants were the first to be trained in change management and helped run and implement the change management methodology on projects. Participants also reported that the consultants' projects were often the first pilot or test groups for change management within the organization.
2. **Subject matter experts**
   Internal consultants acted as subject matter experts in two distinct ways. First, they acted as technology or process experts to assist the change managers with the technical aspects of the change initiative. Second, they advised on messaging and awareness building with specific impacted groups.
3. **Advisors**
   Participants reported that internal consultants acted as change management advisors. They would consistently evaluate, direct and provide feedback on how the change management methodology was or should be deployed within specific departments.

Business Analysts

Participants explained various roles that business analysts played in change management. More than half of respondents reported using business analysts in a change management capacity, and many indicated that analysts supported project management and other responsibilities.

Business analysts as change managers

1. **Impact assessment**
   The change management responsibility most commonly placed on business analysts was assessing the impact change would have on the organization and its employees.
2. **Training**
   Of those who reported that training was a primary responsibility of business analysts, just under two thirds limited it to development of training, and the remainder used analysts for both development and facilitation.
3. **Communication**
   Business analysts were often expected to communicate directly with impacted employees and sponsors to offer support and updates. Communication was primarily with impacted groups and occasionally included creating communication for a project team to deliver.
4. **Change champions**
   In the absence of a dedicated change management resource, the role of change champion occasionally fell solely to a business analyst. This included building the case for change, performing various assessments and applying change management tools and methodology throughout a change.

Business analysts as project managers

1. **Identify current and future states**
   Business analysts identified current and future states and created a process for reaching the future state. This included identifying and developing a solution and developing metrics to gauge success with reaching a future state.
2. **Determine whether change is necessary**
   Many business analysts were tasked with assessing the need for change based on the scope, impact and overall benefit (or lack thereof) of change.
3. **Project team members**
   A small number of participants indicated that business analysts were included as project team members.

Business analysts as external support for project and change management

1. **Subject matter experts**
   Many respondents identified business analysts as subject matter experts reporting that they were often used as consultants to project and change management teams. They frequently supported multiple project teams and worked as liaisons between project teams and stakeholders. Business analysts were responsible for integrating change and project management plans into a holistic project plan.
2. **Research and analysis**
   There were a variety of responses related to business analysts performing research and data analysis. No specific form or subject matter stood out more than the rest, but they included gap analyses, business requirement assessments, on-going feedback during project implementation and best practices research.

Organization Development

Participants identified the role Organization Development (OD) played in change management.

1. **Assist in training**
   OD assisted with and often led training. Participants reported that this was largely due to the OD group having access to the necessary resources and experience with creating and implementing training throughout the organization.

2. **Provide expertise**
   Participants reported utilizing OD's technical and cultural expertise when implementing their change plans. OD provided insights that allowed participants to tailor their change management communications and other activities to specific impacted groups.

3. **Align change management with overall organization strategy**
   OD aligned change management with other change initiatives and overall company strategy. Participants reported using OD to determine the timing of change activities to align them with other company goals and initiatives.

4. **As a resource**
   Participants reported utilizing OD as a resource in their change initiatives. This included defining roles, responsibilities, and organization and job design. OD also provided specialized advice, assistance and a variety of other functions.

PART 4

ADAPTING AND ALIGNING CHANGE MANAGEMENT

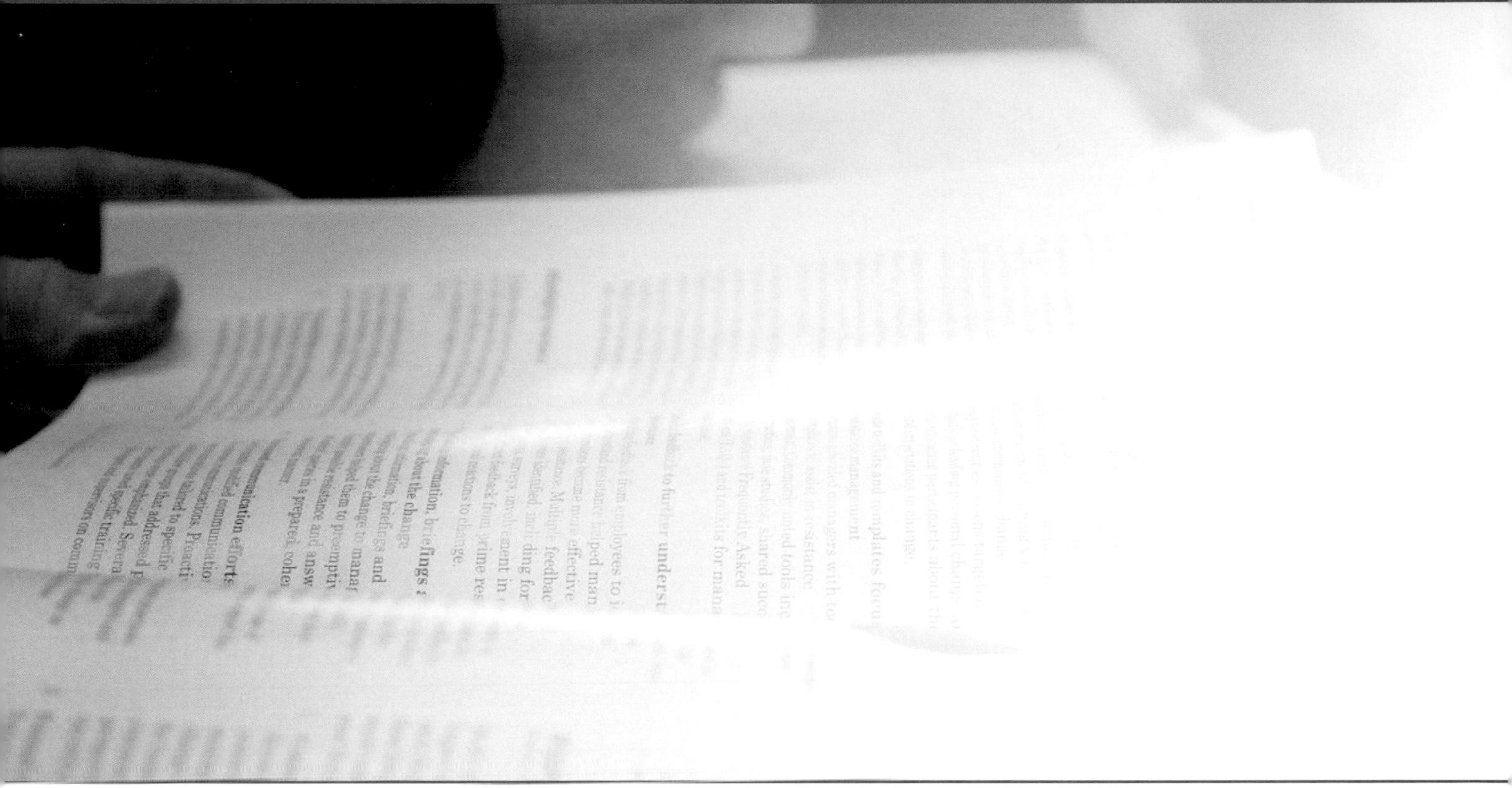

PART 4

ADAPTING AND ALIGNING CHANGE MANAGEMENT

CULTURE AND CHANGE MANAGEMENT

NAVIGATE THE COMPLEXITY OF MANAGING CHANGE WITHIN THE CONTEXT OF CULTURE

SUMMARY

The body of research for understanding the interaction of change and culture takes a step forward in this new, groundbreaking collection of findings. Change management is most effective when the cultural context of impacted employee groups is considered and influences your approach. Building upon established and validated research in the field of intercultural communication, this chapter allows you to benchmark unique challenges and specific adaptations made to change management deployment based on your organization's specific cultural factors.

HIGHLIGHT

The cultural dimensions identified as having the biggest impact on change management were: Individualism/Collectivism, Power Distance and Uncertainty Avoidance.

Cultural awareness

Impact of cultural awareness on change management

Participants in the 2015 study rated the impact of cultural awareness on employing change management. Nine of ten respondents rated cultural awareness as either *important* or *very important* with over half saying *very important* (Figure 15.1).

Figure 15.1 – Impact of cultural awareness on change management

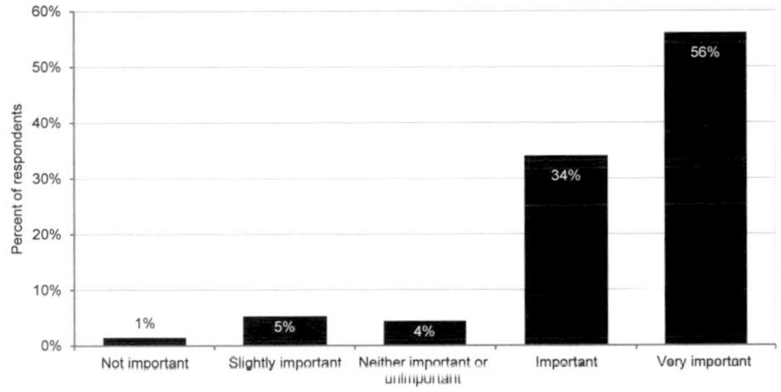

How cultural awareness influenced change management

Participants shared how cultural awareness influenced change management. Participants identified four areas in which cultural awareness impacted change management.

1. **Opportunities for customization**
   Participants felt that change management needed to be customized for the culture in which it was implemented. Change management activities and training needed to be adapted to cultural-specific standards. Change management also needed to be customized to consider disparate cultural values and beliefs.

2. **Cultural-specific adaptations**
   Being culturally aware helped identify areas in which a change management approach needed to be adapted to the culture in order to make it effective. Participants felt that different cultures would view and interact with work relationships differently, and it was important to adapt change management approaches to consider these differences. An understanding of cultural norms allowed change managers to integrate change activities more fully thereby increasing credibility.

3. **Avoid cultural-specific obstacles**
   Participants felt that every culture had obstacles and challenges that could be circumvented or addressed with appropriate cultural insight. These obstacles included cultural-specific norms and taboos that acted as landmines for a change manager and change itself, culture-specific resistance areas that might be unfamiliar to change managers, cross-cultural resentment or bias from either a change manager or organization and culturally disparate ways of experiencing and processing change.

4. **Communication needs to be thought through**
   Participants overwhelmingly identified a need to customize communications for a cultural setting. This included the mode of communication, the sender of messages and the structure and content of a message. Change managers should have a basic understanding of the language of the culture in which they are working. Communication improved through culturally-aware translators.

Global literacy

Participants in the 2015 study were asked to define what it meant to be globally literate.

1. **Awareness**
   Participants reported that awareness of the fact that there were cultural differences and norms was an important aspect of being globally literate. Knowing that other cultures had different modes, methods and beliefs than one's own was a first step in operating within that culture.
2. **Knowledge**
   Participants reported that a spectrum of knowledge about different cultures was needed to be globally literate. This knowledge could take the form of specific cultural knowledge or broad-spectrum, regional knowledge.
3. **Appreciation of cultural differences**
   Participants reported a need for appreciation of culture. Understanding cultural differences was a necessary first step, but participants found that without a degree of appreciation for those differences, understanding alone was not enough to be globally literate.

Participants rated the importance of having globally literate leaders. Nearly half of participants said it was *very important* and 87% reported it was either *important* or *very important* to have globally literate leaders (Figure 15.2).

Figure 15.2 – Importance of globally literate leaders

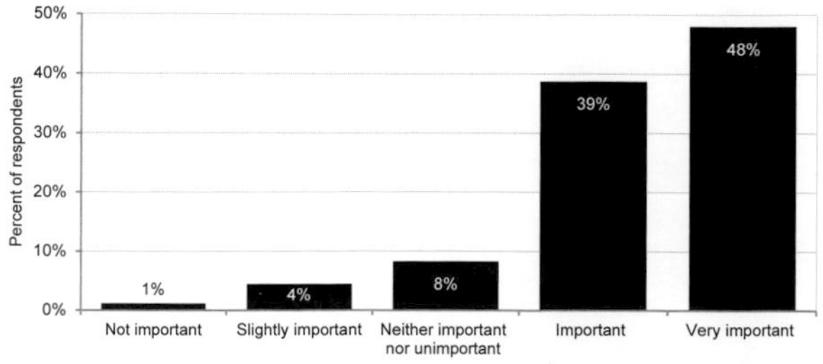

Regional cultural considerations

Perception of change management across regional cultures

Participants in the 2015 study identified perceptions of change management within the culture of their geographic region. The descriptions below present unique challenges and perceptions of change management by geographic region followed by several universal perceptions.

1. **Africa**
   Participants in Africa identified that there is emerging awareness of the need for change management. They also stated that there is still a variance in perceptions and understanding of change management, and it is not yet widespread. Other challenges included change management being perceived as optional or insignificant.
2. **Asia and the Pacific Islands**
   Participants in Asia and the Pacific Islands stated that change management is not appreciated or well understood outside of task-level activities such as communications and training. Although awareness for change management is emerging, some respondents reported challenges with autocratic management styles and the downplaying of the role of change management.
3. **Australia and New Zealand**
   Participants from Australia and New Zealand noted there is emerging awareness for change management. Current challenges to change management in this region include being viewed as useful only for communications and training, or as insignificant or optional. Although change management appears to have some visibility, it is applied inconsistently.
4. **Canada**
   Participants from Canada stated that change management was perceived as accepted and understood. There is also emerging awareness for change management in this region. Challenges to change management include it being used only during communication and training, and being viewed as optional. There are still varied perceptions and understanding of change management even in organizations that use it.
5. **Europe**
   Participants from Europe identified that there is emerging awareness of change management. Although some participants cited that change management is accepted and understood, the region faces challenges regarding perceptions that it is seen as insignificant, optional or for only communications and training.
6. **Latin America**
   Participants from Latin America reported that the region does not yet possess broad awareness of change management, and applications of change management are met with challenges such as tenuous funding or being viewed as optional or "fluffy."
7. **United States**
   The United States contained the largest group of participants. The perception of change management in this region is that it has a positive impact and is an emerging discipline. However, it also faces similar challenges seen in other regions, namely being undervalued, being simply a communication or training task or being viewed as optional or insignificant.

While patterns and trends emerged across individual regions, a range of perceptions from positive to negative were found throughout the data. Below the perceptions are presented from positive to negative.

1. **Favorable, positive impression**
   Participants stated that change management is currently appreciated and accepted in their cultures.
2. **Awareness and acceptance is emerging**
   Participants indicated that there is an upward trend in awareness, acceptance and demand for change management.

3. **Varying perceptions**
   Participants indicated that there was great variance in how change management is viewed. This variance in perception ranges from individual to individual within an organization to localized pockets where change management is considered important.
4. **Undervalued**
   Participants indicated that change management was undervalued, either not fully understood or not fully executed to its potential. Examples of this category span views such as being seen as "soft and fluffy," optional or only filling the role of communication and training.
5. **Lack of value added**
   Participants noted that change management is not currently viewed favorably. Responses included being resistant and cynical and being downplayed due to more authoritarian or autocratic management styles.

Editor's note: Participants from the Middle East contributed survey data. However, there were not a sufficient number of responses to constitute a viable sample for this question, so they are not included here.

Parts of change management that did not fit with various cultures

2015 study participants identified which parts of a change management approach did not fit well within the culture. The two themes that emerged across multiple regions are presented first followed by a breakdown of themes for the specific geographic regions.

Overall themes

1. **Lack of time for necessary activities**
   All cultural regions stressed a lack of time to complete assessments and activities that change management requires. Project teams moved quickly onto other projects, and every level of staff experienced time and energy constraints that prevented them from fully participating in change management.
2. **Current description of change management and its value**
   Participants in the United States, Australia and Canada described a lack of clarity regarding what change management is and the value it brings to a project or organization. U.S. participants cited lack of hard numbers on the Return on Investment (ROI) of change management, and Australian participants described change management as too theoretical. In Canada, employees preferred more details up front and wanted concrete steps concerning how to succeed with change management.

Africa

1. **Sponsorship coaching**
   Cultural emphasis on reputation made sponsor coaching difficult to implement because the need for coaching was seen as a negative reflection on an executive.
2. **Employee engagement**
   Employee engagement experienced low traction because employees felt that the change would impact them negatively. Employees also felt they could not voice their opinions of the change because it could harm their standing in the organization.

Asia

1. **Disruptive**
   Change management activities were interpreted as disruptive especially, as one participant described, if the change affected an "*existing established belief, culture, or social harmony.*"
2. **Open engagement**
   An organization's collectivist culture hindered the effectiveness of employee engagement. Open forum engagement, in particular, was a poor fit because employees would not speak openly or voice disagreement with the change in such a setting.

3. **Distance between executives and employees**
There was little interaction between executives/supervisors and frontline staff members, so change management geared toward sponsors and managers could fail to gain traction.

Australia

1. **Resistance and reinforcement**
Change leaders struggled to address resistance and to reinforce adoption of change. Negative enforcement created coercive resistance, and reinforcement was seen as "spin." This was especially true if resistance management or reinforcement was initiated by an outside change management team or leader instead of by a staff member native to a department.
2. **Frequent and credible communication**
Australian participants highlighted difficulties with communication about a change because leaders were reluctant to share details about change and employees could be distrustful of information when offered.
3. **Executive sponsorship and credibility**
Executives lacked the same level of authority seen in other regional cultures due to more democratic structures, which was especially true in government organizations. High turnover of executives negatively impacted credibility.

Canada

1. **Executive communication**
Due to a culture of self-management and individual responsibility, executive communication and engagement were viewed as less valuable.
2. **Employee or manager coaching**
Employees and managers were accustomed to functioning without involvement from executives or teams outside of their departments. They often viewed a change team's coaching or accountability as an insult or slight.
3. **Independent departments**
Many participants described their organization as silo-ed, with departments or divisions working independently. This conflicted with organizational change competencies if a change methodology was not flexible enough to be tailored to each unique business group.

Europe

1. **Focus on individual transitions**
European participants reported little recognition of the need for individual transitions during change especially when discussing the emotional component of individual transitions. Changes were seen as absolute, requiring adoption without further convincing.
2. **Assessments and feedback**
Receiving completed assessments for early planning or post-change measurements was ineffective because employees were reluctant to criticize their peers or superiors.
3. **Personal and interpersonal communication**
Face-to-face employee engagement was challenging because interpersonal communications about an employee's emotional responses to change were not cultural norms.

United States

1. **In-depth training**
As more autonomous workers, employees preferred training that took up a minimal amount of time or templates they could follow and implement on their own.
2. **Employee coaching**
Participants identified self-reliance as problematic for coaching because employees did not like to be told what to do. Accepting coaching could be perceived as losing independence.
3. **Coaching up**
The hierarchical and silo-ed structure of organizations limited the influence a change management team could have. Leaders

disliked taking advice from those at a lower tier in the organization's hierarchy. Managers and those at or below a change manager's level could be equally resistant to coaching because they considered themselves accountable only to their superiors within their departments or teams.

4. **Rigid change management structure**
The structure of change management was often cited as too complex. Participants highlighted the complexity and rigid structure of organizational change methodologies as hurdles for many parts of their organizations because they failed to account for influential and vocal minorities and autonomous groups that disliked a mandated methodology that was not tailored to them.

Note on stakeholder inclusion:
European, Canadian and Australian participants mentioned the importance of incorporating leaders of all stakeholder into a change management plan. In Europe, unions could have more influence than an organization's executives or change management team. Australian and Canadian participants cited the need to engage indigenous leaders in public or government initiatives because these leaders held more authority than outside officials.

Editor's note: Participants from Latin American and Middle Eastern countries contributed survey data, but there was not a sufficient number of responses to constitute a viable sample for this question. Therefore those regions are not represented here.

Cultural reasons for resisting change management

Participants identified primary reasons people in their region resisted implementation of change management practices.

Across all cultures

1. **Lack of understanding**
Across all countries surveyed, lack of understanding of what change management entails was cited as a main cause of resistance to its practice. Frequently, change management was viewed as project management or only communication and training.

2. **Lack of perceived value**
In addition to a lack of understanding of what change management is, participants from across all cultures noted that change management is not seen as valuable or essential to project success. This included difficultly in measuring the Return on Investment (ROI) and proving change management's contribution to the success of projects.

Regional-specific causes for resistance

Responses were analyzed separately for the global regions. Although there were similarities across some regions regarding causes of resistance, there were unique reasons and variance in the importance of those reasons. The regional-specific reasons for resisting change management are in rank order for each region.

Africa

1. Lack of time and resources to implement change management
2. A top-down approach that forces change and does not involve those impacted
3. Lack of leadership buy-in and involvement
4. Fear of the unknown
5. Lack of credibility for change management and change managers
6. Resistance to a new way of working
7. Fear of losing job security or authority

Asia

1. Lack of time to take on additional work driven by change management
2. Fear of losing job security and authority in role
3. General resistance to a new way of working

Australia

1. A top-down approach that forces change and does not involve those impacted
2. Change saturates organizations that are then unable to adopt change management
3. Negative change management experiences that caused lack of credibility
4. Lack of sponsor involvement and trust in leadership

Canada

1. Daily workloads do not allow for change management practices
2. Change management is too costly or complicated, and resources are not dedicated to it
3. Lack of leadership and management support and involvement
4. Change management takes too much time and effort and delays project timelines
5. Individualistic or top-down approach

Europe

1. Change management is seen as too costly, complicated or difficult; therefore, resources are not dedicated to its application
2. A top-down approach that forces change and does not involve those impacted
3. Change management and its value are not communicated in ways that resonate with the audience
4. Lack of leadership and management support and involvement

United States

1. General resistance to new ways of working
2. Change management is seen as too costly or complicated, and resources are not dedicated to it
3. Daily workloads do not allow change management
4. Lack of leadership and management support and involvement
5. A top-down approach that forces change and does not involve those impacted
6. Belief that change management will slow progress and delay project timelines

Editor's note: Participants from Latin American and Middle Eastern countries contributed survey data, but there was not a sufficient number of responses to constitute a viable sample for this question. Therefore, those regions are not represented here.

Factors that aid adoption

Participants identified with a variety of factors that motivated the use of change management within their culture. The top factors were consistent across various regions.

1. **Motivation**
   The respondents consistently reported that a top reason for applying change management was to motivate employees to adopt the change by helping them understand the impact to them or "what's in it for me?" (WIIFM). A second related reason was to encourage people to be involved by ensuring they had a solid understanding of what the change is and why it is being implemented.
2. **Proven approach**
   A persistent theme reported by the participants was that change management is a proven approach that brings value to the project or organization. Change management is viewed as providing not only direct financial value but also a framework and methodology for implementation and a way to demonstrate consideration for how people will be impacted.
3. **Negative experiences with changes that did not employ change management**
   Participants stated that negative experiences and results from changes initiatives that did not use change management were large factors in their decisions to utilize it now. Additionally, personal testimonials about the positive experiences others had using change management, combined with the failed implementations and painful experiences, often supported the decisions to employ change management.
4. **Preparedness for the future**
   Participants stated that they applied change management to remain competitive in their industry or market. They reported a sense of urgency and an awareness of upcoming changes as factors that made them feel that change management was necessary.
5. **Professional growth**
   A number of participants reported change management as a next step in their professional growth.

Cultural dimensions and change management

For the first time, a section on the culture of the organization was included in the best practices study. Gaining insight into the cultural context of an organization enables understanding and better application of change management practices.

Due to the broad and complex nature of culture, Prosci analysts consulted several independent studies to identify the cultural dimensions that have the greatest impact on change management work. Of the large body of research that exists on cultural dimensions, the following references were leveraged to select the cultural dimensions for the benchmarking study:

- GLOBE (House, Hanges, Javidan, Dorfman & Gupta, 2004)
- Hofstede's Cultural Dimensions Theory (Hofstede, 1980)
- Trompenaar's Seven Dimensions of Culture (Trompenaar & Turner 1997)

Upon reviewing the numerous cultural dimensions presented in these works, Prosci analysts identified six cultural dimensions with the greatest impact on change management.

1. Assertiveness
2. Individualism versus Collectivism
3. Emotional Expressiveness
4. Power Distance
5. Performance Orientation
6. Uncertainty Avoidance

In the 2015 study, respondents indicated where their organization fell on a spectrum for each of the six dimensions. Respondents then identified the unique challenges they faced due to this cultural dimension and specific adaptations to their change management work based on this cultural dimension.

Table 15.3 shows the study population distribution across the six cultural dimensions. Participants' scores on the cultural dimension spectrums were segmented on a scale from extremely low to extremely high. Analysis on the specific challenges and adaptations for each cultural dimension is presented in this section.

Table 15.3 – Respondent distribution across six cultural dimensions

	Extremely Low	Low	Moderately Low	Moderately High	High	Extremely High
Assertiveness	8%	19%	17%	14%	33%	9%
Individualism (low)/ Collectivism (high)	12%	24%	20%	13%	25%	6%
Emotional Expressiveness	14%	27%	20%	15%	18%	6%
Performance Orientation	10%	16%	20%	15%	25%	14%
Power Distance	7%	14%	17%	16%	26%	20%
Uncertainty Avoidance	4%	13%	20%	16%	32%	15%

Assertiveness

Assertiveness is a cultural dimension that describes the degree to which a person is able and expected to advocate his/her personal well-being and goals in their relationships with others. Organizations with low assertiveness communicate in indirect and subtle ways; face-saving is both expected and practiced. Subordinates are expected to be loyal and follow executives' leads. Organizations with high assertiveness communicate in an unambiguous and blunt way, and subordinates are expected to take the initiative during interactions with executives.

Participants indicated their location along the assertiveness spectrum (using a scale from zero to 100) and identified challenges and adaptations for implementing change given their location on the spectrum. Data were analyzed to identify challenges and adaptations for low (spectrum scores of zero to 33), moderate (34 to 67) and high (68 to 100) assertiveness cultures (Figure 15.4).

Figure 15.4 – Average scores for assertiveness across the study

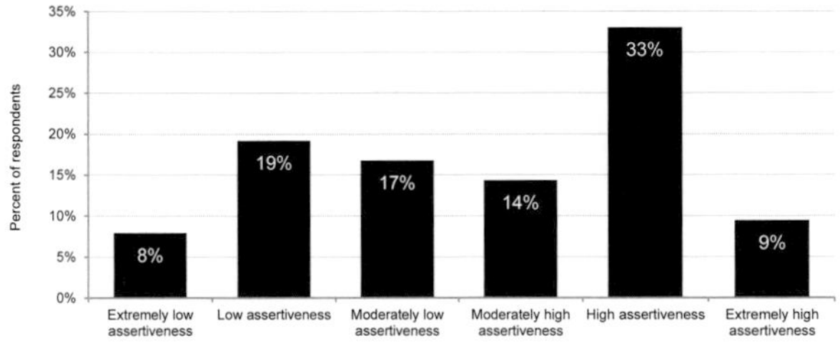

Participants identified challenges they encountered in their change management work and provided adaptations they would make to their change management strategy based on their cultures' assertiveness scores.

Low assertiveness cultures

Challenges

1. **Feedback**
   When provided, feedback was an unreliable measure due to low honesty. Many participants stated that receiving feedback was infeasible, and they were forced to make educated guesses when adjusting or customizing change strategies.
2. **Resistance**
   There was lack of direct accountability at every level and in impacted groups. Participants found this lack of accountability to be prohibitive when managing resistance because there was no one person who could take charge or work with the change team to manage resistance.
3. **Communication**
   Communication was often sanitized to a point at which it lost impact and clarity. Difficult messages were often not sent for fear of upsetting recipients or groups. Participants felt communication was ambiguous or overly complicated and often slowed change.

Adaptations

1. **Communication**
   Respondents reported communicating more frequently and sooner about a change or project. Communication was direct, providing important information about change. Participants collected direct feedback from impacted groups regarding change.
2. **Approach**
   Participants created focus groups or teams for specific projects. These groups worked to customize change management for projects to ensure that the needs of impacted groups were addressed.

Moderate assertiveness cultures

Challenges

1. **Communications**
Impacted groups preferred face-to-face communication, and in larger organizations, this posed logistical problems. Since communication was often more general, participants felt it lost the intended impact with audiences. Impacted groups often dismissed or ignored communication that was not delivered face-to-face.
2. **Resistance**
Respondents had to address both active, vocal resistance and passive, unspoken resistance. Participants had to employ multiple tactics to combat resistance, increasing the amount of work, time and resources spent on resistance management.
3. **Feedback**
Impacted groups were hesitant to give feedback due to a fear of retaliation from management and other executive groups. Participants spent additional time and resources customizing feedback requests for each impacted group to ensure they did not feel threatened.
4. **Sponsorship**
Sponsors struggled with appropriate and effective communication. They would either be too direct, appearing aggressive or angry, or too vague, so impacted groups would receive only small portions of necessary information.

Adaptations

1. **Approach**
The most common execution adaptation was increased time spent during the planning phases of a project. This included the creation of deliverables and the forecasting of potential resistance. This allowed the creation of concrete standards that provided consistency among projects.
2. **Communication**
Participants indicated that effective two-way communication, especially listening, was key. Participants viewed communication as a process of awareness building. Although communication often dealt with impacts to specific groups, it also included more general information about change.
3. **Sponsorship**
Participants felt that the use of sponsors during change led to more effective change management. Participants reported that it was important to first coach a sponsor on how he/she could fulfill the roll effectively, and second to ensure that all sponsors maintained an active and visible presence throughout change.

High assertiveness cultures

Challenges

1. **Communication**
Participants reported assertiveness stifled effective communication efforts. Communication tended to be aggressive or attacking, which resulted in messages being filtered for some groups and not others. This resulted in some impacted groups being informed differently about the initiative. An atmosphere of doubt surrounding the project resulted.
2. **Resistance**
Resistance was often loudly voiced and came from charismatic sources. Resistance was often extreme and seen as the result of the high degree of the assertiveness of the people within the organization. Impacted groups that did not like the change initiative would not adopt the changes and would actively encourage others to do the same.

3. **Feedback**
   Due to the filtering of messages to employees, challenges arose when attempting to gather comparable, meaningful feedback. In some cases, too much feedback contributed to a reduced speed of project execution. Respondents cited potential for retaliation due to the content of the feedback provided, specifically from senior level management. At times there was also a disconnect between the feedback that was being given and the actions that were taken to address the identified problems.

Adaptations

1. **Communication**
   Communication was designed to ensure that members of the organization remained engaged during a project. Communication was informational and dealt with the impact of change over the organization as a whole.
2. **Approach**
   Participants spent more time planning for resistance management and identifying potential sources of resistance. Resistance was viewed as subtle and not outspoken making it important to predict where resistance spots would appear.

Table 15.5 shows the distribution of assertiveness scores by region, and Table 15.6 shows the distribution of scores by industry.

Table 15.5 – Assertiveness scores for each region

Region	Low	Medium	High
Africa	35%	30%	33%
Asia and Pacific Islands	35%	27%	38%
Australia and New Zealand	24%	28%	48%
Canada	30%	37%	33%
Europe	26%	27%	47%
Latin America	62%	24%	14%
Middle East	23%	31%	46%
United States	26%	31%	43%

Table 15.6 – Assertiveness scores for each industry that made up more than 1.5% of the study

Industry	Low	Medium	High
Health Care	31%	27%	42%
Government - State	37%	22%	41%
Banking	25%	30%	45%
Finance	31%	29%	40%
Consulting	21%	25%	54%
Oil and Gas	30%	32%	38%
Government - Federal	25%	38%	37%
Education Services	33%	29%	38%
Insurance	31%	20%	49%
Manufacturing	30%	26%	44%
Utilities	32%	27%	41%
Other	20%	38%	42%
Government - Local & Municipal	32%	37%	31%
Information Services	9%	25%	66%
Retail Trade	24%	21%	55%
Telecommunications	8%	38%	54%
Professional, Scientific & Technical Services	29%	29%	42%
Consumer Goods Manufacturing	30%	30%	40%

Individualism/collectivism

Individualism/collectivism is a cultural spectrum that describes the degree to which people function more as individuals or a collective community. Employees in an organization that is more culturally collective are expected to act in a way that benefits the organization, and in turn, employees expect and trust the organization to meet their needs. Employees in an organization that is more culturally individualistic are expected to take the initiative to ensure their needs and goals are met and to prioritize their own happiness, welfare and fulfillment over those of the organization.

Participants indicated their location along the individualism/collectivism spectrum (using a scale from zero to 100) and identified challenges and adaptations for implementing change given their location on the spectrum. Data were analyzed to identify challenges and adaptations for low (spectrum scores of zero to 33), moderate (34 to 67) and high (68 to 100) individualist/ collectivist cultures (Figure 15.7).

Figure 15.7 – Average scores for individualism/collectivism across the study

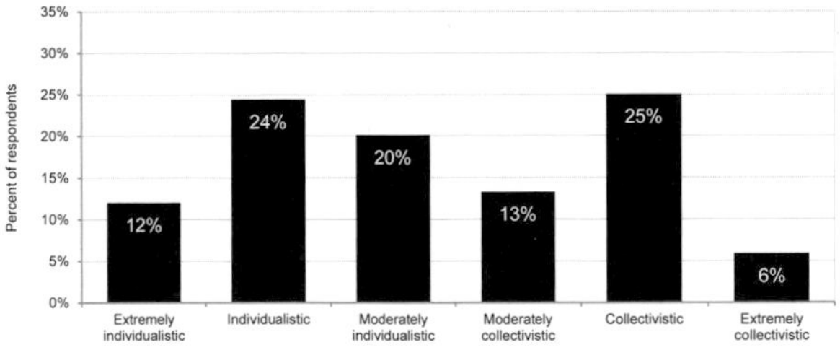

Individualistic cultures

Challenges

1. **Gaining buy-in for initiatives without direct impact**
   Participants felt it was harder to gain buy-in for projects that benefited other groups or the collective good as a whole. Individuals resented giving up their privileges or adjusting their work habits to benefit their colleagues and resisted company-wide initiatives that did not directly impact them in a positive way.
2. **Emphasis on personal satisfaction**
   Participants reported difficulty in identifying and communicating the "what's in it for me?" (WIIFM) for individual employees. The desire for leadership to make a change was not enough to bring employees on board; they needed to understand and believe that a change would personally benefit them to support it. Many participants called attention to the fact that when employees have a decision in how they will participate in the change they often opted out of the change if they did not see any personal benefit in it for them.
3. **Teamwork and collaboration**
   A lack of teamwork was identified as a significant challenge. Employees did not have the desire to collaborate and share ideas because they preferred to do work on their own and in their own way. In highly individualistic cultures, employees often lacked the ability to work effectively as a team toward a common goal. Participants felt this was due in equal parts to employees thinking they could do better on their own and a dislike of having to work on projects that did not affect them.

Adaptations

1. **Understand and target the individual**
   Participants identified the need for the change management team to be cognizant of the motives and views of individuals and to ensure they are taken into consideration throughout the project. Participants adapted their change management work to focus on the individual impact and contribution, reducing emphasis on what is best for the organization. Participants also felt that it was important to conduct impact analyses at the individual level and communicate the "what's in it for me?" (WIIFM). Additional adaptations included targeting individual engagement in the project and providing rewards and recognition at the individual level as part of reinforcement efforts.
2. **Establish small group collaboration and a team focus**
   Participants reported change management efforts required a significant focus on building collective engagement and demonstrating the benefits of working as a team. The frequency of team meetings and development of cross-functional groups was increased, generating representation from diverse audiences and allowing individuals to express their own needs and to be exposed to the needs of others. The influential nature of group dynamics and driving toward consensus were key benefits of working in groups.
3. **Structured communication channels**
   Communication channels needed to be identified up front, providing a consistent approach for tailoring messages and opening structured feedback mechanisms for individuals to be heard. Communication plans required consistency, yet frequency and content was adjusted to incorporate the topics identified in the feedback.

Displaying both collectivist and individualistic tendencies

Challenges

1. **Reduced focus on long-term benefits for the organization**
   Participants felt that employees often would not take into account or be influenced by the changes that solely benefited the long-term success of the organization. Participants felt this often resulted in additional challenges and effort required when the reasons for a change were driven by the potential organizational benefits, and those benefits were communicated at the beginning of the initiative.
2. **Working across business units**
   Participants in a moderate-ranked culture felt there was a lack of information sharing and collaboration across business units. Participants identified a variety of departmental silos resulting from this lack of cross-departmental collaboration. Participants felt this lack of cross-department teamwork made it more difficult for employee and organization-wide change management initiatives, as informal employee groups were formed and created their own unique way of working and were unwilling to adapt their methods to those of other departments resulting in an "us versus them" culture.
3. **Importance of WIIFM**
   Participants in the moderate culture felt that employees focused on "what's in it for me?" (WIIFM) which impacted the degree to which they were willing to participate in the change. Participants felt that employees were more likely not to be engaged and supportive of the change. This resulted in additional work for the change manager to identify the value for each employee and to be prepared to answer their questions when this topic presented ongoing challenges.

Adaptations

1. **Team building and group support**
Participants identified the need to organize teams at the project initiation phase. Participants identified that individuals needed an opportunity to speak up and have a say in the change, while allowing the organization to share project support resources, resulting in a team setting that allowed for collaboration and collective goals with greater buy-in. Additionally, many participants noted the need to communicate the benefits of working together and the specific benefits the change would bring for each group.

2. **Communicate to individuals**
The need to cater to the individual as the recipient of the change management activities was the second most recommended adaptation. The activities described included communicating "what's in it for me?" (WIIFM) for each individual, structuring project updates to target individuals, inviting individuals to participate and have their feedback heard, and scheduling one-on-one meetings for consultation.

3. **Emphasize the greater good of the organization**
Participants reported the need to highlight the greater good of the organization. Participants recommended focusing on the benefit to the organization as a whole and how individual contributions created something larger than any one person or group could do on their own. Recognizing and celebrating "one company" was a common response, as organizations looked to globally standardize a collectivist culture, to reduce the perception of only one department and to emphasize "we're all in it together" messaging.

Collectivist cultures

Challenges

1. **Group decision making**
Participants reported a cultural drive to arrive at a group consensus whenever a decision needed to be made, resulting in slower time frames for decision making and the need to campaign for specific desired outcomes. Additionally, employees desired and expected to be involved in making decisions and having the opportunity to contribute their own view. Participants also reported challenges with accountability as decisions often fell on a group and not an individual person.

2. **Loss of individual input**
Participants felt that the focus on group decision making and reaching consensus often resulted in a loss of individual input, especially dissenting input. Participants reported that employees often resisted speaking up when their input went against the consensus and would often keep quiet and follow the group rather than speak up, even when their insight could have prevented later problems or project failure. Participants also felt that this loss of individual input resulted in a lack or stifling of creativity due to the group's need for a simple solution.

3. **Group influence on decision making**
Group solidarity can lead to implicit support. Participants identified the influence that the collective group could wield over its individual members made it difficult to "turn the ship," as participants reported employees' tendency to rely on the collective voice rather than their own personal beliefs or opinions regarding the change. Participants felt that this reliance on the group voice led to challenges with managing resistance because employees expected to be treated and interacted with as a group rather than on an individual level.

Adaptations

1. **Group representation and deliverables**
   Participants identified an emphasis on group strategy and implementation as the primary adaptions of their change management work. Leveraging organizational value of groups, participants encouraged employees to help their colleagues and looked for volunteers to be champions within the various groups; these actions provided an intra-group dynamic that fostered natural conversion and desire to participate in the change. Creating deliverables for each divisional group and using group facilitation to create a common understanding of the vision of the future state resulted in a rich, collaborative solution.
2. **Request and encourage feedback**
   The collectivist cultural emphasis created a need for a vehicle that allowed feedback to be shared in a structured and safe environment. Impact analysis should be conducted up front. Employees should know how to raise concerns throughout the project, and the change management team should check in more often to identify resistance. Many participants reported that more input provides a more enriched program with unique perspectives and greater organizational buy-in.
3. **Leverage influential advocates**
   Participants provided additional support for key influencers who had potential to impact the group and positioned them as credible local experts to help lead the change effort. Identifying change champions positively affected group adoption and provided additional reinforcement for the message of the sponsor.

Table 15.8 shows the distribution of individualism/collectivism scores by region, and Table 15.9 shows the distribution of scores by industry.

Table 15.8 – Individualism/collectivism scores for each region

Region	Low	Medium	High
Africa	16%	32%	52%
Asia and Pacific Islands	14%	24%	62%
Australia and New Zealand	36%	35%	29%
Canada	31%	40%	29%
Europe	36%	38%	26%
Latin America	38%	43%	19%
Middle East	33%	34%	33%
United States	42%	26%	32%

Table 15.9 – Individualism/collectivism scores for each industry that made up more than 1.5% of the study

Industry	Low	Medium	High
Health Care	39%	32%	29%
Government – State	33%	35%	32%
Banking	29%	36%	35%
Finance	32%	43%	25%
Consulting	45%	23%	32%
Oil and Gas	36%	26%	38%
Government – Federal	35%	43%	22%
Education Services	45%	33%	22%
Insurance	30%	40%	30%
Manufacturing	30%	35%	35%
Utilities	34%	27%	39%
Other	27%	27%	46%
Government - Local & Municipal	37%	25%	38%
Information Services	50%	23%	27%
Retail Trade	31%	38%	31%
Telecommunications	35%	35%	30%
Professional, Scientific & Technical Services	59%	18%	23%
Consumer Goods Manufacturing	26%	48%	26%

Emotional expressiveness

Emotional expressiveness is a cultural dimension that describes the degree to which people are allowed, expected and encouraged to display emotions and emotional states to others. Employees in a low emotionally expressive organization are expected not to display emotions. Although emotions are felt, a person is expected to keep them tightly controlled. Emotional displays in public are seen as awkward and unnecessary. Employees in organizations that are highly emotionally expressive feel able and are encouraged to display their emotional states to others openly and without reservation. Emotional displays are not considered awkward or uncomfortable in the workplace.

Participants indicated their locations along the emotional expressiveness spectrum (using a scale from zero to 100) and identified challenges and adaptations for implementing change given their location on the spectrum. Data were analyzed to identify challenges and adaptations for low (spectrum scores of zero to 33), moderate (34 to 67) and high (68 to 100) emotional expressiveness cultures (Figure 15.10).

Figure 15.10 – Average scores for emotional expressiveness across the study

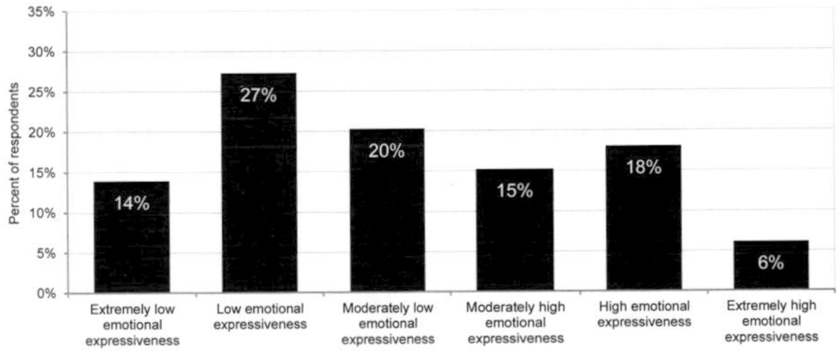

Low emotional expressiveness cultures

Challenges

1. **Fear and avoidance behavior**
   Participants reported that fear of conflict or upsetting anyone often derailed plans and masked resistance to the change. Participants also reported that impacted groups often struggled to express their concerns around the change.
2. **Passive-aggressive behaviors**
   Due to a lack of desire to express their feelings, impacted groups often resorted to passive-aggressive behaviors during the change. This caused a buildup of resentment whenever anyone had to work with the change.

Adaptations

1. **Create an open communication/feedback channel**
   Creating an open communication and feedback channel and encouraging employees to provide feedback without fear of consequences allowed trust building and a feeling of participation rather than merely being subject to change.
2. **Use one-on-one communications**
   Participants reported using one-on-one sessions to gather concerns and input from employees. With groups that are less prone to emotional expressiveness, reading secondary signals like body language and "reading between the lines" to get to the true feelings of an employee during feedback was important.
3. **Engage with managers/supervisors**
   Participants engaged managers and supervisors of employees to gather observed feedback and responses from teams. A more accurate account of perceptions from the "ground level" was gained by leveraging the proximity of managers and supervisors. Engaging managers and supervisors served the dual purpose of expanding their role as change agents.

Moderate emotional expressiveness cultures

Challenges

1. **Bottling up emotions**
   Emotional displays tended to occur only in their extremes. Impacted groups bottled up their negative feelings about the change and would unleash them at a later point when any chance for a change of course had passed.
2. **Identifying resistance**
   Participants reported they had a difficult time identifying resistance because resistant groups were adept at hiding their feelings regarding the change. Participants reported identifying resistance to the change much later than would be ideal during the change initiative.

Adaptations

1. **Create an open, safe environment**
   Participants created an open channel and encouraged employees to provide feedback. By creating this open, safe environment, participants paved the way for smoother change management with a foundation of mutual respect and integrity.
2. **Use one-on-one communication**
   Participants engaged with impacted employees individually. Although drawing emotional responses was not the goal, participants felt that emotional responses during meetings were indicative of honest feedback about change. One-on-one communications also served as opportunities to assist individuals through change and to address personal concerns or fears.

High emotional expressiveness cultures

Challenges

1. **Difficulty communicating about change**
   A high degree of emotional expressiveness meant that every communication regarding the change would potentially have a large emotional response. Participants reported that attempting to customize communication not to elicit an emotional response was very difficult.
2. **Cross-cultural communication**
   Participants reported that communication across cultural lines was very difficult, especially when one group was highly emotionally expressive and the other was not. Participants reported both sides in the interaction would think the other side was being offensive.

Adaptations

1. **Create opportunities for feelings to be heard**
   Participants reported that it was critical to build time into a project to interact with impacted groups and employees at multiple points to allow feelings and feedback to be heard. Limits and a common language were created to communicate feedback clearly and constructively.
2. **Tailor communication to be clear and focused on business objectives**
   Communication should strive to be concise and informative while not evoking emotional responses. Providing information in a clear, neutral manner allowed employees to quickly understand why, how and what a change was, reducing misunderstandings and information distortion.
3. **Address concerns and questions promptly**
   Participants identified a need to quickly and appropriately address concerns, questions or fears that surfaced to reduce both personally and publicly-voiced anxieties. Listening to and addressing questions quickly from employees supported them through change, and reduced resistance.

Table 15.11 shows the distribution of emotional expressiveness scores by region, and Table 15.12 shows the distribution of scores by industry.

Table 15.11 – Emotional expressiveness scores for each region

Region	Low	Medium	High
Africa	42%	45%	13%
Asia and Pacific Islands	34%	29%	37%
Australia and New Zealand	42%	34%	24%
Canada	40%	36%	24%
Europe	38%	36%	26%
Latin America	33%	34%	33%
Middle East	27%	18%	55%
United States	43%	35%	22%

Table 15.12 – Emotional expressiveness scores for each industry that made up more than 1.5% of the study

Industry	Low	Medium	High
Health Care	44%	27%	29%
Government - State	51%	27%	22%
Banking	35%	42%	23%
Finance	39%	44%	17%
Consulting	47%	29%	24%
Oil and Gas	44%	33%	23%
Government - Federal	49%	30%	21%
Education Services	40%	33%	26%
Insurance	42%	36%	22%
Manufacturing	33%	31%	36%
Utilities	46%	32%	22%
Other	28%	49%	23%
Government - Local & Municipal	43%	38%	19%
Information Services	39%	32%	29%
Retail Trade	31%	35%	34%
Telecommunications	14%	53%	33%
Professional, Scientific & Technical Services	45%	40%	15%
Consumer Goods Manufacturing	26%	32%	42%

Performance orientation

Performance orientation is a cultural dimension that describes the degree to which a person is rewarded for and expected to be innovative and the level of performance and continuous improvement expected from that individual. In a low performance-orientation organization, societal and family relationships are more important than improving performance. Formal feedback is viewed as judgmental and discomforting. Communication is subtle and indirect. In high performance-orientation organizations, training, personal development, competitiveness and formal feedback are seen as necessary for improving performance. Communication is direct and unambiguous, and employees are expected to strive for and demonstrate improvements in their work.

Participants indicated their location along the performance orientation spectrum (using a scale from zero to 100) and identified challenges and adaptations for implementing change given their location on the spectrum. Data were analyzed to identify challenges and adaptations for low (spectrum scores of zero to 33), moderate (34 to 67) and high (68 to 100) performance oriented cultures (Figure 15.13).

Figure 15.13 – Average scores for performance orientation across the study

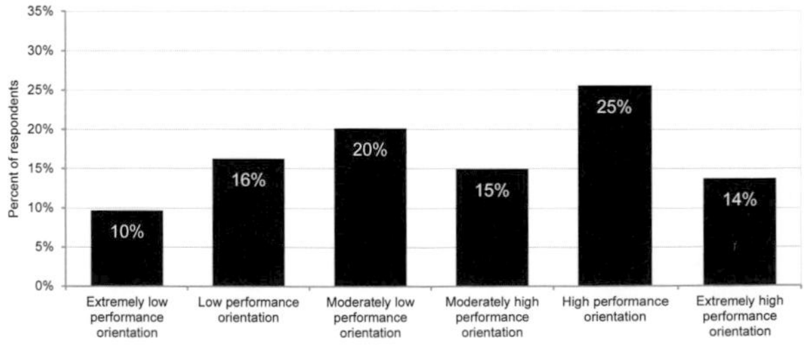

Participants identified challenges they encountered in their change management work, and provided adaptations they would make to their change management strategies based on their cultures' performance orientation scores.

Low performance orientation cultures

Challenges

1. **Lack of effective communication**
   Gaps in communication between upper management and frontline employees were reported. Employees did not like hearing negative feedback about their job performance nor did they have a desire to increase performance, and the lines of communication were effectively closed.
2. **Lack of accountability**
   No one was willing to take responsibility for stages of the project. There was no clear goal-setting or team responsible to ensure goals were met. Low performance-orientated employees saw no repercussions for staying with the old systems and choosing not to change.
3. **Lack of performance metrics**
   Many teams did not have formal metrics in place to evaluate performance. This lack of measurement resulted in challenges to positive and negative reinforcement.

Adaptations

1. **Let impacted groups choose their incentives**
   Participants let impacted groups pick and design their own incentives during the change intuitive. Participants reported that these incentives were often not business related and were more enjoyment oriented, such as trips to theme parks and other recreational activities.
2. **Desire building focused on individual impact**
   Participants focused their desire and awareness messages on how the change would improve their day-to-day work. Participant messages were customized for individuals or small impacted groups.

Moderate performance orientation cultures

Challenges

1. **Lack of accountability**
   A large number of projects were left without someone taking responsibility for successes and failures. No one wanted to own the change in case anything went wrong. This left team members uncertain of whom to ask when they had questions about a change or process.
2. **Lack of adoption metrics**
   Without the ability to measure adoption and usage among impacted groups, there was no way to adapt or adjust course once a project began. Adoption or usage metrics were also viewed as performance metrics and were not received well by impacted groups.
3. **No place for employee feedback**
   Employees wanted a forum in which questions or concerns could be heard. Employees wanted to talk to someone directly and have a liaison that would help get questions answered.

Adaptations

1. **Gathering feedback**
   Allowing space for and seeking out feedback from impacted groups regarding the change allowed participants to actively monitor resistance and customize communication and incentives around the change.
2. **Acknowledgement**
   Participants reported that the most effective form of incentives was personal acknowledgement. Participants built in and actively worked to acknowledge high performers and early adopters. This acknowledgement often went in parallel with performance and personal incentives as well.

High performance orientation cultures

Challenges

1. **Employee resistance**
   Participants reported that high performance-oriented employees did not welcome the state of uncertainty that comes with a change and were comfortable with their current jobs. Some employees feared a decrease of productivity during change.
2. **Lack of effective training**
   Employees at all levels did not feel prepared for change after they had been through training, though participants felt that the training was more than adequate. Employees lacked confidence in their ability to apply new skills in the future state.
3. **Lack of employee motivation**
   Employees from every level of the organization did not understand why the change was happening and how adoption of change would improve their performance metrics. High performance-oriented employees were frustrated when they felt they had wasted time and energy on a change they believed to be unnecessary.

Adaptations

1. **Tie performance metrics to adoption**
   Participants tied specific performance measures to specific adoption activities in impacted groups. These groups responded better to incentives that linked to their performance metrics rather than outside enjoyable activities.
2. **Unambiguous communication**
   Participants reported that impacted groups responded the best to unambiguous and technical communication about the change. Further, impacted groups tended to digest and act on more technical and un-watered-down information rather than personal communication about the change.

Table 15.14 shows the distribution of performance orientation scores by region, and Table 15.15 shows the distribution of scores by industry.

Table 15.14 – Performance orientation scores for each region

Region	Low	Medium	High
Africa	37%	26%	37%
Asia and Pacific Islands	29%	29%	42%
Australia and New Zealand	26%	40%	34%
Canada	24%	36%	40%
Europe	25%	34%	41%
Latin America	43%	38%	19%
Middle East	27%	46%	27%
United States	24%	27%	49%

Table 15.15 – Performance orientation scores for each industry that made up more than 1.5% of the study

Industry	Low	Medium	High
Health Care	28%	32%	40%
Government - State	38%	32%	30%
Banking	28%	25%	47%
Finance	23%	35%	42%
Consulting	23%	23%	54%
Oil and Gas	20%	37%	43%
Government - Federal	35%	34%	31%
Education Services	33%	38%	29%
Insurance	28%	37%	35%
Manufacturing	26%	31%	43%
Utilities	35%	40%	25%
Other	14%	27%	59%
Government - Local & Municipal	37%	46%	17%
Information Services	19%	43%	38%
Retail Trade	13%	23%	64%
Telecommunications	19%	19%	62%
Professional, Scientific & Technical Services	36%	32%	32%
Consumer Goods Manufacturing	15%	35%	50%

Power distance

Power distance is a cultural dimension that describes the degree to which power is distributed (equally versus unequally) with people at the bottom accepting their position. Organizations with low power distance allow employees access to higher-level members with little to no formal rules or chain of command. Employees expect company-wide decisions to be made democratically and for each voice to be heard. Organizations with high power distance have formal and strictly defined rules for accessing high-level executives. Employees do not expect to be consulted on company-wide decisions.

Participants indicated their locations along the power distance spectrum (using a scale from zero to 100) and identified challenges and adaptations for implementing change given their location on the spectrum. Data were analyzed to identify challenges and adaptations for low (spectrum scores of zero to 33), moderate (34 to 67) and high (68 to 100) power distance cultures (Figure 15.16).

Figure 15.16 – Average scores for power distance across the study

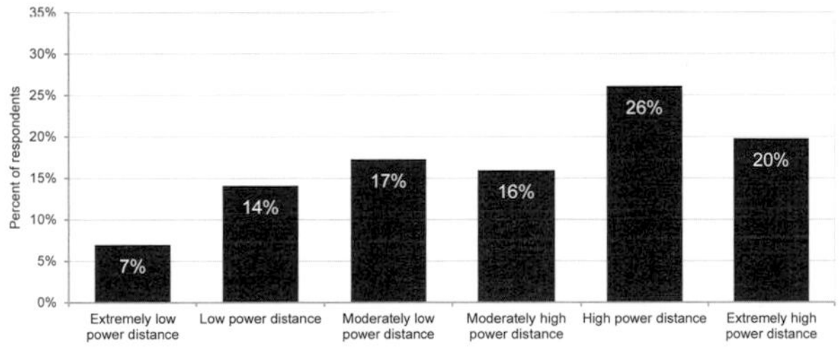

Low power distance cultures

Challenges

1. **Impaired communication**
   Due to extensive access, information often skipped levels of the organization which resulted in repeating information several times. Informal communications led to rumors and decreased the credibility of information surrounding change.

2. **Increased resistance**
   Low power distance structures resulted in a large amount of resistance because individuals from all levels of the organization constantly challenged ideas. Employees often did not adhere to changes, and messages were not uniform across the organization. Conflicts arose between levels of management, and productivity suffered consequently.

3. **Decreased productivity**
   Productivity decreased due to more time being spent on gaining buy-in, lack of governance and slower decision processes.

Adaptations

1. **Increase engagement**
   Employee engagement was achieved with an increase in functions and meetings that were used to ensure alignment of the organization across all levels. The quantity of meetings ensured that employees had multiple opportunities to encounter and engage with the change project.

2. **Structure communication channels**
   Communication channels needed to be identified up front to provide a consistent approach for tailoring messages and to open structured feedback from individuals. Communication plans required consistency and frequency, so content could be adjusted to incorporate the topics identified from feedback.

3. **Enhance change management plans**
   Participants in low power distance organizations added structure to change management by placing stakeholders in key positions, including establishing guidelines to ensure all levels were being communicated with and clearly defining roles and responsibilities.

Moderate power distance cultures

Challenges

1. **Decreased ability to drive change**
   Leadership had a decreased capability to direct change, had to put more effort into gaining buy-in for change and had to engage managers more thoroughly.
2. **Increased resistance**
   Resistance occurred because senior leaders did not account for employees' input and concerns when dealing with issues centered on change. Employees were then more likely to resist any aspect of change. Senior leaders appeared to think they had more sway over employees than they did.
3. **Poor structure**
   Participants with moderate power distance organizations reported a need to tailor change plans more specifically to groups as opposed to using a uniform approach. Creating individual plans required more time on the change manager's part and lowered the effectiveness of mass communication regarding change.

Adaptations

1. **Balance communication**
   Participants expressed the need to establish balanced communication during change management. Open and honest feedback was balanced with a clear boundary and understanding of "who has the final say."
2. **Gain buy-in**
   Participants reported putting more effort toward gaining employee buy-in. Awareness of the need for and importance of change management was created by using more meetings and team activities. Other activities to gain buy-in included visible sponsorship engagement, involvement of key stakeholders, creation of plans for various groups and demonstration of the value of change management.
3. **Empower sponsors**
   Sponsors in moderate power distance organizations were encouraged to take charge of change as an adaption to the position on the power distance spectrum. Empowered sponsors bridged the gap between leaders' direction and employees' concerns and feedback.

High power distance cultures

Challenges

1. **Restricted communication**
   Participants identified too few and poor levels of communication occurring in high power distance organizations. A large gap was described between senior leaders and frontline employees which resulted in a loss of productivity and increased time for implementation. Fear among employees and executives appearing unapproachable were primary limitations to communication from lower levels to executives.
2. **Isolated decision making**
   Isolated decision making was challenging. Executives made decisions without considering the impact to employees. Consequently, the alignment of the organization suffered because different levels and groups had different directions.
3. **Lack of employee engagement**
   Lack of commitment and trust were other challenges for organizations with high power structures. Passive resistance resulted from these issues because employees felt powerless, unheard and not cared about. Resources had to be reallocated to account for these avoidable problems.

Adaptations

1. **Communicate openly and directly**
   Participants reported using executive and senior leaders more often during communications. Higher-level leadership lent authority to communication, and resistant employees were more likely to adopt change when instructed.

2. **Engage leadership**
   Leadership visibility and engagement ensured that impacted groups understood that company leadership was supportive of and behind change from the beginning. Early leadership involvement encouraged and promoted early adopters.

Table 15.17 shows the distribution of power distance scores by region, and Table 15.18 shows the distribution of scores by industry.

Table 15.17 – Power distance scores for each region

Region	Low	Medium	High
Africa	6%	19%	75%
Asia and Pacific Islands	9%	18%	73%
Australia and New Zealand	20%	31%	49%
Canada	13%	37%	50%
Europe	33%	33%	34%
Latin America	10%	33%	57%
Middle East	9%	27%	64%
United States	23%	29%	48%

Table 15.18 – Power distance scores for each industry that made up more than 1.5% of the study

Industry	Low	Medium	High
Health Care	16%	30%	54%
Government - State	21%	27%	52%
Banking	14%	29%	57%
Finance	27%	25%	48%
Consulting	27%	37%	36%
Oil and Gas	17%	37%	46%
Government - Federal	2%	29%	69%
Education Services	16%	37%	47%
Insurance	27%	27%	46%
Manufacturing	26%	21%	53%
Utilities	12%	37%	51%
Other	11%	56%	33%
Government - Local & Municipal	18%	25%	57%
Information Services	42%	35%	23%
Retail Trade	13%	26%	61%
Telecommunications	15%	45%	40%
Professional, Scientific & Technical Services	32%	32%	36%
Consumer Goods Manufacturing	32%	36%	32%

Uncertainty avoidance

Uncertainty avoidance is a cultural dimension that describes a culture's tolerance for ambiguity and uncertainty. Low uncertainty avoidance organizations do not prefer unknown or unusual situations, but do not avoid them and feel comfortable in new situations. These organizations are pragmatic and are tolerant of change. High uncertainty avoidance organizations try to minimize or avoid unusual or unknown circumstances. Step-by-step planning, rule implementation and attention to detail precede change.

Participants indicated their locations along the uncertainty avoidance spectrum (using a scale from zero to 100) and identified challenges and adaptations for implementing change given their location on the spectrum. Data were analyzed to identify challenges and adaptations for low (spectrum scores of zero to 33), moderate (34 to 67) and high (68 to 100) uncertainty avoidance cultures (Figure 15.19).

Figure 15.19 – Average scores for uncertainty avoidance across the study

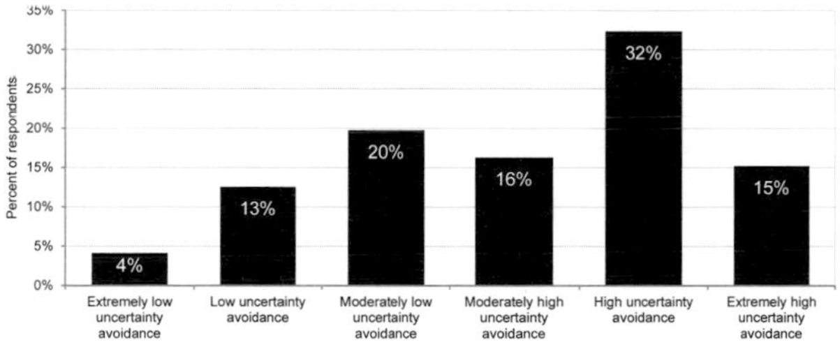

Participants identified challenges they encountered to their change management work, and provided adaptations they would make to their change management strategies based on their cultures' uncertainty avoidance scores.

Low uncertainty avoidance cultures

Challenges

1. **Too much ambiguity**
   Too much ambiguity regarding change emerged in low uncertainty-avoidance cultures. Senior leaders were content to take a "see what happens" approach to change. Impacted groups did not see change as having an impact on them and were less likely to care about change initiatives.
2. **Lack of consistency and follow through**
   Organizations were too willing to switch to a new technology or process at any indication that it could be an improvement. Changes were initiated frequently, leading to high change saturation which negatively impacted productivity.
3. **Lack of respect for change**
   Changes were not perceived as something that impacted the organization. Acquiring resources and support was more difficult because the impact of the change and the need for structure and resources for change management were underappreciated.

Adaptations

1. **Communication**
   Participants cited altering communications to reflect their culture's tendency to avoid unusual or unknown circumstances. This included communicating earlier and more often, addressing "what's in it for me?" (WIIFM), providing clarity, setting expectations, ensuring messaging was consistent and providing the right amount of detail.
2. **Identify and mitigate uncertainty**
   Participants identified uncertainty through analysis, responded quickly to concerns, provided additional information and training for those who needed it and created awareness regarding uncertainty to let people know that some uncertainty was acceptable.

3. **Training and support**
   Participants increased the amount of training provided regarding changes, provided additional coaching to people who were struggling with change, created practice scenarios for people to try out change in advance and rewarded increased effort and early adoption of change.
4. **Planning**
   Participants increased the amount of planning for change, increased details and documentation within their plans, recognized the need to change a plan due to organizational culture and allowed flexibility within a plan during change.

Moderate uncertainty avoidance cultures

Challenges

1. **Uncertainty**
   Impacted groups become paralyzed and unable to respond to uncertain situations. Participants reported a tendency for executives to be more reproachful during uncertainty leading to poorly executed change.
2. **Resistance**
   When changes were announced, participants reported difficulties in getting change started. Impacted groups had difficulty embracing changes, which required pulling people along. This difficulty was most often a result of fighting a legacy of change resistance.
3. **Change fatigue**
   Change fatigue caused missed deadlines and an overall fear of future changes. Ambiguity and poor adoption of future changes resulted from change fatigue and lack of reinforcement of previous changes.
4. **Confusion**
   Last minute execution and lack of clarity on current projects led to confusion within impacted groups. Lack of awareness and mixed messages added to the confusion during change.

Adaptations

1. **Communication**
   Participants communicated more regularly with increased emphasis on the vision, benefits and solutions surrounding change. They stated that they commonly addressed "what's in it for me?" (WIIFM), provided clarification concerning job roles and promoted more one-on-one communication.
2. **Increased coaching, training and support**
   Participants implemented more check-ins and accountability measures and provided additional coaching and support where needed. Participants provided training to supervisors and managers on dealing with ambiguity and uncertainty in the workplace.
3. **Planning**
   Participants planned fewer changes at once, created better plans with increased detail and documentation and built clearer and more robust communication plans. They also modified plans to account for reactions based on their culture.
4. **Identify and mitigate uncertainty**
   Participants analyzed change to identify uncertainty and resistance and reinforced key messages among impacted groups to bolster awareness of the need for change and mitigate concerns.

High uncertainty avoidance cultures

Challenges

1. **Need for detailed communications**
   The most frequently stated challenge was the need for significant details to be spelled out upfront prior to the start of change. This fueled a desire for a clearly-articulated vision and a detailed description of the future state prior to employees committing to participate in change. Communication and preparation for change needed to involve a wider audience, so it was comfortable and ready for change and had the knowledge and tools to support it.

2. **Fear of the unknown**
   Change brings uncertainty, and participants indicated that fear of the unknown associated with change led to a lack of tolerance for ambiguity. Many questions arose and frustrations set in when answers were not readily available. An unwillingness to change when people were uncertain about what was expected in the new system was a challenge that stemmed from fear of the unknown.

3. **Risk aversion**
   High uncertainty-avoidance environments were marked by a desire to avoid risk and mitigate potential negative consequences of change. Participants noted that risk aversion often led to "analysis paralysis" and inaction. Risk aversion also led to bias toward maintaining the status quo until numerous risks had been addressed clearly. Decision making was formal requiring rules and standards.

4. **Slow pace of change**
   Participants indicated that the slow pace of change was especially challenging in cultures of high uncertainty avoidance. Detailed planning, frequent questioning and clarifying expectations repeatedly extended timelines for change.

Adaptations

1. **Communication**
   Participants looked for innovative and creative ways to communicate and increased communications regarding the business value of change. They included more one-on-one communication in their communication plans.

2. **Adapting change**
   Participants slowed change, staggered changes or limited the number of changes occurring in the organization. Participants also mentioned more planning, increased flexibility and simplifying the change.

3. **Increased training and support**
   Participants increased training and found new ways to coach employees through change. They used ADKAR® to discover where additional skill building was necessary and provided the support needed.

Table 15.20 shows the distribution of uncertainty avoidance scores by region, and Table 15.21 shows the distribution of scores by industry.

Table 15.20 – Uncertainty avoidance scores for each region

Region	Low	Medium	High
Africa	17%	46%	37%
Asia and Pacific Islands	27%	15%	58%
Australia and New Zealand	13%	39%	48%
Canada	13%	27%	60%
Europe	20%	37%	43%
Latin America	15%	40%	45%
Middle East	9%	36%	55%
United States	18%	35%	47%

Table 15.21 – Uncertainty avoidance scores for each industry that made up more than 1.5% of the study

Industry	Low	Medium	High
Health Care	20%	39%	41%
Government - State	13%	29%	58%
Banking	20%	34%	46%
Finance	17%	40%	43%
Consulting	33%	26%	41%
Oil and Gas	14%	37%	49%
Government - Federal	13%	23%	64%
Education Services	7%	30%	63%
Insurance	10%	40%	50%
Manufacturing	16%	32%	52%
Utilities	13%	25%	63%
Other	26%	40%	34%
Government - Local & Municipal	16%	31%	53%
Information Services	19%	43%	38%
Retail Trade	18%	32%	50%
Telecommunications	29%	33%	38%
Professional, Scientific & Technical Services	4%	35%	61%
Consumer Goods Manufacturing	22%	45%	33%

Relative impact of cultural dimensions on change management work

After providing input on the six cultural dimensions, participants rank ordered the cultural dimensions based on the impact they had on change management. A rank of *1* meant the dimension had the largest impact on change management, and *6* meant it had the least.

Figure 15.22 shows the rank ordering of impact of the cultural dimensions of change management work. Responses were weighted and indexed. Individualism versus collectivism, power distance and uncertainly avoidance had the greatest impact on change management work, and emotional expressiveness had the least impact.

Figure 15.22 – Weighted scores for most impactful cultural dimensions

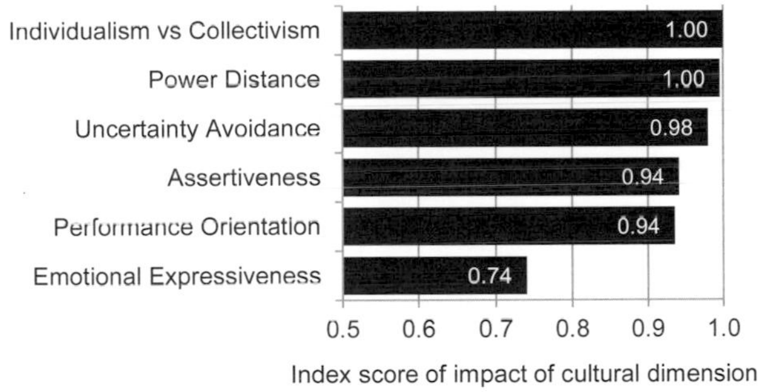

Looking just at the dimensions participants ranked as having the greatest impact, Figure 15.23 shows that although the top three remain the same, the order shifted. Twenty-four percent of respondents ranked uncertainty avoidance as having the greatest impact on change management, followed by power distance (21%) and individualism versus collectivism (18%).

Figure 15.23 – Cultural dimensions rated as having the largest impact (ranked 1)

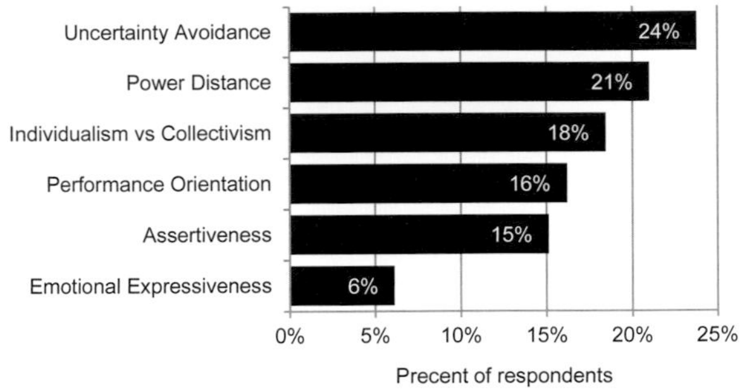

Figure 15.24 shows the distribution of cultural dimension impact rankings. The percentage that ranked individualism versus collectivism (38%), power distance (39%) and uncertainty avoidance (41%) as *1* or *2* was higher than for the other cultural dimensions. Nearly half (49%) of all respondents indicated that emotional expressiveness was a low-impact dimension.

Figure 15.24 – Distribution of cultural dimension impact rankings

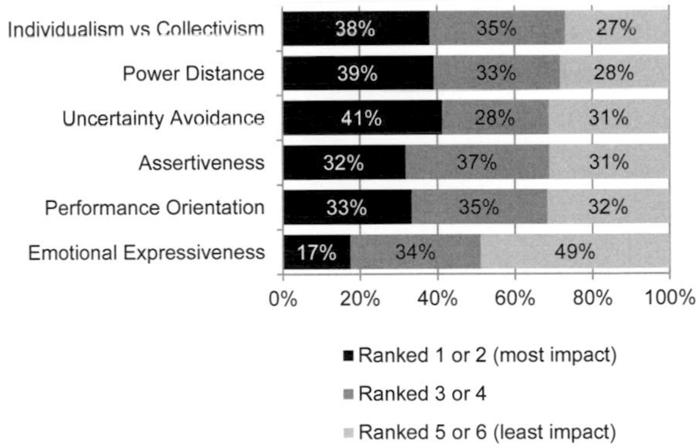

CUSTOMIZING CM BY INDUSTRY

ADAPT CHANGE ACTIVITIES TO THE UNIQUE CHALLENGES OF YOUR INDUSTRY

SUMMARY

Industries share characteristics that create unique challenges for managing people through change. How is change management different in banking? How must it be adapted in health care? What can practitioners account for when managing change in government? For the first time in the change management context, research data sheds light into patterns of prevalent challenges and common types of change faced by vertical industries. Customize your change management planning and implementation with actionable adaptations benchmarked from change leaders in your own industry.

HIGHLIGHT

Meaningful differences between industries emerged that influenced how change management was applied, such as technology adaptiveness, tenure of workforce and risk tolerance.

Industry-specific challenges when employing change management

For the first time, participants identified challenges they faced due to their industry when employing change management. To report accurately on industry-specific challenges, industries that made up at least 2% of the study's participants were analyzed individually, and the remaining industries were analyzed together and listed in the *other* category.

In the interest of clarity, industries were grouped into five broad categories based on similarities.

Group 1

- Government – Federal
- Government – State
- Government – Local/Municipal

Group 2

- Banking
- Finance
- Consulting
- Insurance

Group 3

- Information Services
- Telecommunications
- Professional, Scientific and Technical Services

Group 4

- Health Care
- Educational Services

Group 5

- Oil and Gas
- Manufacturing
- Utilities
- Retail Trade
- Consumer Goods and Manufacturing

Government Organizations: Federal, State and Local/Municipal

Challenges

1. **Concerns unique to government organizations**
   Participants identified factors particular to government organizations as top barriers to implementing change management. These were variables that exist almost exclusively in government organizations as opposed to private companies and organizations. Examples included government bureaucracy such as lengthy procedures, complicated rules and regulations, and long chains of command; political motivations that do not necessarily contribute to the efficiency of change management projects; and election cycles that occur every two to five years and cause changes to political regimes and priorities.
2. **Lack of resources and specialty knowledge**
   Lack of resources was a challenge to change management. Participants identified lack of funding, specialized knowledge and adequate time to implement change.

Adaptations

1. **Communication**
   Respondents identified a number of adaptations to the style and frequency of communication surrounding change management to account for unique characteristics of government. This included addressing government protocols regarding communication structure, frequency and norms concerning who to include in specific communications and how to address them.
2. **Account for cultural context**
   Respondents adapted change management to suit the cultural context of their government organization. For example, taking a "tailored-to-fit" approach to change management and demonstrating extreme flexibility.

Banking, Finance, Consulting and Insurance

Challenges

1. **Traditional and non-people-centric culture**
A traditional culture attached to status quo within a well-established and successful industry made change management difficult. These industries tended not to have people-centric cultures and focused on technical solutions and measurable success (ROI, profits) as opposed to interpersonal relations/human variables. These organizations had historically known success and were reluctant to deviate from established systems/processes.
2. **Required quantifiable return and organizational priorities**
These industries focused on profit and the monetary benefits of adopting change management. Sponsorship and resources were contingent on proving quantifiable Return on Investment (ROI) of change management. Time to market and diverting resources from the organization's main products were also key concerns. These organizations placed high importance on guarding their competitive edge; it was difficult to convince executives to divert resources to change management.

Adaptations

1. **Emphasize the benefits of change management in a business-specific way**
Many respondents noted that an effective way to sell change management was to put the benefits in the language of the organization. Examples included using cost benefit analysis, highlighting that Return on Investment (ROI) depended on people and using business language to discuss change management.
2. **Account for cultural context**
Respondents needed to consider the cultural contexts of their organizations when working on change management, including an increase in transparency of communications in response to a culture of secrecy and accounting for an egocentric culture.

Information Services; Telecommunications; and Professional, Scientific and Technical Services

Challenges

1. **Organizational focus on technology over people**
Respondents from these industries identified challenges related to culture, barriers and changes they expect to face. These organizations focused on technical solutions over interpersonal relations/human variables. Respondents also felt that employees lacked emotional intelligence skills and training.
2. **Industry pace**
Participants from these industries frequently cited the fast pace of the industry and the resulting shortened deadlines for change management as factors that impeded success.

Adaptations

1. **Adaptable and flexible methodology**
Using a highly adaptable and flexible methodology for change management allowed participants to address the challenges of the organization's culture and pace of the industry.
2. **Communication**
Participants noted a number of adaptations to both frequency and style of communication to account for the fast pace of the industry and the culture of the organization. Communication was frequent and brief to ensure impacted groups would digest it; lengthy communications often went unopened.

Health Care and Education Services

Challenges

1. **Autonomous nature of employees**
   In both health care and education services industries, the unique responsibilities of employees demanded a high degree of autonomy and independent thinking. Physicians, nurses, academics and educators were identified as employees for whom it is difficult to accept change at face value without convincing and clear evidence.
2. **Lack of designated resources**
   Lack of resources was noted as the second most common challenge when trying to implement change management, including monetary and non-monetary resources. Participants noted a lack of funding designated specifically for change management. Inadequate non-monetary resources included specialized change management training, dedicated change management practitioners and time away from daily priorities to focus on change management.

Adaptations

1. **Alignment with employee characteristics**
   Participants identified various ways in which change management methodology was adapted to work with employees in health care and education services industries. Examples were to include physicians/ professors on change management teams, to meet expectations of a high degree of collaboration and to increase stakeholder engagement.
2. **Communication**
   Participants described ways in which communication was adapted to be most effective in health care and education services industries. Examples included adapting communication to resemble academic discourse in education services industries and linking change to improvements in patient care in health care industries.

Oil and Gas; Manufacturing; Utilities; Retail Trade; and Consumer Goods and Manufacturing

Challenges

1. **Aging and tenured employee base**
   Participants identified employee demographics as the top challenge when employing change management. Many respondents noted an aging employee demographic as being particularly resistant to change. Employees who have been with the same company for many years were often reluctant to deviate from established practices and procedures.
2. **Decentralized and dispersed organizations**
   Participants identified elements of their respective organizational structures as a top challenge to overcome. The most common was organizational decentralization in terms of both decentralized authority structures and geographic dispersal.

Adaptations

1. **Account for cultural context**
   Respondents identified a need to consider cultural contexts in an organization. Examples included adapting to the global nature of an industry and adjusting the approach to work with employee demographics.
2. **Communication**
   Participants described ways they adapted communication techniques to fit their organizations best. Examples included using clear analyses, documentation and business language and ensuring messages came from an appropriate level of leadership.

Other industries

Challenges

1. **Cultural characteristics**
   Due to various industries included in this category, responses ranged wildly.
   - **Non people-centric industry**: Some industries emphasized solutions, quantifiable variables and technological innovation over people-centric variables.
   - **Little history of change management**: Some companies in established industries that have known historical success identified a culture of complacency and resistance to change. Their history of success led to resistance to change and lack of familiarity with change management.
   - **Risk-averse culture**: Companies that have known success or operated in volatile markets were reluctant to expose themselves to risk by changing practices or devoting resources to change management.
2. **Lack of resources**
   Lack of resources was identified as a significant challenge when employing change management. Responses ranged from general to specific lack of resources.
   - **Lack of time**: Short/strict deadlines were imposed on change management projects, and organizations expected change management to be undertaken in addition to daily responsibilities.
   - **Lack of funding for change management:** Funding designated specifically for change management was scarce.
   - **Lack of designated change management resources (non-monetary)**: Specialized change management training, dedicated change management practitioners and time away from daily priorities to use change management resources were commonly lacking.

Adaptations

1. **Communication**
   Participants noted that it was often necessary to modify the style and frequency of communication regarding change management. Adaptability was the most important factor; communication needed to be adapted to each organization.
2. **Account for cultural context**
   Participants spoke of a need to adapt change management methodologies and strategies to accommodate unique cultural dimensions of their organizations, such as the global nature of an organization or traits inherent to an organization in public versus private sectors.

Top three industry-specific changes on the horizon

For the first time, participants identified the top three changes they believed were on the horizon in their industries. Each industry was analyzed to identify trends related to the characteristics of each. Industries are listed alphabetically.

Aerospace:

1. **Technological changes**
   Participants anticipated changes in the technology used in their industry and challenges associated with integrating new technology. Examples included new aircraft models and technology and new applications for industry technology such as space-based surveillance.
2. **Market changes**
   Participants identified changes to markets including overall economic climates, oil prices and changes to demand.
3. **Operational changes**
   Examples included reductions in budgets and resources, changes in daily procedures and revisions to business models.

Arts, Entertainment and Recreation:

1. **Technological changes**
   Technological changes in this industry related nearly exclusively to digitalization. Respondents spoke of the "*impact of digital technology*" and a "*movement away from standard TV and use of* [various] *technologies.*"
2. **Market changes**
   The most common market change was an increase in competition in the industry. Other changes to markets included decreased profit margins, shifts in customer demographics and industry consolidations.

Banking:

1. **Market changes**
   The most common market change was an increase in regulations and government oversight. Other changes included new market emergence, changes to demand related to shifts in customer expectations and traditional markets closing and increased competition in the industry.
2. **Operational changes**
   Participants most frequently identified changes related to operations including changes to customer/user relationships, shifting priorities and business strategies such as "*consolidation of operations and focus on profitability.*"
3. **Technological changes**
   Technological changes were identified nearly as frequently as operational changes. Technological changes to the industry included digital banking, automation and the increased need for cyber security.

Consulting:

1. **Operational changes**
   Primary operational changes identified included changes in business focus and cost reductions. The consulting industry was one of the few that identified institutionalizing change management as an upcoming change in the industry.
2. **Technological changes**
   Participants identified changes to technology including a move to cloud computing, digitalization and "big data analytics."
3. **Organizational changes**
   Participants identified changes in the organizational structure of the company. Examples included changes to upper management, outsourcing and changes to the internal structure of the organization.

Consumer Goods and Manufacturing:

1. **Operational changes**
   Examples included new procedures and processes, automation of processes and increased focus on customer/client relationships.
2. **Market changes**
   Changes to markets were identified as important upcoming changes in the industry. The most frequent changes focused on industry consolidation and an increase in mergers and acquisitions. Other responses included increased competition, changes to demand and increased focus on innovation.
3. **Organizational changes**
   Participants identified organizational changes to the structure of companies, examples of which included growth and expansion and changes to the internal structures of the organizations.

Education Services:

1. **Market changes**
The most commonly identified market change was an increase in competition. Other market changes included industry consolidation, an increase in government regulations and a change to demand. One example was a "*continued swing away from* [the] *traditional four-year student model.*" Responses related to change in demand frequently mentioned an increase in demand for eLearning and virtual products.
2. **Operational changes**
Participants identified changes to the operations of the educational institutions of which they were part. Examples included changes to curricula, changes to student relations related to increased diversity, shifting student demographics and increased collaboration with commercial sponsors.
3. **Budget changes**
Participants identified budget changes and changes to federal/state funding.

Finance:

1. **Market changes**
The most frequently identified market change was an increase in government regulations, legislation and disclosure requirements. Other changes included increased competition, increases in pace and "*consolidation as industry players try to bulk up in an effort to gain size and survive.*"
2. **Technological changes**
Changes in the technology used in the finance industry including digitalization and online self-service portals.
3. **Operational changes**
Participants identified changes related to operations including new procedures, business models such as a "*move toward lower cost investment vehicles,*" changes to customer relations, specifically a reduction in personal interactions, and a new focus on budgets and cost structures.

Government – Federal:

1. **Organizational changes**
Organizational changes included changes to upper level management, change to hierarchy and chain of command and internal restructuring of departments.
2. **Technological changes**
Participants identified changes in technologies. Examples included digitalization of records, moves to cloud computing and an increase in using data analytics for decision making.
3. **Operational changes**
Operational changes included changes to training frameworks, institutionalization of change management and changes in client/customer relationships.

Government – Local/Municipal:

1. **Operational changes**
Operational changes included new priorities, changes to customer/client relationships and an increase in merit-based pay.
2. **External controlling forces**
The category of external controlling forces identified regulations and variables that are outside the control of individual organizations, such as government reforms, changes in political leadership, an increase in public accountability and disclosure requirements.
3. **Technological changes**
Technological changes included digitalization of records and an increase in cloud-based computing and virtual tools, such as an "*online citizen portal—applying for permits, licensing through the Internet.*"

Government – Military:

1. **Operational changes**
The operational change most frequently identified was a change in training techniques and priorities. Other operational changes were institutionalization of change management and increased regulations.
2. **Organizational changes**
Participants identified changes to organizational structures. Responses included staff reductions, increased turnover and large numbers of new employees.
3. **Technological changes**
Participants identified changes to the technology used in military organizations including moves to cloud computing and "*more mobile applications in development.*"

Government – State:

1. **Technological changes**
Technological changes were the most frequent responses from participants in state governments. Examples included digitalization, updates to computer systems and virtual tools such as "*cloud eLearning modules.*"
2. **Organizational changes**
The organizational change most frequently identified was reducing employee headcount. Other responses included an increase in privatization and outsourcing.
3. **Operational changes**
The most frequently identified operational change was a move toward a new or restructured business model. Other responses included changes to priorities, changes to user/citizen relationships, leadership development and increased need for employee engagement.

Health Care:

1. **Health care paradigm shift**
This category described changes in the fundamental nature of the health care industry. Examples included a move toward an individual or self-managed health care model, increases in regulations or legislation (specifically the Affordable Care Act in the United States), industry consolidation through mergers and acquisitions and standardization of patient care. Responses in this category were more than double those in any other category.
2. **Technological changes**
Technological changes in the health care industry included increased use of electronic records, new drugs and technology designed for patient care and automation.
3. **Budgetary concerns**
Budgetary concerns referred primarily to budget cuts, loss of funding and a move toward profit-focused business models.

Information Services:

1. **Operational changes**
Participants identified changes to implementation models, reduction in paper dependency, changes to customer/client relationships and an increase in the use of performance metrics.
2. **Technological changes**
Technological changes included digitalization, automation and increased use of big data analytics.
3. **Market changes**
Market changes included industry consolidation through mergers and acquisitions, maturing markets with decreasing profit margins and increased competition illustrated by "*decreased differentiation based upon product alone.*"

Insurance:

1. **Market changes**
   The most frequent response identified increases in regulations and government oversight (specifically related to the Affordable Care Act in the United States). Other responses included increases in competition, changes in demand and the general economic climate related to recovery from the recession.
2. **Operational changes**
   Operational changes included changes to business plans, evolving processing systems, changes to goods/services and increased emphasis on client relationships.
3. **Technological changes**
   Technological changes included increases in the use of digital self-service platforms, automation and an increase in the use of multimedia techniques.

Manufacturing:

1. **Market changes**
   Market changes included an accelerated pace within the industry, increased costs, changes to demand, increased competition and greater government regulation.
2. **Operational changes**
   Participants identified operational changes such as changes to business plans and established systems, increased focus on adaptability, a rise in non-traditional products and shifts in company priorities such as increased focus on managing environmental impact.
3. **Technological changes**
   Technological changes included digitalization, automation of systems and a move toward cloud computing systems.

Mining:

1. **Market changes**
   Changes resulting from overall shifts in the market included an increase in competition, falling prices of ore, expansion into new markets and changes to regulations.
2. **Operational changes**
   Examples included reworking of existing business models, increased focus on cost management and changes in employee demographics.

Non-profit:

1. **Operational changes**
   The most commonly mentioned operational changes were changes in business models and modernization of business processes. Other responses included increased focus on cost management and budgetary concerns, a change in products and services and a formalization of methodologies.
2. **Market changes**
   Market changes included demand changes related to customer expectations, increased competition and greater industry regulation.
3. **Organizational changes**
   Organizational changes included internal restructuring, new leadership, new partnerships and global expansion of organizations.

Oil and Gas:

1. **Market changes**
   Participants identified market changes such as volatility of oil prices, emerging markets, alternative energy sources and changes to demand, for example "*reduced drilling needs due to a decline in oil prices.*"
2. **Operational changes**
   The most common operational changes were a shift in the priorities of the organization, specifically pressures to lower greenhouse gas emissions, and a focus on safety and compliance. Other operational changes included institutionalizing change management, improving information management and changes to role/capability.
3. **Technological changes**
   Technological changes included automation of processes, an increase in data-driven decision making and advances in the tools the industry uses.

Pharmaceutical:

1. **Market changes**
   The top change was an increase in regulations and government oversight. Other changes included increased competition, expansion into new markets and increased consumer power.
2. **Operational changes**
   Operational changes included advances such as remote monitoring, a rise in patient safety as a priority and advances in industry technology such as "*molecule/drug development.*"

Professional, Scientific and Technical Services:

1. **Operational changes**
   Operational changes included changes to business models and procedures, institutionalization of change management and pressure to increase profits.
2. **Technological changes**
   Technological changes included the move to cloud computing, new information technology systems and a shift to electronic files.
3. **Market changes**
   Respondents identified market changes such as changes in customer expectations, acceptance of change as a constant within the industry and changes to the availability of external resources.

Retail Trade:

1. **Technological changes**
   Technological changes were the most frequently identified areas of upcoming change. Examples included e-commerce, a move toward cloud computing and increased popularity of omni-channel commerce.
2. **Changes to customer/client relationship**
   Changes to customer relations included increased focus on the customer experience, increased online interaction and a move toward personalized experiences for customers.
3. **Organizational changes**
   Changes included employee downsizing and changes to organizational leadership.

Telecommunications:

1. **Market changes**
   Market changes included a rise in national broadband networks, industry consolidation, increased competition, greater need for agility and adaptability and a "*reduction of need for a landline and traditional communications.*"
2. **Technological changes**
   Technological changes included increases in digitalization and cloud computing.
3. **Operational changes**
   Operational changes included changes to systems and industry tools, new goods/services and greater focus on customer satisfaction.

Transportation and Warehousing:

1. **Operational changes**
   Operational changes included changing systems/processes to increase efficiency, increased innovation in the industry, changes to customer/client relations and changes to priorities.
2. **Market changes**
   Market changes included changes to the overall economic climate (e.g., fuel prices), increased competition and industry consolidation.
3. **Technological changes**
   Technological changes, such as moves to cloud computing, were common.

Utilities:

1. **Market changes**
   The most common market changes were a rise in the popularity of renewable energy and further government regulation related to carbon dioxide emissions. Other changes included changes to demand, industry consolidation and increased competition particularly from the renewable energy industry.
2. **Operational changes**
   Operational changes included changes to processes and business models, increased attention to environmental concerns and changes to customer relations.
3. **Technological changes**
   Technological changes included digitalization of the energy market, remote meter reading and popularization of smart-grid technology.

Editor's Note: Some industries did not have sufficient responses to justify drawing conclusions about future market trends. These industries included administrative and support services, agriculture, forestry, fishing and hunting, construction, food/beverage, real estate, rental and leasing, other services (except public administration), social assistance, waste management, remediation services and wholesale trade.

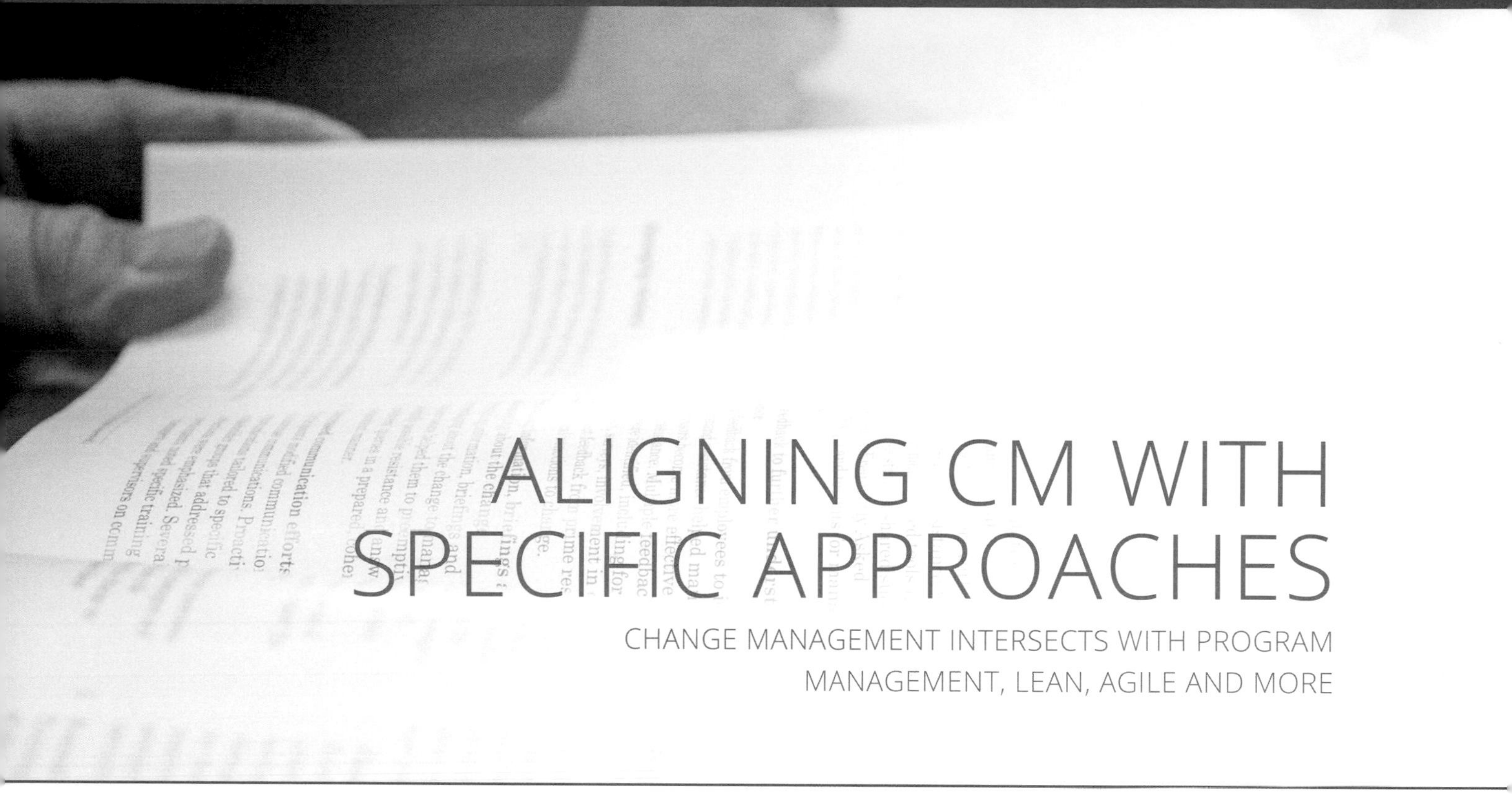

ALIGNING CM WITH SPECIFIC APPROACHES

CHANGE MANAGEMENT INTERSECTS WITH PROGRAM MANAGEMENT, LEAN, AGILE AND MORE

SUMMARY

How do change professionals execute change efforts in alignment with common improvement disciplines? How can you optimize change management application within the context of program management? What adaptations should you make when applying change management in conjunction with Agile? Lean? Six Sigma? Leverage best practices for effectively working at the intersection of change management and these valuable and prevalent improvement methods. Examine practical advice about the complexities encountered and recommended actions to support a successful alignment of your change management work. Tap into the accelerating power of a strategically-aligned approach to change.

HIGHLIGHT

44% of participants shared challenges and recommendations for applying change management to a program.

Change management with specific approaches

Participants reported on aligning change management with specific approaches including:

- **Program management**
  Forty-four percent of participants were managing the people side of change at a program level or on a project that was part of a larger program.
- **Continuous process improvement (CPI)**
  Just over 20% of participants were applying change management in conjunction with CPI.
- **Lean**
  Fourteen percent of participants reported applying change management in conjunction with a Lean effort.
- **Agile**
  Just more than one in ten participants reported on a change that was happening in conjunction with the application of an Agile methodology.
- **Six Sigma**
  Eight percent of participants were applying change management in conjunction with Six Sigma.

Figure 17.1 shows participants' experiences with change management using specific approaches. The most frequent approaches were program change management and continuous process improvement (CPI).

Figure 17.1 – Aligning change management with specific approaches

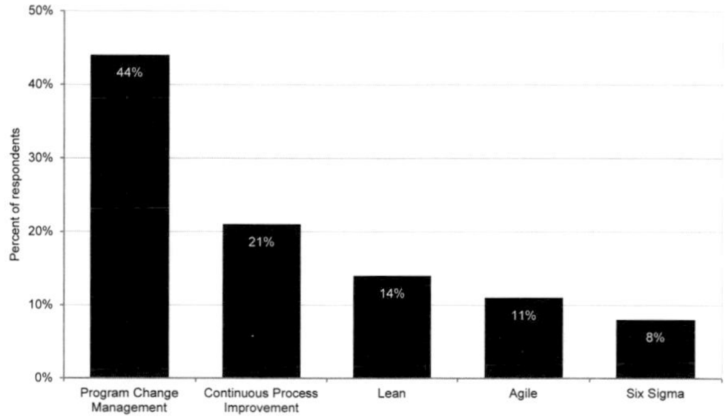

Aligning with program management

Source date: 2013

Challenges

Participants shared insights and experiences related to change management for programs or projects that were part of a program. Participants identified the complexities or issues they faced from a people side of the change perspective in a program setting. The top complexities or issues identified by participants were:

1. **Impact and stakeholder management**
   The greatest challenge identified for managing change in a program setting was managing the impact on employees. The quantity of impacted groups and variation in impact to those groups posed a challenge as did the nature of impacts across the lifecycle of the program. Poor coordination of overlapping impacts affected end users and constituents negatively.
2. **Coordination of various program aspects**
   Coordinating various projects that comprised a program was an issue participants faced. In many instances projects were managed in a "hodgepodge" manner without coordination or integration at the program level. Without a portfolio view silos emerged and alignment did not occur. Some projects advanced faster than others did, and there was insufficient knowledge of each project. Without coordination there were inconsistencies in the application of change management across the program.
3. **Complexity**
   The general complexity of a program created change management challenges. In particular, impact dependencies and interconnectivity of various aspects had to be addressed. Variations in culture, geographic location, time zones and language required attention. The timing of a program created additional complexities which included sequencing, maintaining momentum and operating in an environment with multiple systems during transition.
4. **Resource shortages**
   Resource availability for change management was an issue in a program setting. Participants noted loss or replacement of resources over the lifecycle of a program, which created continuity challenges.
5. **Communications**
   Coordinating communication in a program was challenging. Inconsistent communications created confusion within the organization, and differing backgrounds and varying communication needs created additional issues. Without coordination there was risk of communication overload for employees.
6. **Conflicting priorities**
   Participants identified projects moving in different directions, failing to be aligned or competing for priority as issues in a program.
7. **Lack of cohesive vision**
   Within a large program participants reported a need for a cohesive vision and clear future state that each project supported. Creating a single, shared vision was a challenge particularly when a systematic, big-picture perspective was missing.
8. **Saturation**
   Given the amount of change created by a program comprised of many projects or phases, there was significant risk of saturation and deteriorated engagement.
9. **Resistance**
   Although resistance to any type of change is challenging, participants in a program highlighted the risk of "spillover resistance" when resistance to one aspect of a program impacted other aspects of the program.

Recommendations

Participants provided recommendations for applying change management within a program. Top recommendations were:

1. **Implement program-level change management**
   Participants recommended applying program-level change management. This included a program-level change plan that addressed program-level awareness. A program-level plan served as an anchor for connecting each program element, clarified the vision and provided a big-picture view which enabled alignment of each project aspect. The program-level view resulted in a single mapping of program impacts, including answers to what, who and when. The program perspective enabled identification of dependencies and segmentation of program and project-level work.
2. **Coordinate change management**
   Change management regarding various aspects of a program had to be coordinated and integrated to be effective. Use of a common approach was encouraged, but localization and tailoring of the approach to the change aspects or audience were highlighted. Each aspect of the program needed a change management presence and resources. Early involvement of change management was critical.
3. **Enhance stakeholder management**
   In a program, participants reported the importance of gaining a clear understanding of the unique impacts of change on various groups. A more robust stakeholder analysis that incorporates timing and degree of impact is required. Participants also emphasized the importance of research and learning about unique attributes of each group. Gathering input and enabling participation were important stakeholder management techniques.
4. **Coordinate communications**
   Communication must be coordinated in a program setting. The scale of change requires an increase in overall communications. Participants recommended mapping anticipated communications, so messages and senders could be coordinated. Consistency of messaging, including identification of a single point of contact for information, aided communication in a program.
5. **Clarify governance, roles and reporting relationships**
   Due to the complexity of programs that have many moving parts, participants highlighted the importance of clarity regarding governance, roles and reporting relationships for project teams and change management resources.
6. **Leverage change networks**
   Given the broad scope of a program, participants recommended building and leveraging the support of a change network. Managers and supervisors were key members of the network. Change champions within impacted parts of the organization were valuable assets to a change network.
7. **Ensure sponsorship**
   Similar to findings related to general change, sponsor support was critical in a program. Participants stressed the importance of accessible, program-level sponsorship. The broad nature of a program also elevates the importance of alignment within the sponsor coalition.

Aligning with continuous process improvement

Source date: 2013

Steps to align

Participants who applied change management in conjunction with continuous process improvement (CPI) explained how they aligned the two.

1. **Aligned or integrated plans and methodologies**
   Change management and CPI plans were aligned. Examples of components that were aligned included timelines and terminology. Other participants strived for integration rather than alignment which included integration of toolkits, documentation processes, training plans and communication plans. In some cases overarching change management and CPI methodologies were integrated. Integration also occurred at the job-role level, at which the CPI team was assigned change management responsibilities.
2. **Supplement CPI with change management steps and principles**
   Participants integrated change management steps into the CPI project plan or process. As an example, impacts to employees were reassessed at each phase or gate of the CPI or project process. Participants incorporated current and future state analyses during early stages of the CPI or project process, and others built in a resistance management plan.
3. **Encouraged collaboration of teams and key individuals**
   Participants collaborated with the CPI project team and communicated regularly. Both teams attended performance and review meetings and shared frequent project updates. Teams collaborated on activities such as identifying impacted groups and creating communication plans. In some cases, the change team took on a support role for the CPI project team.
4. **Focused on awareness and buy-in**
   Participants focused on raising awareness regarding the need for alignment. Future-state benefits were shared to gain buy-in from employees. Participants also focused on gaining buy-in from sponsors and managers by engaging them in the initiative. Participants pointed out similarities between common change management practices and the CPI strategy to help impacted groups become comfortable with the initiative and more likely to get on board.
5. **Focused on reinforcement and sustainability**
   Participants emphasized reinforcement and sustainability during CPI applications. This was accomplished by creating feedback channels for end users and holding lessons-learned sessions. A great deal of emphasis was placed on monitoring sustainment and using metrics to identify gaps that needed to be addressed.

Recommendations

Participants who applied change management in conjunction with CPI provided recommendations for others in similar situations.

1. **Align and integrate change management with CPI**
   Participants emphasized the importance of understanding the inputs, outputs and overall process of CPI as the first step in aligning it with change management. Alignment included coordinating with project leaders on decisions impacting each group through discussions and regular updates and ensuring functions aligned strategically. Participants also recommended integrating CPI and change management methodologies, timelines, activities and tools. Recommendations included involving thought and skill leaders to identify ways to integrate and to build change management into the CPI approach.

2. **Focus on building awareness and buy-in**
Participants recommended building awareness of the need for change management and aligning it with CPI. Communicate the personal benefits and business reasons for the initiative, and explain what the change will look like. Participants considered transparency critical. As an approach to gaining buy-in, participants recommended explaining the complementary nature of change management and CPI. Communicating the links between the two functions, pointing out that they cannot be conducted in isolation and tying the CPI philosophy to change management to "*demystify change*" was recommended.

3. **Apply a structured change management approach**
Participants stressed the importance of getting involved in the initiative early and applying a structured approach throughout. They also recommended applying the approach with flexibility. Participants drew attention to the need for planning which included assessing the current state, identifying what the change will look like, discussing lessons learned from previous changes and holding focus-group sessions to reflect on previous changes.

4. **Leverage change management best practices**
Participants recommended paying special attention to the following change management best practices:

    - Managing resistance by leveraging influential parties to advocate change, identifying potential areas of resistance and understanding what actions or events might cause resistance
    - Engaging executive sponsors and ensuring that they stay visible and involved throughout the initiative
    - Providing support and coaching to managers and supervisors
    - Developing a communications plan and ensuring there are a variety of communication channels in place

5. **Engage frontline employees**
Participants emphasized the importance of engaging frontline employees throughout the initiative. Recommendations included engaging end users in the solution design, giving them ownership over part of the process and giving frontline employees plenty of opportunities to participate.

6. **Focus on reinforcement and sustainment**
Participants stressed the importance of planning for reinforcement and sustainment. Participants identified reinforcement activities including communicating early successes and creating channels to collect feedback from frontline employees.

Aligning with Lean

Source date: 2013

Steps to align

Participants applying change management in conjunction with a Lean effort (14%) took the following actions to align the two.

1. **Aligned and integrated processes and methodologies**
   Participants aligned Lean and change management methodologies. Participants integrated them by incorporating the change management methodology into the Lean process; "*built managing change into the Lean methodology.*" Participants also integrated Lean activities and terminology into stages of the change management plan.
2. **Leveraged change management best practices**
   Participants leveraged change management best practices when working in conjunction with Lean. They focused on building awareness by communicating the benefits of change, engaged middle managers during design, obtained active and visible sponsorship and focused on reinforcing and sustaining change.
3. **Built knowledge and integrated training**
   Practitioners focused on building their own and teammates' knowledge of Lean. Change management resources and the project team were trained in Lean.
4. **Assessed the change**
   Participants assessed the current and future states of change using process mapping, root cause analysis, as-is/to-be analysis and current-state analysis. Participants also analyzed the impact of change, assessed the organization's readiness for change and identified potential areas of resistance.
5. **Collaborated and integrated teams**
   Participants reported engaging the Lean team in change management, collaborating on establishing objectives, including Lean experts on change and project management teams and creating a steering committee with representation from the Lean, project and change management teams.
6. **Integrated tools**
   Participants integrated tools including value stream mapping, communications plans and training plans.

Recommendations

Participants applying change management in conjunction with Lean provided the following recommendations for others in similar situations.

1. **Integrate change management and Lean**
   Participants recommended integrating change management and Lean as early in the project lifecycle as possible. Participants suggested incorporating Lean terminology and concepts in the change management methodology. Evaluate and address waste in the change management process, and apply plan-do-check-act (PDCA) throughout change.
2. **Draw attention to the complementary nature of change management**
   Participants stressed the importance of showing that change management and Lean are complementary. They recommended linking change management and waste reduction to appeal to Lean professionals.
3. **Leverage change management best practices**
   Generally, participants recommended increasing the level of change management. Change management best practices were especially important when working in conjunction with Lean. Participants emphasized using a structured approach, building awareness, communicating how change will benefit employees and the organization, delivering consistent messaging, ensuring active and visible sponsorship and involving impacted groups.

4. **Adjust the change management plan**
   Participants conveyed the importance of early planning and establishing objectives. They recommended creating a plan that is simple and supports flexibility. Create a series of projects that are focused and have shorter-term goals than the overall initiative.

5. **Collaborate frequently with the Lean team**
   Participants emphasized the importance of establishing a relationship with Lean experts and project leads; "*Change management and Lean experts need to be side-by-side on the project team.*" Meet regularly with Lean and project teams and communicate frequently.

6. **Build knowledge and integrate training**
   Participants recommended integrating Lean and change management training. They stressed the importance of change management practitioners having a solid understanding of Lean and knowing how to incorporate it during change management.

7. **Assess the current state**
   When applying change management in conjunction with Lean, participants recommended completing a current-state or gap assessment at the beginning of a project. They conveyed the importance of understanding why current processes or systems are in place and what impacts the change initiative will have.

Aligning with Agile

Source date: 2013

Steps to align

Participants who applied change management in conjunction with Agile software development (11%) took the following actions to align the disciplines.

1. **Aligned methodologies and processes**
Participants aligned change management steps with the Agile methodology or renamed change management activities to align with Agile terminology and phases. Participants aligned change management with sprint deliverables. Change management milestones were aligned with Agile milestones and deliverables. Some participants scheduled change management steps after each Agile iteration.
2. **Collaborated and integrated teams**
Participants supported collaboration and integration of teams. Participants involved change management resources in Agile design iterations, collaborated with project teams when defining change, involved change management resources in Scrum sessions, added change management resources to the project team and collocated change and project management teams.
3. **Applied Agile concepts to change management**
Change management teams internalized Agile concepts and applied them to their own processes and activities. Examples included chunking change activities and milestones into smaller tasks, breaking change management project cycles into iterative stages and creating an overall flexible change management plan. These steps were taken to tailor change management to the cyclical nature of Agile.
4. **Aligned or integrated communications and training plans**
Participants aligned the change management communication plan with Agile deliverables. They also altered change management training methods to align with the Agile process or divided delivery of training content to align with what was being delivered during an Agile phase. Some participants integrated communications and training plans. "*We reported to internal stakeholders the results of each Agile increment via a project stakeholder newsletter.*" "*Translated Agile requirements into UAT* [User Acceptance Testing] *scripts and training materials.*"
5. **Shared and integrated tools**
Participants reporting sharing and integrating tools as a step to align change management with Agile. Participants referenced and contributed to the Agile project wall, linked Agile user stories to change urgency and joined impact assessments with to-be process mapping. "[We] *adapted traditional OCM toolkit to support Agile project phases and sprints.*"

Recommendations

Participants who applied change management in conjunction with Agile provided recommendations for others in similar situations.

1. **Adjust the overall change management approach**
Creating a flexible, fluid change management approach was suggested twice as often as other recommendations. This included creating just-in-time change management plans with short-term goals, and consistently revisiting them to account for iterations in Agile time frames. Participants also recommended assessing the organization's level of Agile maturity before undertaking a new change.

2. **Define roles and collaborate**
   Participants emphasized the importance of clearly defining the roles of Agile and change management practitioners. Focus on early collaboration between the Agile, project and change management teams. Include a change management resource in Sprint team meetings or Scrum sessions and involve Agile practitioners in change management.

3. **Emphasize communications and training**
   Provide sufficient training and increase communications. Educate employees "*on what it means to be 'Agile' in order to be nimble about the work and timing of change deliverables*" and "*provide coaching and training to address shortfalls.*" Consistent communication and regular updates on project progress during a project was recommended.

Aligning with Six Sigma

Source date 2013

Steps to align

Participants who were applying change management in conjunction with Six Sigma (8%) identified actions taken to align the two.

1. **Embedded change management in Six Sigma processes**
   Participants embedded change management activities and principles in Six Sigma. Change management was added to DMAIC (define, measure, analyze, improve, control) roadmaps and process mapping. Participants embedded change management principles such as building awareness, encouraging employee engagement and ensuring impacted groups were represented throughout Six Sigma.
2. **Supported collaboration and interaction between teams**
   Participants collaborated with Six Sigma resources which included keeping them updated on change management and working closely with the Six Sigma lead throughout the project lifecycle. It was common for change management and Six Sigma resources to collaborate with the project management team. Change management resources also provided support to the Six Sigma team throughout the project.
3. **Integrated tools**
   Integration of change management and Six Sigma tools was reported by participants. Integrated tools included root-cause analyses, failure mode effects analyses, control charting and communications plans.
4. **Aligned methodologies**
   Participants aligned change management and Six Sigma including coordinating phases of DMAIC with and using Six Sigma language in the change management methodology.
5. **Integrated training**
   Participants incorporated change management concepts in Six Sigma training and trained change management resources in Six Sigma.
6. **Integrated metrics and measurement**
   Participants incorporated Six Sigma measures into the change management methodology. Others integrated adoption measurement into Six Sigma measures.
7. **Embedded Six Sigma in change management**
   Participants included DMAIC phases and principles in change and project management.

Recommendations

Participants who applied change management in conjunction with Six Sigma provided change management recommendations for others in similar situations.

1. **Focus on building collaborative relationships**
   Participants emphasized the importance of building strong relationships with project management leads and Six Sigma experts. Participants recommended establishing role clarity and having change management resources support project and Six Sigma teams.
2. **Apply change management best practices**
   Participants recommended applying change management best practices throughout the initiative. Ensure a structured change management approach is in place and that dedicated resources focus on change management and align with Six Sigma. Engage change management early in the project lifecycle, and focus on reinforcing and sustaining the change.

3. **Focus on general alignment of change management and Six Sigma**
   Recommendations included:
   - Make change management part of Six Sigma
   - Coordinate DMAIC and change management phases
   - Align the change management methodology with DMAIC
   - Integrate change management gates with Six Sigma tollgates
   - Ensure activities of both practices have been completed before passing gates
4. **Focus on building awareness and gaining buy-in**
   Participants recommended focusing on communicating the benefits of the initiative, explaining the changes required by individuals early and describing what the change will look like when applied. Emphasize transparency and timely communications.
5. **Make change management measurable**
   Participants recommended establishing clear change goals and using metrics, so change management progress can be measured; "what gets measured gets done." Participants stressed the importance of making change management activities and goals measurable and quantifiable to align with Six Sigma practices that emphasized measurement.

MANAGING COMPLEX CHANGES

HOW TO ADAPT WHEN THE PROJECT PRESENTS DIFFICULT CHANGE MANAGEMENT SCENARIOS

SUMMARY

Study participants provide actionable insights for navigating ten specific project types that make change management complex, such as change that spans wide geographic areas or change with little or no WIIFM (What's In It For Me). Benchmark the issues others have encountered and investigate recommendations for applying change management effectively in these complex and complicated changes. Adapt your change management efforts to the size and scale of the project and plan proactively for the unique complexities that some changes produce.

HIGHLIGHT

Over half of participants (53%) provided direction for managing a change with little or no WIIFM (What's In It for Me).

Complex changes managed

Participants provided details about issues and recommendations for managing the people side of change for these complex change types:

- Spanning wide geographic areas
- Little or no WIIFM
- Impact across various cultures
- Long time frame
- Reorganization
- Union environment
- Layoffs or significant staff reductions
- Enterprise resource planning
- Cloud-based computing
- Merger or acquisition

Figure 18.1 shows participants' experiences with handling complex changes from the 2011, 2013 and 2015 studies. The most frequent complex changes participants managed were those spanning geographic areas (59%), little or no WIIFM (53%) and impacts across various cultures (50%).

Figure 18.1 – Complex changes managed

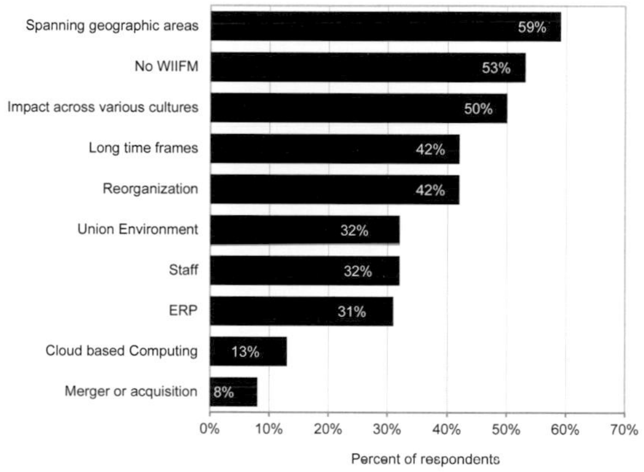

Spanning wide geographic areas

Source date: 2013

Issues

Participants involved in change that spanned a wide geographic area experienced the following complexities and issues.

1. **Cultural differences**
   Participants managing change across wide geographic areas experienced varied management styles, perceptions of change, personal values and motivation, legal restrictions or political affiliations and levels of change saturation.
2. **Coordination complexities**
   Coordinating between time zones was complicated. This issue was exacerbated when travel restrictions prevented face-to-face communications between key individuals. Coordinating training became complex, requiring new, usually web-based, training methods or extensive planning for logistical considerations.
3. **Communication complexities**
   Communicating across geographic areas presented challenges. Practitioners relied on onsite managers to relay change messages. However, managers did not always deliver the intended message due to misunderstanding or language differences. Gaining access to communication technology or a lack of competency with these technologies created additional complexities.
4. **Alienation of physically separate locations**
   Geographically separated divisions were prone to alienation, and developed an "us versus them" mentality. This was exacerbated by a lack of sponsor visibility and poorly executed awareness campaigns. As a result, distant locations were not engaged, had a low sense of team cohesion and felt imposed on by central headquarters.

Recommendations

Participants involved in change that spanned a wide geographic area provided seven recommendations for addressing unique change management challenges.

1. **Develop an extended change team**
   The top recommendation was to build a change network. Networks can be created by identifying influential individuals, not necessarily formal change team members, at each location who are capable and willing to advocate change and oversee its execution. Potential candidates for these positions should be identified onsite and educated in change management.
2. **Adjust communications plan**
   Participants recommended establishing multiple communication channels to allow open, two-way feedback. This also encourages clear, consistent communication between all geographic locations. Complexities arising from physical distance were mitigated when clear and open communication occurred regularly. Additional recommendations to facilitate communication between groups included centralizing communication to coordinate and unify messages, delivering simultaneous communications to all locations and using the most effective communication channels.
3. **Make frequent physical appearances**
   Many participants noted there was no substitute for face time with impacted employees and recommended physical appearances at each location. If budget restrictions prevented this, participants recommended making a physical appearance at project initiation. Others suggested choosing project sponsors based on their proximity to impacted parties or positioning subject matter experts at each location.

4. **Allow for cultural adaptations**
   Participants indicated that creating a flexible approach allowing for adaptations to various cultural needs was an important consideration for global change managers. Completing a thorough cultural evaluation to assess managerial styles, motivations, communication styles and personal values was recommended prior to executing change. Educating global teams in cultural workshops to provide a clear understanding of cultural impacts was also recommended.

5. **Adapt change plan and approach**
   Recommendations were made by participants to adapt the change management plan when considering a global change project. The most common included:

   - Allocate budget and time resources to allow adequate training
   - Meet virtually with key leaders regularly
   - Share successes of one outpost with the entire network
   - Group projects by time zone
   - Promptly address concerns from all locations
   - Establish separate sponsors based on region

6. **Incorporate technology**
   Participants recommended investing in and using current virtual technology such as corporate social media, webinars, online learning tools, teleconferencing and virtual collaboration tools.

7. **Emphasize key change management activities**
   Participants recommended emphasizing these common change management activities:

   - Impact analysis
   - Readiness assessment
   - Change benefits at the organizational level
   - Change benefits at the personal level
   - Sponsor engagement as early in the change process as possible
   - Relationship building and team cohesiveness
   - Comprehensive risk management strategy

Little or no WIIFM

Issues

Participants managing change in which outcomes were negative or perceived negatively from the employee perspective, with little or no "what's in it for me?" (WIIFM), experienced three complexities related to change management.

1. **Overcoming resistance and gaining buy-in**
   Mentioned nearly six times more often than other complexities, participants experienced high passive and active employee resistance. Resistance resulted due to the intensified challenge of gaining employee buy-in. Feelings of "*more work, less efficiency,*" "*I'm not impacted*" and "*it's not my job*" were prevalent among employees, making them less likely to adopt change.

2. **Addressing employee fears**
   When the outcomes of change were negative or perceived negatively, employees had greater concerns and fears for the future. The most common concerns included compromised job security, increased monitoring of activities, working with unfamiliar systems and periodic declines in productivity. Feelings of uncertainty led to high stress and anxiety among employees. As a result, participants experienced higher employee turnover.

3. **Depending solely on organizational benefits**
   Participants had difficulty portraying the benefits of change when trying to build awareness of why change was needed. Since only organizational benefits would result (or it was perceived as such by employees), participants experienced difficulties articulating why change was necessary. They relied on translating the organizational benefits into individual benefits, which was not always successful. This complexity was exacerbated when communications were not transparent, employees did not trust their managers or supervisors and higher levels of the organization appeared to benefit from change.

Recommendations

Participants in the 2015 study provided recommendations for change projects when there was little or no WIIFM. The top three recommendations were:

1. **Communicating frequently and transparently**
   Participants cited the need for open, honest and transparent communication. Impacted groups had a negative view of change, and participants felt that communicating often and with transparency helped negative views not worsen.
2. **Explain the business reason for change**
   With little or no WIIFM, it was important to fully explain why change was necessary for the organization. Impacted groups could then recognize secondary benefits by understanding that if the organization benefited from change they benefited from the organization's improved position.
3. **Listen to and address concerns**
   Listen to concerns and address them whenever possible. Do not downplay negative implications associated with change, and do not try to make it sound better than it is.

Impact across various cultures

Source date: 2013

Issues

Participants involved in change that impacted various cultures experienced four primary issues or complexities from a people side of the change perspective.

1. **Cultural differences**
   The majority of participants reported that overcoming cultural differences was the greatest challenge. Cultural differences and resulting challenges included varied ways of doing work, different perceptions of the change, different forms of resistance, different styles of communication, different backgrounds (e.g. Information Technology, academia, etc.), cultural unawareness and different work ethics.
2. **Adapting to regional/cultural circumstances**
   Participants reported that understanding and adapting to the diverse needs of each impacted group was the second largest challenge.
3. **Changes to how work was done**
   Changes to how work was done included changes to business or organizational processes, integration of different cultures or different business units, changes to reporting structures and roles and changes to expectations and requirements.
4. **Language implications**
   Using simple language, translating into different languages and overcoming language barriers was the fourth challenge.

Recommendations

Participants who experienced change across various cultures reported four recommendations.

1. **Build cultural awareness**
   Participants stated that building cultural awareness is a primary recommendation for others managing intercultural change. Participants suggested acknowledging, honoring and understanding different languages, values and needs. Training to support this effort should include building cultural awareness through cultural workshops, cross-cultural interaction and change management training.
2. **Create a cross-cultural change team**
   Participants recommended building a cross-cultural change team that included local change leaders who were active and committed to change. Cultural experts who specialized in intercultural changes could also be used on the team.
3. **Customize plans for each group**
   A third recommendation included adopting and sticking to a method or change plan that could be adapted to meet the unique needs and preferences of each group. Participants also suggested representing all groups or cultures on teams and in plans.
4. **Communicate clear and consistent messages for each group**
   Participants recommended communicating transparently and consistently about the change and about cultural differences and challenges faced by each group, including listening to employees experiencing these challenges.

Long time frame

Source Date: 2013

Issues

Participants who experienced change over a long time frame (over two years) reported three complexities.

1. **Retaining focus**
   Participants cited numerous reasons for losing focus including change saturation, change fatigue, other changes interfering, changing or interfering priorities, inconsistency of plan or approach and frequent changes to vision, direction, timeline, content or scope.
2. **Maintaining momentum**
   Maintaining momentum or motivation were major issues in changes occurring over a long time frame. Lack of commitment, loss of interest or burn-out occurred in the long period of moving toward a future state.
3. **Retaining people**
   The third complexity was retention of key people and knowledge holders due to staffing changes, role changes, employee turnover or management replacements including losing sponsors during change.

Recommendations

Participants who reported involvement in long-term change provided four recommendations for others applying change management in a similar context.

1. **Develop a structured approach**
   Develop a structured plan that is realistic, flexible and sustainable. Participants recommended communicating about the change and vision as soon as possible. Regular updates and reviews of the strategy were included in this structured approach.
2. **Break change into manageable phases**
   Participants recommended building clearly defined milestones and manageable phases, so short-term successes and progress could be recognized, celebrated and sustained.
3. **Communicate throughout**
   The third recommendation encouraged planned, sustained communication regarding change. These communications should be transparent and maintain key messages. Communications that were fresh and informative were most effective.
4. **Identify and ensure support from sponsorship and leadership**
   Assess sponsor commitment and confirm both engagement and continuity.

Reorganization

Aligning change management during reorganization projects

Participants in the 2015 study identified how they aligned change management with a reorganization effort.

1. **Communication**
The top recommendations related to communications; "*be clear and honest about the negative impacts of the change as early in the project as feasible.*" Common themes included honesty and transparency in communications, the importance of managing rumors and addressing gossip, the importance of face-to-face communications and the value of social media as a tool to keep the organization updated about change.
2. **Engage and support leadership**
Many participants noted the importance of having full support from leadership. This meant having an engaged and committed sponsor for the project, having the support of middle managers and supervisors and having leadership that values change management. Providing support for leadership in the form of leadership training or talking, for example, had a large, positive impact on the engagement of leadership.
3. **Structured plan**
Participants identified the presence of a structured plan as a crucial element when applying change management on a reorganization project. Recommendations included using a structured and formalized methodology, clearly defining the scope, goals and future state of change, building flexibility into the plan and reinforcing change.
4. **Stakeholder engagement**
Active stakeholder engagement during change was essential to the success of a reorganization project. Respondents suggested holding open forums as a way to engage large numbers of impacted groups.

Recommendations

Participants also provided specific recommendations for change management on a reorganization effort.

1. **Communication**
Communicating about reorganization was necessary, and there can be too much or bad communication about reorganization. Meticulous planning of communication was paramount.
2. **Fight the rumor mill**
Participants planned for and addressed how they would fight the rumor mill regarding reorganization. Tactics included controlling communication about the initiative, ensuring alignment in communication by every person involved and correcting misinformation quickly and efficiently.
3. **Awareness and engagement**
Participants reported the importance of building awareness of both the change itself and the need for it far in advance of the change. Participants used awareness building to engage impacted groups and senior leaders early, before change began, allowing change managers more time to address resistance.

Union environment

Source date: 2013

Issues

Participants managing the people side of change that occurred in a union environment explained the complexities they experienced. The majority reported four common issues.

1. **Difficulty engaging the union**
   Participants managing change in union environments experienced difficulty balancing union involvement. Striking a balance and engaging unions lengthened the timeline of change. In some cases, the union was uninterested, disengaged or passively resistant, which slowed progress in organizations in which negotiation and project acceptance from unions were required. In other cases, a union was over-engaged, which also slowed progress. Some participants experienced hostility, resistance and an "us versus them" mentality from unions.
2. **Complexities in communications**
   Additional communication was necessary. Participants had to account for seeking union approval in their communications plan. Confusion and inconsistent messaging resulted because either union approval was required before communicating with employees about change or the union was responsible for mediating and communicating with employees. Participants occasionally felt that unions misrepresented the change through communications and supported rumors about change.
3. **Negative employee impacts**
   Union involvement sometimes exacerbated employees' fears of job loss, which lowered their motivation and created concerns about employee strikes. Tenured employees were comfortable resisting change because the union protected their job positions.
4. **Collective bargaining agreement (CBA) considerations**
   Participants had to work around contract restrictions and collective bargaining agreements (CBAs). Employees would not accept new job role responsibilities unless they were added to the CBA. Renegotiating CBAs extended the project timeline. Failing to comply with the CBA could lead to legal complexities. When litigation occurred, the project was blamed.

Recommendations

Participants managing the people side of change during an initiative taking place in a union environment provided five change management recommendations.

1. **Engage union leaders early**
   Participants recommended engaging unions early and consistently throughout change. Consistently engaging union leaders or representatives strengthened the working relationship. One method for ensuring consistent engagement was assigning a change management liaison to the union.
2. **Collaborate with unions**
   Working collaboratively with unions was recommended. Partnering with a union and using its feedback during decision making and planning phases were suggested. Participants recommended being flexible, patient and highly organized to get the most benefit from collaborating.
3. **Communicate early and often**
   Participants recommended communicating early, frequently and transparently with a union. Specific recommendations included clearly communicating project scopes and new role responsibilities to avoid confusion and rumors.

4. **Educate union leaders**
   Educating union leaders about change management was recommended. Providing basic education encouraged union leaders to engage employees, build awareness and increase buy-in.

5. **Become familiar with union regulations**
   Participants also recommended becoming familiar with union contracts and regulations to allow practitioners to understand union impacts and provide a more complete vision of the impact of change.

Layoffs or significant staff reductions

Issues

Participants described the employee-based resistance they faced when managing a change that required layoffs and/or significant staff reduction.

1. **Fear**
   Participants reported that employees feared losing their jobs. They were less likely to take risks, fearing they would make a mistake. This fear affected the atmosphere and made employees much less likely to embrace change because doing so appeared synonymous with embracing layoffs.
2. **Loss of productivity**
   Participants reported decreases in productivity due initially to a sense of futility among employees because they saw themselves as the next people to be let go. Participants reported that high performers would quit for fear of losing their jobs. This left the remaining workforce without the high performers' knowledge and expertise. Some participants reported that when the high performers left, it was to work for competitors.
3. **Absenteeism**
   Participants reported cases of absenteeism that manifested in several ways. First, employees would not show up to meetings, activities or events related to change. Second, employees would not show up to general meetings or everyday working activities. Last, employees would begin using all of their paid time off. Participants also reported a large spike in the number of sick days claimed during change.
4. **Working against change**
   Participants reported that employees would subvert change and/or retaliate. This included sabotaging both change or company property, making other employees feel guilty for participating in and supporting change and, in some cases, spreading false information and encouraging gossip about change.

Recommendations

Participants that managed change involving layoffs or significant staff reductions provided three recommendations.

1. **Constant communication**
   Near-constant communication about change quelled current or potential rumors. Participants reported that impacted groups were prone to speculation regarding change. Ensuring a reliable culture of immediate communication eased fears.
2. **Addressing concerns**
   Impacted groups had many concerns and questions regarding change that needed to be addressed. Participants reported addressing concerns promptly, efficiently and articulately. Impacted groups were more likely to be accepting of change if they saw their concerns being addressed from the beginning.
3. **Communicate the business need for change**
   Participants reported that impacted groups should understand the business need for change. Although change resulted in layoffs that affected some employees negatively, participants reported the need to clarify that the change was not superfluous and was a necessary step for the organization.

Enterprise resource planning (ERP)

Participants in the 2015 study identified actions taken to align change management with enterprise resource planning (ERP) system implementation and recommendations.

Aligning CM with ERP

1. **Integrate change management early**
   Participants reported the importance of integrating change management early with project teams. ERP was complex and required a majority of resources to implement. If change management was not integrated from the beginning, participants struggled to do so later.
2. **Clear communication**
   Due to the technical nature of change, project participants stressed the importance of clear and digestible communication. Technical information had to be repurposed, so multiple audiences with a variety of technical understanding could comprehend changes.
3. **Understanding the methodology**
   Participants worked to ensure there was an understanding of both the goals of implementing ERP and the change methodology used to reach those goals. Participants felt this was in line with how ERP was presented and worked to create a cohesive approach.
5. **Become a change management liaison**
   Participants reported being liaisons between technical and project teams, improving communication and helping stakeholders agree on methods. Change managers ensured each team was communicating often and effectively. The change management team included employees from across the organization and solicited direct feedback. Respondents also noted that it was paramount to support employees through reorganization, particularly were downsizing part of the reorganization project.
6. **Understand the change fully**
   Participants noted the importance of fully understanding both the change and its various impacts throughout the company. Participants recommended conducting risk and impact assessments to understand motivations behind the change and resistance that might arise in response.
7. **Early engagement**
   Participants recommended early engagement of change management on reorganization projects to manage change. Early engagement helped manage employee anxiety over change, establish a structured plan/framework for change and secure strong sponsorship for a change project.

Recommendations

1. **More change management**
   Participants stressed, "*The more change management, the better*" when implementing an ERP system. Participants reported a tendency for project teams to get lost in the technical aspects of the implementation and neglect change management. Participants reported that change management was more crucial to the success of a project because it depended highly on successful adoption and use by impacted groups.
2. **Identified needed versus desired outcomes**
   Participants felt that an ERP system rarely delivered on every desired outcome; it was necessary to identify needed outcomes and then focus change management on ensuring adoption, use and implementation of those specific outcomes.
3. **Above-average understanding of the ERP system**
   Due to the technical nature of change, participants reported needing above-average understanding of the ERP system they were responsible for implementing. Without technical knowledge, communication, credibility and cohesion suffered.

Cloud-based computing

Aligning change management with cloud-based computing efforts

Participants identified actions to align change management with a move to cloud computing.

1. **Strong communications regarding change**
Due to the technical and sometimes confusing nature of cloud computing, participants emphasized the importance of strong, clear and frequent communication concerning change. Participants noted the effectiveness of demonstrating product capabilities ahead of the go-live period to show benefits and create narrative surrounding change.
2. **Integration and stakeholder engagement**
Actions included identifying super users or change champions, engaging sponsors in change and integrating technology into the change management and project plans.
3. **Increased emphasis on training and preparation**
Participants identified several actions related to training and preparing for change as crucial when aligning change management and a move to cloud computing. These actions included offering strong and frequent training programs on cloud functionality and technological knowledge, developing a pilot program to test systems and tailoring systems to minimize change's impact on the user.
4. **Methodology tailored to change**
Many participants noted techniques and elements of the methodology that were adapted to address a project related to cloud computing. Particular emphasis was placed on use of an adaptable and flexible methodology. Other examples included using a gradual, step-by-step transition to the future state, considering web security and using an external technology consultant to facilitate transition.
5. **Understanding change impact**
Respondents identified several aspects of change that they felt it was necessary to understand fully, including transformation of the role of information technology, the impact of change on business scenarios and the impact on internal Information Technology (IT) such as loss of power or relevance.

Recommendations

1. **Fully understanding the change and the new interface**
Participants recommended conducting impact assessments prior to go-live in order to fully understand the scope of the change and its impact on the organization.
Recommendations for understanding the new interface included placing a heavy emphasis on understanding, being able to explain the cloud computing technology, and engaging experts on the technology.
2. **Implementation plan**
Several respondents noted the importance of using a phased or gradual implementation plan to gradually acclimate employees to the new system and technology. Other recommended adaptations included addressing concerns around web security, engaging stakeholders specifically internal Information Technology (IT), using a pilot program to test the system and using incentives to encourage adoption.
3. **Clarifying communications**
Participants recommended various communication strategies to clarify expectations and goals surrounding the change and to address concerns that frequently arose from the complicated and technical nature of a move to cloud computing. Participants recommended beginning communications early, actively addressing the possibility of staff reductions as a result of the change and clearly communicating both the vision and benefits of the change.

4. **Demonstrate benefits of change**
   Participants recommended placing a heavy emphasis on the benefits of the change as a way of selling the change and gaining both stakeholder and executive engagement. Specific recommendations included demonstrating the new platform/technology prior to go-live, tying the usage to the business case, explaining the business impact of the change and emphasizing the "what's in it for me?" (WIIFM) benefit.

5. **Training on the new system**
   Participants noted the particular importance of providing training for the new system. Respondents noted that it was helpful to first identify what new skills were needed, such as increased computer literacy among employees, before providing training sessions and resources.

Merger or acquisition

Source date: 2011

Issues

The 8% of participants that experienced a merger or acquisition listed three main issues or complexities when undertaking change.

1. **Cultural differences**
   Participants reported that cultural differences were the greatest issue during a merger or acquisition. This issue often manifested in "us versus them" attitudes or internal rivalries.
2. **Changes to structure**
   Participants faced issues regarding changes to the internal or external structure of the business or organization, including different terminology, expectations, leadership and languages used for business transactions or in the work environment.
3. **Insecurity about the future**
   Participants cited that insecurity about the future complicated change management on mergers or acquisitions noting that this type of change was often met with fear and skepticism.

Recommendations

Participants who experienced a change involving a merger or acquisition provided three primary change management recommendations.

1. **Communicate**
   Participants cited open and honest communication as a primary recommendation when undertaking a merger or acquisition. Recommendations included transparent communications focused on the individual, communications that included the rationale and benefits and communications that brought the audience back to the vision of change.
2. **Know the people and cultures influenced by change**
   This recommendation included understanding strengths and constraints of employees, conducting cultural assessments and stakeholder analyses and understanding the change from different perspectives.
3. **Invest in change management early**
   Participants recommended incorporating change management at the beginning or early during a merger or acquisition in addition to elevating change management to the strategic business level.

SATURATION AND PORTFOLIO MANAGEMENT

MITIGATE THE CUMULATIVE AND COLLECTIVE IMPACT OF AN EVER-INCREASING VOLUME OF CHANGE

SUMMARY

The amount of change is expected to continue to increase across all industries. Benchmark who is experiencing change saturation and who is responsible for identifying and mitigating its negative consequences. Learn tactics for actively managing the portfolio of change and best practices for addressing the time and resource collisions of multiple simultaneous projects. Increase efficiency, effectively allocate resources and maintain employee engagement with a proactive and strategic approach to change portfolio management.

HIGHLIGHT

79% of organizations were nearing, at or past the point of change saturation, an increase from previous studies.

Change expected in the next two years

As in the 2011 and 2013 studies, participants indicated the amount of change expected in the next two years (Figure 19.1). In the 2015 study, 72% of participants expected a slight or significant increase, in comparison to 70% in 2013 and 71% in 2011. In each of the 2013, 2011 and 2009 studies, fewer than 10% of participants expected the amount of change to decrease in the coming two years.

Figure 19.1 – Amount of change expected in the next two years

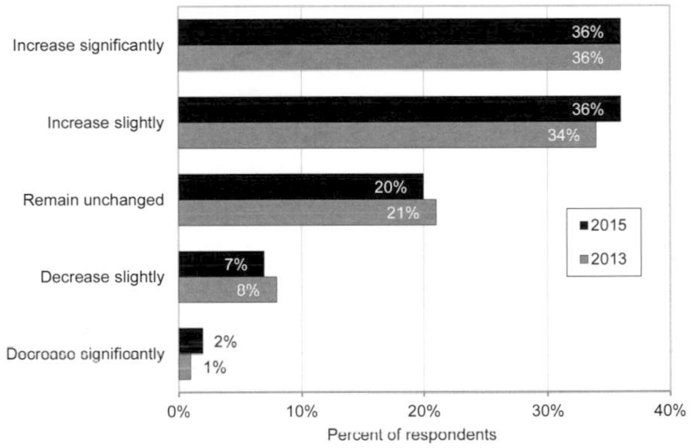

Level of saturation

The percentage of participants near, at or past the point of saturation continued to increase. Seventy-eight percent of participants in the 2015 study identified being near, at or past the point of saturation, up from 77% in 2013 and 73% in 2011 (Figure 19.2).

Figure 19.2 – Level of change saturation

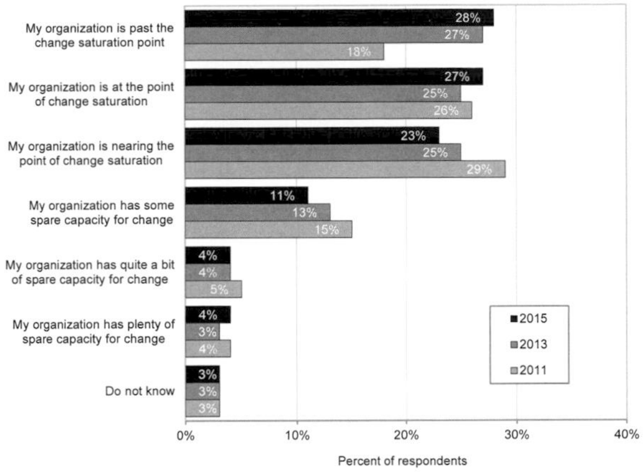

The number of organizations nearing, at or past the level of change saturation has been increasing over time, as shown in Figure 19.3.

Figure 19.3 - Percentage of participants near or past the change saturation point

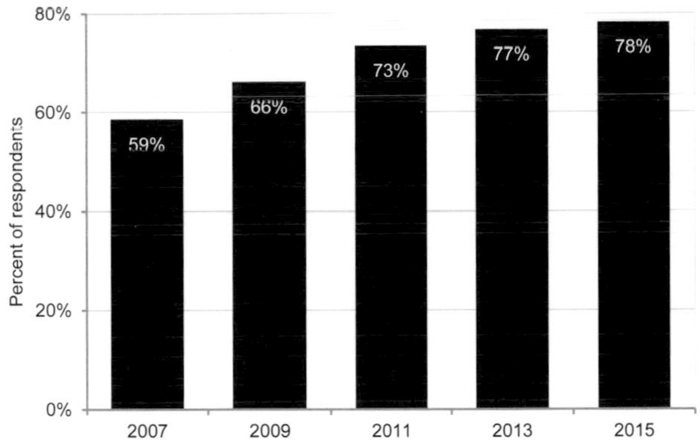

Level of change saturation by region

Figure 19.4 shows the percentage of participants that indicated being near, at or past the point of saturation by region. The regions are ordered based on the greatest occurrence of change saturation.

Figure 19.4 – Change saturation by region

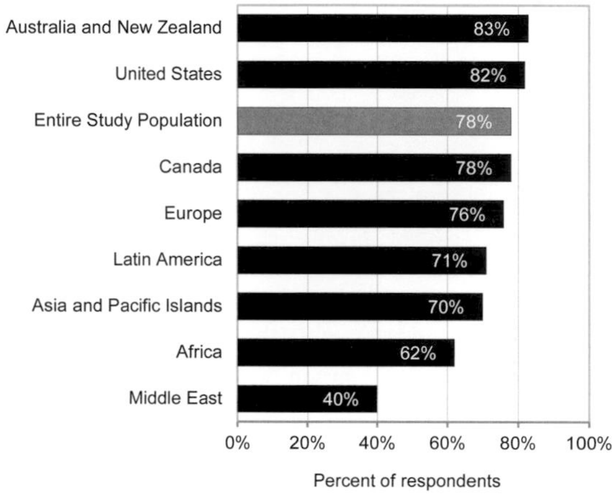

Level of change saturation by industry

Figure 19.5 shows the percentage of participants that indicated being near, at or past the point of saturation by industry. Data were provided for industries represented by 2% or more of participants. Industries are ordered based on greatest occurrence of change saturation.

Figure 19.5 – Change saturation by industry

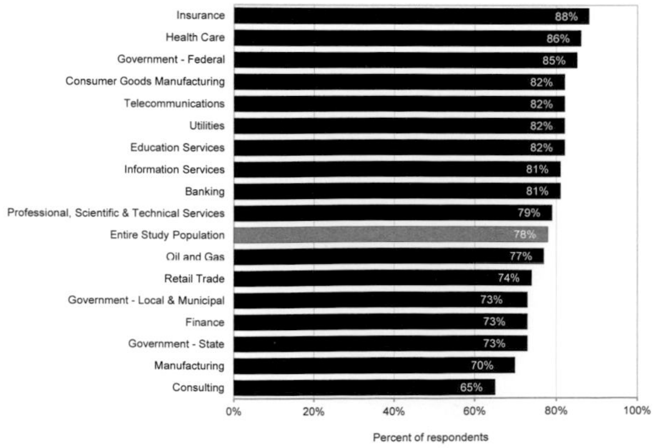

Level of change saturation by organization size

Figures 19.6 and 19.7 show the percentage of participants that indicated being near, at or past the point of saturation by organization size, both annual revenue and number of employees, in comparison to the entire study.

Figure 19.6 – Change saturation by annual revenue of organization

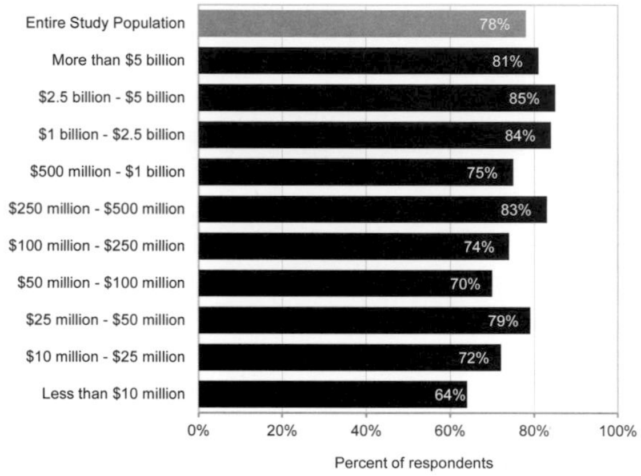

Figure 19.7 – Change saturation by number of employees in organization

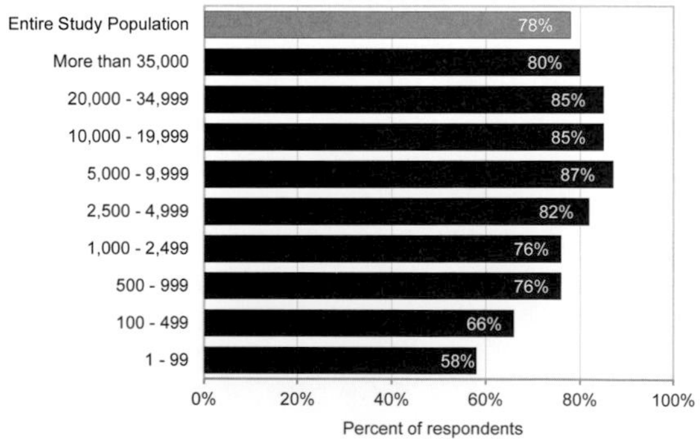

Parts of the organization experiencing the greatest change saturation

Participants identified which parts of their organizations experienced the greatest change saturation. Participants reported that change saturation was occurring across the organizations as a whole. This was either due to too many changes that affected the whole organization or to the fact that every department was undergoing a variety of change projects.

1. **Frontline employees**
   Frontline employees were cited as experiencing high degrees of saturation. This was due largely to the fact that any change in structure or operations had cascading impacts on the daily work of frontline employees. Participants also reported that, to keep up in their respective markets, the need for change had become constant, and frontline employees are first and most impacted by these changes.
2. **Middle managers**
   Middle managers were also cited as experiencing high degrees of change saturation. Middle managers were often tasked with the implementation of change and were the first to feel the impacts in the work group.

Other functional areas experiencing saturation as reported by participants included:

- Operations
- Customer service
- Customer facing roles
- Sales
- Shared services
- Human Resources (HR)
- Support staff
- Corporate services
- Change Management Office

Universal and localized saturation

Source date: 2013

Participants identified whether saturation was universal across the organization or localized within small areas or pockets. More participants (48%) expressed that saturation was universal (Figure 19.8).

Figure 19.8 – Spread of change saturation

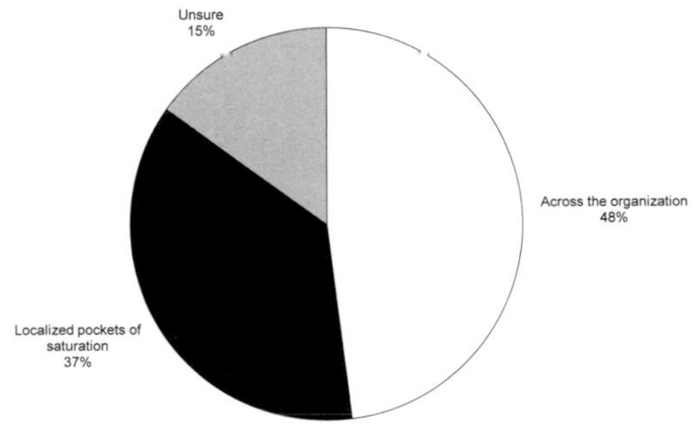

The 37% of participants who indicated saturation was concentrated in localized areas within the organization identified the areas experiencing the greatest levels. Participants reported that Information Technology (IT) was the most saturated area. Human Resources (HR) and customer-facing roles, such as sales, were also areas commonly experiencing saturation. Other notable areas of saturation were finance and the Project Management Office (PMO). Some participants identified employee groups that were experiencing high levels of change saturation, including frontline employees and leadership.

Understanding/measuring saturation

Participants in the 2015 study described how they measured/understood their employees' level of change saturation.

1. **Saturation behaviors**
   Participants cited several behaviors that were viewed as either demonstrating or caused by change saturation. These behaviors included: higher volume of sick leave,

resistance to the change via talk or behavior, gossip and refusal to attend informational meetings about the change.

2. **Feedback**
Participants utilized formal and informal feedback channels to evaluate their employees' saturation levels. While a variety of assessment types were used, participants stressed the importance of routine checkups throughout the course projects.

3. **Observation**
Participants actively observed and monitored the amount and complexity of changes that impacted groups were experiencing. This required participants to actively monitor and keep track of the changes that were being implemented in their organization and the groups affected by those changes.

4. **Intuition**
Participants often cited "gut feelings" or the importance of keeping their "finger on the pulse" of their organization's change culture.

Change management actions taken to address saturation

Source date: 2013

Participants described what they did in response to saturation. Some participants did not address change saturation for a number of reasons. The most common reason was that the activity fell outside of established change management responsibilities. Other reasons included that the organization was not viewed as saturated or that the sponsor did not request saturation analysis.

Remaining participants indicated that the following actions were taken in response to saturation:

1. **Communicate clearly and consistently**
Participants engaged in clear and consistent communications for each change. Some participants marketed the change internally, so it stood out from other initiatives.

2. **Engage the sponsor**
Sponsors were engaged by the change manager to prioritize which changes required immediate attention and which could wait or be discontinued. Participants also engaged sponsors to allocate more resources and funding to change.

3. **Adjust the schedule**
Changes were rescheduled, if possible, to give impacted groups more time to deal with changes in progress. This included cancelling projects, staggering go-live dates and heat-mapping affected groups to identify groups experiencing saturation and change fatigue.

4. **Integrate**
Participants integrated similar changes and placed them under the umbrella of a program. They also tried to identify overlap between projects and to minimize redundancies when possible.

Addressing saturation and collision

When participants were asked to identify how their organization addressed change saturation and the collision between multiple changes, the top response was "*nothing*," as many organizations did not address this issue. The top responses for those who did state specific solutions were:

1. **Apply portfolio management techniques**
The most frequent response was to take an objective view of the changes taking place and utilize formal tools to manage the changes. Having a portfolio of changes allowed participants to streamline work flows, efficiently allocate change resources and coordinate plans among different projects. Assessments like heat maps and questionnaires were frequently used to identify the change capacity of and impact to people in the organization.

2. **Support prioritization**
Participants noted that prioritizing changes helped address the issue of change saturation and collision. Prioritization ensured that

changes were aligned with the direction of the organization and were both created from and enhanced by previous experiences.

3. **Use of structures**
   Another frequent solution to change saturation and collision was to use a dedicated resource. Project Management Offices (PMOs) and steering committees were most often used to oversee, manage and decide on collision and saturation issues.
4. **Adjust the portfolio**
   The main adjustments to the change portfolio that addressed change saturation and collision were to limit the number of changes happening at a single time, modify the time frames of different projects of different priorities and distribute resources to the necessary areas.
5. **Increase communication efforts**
   Participants noted that communication efforts helped address saturation and collision by providing a roadmap and status of the portfolio of change, understanding of the amount of change underway and alignment with the organization.

Managing the change portfolio

Participants in the 2015 study indicated whether they managed the change portfolio (Figure 19.9). Forty-two percent reported that the portfolio was being managed in 2015 in comparison to only 32% in 2013.

Figure 19.9 – Managing the change portfolio

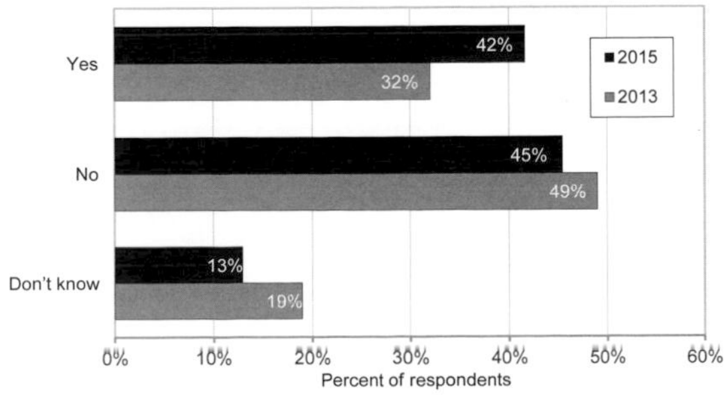

Location of portfolio management

Participants in the 2015 study identified where portfolio management was taking place within the organization with the Project Management Office (PMO) being the most common location (Figure 19.10). Top responses in the *other* category were change management departments, general business units and specific management positions.

Figure 19.10 – Location of portfolio management

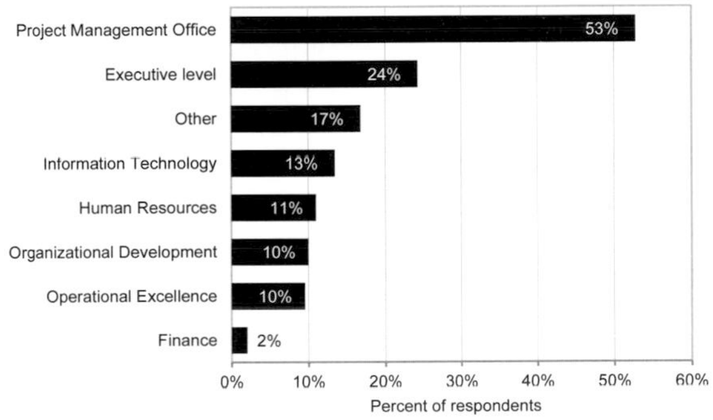

Interest in portfolio management

Source date: 2013

Participants in the 2013 study rated the organization's level of interest in managing the change portfolio. Only 20% reported high to extremely high interest, and 40% expressed low or extremely low interest (Figure 19.11).

Figure 19.11 – Organizational interest in managing the change portfolio

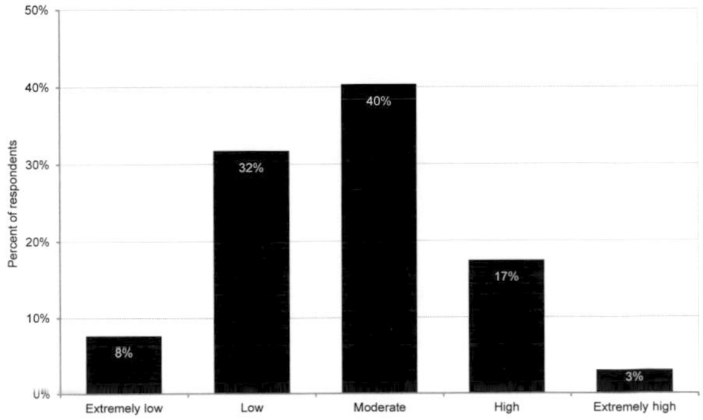

Primary motivations for managing the change portfolio

Source date: 2013

Participants in the 2013 study reported on motivations for managing the change portfolio. The most common, in rank order, were:

1. **Mitigate or alleviate change saturation**
   The primary motivation for managing the portfolio of change was managing change saturation. Participants managed the portfolio of change as a step to increase and monitor the organization's capacity for change. Participants emphasized the need to manage the saturation that affected various groups at the employee and leadership levels. Portfolio management was also conducted to handle or resolve competing change initiatives better.
2. **Ensure project success**
   Participants managed the change portfolio to increase the likelihood of success on each project and achieve the desired Return on Investment (ROI) for projects that comprised the portfolio. Ensuring project results were sustained, avoiding project failures and setting up future projects for success were also reasons for managing the change portfolio.
3. **Increase organizational effectiveness**
   Managing the portfolio of change was driven by a desire to increase strategic effectiveness, process efficiencies, productivity and organizational growth. Participants were motivated to manage the portfolio to ensure efforts were not duplicated. Participants also noted the role portfolio management plays in aligning change initiatives with the organization's strategic goals.
4. **Allocate resources and budget**
   Participants managed the portfolio of change to allocate resources and funding to change initiatives more effectively. Participants drew attention to tracking and monitoring portfolio management to support allocation.
5. **Maintain or improve employee satisfaction**
   Managing the portfolio of change allowed organizations to improve employee satisfaction and engagement. Participants were motivated to manage the portfolio to minimize change fatigue experienced by employees and mitigate resistance stemming from oversaturation of individuals.

Tactics for managing the change portfolio

Source date: 2013

Participants reported on tactics used to manage the change portfolio. The top four responses were:

1. **Monitor changes underway**
   Participants created an umbrella of oversight to monitor multiple changes underway in the organization. Functions included tracking progress of multiple projects, tracking resources assigned to projects, monitoring management's capacity for change and gauging the degree of impact on other groups and individuals. Monitoring projects allowed mapping of projects including prioritization and the staggering of timelines. Tools included heat maps, calendar maps and impact surveys.
2. **Centralize information and reporting**
   Participants created systems for openly exchanging and coordinating information. Central locations or databases were created to share information regarding resource availability, project details, communication plans and general change plans. Reporting was centralized so that all project reports were viewed by the change management lead, Change Management Office (CMO) or other lead individual or functional group. "*There are change management communities across projects that meet to compare plans and impacts. All change management plans are also reviewed by the central Change Office.*" "*All of the change management and project management teams report initiatives to a single database.*"

3. **Formalize portfolio management**
A common tactic for managing the portfolio of change was formalizing it as an initiative. Activities included:
    - Establishing a formal strategy and creating a project plan that outlined portfolio management
    - Developing a communications plan focused on sharing information about portfolio management
    - Building a business case and justifying the need for managing the change portfolio
4. **Collaborate with leadership and other groups**
Participants emphasized leadership involvement as an important step in managing the portfolio of change. Leadership was called on to allocate funding and resources to portfolio management. Leadership meetings allowed participants to give updates and guide discussions about the portfolio. Participants delivered formal reports to leadership, including tracking and monitoring reports. Participants involved other groups, such as the Project Management Office (PMO) and frontline employees, through informal discussions, cross-functional meetings, networking and engagement.

Resolving conflicts when there is competition for resources

Participants defined how their organizations resolved conflicts between projects when there was competition for resources, budgets or impacts on people.

1. **Prioritization**
Prioritization methods were used in both formal and informal settings to resolve project conflicts. Formal prioritization took place ahead of project launch and involved criteria for comparing projects. Informal prioritization typically occurred after a project launch and did not involve methods for comparison. The most frequently cited prioritization criteria included highest value, highest impact, highest expected Return on Investment (ROI), strategic alignment, importance to the business, business urgency and regulatory or legislative mandates.
2. **Senior leadership decisions**
In some cases, decisions were simply made by the CEO, while other cases involved discussions with senior management teams. When conflicts arose and could not be resolved, they were escalated to senior management.
3. **Negotiation**
Negotiation and collaboration directly among teams resolved conflicts between projects. These tactics were used in face-to-face meetings, in discussions with project teams, with leaders and with representatives from the business.
4. **Use of oversight committees**
Project conflicts were addressed by the collective work of an oversight group. Participants shared a number of names for this group including steering group, steering committee, management review board, project control board, business exchange team, change control board and advisory board. This group had visibility across multiple projects and made decisions to resolve conflict.
5. **Increased resources**
Conflicts between projects were resolved by increasing the amount of resources and typically included a larger budget or workload for employees.

A number of participants cited the role of individuals in influencing decisions when conflict occurred. Politics and the use of influence and clout resulted in projects moving forward. Several participants also cited, with a negative connotation, that the loudest people ("squeaky wheels") were the ones who were heard. Finally, several participants indicated that projects with the strongest sponsor were favored in times of conflict.

Appendices

Appendix A – Participant demographics

Geographic representation

Figure A.1 shows the geographic distribution of participants in the 2015 study. Representation was global with 65% of participants located outside of the United States.

Figure A.1 – Geographic representation of participants

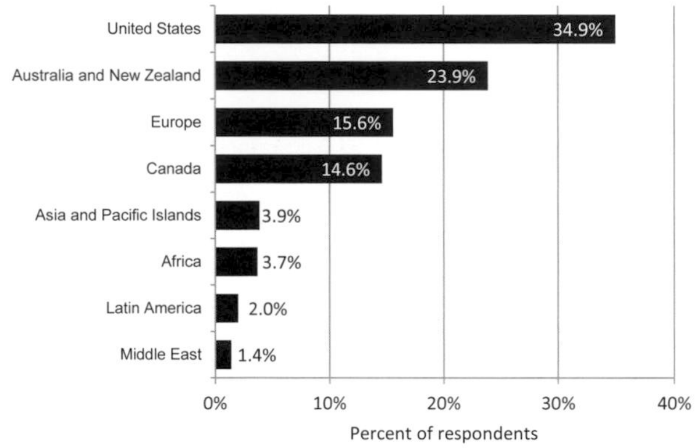

Geographic presence

Nearly half of participants had a presence in multiple countries, similar to findings in the 2013 study (Figure A.2).

Figure A.2 – Geographic presence

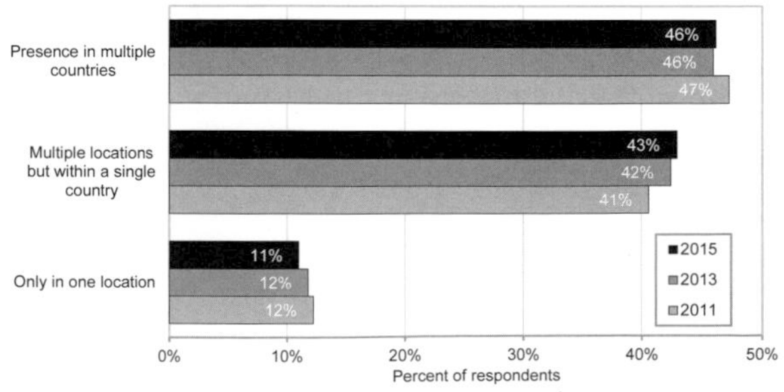

Industry representation

The top responding industries in the 2015 report mirrored those from previous studies. The top responding industries (those with more than 5% of total study respondents) were Health Care, Government – State, Banking, Finance, Consulting, Oil and Gas, and Government – Federal (Figure A.3). Any industries representing less than 1.5% of participants were included in the *other* category.

Figure A.3 – Industry segment

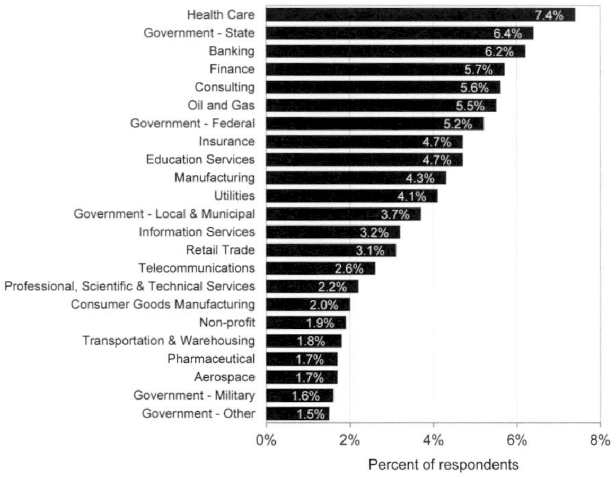

While the top three industries were the same in the 2015 study as in 2013, the order did shift. Banking moved from number one on the list in 2013 to number three in 2015, while Health Care moved up from number two in 2013 to be the most represented industry in 2015.

In this iteration of the benchmarking study (as in the 2013 and 2011 editions), external consultants were specifically instructed to indicate the industry of the client they were representing.

Annual revenue of the organization

Participants in the 2015 study represented a wide range of organizations based on overall organization size measured by annual revenue (or budget for non-profit and government institutions) as shown in Figure A.4. As with the 2013 study, the largest participation came from organizations with more than $5 billion in annual revenue, representing over one quarter of participants.

Figure A.4 – Annual revenue or budget of participating organizations

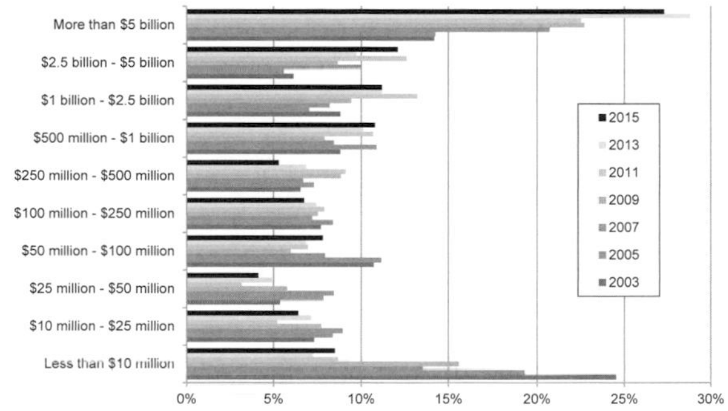

Total number of employees in the organization

Participants indicated the total number of employees in their organization (Figure A.5). Nearly one in five organizations represented in the study had more than 35,000 employees, the most represented group. Organizations with fewer than 1,000 employees made up 26% of study representation.

Figure A.5 – Total number of employees in participating organizations

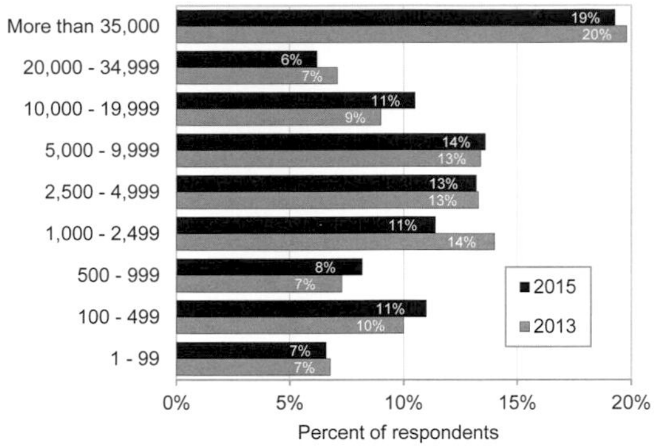

Number of projects underway

Participants in the 2015 study indicated how many projects were currently underway in their organization (Figure A.6). Twenty percent of participants said there were ten or fewer changes underway in their organization, and just over one quarter indicated more than 100 projects.

Figure A.6 – Number of projects underway

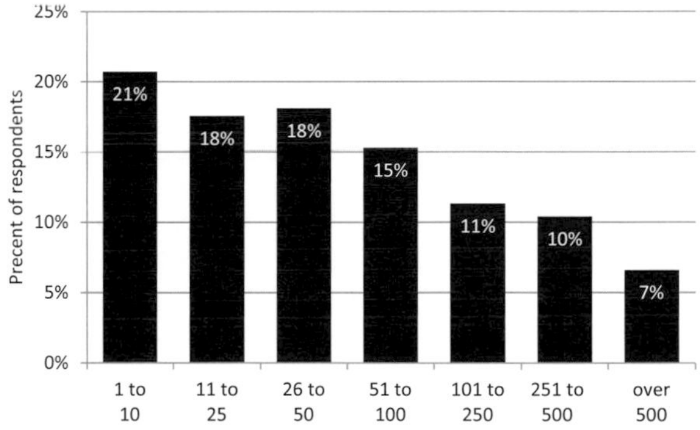

Further analysis showed an expected trend that larger organizations, in terms of both revenue and number of employees, had more projects underway than smaller organizations.

Percentage of projects applying change management

Participants in the 2015 benchmarking study shared the percentage of projects in their organization that were applying change management (Figure A.7). Participants reported, on average, that just over one in three (35%) of the projects in their organization were applying change management. Data labels are shown for data from the 2015 study.

Figure A.7 – Percent of projects applying change management

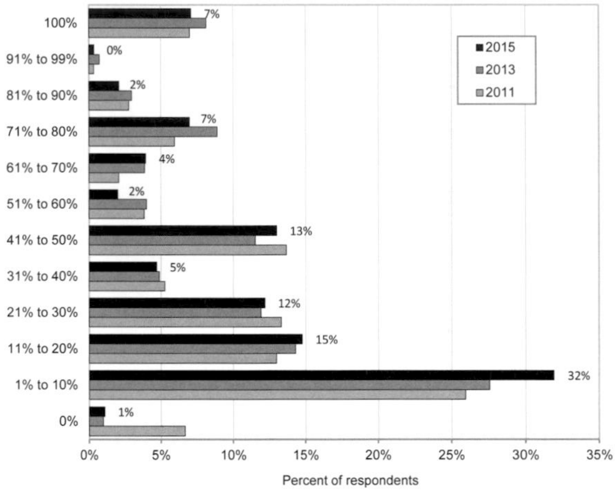

Table A.8 shows a more granular view of the percent of participants reporting that 50% or fewer, 25% or fewer or 10% or fewer projects in the organization were applying change management. The data show a slight decrease in change management application between the 2013 and 2015 benchmarking studies.

Table A.8 – Percent of projects applying change management

Percent of projects applying change management	Percent of participants in 2013 study	Percent of participants in 2015 study
50% or fewer	71%	78%
25% or fewer	49%	55%
10% or fewer	29%	33%

The following graphs show the percentage of projects in the organization applying change management relative to demographic data about the organization.

Figure A.9 shows the breakdown by region relative to the overall average of 35%. Participants from Europe, Canada, the United States and Latin America reported a lower percentage of projects applying change management than the overall study population average.

Figure A.9 – Percentage of projects applying change management by region

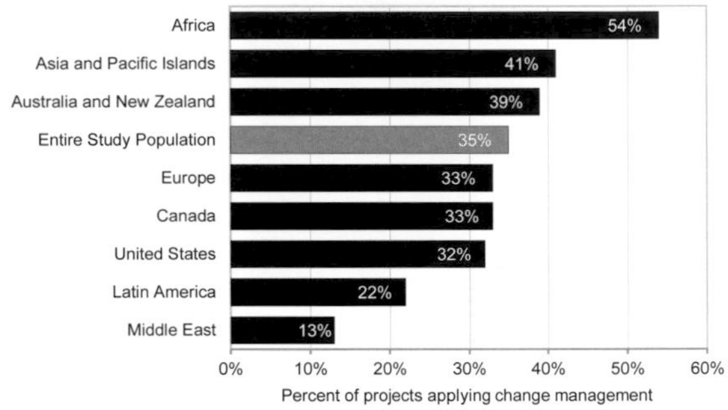

Figure A.10 shows the average percentage of projects applying change management by industry. Banking, services, consulting, finance and retail trade topped the list.

Figure A.10 – Percentage of projects applying change management by industry

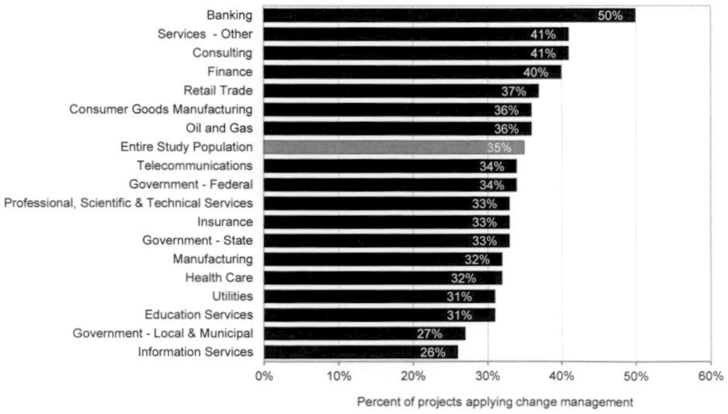

Figure A.11 shows the percentage of those applying change management relative to the annual revenue of the organization.

Figure A.11 – Percentage of projects applying change management by revenue

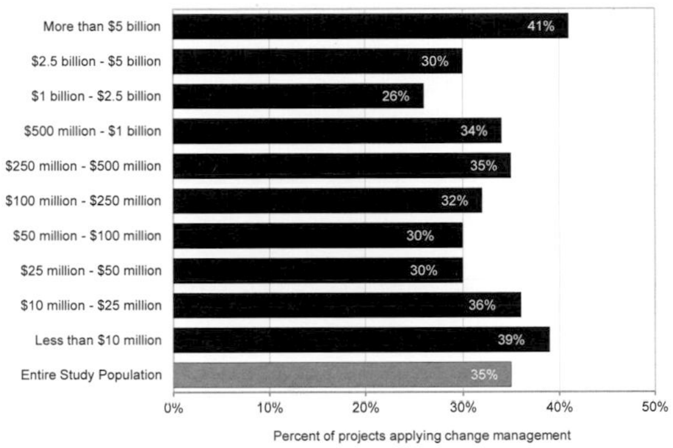

Figure A.12 shows the percentage of those applying change management relative to the number of employees in the organization.

Figure A.12 – Percentage of projects applying change management by number of employees

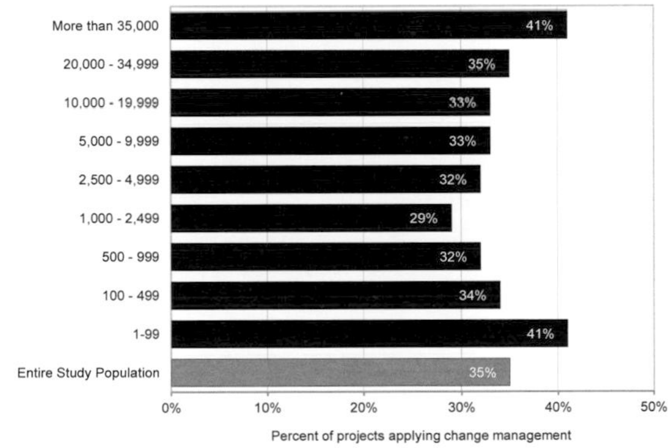

Figure A.13 shows the percentage of those applying change management relative to organizational change management maturity. Organizations with higher maturity in change management had higher percentages of projects applying change management than those with lower maturity scores.

Figure A.13 – Percentage of projects applying change management by organizational maturity

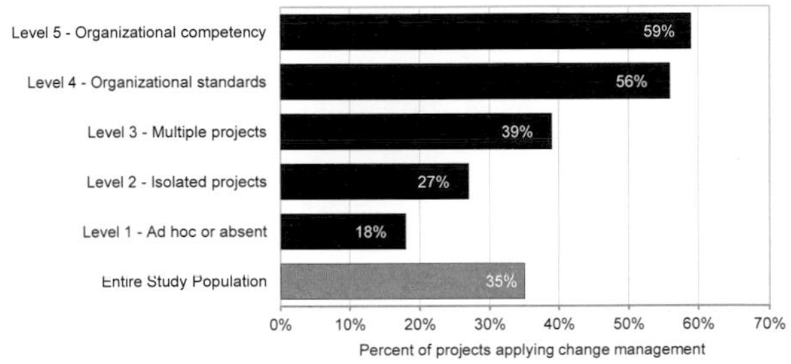

Percentage of projects considered successful

For the second time, participants in the 2015 benchmarking study identified the percentage of projects in their organization that were considered successful in terms of meeting objectives and delivering intended results and outcomes. The overall average for the entire study population was 49% – meaning that about half of the projects undertaken in organizations that participated in the study were considered successful in terms of meeting objectives and delivering intended results.

Figure A.14 shows the breakdown of participants and the percentage of projects deemed as successful in their organization in terms of meeting objectives and delivering intended results. Nearly one quarter of participants stated that between 41% and 50% of their projects were successful.

Figure A.14 – Percentage of projects considered successful

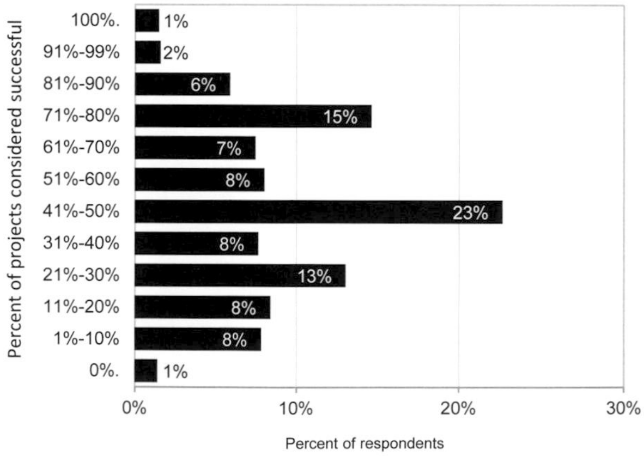

Figure A.15 shows average successful projects by region relative to the overall study average.

Figure A.15 – Percentage of projects considered successful by region

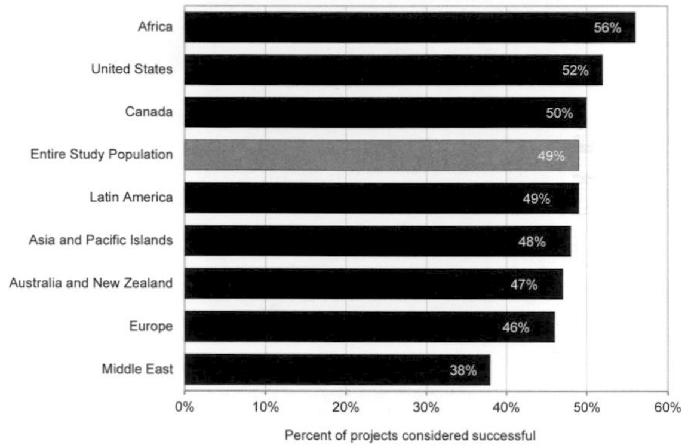

Figure A.16 shows average successful projects relative to annual revenue of the organization.

Figure A.16 – Percentage of projects considered successful by revenue

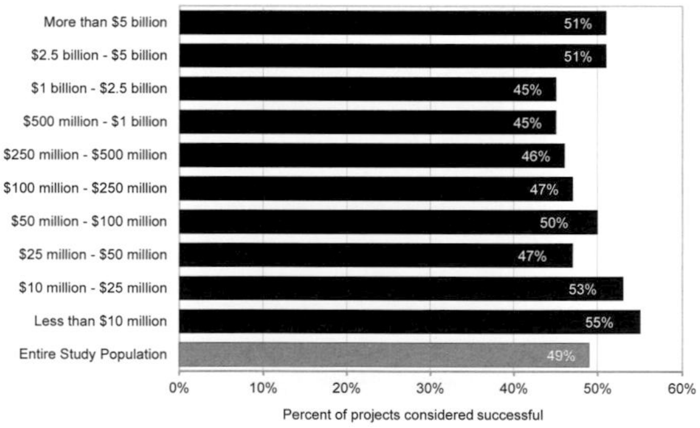

Figure A.17 shows average successful projects relative to the number of employees in the organization.

Figure A.17 – Percentage of projects considered successful by number of employees

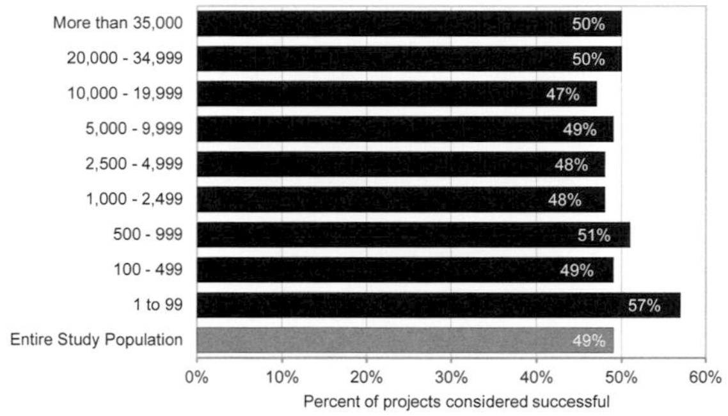

Figure A.18 shows average successful projects relative to organizational change management maturity.

Figure A.18 – Percentage of projects considered successful by organizational maturity level

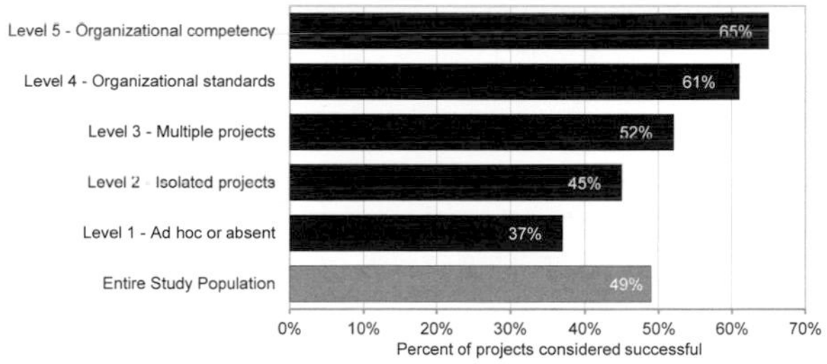

Figure A.19 shows average successful projects by industry.

Figure A.19 – Percentage of projects considered successful by industry

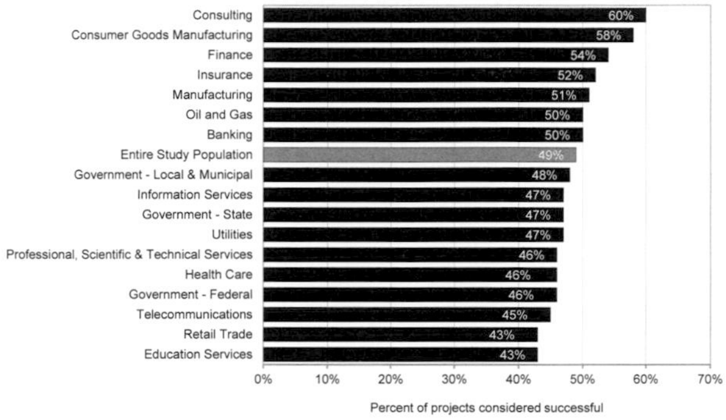

Participant experience

Participants in the 2015 benchmarking study shared how many years they had been involved in applying change management (Figure A.20). The most common response was more than twelve years of experience (29%). Forty-seven percent reported more than eight years of experience, while only 5% had one year or less of experience.

Figure A.20 – Years of change management experience

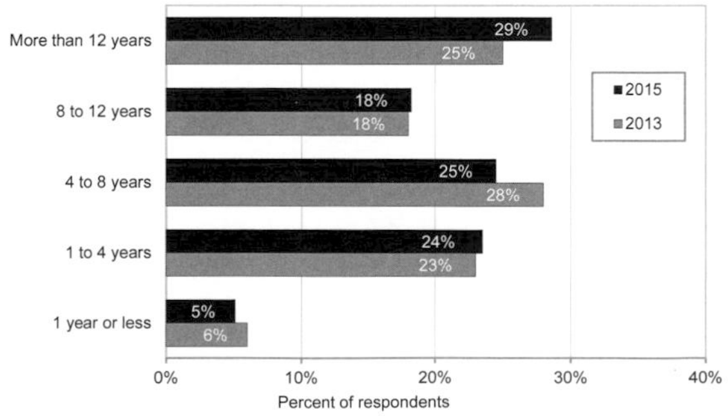

Involvement in change management

Participants indicated their job role in relation to change management. Participants selected one of the five following choices:

- My role is exclusively as a change management practitioner supporting various projects
- I am primarily a change management practitioner, with some other responsibilities
- I was tasked with change management on a project but have other primary responsibilities
- I am a project leader or team member familiar with change management on the project but do not consider myself a change management practitioner
- Other

Figure A.21 presents the breakdown of participants' roles related to change management. Over one third of participants (38%) stated that their role was exclusively as a change management practitioner, and 26% indicated that their role was primarily as a change management practitioner, with some other responsibilities.

Figure A.21 – Participants' roles in change management

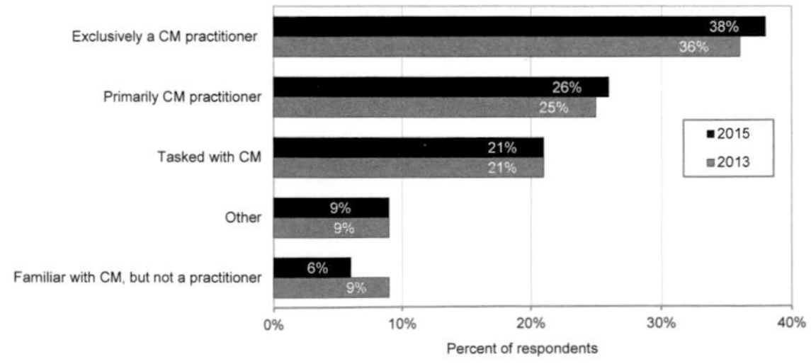

Practitioners who indicated they were *primarily a change management practitioner, with some other responsibilities* (26%) indicated the percentage of their job that was dedicated to change management (Figure A.22).

Over three quarters of participants indicated that more than half of their job focused specifically on change management.

Figure A.22 – Percentage of job dedicated specifically to change management

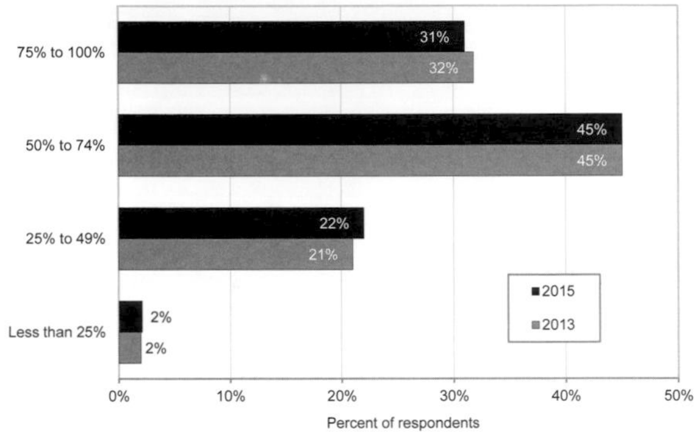

Participants who were exclusively or primarily change management practitioners also estimated the number of projects on which they provided change management support each year (Figure A.23). Only 13% supported more than 10 projects per year. Forty-three percent supported between three and five projects per year.

Figure A.23 – Number of projects supported by change management practitioners

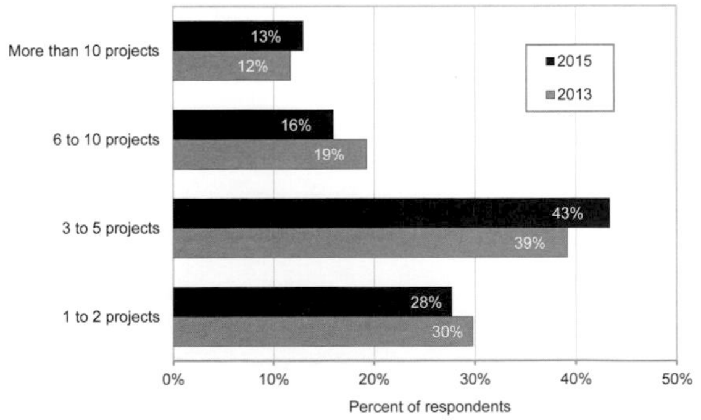

Appendix B – Project profiles

Project stage

Sixty-one percent of participants were reporting on projects that were completed or in the implementation phase. (Figure B.1).

Figure B.1 – Project stage

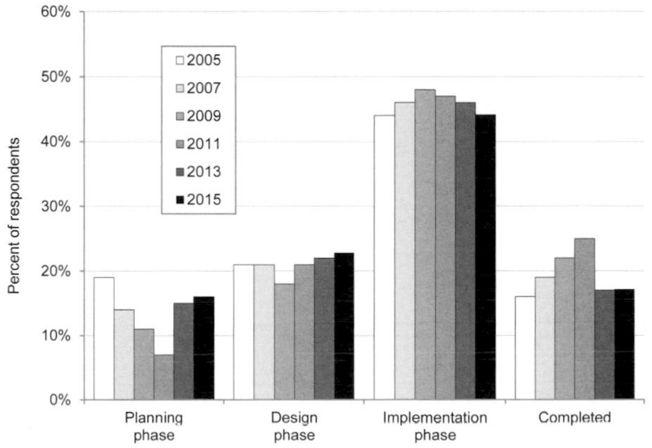

Type of change

Participants indicated the type of change they were reporting on in the benchmarking study by selecting from a list of: *process changes, system changes, job role changes, organizational structure changes* or *other* (Figure B.2).

Figure B.2 – Change type

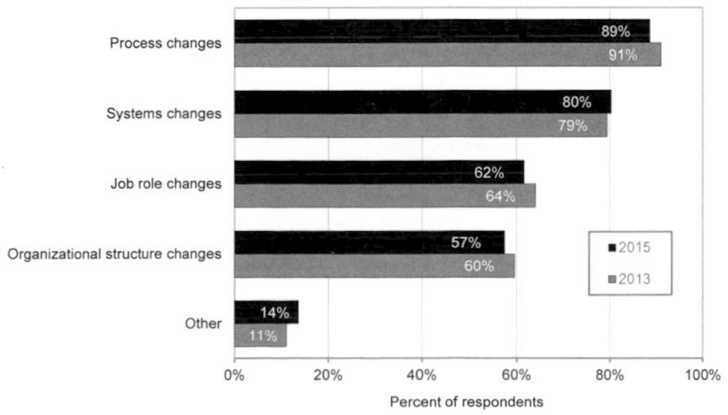

Editor's note: Participants were able to select multiple responses, resulting in a total of more than 100%.

Over 60% of participants selected three change types (26%) or four change types (35%). Only 11% selected a single change type (Figure B.3).

Figure B.3 – Number of change types selected

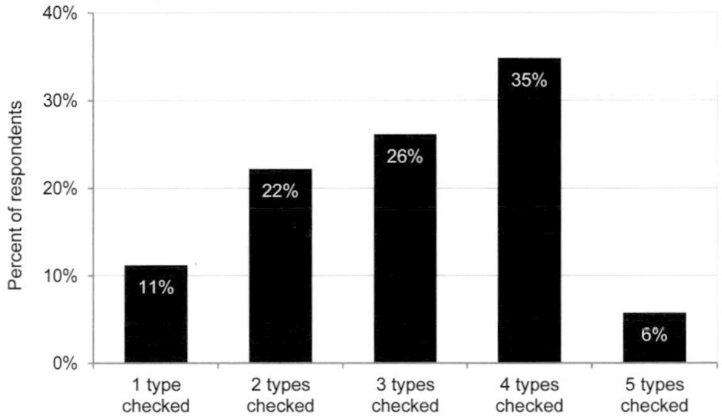

For those who selected multiple project types, the most common combination was process + system + org + job role at 37%, followed by 19% that were reporting on process + system changes. Figure B.4 shows the most frequent combinations.

Figure B.4 – Combinations of change types

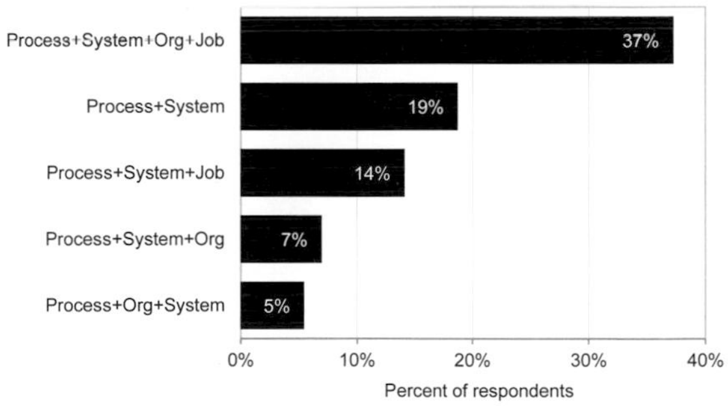

Project classification

Participants in the 2015 study identified a specific classification for the project on which they were reporting (Figure B.5). As in the 2013 study, *IT software upgrade/installation*, *culture change* and *Enterprise Resource Planning (ERP) system* were the three most common initiatives reported. Figure B.5 shows only the initiatives representing more than 1.7% of the study population.

Figure B.5 – Initiatives reported on

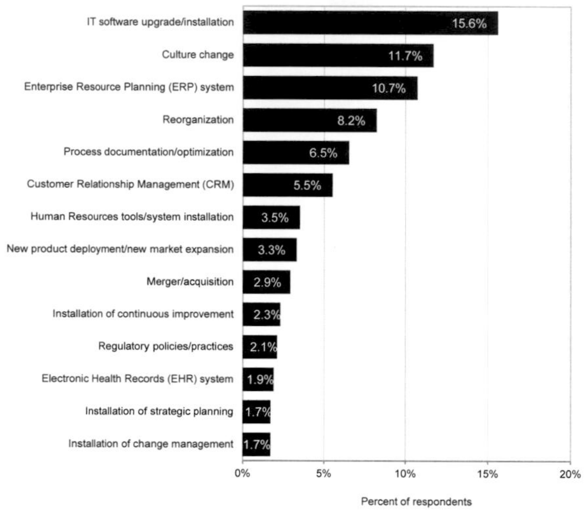

Size of change

Participants provided several data points on the size of the project on which they reported. Participants indicated:

- Scope of the change
- Project investment
- Number of employees impacted

In terms of scope of the change, projects in the 2015 study matched those of previous studies with the largest representation from projects impacting the entire enterprise (Figure B.6).

Figure B.6 – Scope of the change

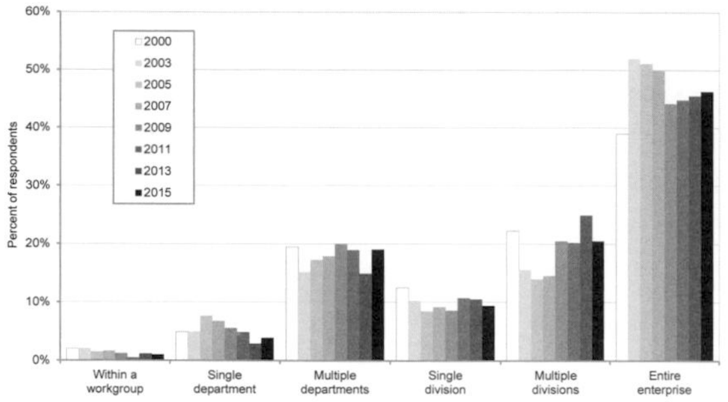

From a project investment standpoint, the 2015 study had fewer projects of less than a $500,000 investment, with a corresponding increase in the number of projects with over a $5 million budget (Figure B.7).

Figure B.7 – Project investment

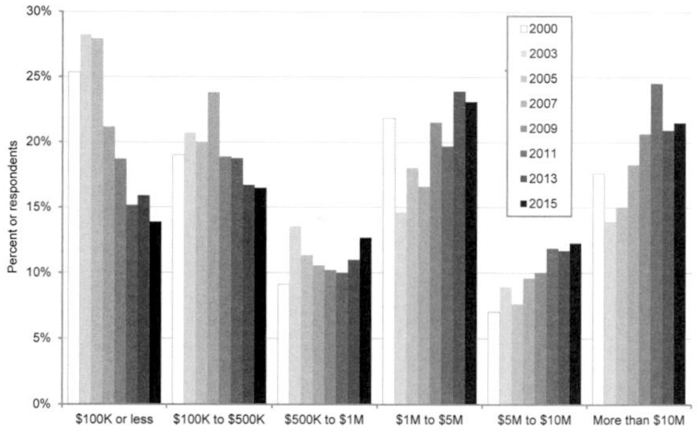

The 2015 study included reporting on more projects that impacted more than 1000 employees than previous benchmarking studies. In total, nearly half (48%) of the projects represented in the 2015 study impacted more than 1000 employees (Figure B.8).

Figure B.8 – Number of employees impacted

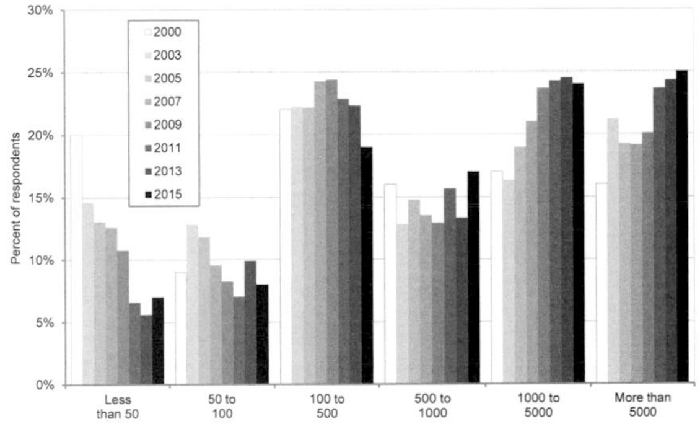

Duration of the change

For the third time, participants shared data on the duration or length of the project on which they were reporting. As in the 2011 and 2013 studies, nearly 40% of participants reported on projects lasting more than 24 months, and over 70% reported on projects lasting more than 12 months (Figure B.9).

Figure B.9 – Duration of the change effort

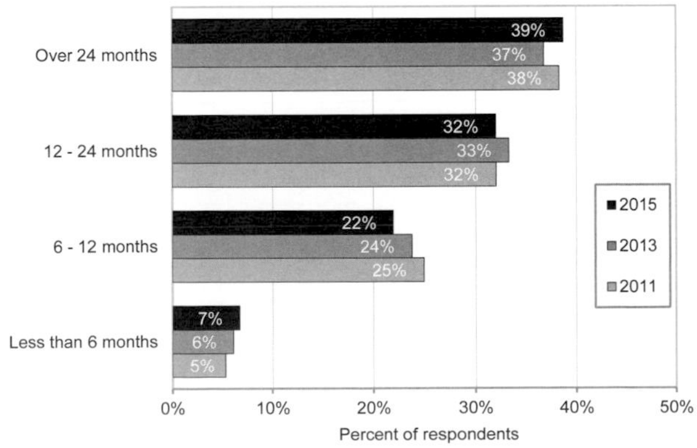

Measures of success: meeting project objectives, schedule and budget

As in previous studies, participants indicated the degree to which the project succeeded based on three criteria: meeting objectives, staying on schedule and staying on budget (Figures B.10, B.11 and B.12).

Overall, 40.7% of participants reported that the project they were reporting on met, exceeded or greatly exceeded objectives – a slight drop from 42.9% in the 2013 study. Thirty-six percent reported being on schedule, slightly ahead of schedule or drastically ahead of schedule – just slightly below the 37% reporting this in 2013. Over half of participants (54%) reported being on or under budget, dropping from 58% in the 2013 study.

Data on project success in terms of meeting objectives, finishing on schedule and staying on budget were used in a correlation with the overall change management effectiveness to evaluate the impact of more effective change management on the achievement of results and outcomes of the project. These correlation results can be found in the Effectiveness section.

Figure B.10 – Meeting objectives

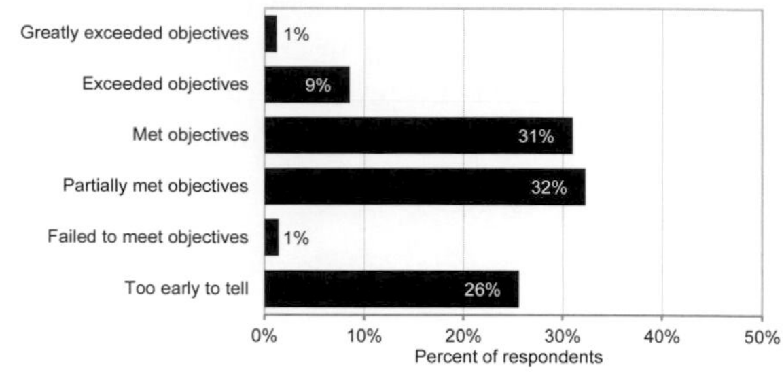

Figure B.11 – Projects on schedule

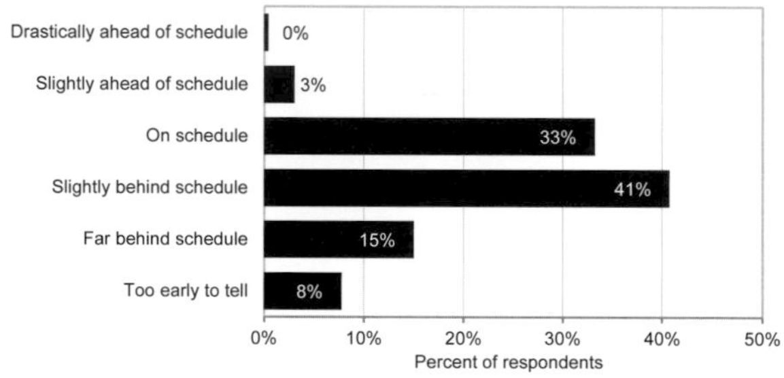

Figure B.12 – Projects on budget

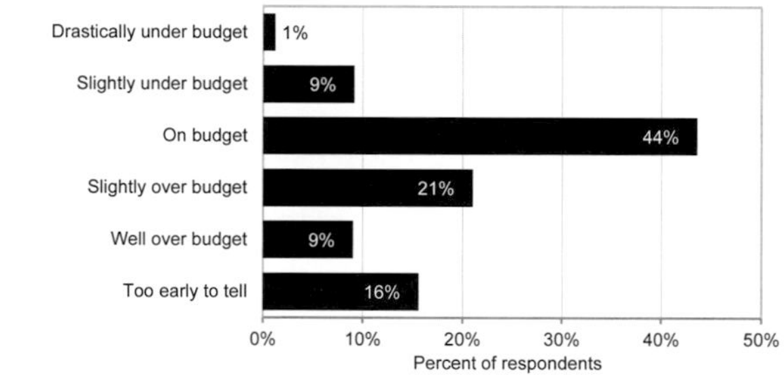

Appendix C – List of certification programs participants attended

Participants wrote in answers to the question "Whose certification program did you attend?" Due to this open ended entry, some provider names were abbreviated. All responses are listed as provided by study participants with no changes including abbreviations. This list includes every certification provider reported by participants in alphabetical order.

- Accelerating Change & Transition (ACT) methodology
- Accenture Change Management Program
- ACMP
- Acuity Institute
- AdPro
- AGPM Change Foundation and Practitioner
- AGSM
- AIM
- Amwaj, Khalid Al-Mobarak
- APMG International
- ASTD CPLP; Northwestern University Master's Degree in Learning & Organizational Change
- Being Human
- Bridges
- Bridges Transitions
- Changability
- Change First
- Change Guides LLC
- CMC
- CMI
- CMR
- CSUS
- De Baak
- FAIMER
- GE Healthcare (CAP, WO)
- Georgetown University
- Google Apps LCS 400 Change Management Mastery
- Human Univerz
- IBM
- IMA
- LaMarsh
- Mawj IT
- MCSI
- Mount Royal University
- MSOD Pepperdine
- PCI
- Proacteur
- Procsi
- Ricoh
- Rimer
- University of Houston
- University of Sydney
- Utrecht University
- Worldsview Academy
- Yellowhouse

Appendix D – Consultants used

The list below includes consultants referenced by participants in the 2015, 2013, 2011 and 2009 benchmarking studies. Those mentioned by more than one participant are indicated with an asterisk (*).

- 1765621 Ontario Limited*
- 2BM Mejor Cambio
- 451 Consulting Pty Ltd
- Abglobal partners, LLC
- Abreon Group
- Acando
- Accenture*
- Access Sciences
- ACME Business Consulting*
- Adaptus Consulting
- Adobe connect
- AdPro Change Systems Inc.
- Aitch Limited
- Alignea Consulting Limited
- AlignED, LLC
- Alitra
- Allegra Consulting
- Alvarez & Marsal
- AMBiT Consulting*
- Ampersand
- Annex
- Aon Hewitt*
- Ariba
- Aspiri Consulting Inc
- Atkins
- Atos
- Avanade*
- Avocette Technologies
- Axia
- BakerTilly
- Barrett Partners Inc
- BCG
- Being Human
- Bellrock Benchmarking Inc.
- Bevington
- BHFL Group
- Biggest Room Of All
- Birgit Maier Consultancy
- Bizmod
- Blue Beyond Consulting
- Bluewolf
- Boomerang Management Inc.
- Boston Consulting Group
- Boxley Group
- Breo Consulting
- Brio Conseils
- BSM & ASSOCIADOS LTDA
- Callida Consulting
- Canberra Consulting
- Capgemini*
- CARA Group
- CCHPO
- Centric Consulting
- CGI*
- Chamonix Consulting*
- Chandler Macleod
- Change Elements
- Change Guides*
- Change Logic
- ChangeWright Consulting
- Chartier Management Consulting
- Cloud Sherpas
- CMC Partnership (UK) Ltd*
- CMC Partnership*
- CMC*
- Cogitate Consulting Pty Ltd*
- Cognizant Business Consulting*
- Cohesive Solutions, Inc
- Comunicacion y Cambio S.A.S
- Conister Consulting Inc.
- Connect the Dots Consulting
- Coradix
- Cosmectra
- Creative Workforce Solutions, LLC
- Crowe Change Specialist Services
- Crowe Horwath LLP
- CTCS Consulting, LLC
- Customer Reach Pty Ltd
- Daniels Consulting Group
- Daston
- David Clarke
- DB Results*
- Dearborn
- Decision Processes International
- Deloitte*
- Denis Corthier BVBA
- Dhanush Infotech
- Dialog IT
- Dimension Data
- Diversified Consulting*
- DSD Laboratories
- Eagle Hill Consulting, LLC

- Elevate Consulting Services
- Empact
- Enabling Excellence
- Enaxis Consulting*
- EOH
- Ethree Consulting
- Evolve! People and Process Management
- Expressworks International
- EY*
- Ferguson Leadership
- Forpath, Bluestar, PWC, Axia, Navigator, Centric
- Free To Grow SA
- Freelance change management consultant engaged by Soltius Indonesia
- Freelancer
- Frontit*
- FSS + Avanxo
- G J Sharp Consulting, Inc
- Gagen MacDonald
- Gensler
- Gorman Project Consulting
- Growth Guiders, LLC
- Grupa Eco Biznes Sp. z o.o.
- H4 Consulting
- Hackett Group
- HCL
- Highlands Consulting
- Hitachi Consulting*
- HOK*
- HP - Canada
- Human Univerz*
- Hunziker Consulting
- Ibiska
- IBM*
- ICF-GHK
- ICI Sevices, Inc.
- Ilik
- Inclusive Cultures
- Informatix Inc.
- Infosys Management Consulting Services*
- InfoWorks, Inc.
- Innolead
- Insight Consultants
- Integral Assets
- Intent Group
- Interis
- International Strategy & Consulting
- IPG
- Jacqueline Ross Consulting
- JCI Business Services Pty Ltd
- JFT Management Consulting Inc.
- Joanna Tropp-Bluestone
- JPkonsulting
- Kate Pascale and Associates Pty Ltd
- Kathalys
- KBACE (Training), AlignOrg Solutions (CM)
- Keogh Consulting*
- Kepnor Tregoe
- KMD
- KnowledgeConsult
- KnowledgeWorx
- Koach S. A.
- KPMG*
- Kronos, Inc.
- LaMarsh Global
- LaMarsh Global
- Libero
- Life Cycle Engineering
- Life Cycle Institute
- Link2Change
- Loboh Enterprises Pty Ltd
- Lonadek Oil and Gas company
- Luebbert Hill LLC
- Lykken Change Management Resources
- Macanta Consulting
- Maryville Techologies
- Mass Ingenuity
- McKinsey
- Mediabloc Consulting (Afrissance)
- Mercer
- Meridian Consulting LLC
- Methodos*
- Microsoft
- Mind4IT
- Mindpeace Consulting
- MNP Consulting*
- Momentum Inc
- Mosaic
- MSS
- MUTAREE
- MYRA Systems Corp.
- Mythios Group, Inc
- N9NE Limited
- Navigant
- Navigator Management Partners*
- Navigator Mgmt Partners
- Navigo Consulting and Coaching*
- Neoris Consulting Services*
- NISG India
- Nish Consulting
- No Bull
- Noah Consulting*
- North Highland*
- Nous Group*

- NTT Data / Accenture
- OBS
- Octo Consulting Group
- Omnifocus Best Practice Solutions
- One Brit
- OneSource Virtual
- Online Business Systems*
- Ophelo*
- PA Consulting
- Pactera*
- Panorama Consulting Solutions
- Patina Solutions
- Pcubed
- Peacebridge Performance Inc.
- Pearson Trueman*
- People & Performance
- People Change
- People Dynamics Ltd,
- People Flourishing
- PeopleFirm LLC
- PeopleQuest Consulting
- Picourseware-Training
- Pi-CPI, LLC
- Point B Consulting
- PorterAuthority
- Presence of IT
- Proacteur*
- Process Solutions
- Project Corporation
- Prosci
- PTC inc.
- PWC*
- Quora Consulting
- R3 Government Solutions LLC
- Ramse Consulting Oy
- Raytheon
- Red Wing
- Results in HR
- RJS & ASSociates
- Roar Change
- ROTOR CONSULTING
- Saba
- Safe Bridge
- SAJE Consulting, Inc
- SAP Business Transformation Services*
- Schafer Consulting
- SCNC
- Shad Consultancy
- Sierra Systems
- Sierra-Cedar*
- Six Sigma Philippines
- Slalom*
- SMS Management & Technology*
- Sorgema CRC
- SPP, INSYNC
- Spring Management Consulting Inc.
- STAR Collaborative
- Stegmeier Consulting Group
- Strategy&*
- StrikConsulting
- SurePower
- Sustainable Performance Group, A Phase 5 Group Inc. Company
- Sustaining Change Ltd. NZ.
- SYSDOC*
- Systemscope
- TASC Management Consulting
- Tascot Global, LLC
- Tata Consulting Firm
- TEKSystems
- The Change Collaborative LLC*
- The Highlands Consulting Group, LLC
- The Pillars
- theBigRocks.com
- ThoughtWorks
- Tiba Managementberatung
- Tier 1 global SI company
- Towers Watson
- Transformation Sciences Inc.
- Transformational Change Leadership
- TranZeal Consulting
- Tyler Change Management Solution
- Veldhoen + Company
- WIPRO*
- Zelos

Appendix E – Prosci Change Management Maturity Model

Below are the complete descriptions of the five levels of the Prosci® Change Management Maturity Model™ provided to study participants.

Level 1 – Ad hoc or absent

At Level 1 of the Maturity Model, project teams are not aware of and do not consider change management as a formal approach for managing the people side of change. Projects at this level can have one or more of the following characteristics:

- Project leadership is focused only on the "concrete" or tangible aspects of the project, including funding, schedule, issue tracking and resource management.
- Communications from the project are on a "need to know" basis only and are typically infrequent.
- Employees find out about the change first through rumors and gossip rather than structured presentations.
- Executive support is in the background, as evidenced through funding authorization and resource allocation, but active and visible sponsorship is not present.
- Supervisors and managers have little or no information about the change and have no change management skills to coach their employees through the change process.
- Employees react to change with surprise; resistance can be widespread.
- Productivity slows and turnover increases as the change nears full implementation.

When is change management used on a project at this level?

Change management is applied on a project at this level only as a last resort when employee resistance jeopardizes the success of the project.

Level of integration between project management and change management

At this level, change management is reactive and an add-on to the project. No integration with project management takes place at the beginning of the project.

Level 2 – Isolated projects

In Level 2, elements of change management begin to emerge in isolated parts of the organization. The effort to manage the people side of change is infrequent and not centralized. Characteristics of this level are:

- A large variation of change management practices exists between projects with many different change management approaches applied sporadically throughout the organization; some projects may be effectively managing change while others are still in Level 1.
- Elements of communication planning are evident, but there is little sponsorship or coaching as part of change management.
- Managers and supervisors have no formal change management training to coach their employees through the change process.
- Change management is typically used in response to a negative event.
- Little interaction occurs between the isolated project teams using change management; each new project "relearns" the basic change management skills.

When is change management used on a project at this level?

At this level change management is applied on a project when resistance emerges or when the project nears implementation, with only isolated projects using change management at inception. Some elements of communication planning occur early in the lifecycle.

Level of integration between project management and change management

In Level 2, change management is not fully integrated into project management. On projects that use change management, the project team is aware and knowledgeable of change management. In certain instances, a change management advocate can encourage the integration of change management and project management.

Level 3 – Multiple projects

At Level 3, groups emerge that begin using a structured change management process. Change management is still localized to particular teams or areas in the organization. Organizations at this level can have one or more of the following characteristics:

- Structured change management processes are being used across multiple projects; multiple approaches and methodologies are being utilized.
- Some elements of knowledge sharing emerge between teams in the organization; experiences are shared between teams in some departments or divisions.
- While change management is applied more frequently, no organizational standards or requirements exist; pockets of excellence in change management co-exist with projects that use no change management.
- Senior leadership takes on a more active role in sponsoring change and considers this role part of their responsibilities, but no formal company-wide program exists to train project leaders, managers or coaches on change management.
- Training and tools become available to project leaders and team members; managers are provided with training and tools to coach frontline employees through future changes.

When is change management used on a project at this level?

Change management is initiated at the start of some projects, with a large fraction still applying change management as a reaction to employee resistance during implementation.

Level of integration between project management and change management

In Level 3, teams that are successful at change management integrate change management with their overall project management methodology at the inception of the project. Communication planning is integrated at the planning phase, and other plans are developed prior to implementation.

Level 4 – Organizational standards

In Level 4, the organization has selected a common approach and implemented standards for using change management on every new project or change. Note: a common methodology does not mean a "one-size-fits-all" recipe. Effective methodologies use repeatable steps but are built on understanding the situation and using the appropriate tools for the specific change. Organizations at this level can have one or more of the following characteristics:

- There is an enterprise-wide acknowledgement of what change management is and why it is important to project success.
- A common change management methodology has been selected and plans are developed for introducing the methodology into the organization.

- Training and tools are available for executives, project teams, change leaders, managers and supervisors. Managers and supervisors are provided formal training in change management.
- A functional group may be created to support change initiatives, with roles like Director of Change Management. Organizations may create a Center of Excellence with individuals, groups or administrative positions dedicated to supporting change management efforts and building change management skills.
- Executives assume the role of change sponsors on every new project and are active and visible sponsors of change.
- Resistance and non-compliance is expected in isolated instances. Some project teams still do not understand why they are using change management. Adoption is not yet at 100%, and the organization is in the process of building change management skills throughout the organization.

When is change management used on a project at this level?

At Level 4, teams regularly use a change management approach from the beginning of their projects. Change management work begins at the planning phase of the project.

Level of integration between project management and change management

Project management and change management are integrated from the beginning to the point where they are not separable. Project teams follow both project and change management milestones.

Level 5 – Organizational competency

Level 5 is having change management competency as part of the skill set of the organization. Organizations at this level can have one or more of the following characteristics:

- Effectively managing change is an explicitly stated strategic goal and executives have made this a priority.
- Employees across the enterprise understand change management, why it is important to project success and how they play a role in making change successful.
- Change management is second nature – it is so commonplace that it is nearly inseparable from the initiatives.
- Managers and supervisors routinely use change management techniques to help support a broad range of initiatives, from strategy changes to individual employee improvement.
- The organization gathers data to enable continuous improvements to the common change management methodology, tools and training.
- Extensive training exists at all levels of the organization.
- Higher Return on Investment (ROI), lower productivity loss and less employee resistance are evident across the organization.

When and how is change management used on a project at this level?

Change management begins before projects begin.

Level of integration between project management and change management

When organizations have developed a high level of change management competency, change management steps are completely integrated into project management. Planning and design phases have both project and change management elements and are viewed as standard practice.

Appendix F – Regression analysis

Relationships between various aspects of change management and measures of outcomes were analyzed using multivariate linear regression (ordinary least squares). Original qualitative responses were quantified by scaling answers into an appropriate range for the number of categories provided to reduce bias. Factors controlled for in all models included change management experience, formal change management certification, change management role, relationship to the organization, size of the organization, location of the organization, geographic presence of the organization and industry. These factors were controlled for by including the variables in the model.

Limitations included:

- Questions were designed for qualitative analysis.
- Values are relative, not absolute.
- Participants had disparate preferences and perceptions.
- The sample was not from a random distribution; individuals who were strong believers in change management were more likely to participate (sample selection).
- Organizations that had better responses were more likely to be proficient at change management (reverse causality).
- Results might be driven by factors not assessed in the model (omitted variable bias).
- Models were restricted to linear relationships.

Applications, strengths and usefulness of analyses:

- Places a magnitude on crucial variables that influence the effectiveness of change management.
- Value is gained by contextualizing the strengths and significance of results.
- Useful predictive capability and application.
- Although cardinal scales were used, compounding significant results in different relationships enhances the value and credibility of findings.

Missing data for control variables or variable effectiveness of the change management program were dropped from analysis. Mean analysis was performed to compare observable characteristics between observations used in the analysis and observations that were dropped. Although mean analysis on control characteristics is more conventional, the categorical nature of these variables compromises those types of comparisons. As a result, mean analysis was conducted on the quantified variables that were available. Although the group that was dropped had slightly lower values than the group used, the two groups were found to be similar, as shown in Table F.1. Participants who did not complete the survey are less likely to be entrenched in change management and, thus, less likely to have an effective change management program and less likely to have the strength of change management factors. Therefore, dropping observations does not bias results substantially and is the more conservative approach.

Table F.1 – Analysis of means between observations used and not used during analyses

Categories	Group used	Group not used
Effectiveness	5.053	4.571
Dedicated change resource	0.76	0.721
Use of a particular change method	0.728	0.686
Level of a structured change management methodology	6.449	6.018
Level of sufficient resources	4.95	4.893
Level of project and change management integration	6.463	6.08
Sample size	981	141

The outcome variable used during analyses was the response to the question "Rate the overall effectiveness of the change management program." Participants selected from responses *poor*, *fair*, *good* and *excellent* depending on how effectively they perceived the change management program in their organization was operating. Under the assumption that all of the individuals intuitively used a linear system when deciding on their responses, these four categories were split into equal range values on a scale from zero to 10. An example of how these qualitative responses were quantified is: if a participant indicated that the program was good, he/she was randomly assigned a value between 5 and 7.5. This process was repeated 500 times and then averaged to achieve a value that was as unbiased and consistent as possible. Analysis was also performed on samples with 1 and 10 iterations, and similar results were found. An identical quantification methodology was applied to each variable used to inspect relationships. The Breusch-Pagan test for heteroscedasticity was used to determine whether residuals were correlated with the dependent variables in all models and for all analysis. To correct for heteroscedasticity and ensure the standard errors, and thus hypothesis tests, were unbiased, White or Robust standard errors were used, and corrected values are shown in the report. ANOVAs (analysis of variances) were conducted on models with different variables to ensure all variables included in each respective model were significant to maximize explained variation and minimize multicollinearity to find the best fit line for the model. A balance was struck between maximizing the amount of variation that could be explained by the model and minimizing confounding variation.

Dedicated change resource and effectiveness

The model tested regarding the relationship between having a dedicated change resource on the project team and overall effectiveness of a change management program was found significant, with an $F(138, 841)$ of 3.17 and a p-value less than 0.01 which is below conventional standards of significance at the 99% confidence level. The model had an R^2 of 0.35 and adjusted R^2 of 0.24. Although small, the R^2 values are due partially to the fact that the independent variable was binary. Responses of *I don't know* were dropped. Sensitivity checks suggested that nearly identical results are obtained when regressions are conducted with the 74 observations that include the response *I don't know*, coded as zero, in comparison to the analysis in which the responses were removed from the data.

Use of a methodology and effectiveness

The model tested regarding the relationship between use of a methodology and overall effectiveness of a change management program was significant at the 99% confidence level with an $F(138, 8241)$ of 2.98 and p-value less than 0.01. The model had an R^2 of 0.33 and adjusted R^2 of 0.22. Although small, the R^2 values are due partially to the fact that the independent variable was binary. Twenty responses of *I don't know* were dropped from analysis. Sensitivity checks suggested that nearly identical results are obtained when regressions are conducted with analyses that include the response *I don't know*, coded as zero, in comparison to the analysis in which the responses were removed from the data.

Level of a structured model used and effectiveness

The model tested regarding the relationship between degree of structured methodology and overall effectiveness of a change management program was significant at the 99% confidence level, with an $F(138, 841)$ of 5.08 and p-value less than 0.01. The model had an R^2 of 0.45 and adjusted R^2 of 0.37, thus the model explained much variation. More variation was explained by this model in comparison to the first two models due to the structure of the data and because the independent variable was continuous. There were no missing data during this analysis.

Level of sufficient resources and effectiveness

The model tested regarding the relationship between degree of sufficient resources and overall effectiveness of a change management program was significant at the 99% confidence level with an $F(138, 838)$ of 4.07 and p-value less than 0.01. The model had an R^2 of 0.40 and adjusted R^2 of 0.30, and thus the model explained much variation. More variation was explained by this model in comparison to the first two models due to the structure of the data and because the independent variable was continuous. Three observations were removed due to missing responses.

Level of integration and effectiveness

The model tested regarding the relationship between degree of sufficient resources and overall effectiveness of a change management program was significant at the 99% confidence level with an $F(138, 836)$ of 4.71 and p-value less than 0.01. The model had an R^2 of 0.44 and adjusted R^2 of 0.34, and thus the model explained much variation. More variation was explained by this model in comparison to the first two models due to the structure of the data and because the independent variable was continuous. Five observations were removed due to missing responses.

Study participants

The list of study participants from the 2007, 2009, 2011, 2013 and 2015 studies can be found online at www.prosci.com/research-participants